940.315 B /BHPA/357984
W9-CTR-386

BEHIND THE LINES

Behind the Lines

Gender and the Two World Wars

MARGARET RANDOLPH HIGONNET
JANE JENSON
SONYA MICHEL
MARGARET COLLINS WEITZ
Editors

YALE UNIVERSITY PRESS
New Haven and London

Designed by Nancy Ovedovitz and set in Galliard type by Keystone Typesetting Co., Orwigsburg, Penn. Printed in the United States of America by Murray Printing Co., Westford, Mass.

Library of Congress Cataloging-in-Publication Data

Behind the lines.
Includes index.
1. World War, 1914–1918—Women. 2. World War, 1939–1945—Women. 3. Women—History—20th century. I. Higonnet, Margaret R.
D639.W4B43 1987 940.3′15′03042 86–28102

The paper in this book meets the guidelines for permanence and durability of the Committee on Production Guidelines for Book Longevity of the Council on Library Resources.

10 9 8 7 6 5 4 3 2 1

CONTENTS

ACKNOWLEDGMENTS

Most of the articles collected in this anthology were first presented as papers at the Workshop on Women and War held at the Center for European Studies at Harvard University, January 8–10, 1984. Together, the panelists and members of the audience created an intellectual climate in which the major themes of this collective study could develop. We are grateful to all those who participated, as well as to the institutions whose support made the workshop possible: the Center for European Studies, the Council for European Studies, the Government of France, and Radcliffe College. Our special thanks go to Dr. Marietta Lutze for her faith in our objectives and her generous assistance.

Due to limitations of space, we have not been able to include here all of the papers presented originally or gathered later from participants. We would like to thank those who gave us the benefit of their thinking on gender and war, but whose work does not appear in these pages: Paola di Cori, Jean Bethke Elshtain, Mary Felstiner, Carla Johnston, Charles Maier, Joan Ringelheim, and Andrea Walsh. We would also like to thank Miriam Abramowicz for sharing with us her film, *As if It Were Yesterday*.

One of the primary aims of the workshop was to bring together European and American scholars who were doing research on similar questions. Paola di Cori, a research associate at the Center for European Studies in 1981, graciously served as our ambassador to the network of European women's historians; regrettably, she had to return to her teaching duties at the University of Rome before her colleagues arrived for the workshop.

Throughout this project, we relied on the efforts of many people. Philippa Bovet, dean of Radcliffe, ably assisted us in handling arrangements for the workshop. Over the years, members of the staff of the Center for European Studies have helped us—and humored us—in countless ways. Colleagues at the Center have provided references, translations, and intellectual stimulation. And we were fortunate to find in Charles Grench of Yale University Press a most discerning and encouraging editor.

Abby Collins, assistant director of the center, has made invaluable contributions at every stage; perhaps most important, she provided the initial concept for the workshop. We are pleased to be able to acknowledge in print her vision, sound judgment, and commitment, all of which were essential to the process that gave rise to this book.

BEHIND THE LINES

INTRODUCTION

"War is men's business, not ladies'," we are told in *Gone With the Wind*, but the total wars of the twentieth century force us to acknowledge that it is women's concern as well. Advances in military technology and strategy have blurred the boundaries between war zones and the homefront. Mass communication and psychological warfare affect all sectors of belligerent societies.[1] Women, like men, have been mobilized for both civilian and military work. They have moved from auxiliary and support roles such as nursing to sabotage and combat. As defense workers producing armaments, they may be said both to complement and to expand the reach of the predominantly male armed forces.[2] Moreover, employed or not, all women have had to contend with food shortages, rationing, and evacuation. In all these ways, then, the realities of the two world wars contradicted the myth that war compels men to go forth and fight in order to protect their women, who remain passive and secure at home with the children.

Underlying this myth is the belief that men are naturally fierce and warlike, while women, as mothers, have an affinity for peace. It might be argued that this opposition of masculinity to femininity, like that of battlefront to homefront, helps to guarantee social stability. For, paradoxically, war unleashes aggressiveness in defense of civilization—violence intended to contain violence. Images of femininity, nurturance, and the family can be invoked to restore the balance and protect our faith in the social order. Jean Bethke Elshtain suggests that "the image of woman as Other, as the Goddess of Peace," retains its power in spite of women's active military involvement because it symbolizes qualities that fend off the barbarism implicit in war.[3] The

1. See Raymond Aron, *The Century of Total War* (Garden City, N.Y.: Doubleday, 1954), 19–22, 37–44; and Gordon Wright, *The Ordeal of Total War, 1939–1945* (New York: Harper, 1968), 174–82 and chap. 11.

2. Wright, *Ordeal,* 52–56; see also Alan S. Milward, *War, Economy and Society, 1939–1945* (Berkeley: University of California Press, 1979), 60–63.

3. Jean Bethke Elshtain, "Women as Mirror and Other: Toward a Theory of Women, War, and Feminism," *Humanities in Society* 5, 2 (Winter–Spring 1982), 32.

"otherness" of femininity, like the "liminality" of the warrior figure,[4] establishes the social limits of war and guarantees the possibility of postwar normalization.

The Goddess of Peace took many forms in the propaganda and mass culture of the two world wars. The Great War linked women's patriotic duty to motherhood: legions of nationalistic mothers were pictured bravely sending their boys off to war. The Second World War eroticized images of femininity, producing not only Mrs. Miniver but romantic and kittenish sexual partners and Hollywood pinups. No matter how she is manifest, though, this goddess always contrasts with, even while supporting, Mars.

Despite periods of questioning and reassessment after both 1918 and 1945, the mythical differentiation between men and women in relation to war persisted, in part because scholars employed categories that masked the realities and complexities of women's participation in the conflicts. Many historical accounts of these wars focus on traditional military, diplomatic, or narrowly defined economic topics. When social historians discuss the homefront, they generally subsume women under aggregate statistics, typologize them as social problems (for example, those requiring evacuation and daycare), or characterize women filling men's prewar roles as interesting but temporary anomalies.[5] Even those alert to the historiography of women find it difficult to integrate their chapters on the "new woman" into the larger picture.[6] Similarly, literary scholars customarily exclude women's voices from the canon of war literature, favoring writings based on the actual experience of combat.

Two recent waves of scholarship have, however, begun to question the mythology of war's gender. The first explores the cultural construction of soldiering and its psychological implications for men. In *The Face of Battle* John Keegan breaks with the tendency of previous military historians to treat soldiers in the aggregate and investigates the experience of individual men in specific battles. At the Somme in 1916, Keegan discovered, the "will to fight" was, for many men, an uncertain phenomenon at best.[7] Paul Fussell and Eric

4. Eric Leed, *No Man's Land: Combat and Identity in World War I* (Cambridge: Cambridge University Press, 1979), 19.

5. See, for example, Angus Calder, *The People's War: Britain 1939–1945* (New York: Pantheon, 1969), 388–90, 400–04; Richard M. Titmuss, *Problems of Social Policy* (London: His Majesty's Stationery Office and Longmans, Green, 1950), chaps. 19–20; and Richard Polenberg, *War and Society: The United States, 1941–1945* (Philadelphia: Lippincott, 1972), chap. 5.

6. See, for example, Arthur Marwick, *The Deluge: British Society and the First World War* (Boston: Little, Brown, 1965).

7. John Keegan, *The Face of Battle: A Study of Agincourt, Waterloo and the Somme* (New York: Viking Penguin, 1985), 274–84.

Leed take up the same theme in their studies of soldiers' cultural and literary responses to the Great War, showing that their ambivalent attitudes toward aggression were coupled with deep fear, disorientation, and passivity.[8] By revealing a crisis of masculinity, they alert other scholars to the problematic relationship between war and the construction of gender. Although these works concentrate on war's effect on men, they provide one model for the study of women and war by showing how soldiers drew upon "the cultural repertoire of meaning . . . to define felt alterations in themselves."[9] The interplay between cultural forms and self-definition is one of the central themes of this book.

In the second wave of new scholarship, feminist historians challenge the assertion that the two wars were entirely male enterprises. Their studies describe the many roles women played in the military, resistance, and medical corps, as well as in heavy industry at home.[10] These historians find, however, that in war as well as in peace there were sharp differences in the activities, responses, and status of women and men. While wartime may have impelled women out of the domestic sphere, they nonetheless tended to remain in subordinate relationships to men, who continued to dominate the labor market and monopolize political power.

Both of these trends in the historiography of war raise questions about gender. The discovery of the crisis of masculinity reveals that so-called masculine traits are not universal, natural attributes of men; the perception that women's subordination persists despite profound changes in their economic and political activities suggests that status does not depend on reaching a fixed position in the social order. How, then, is gender designated? A number of scholars (many of them represented here) have adopted a theoretical stance asserting that social differences between women and men are produced by

8. Leed, *No Man's Land,* chap. 5; Paul Fussell, *The Great War and Modern Memory* (New York: Oxford University Press, 1975). Leed stresses soldiers' psychological reactions; through their letters and diaries, Klaus Theweleit traces the sources of fantasy of members of the German elite Freikorps in *Männerphantasien,* 2 vols. (Frankfurt/Main: Roter Stern, 1977–78).

9. Leed, *No Man's Land,* ix.

10. See for example Maurine Greenwald, *Women, War, and Work: The Impact of World War I on Women Workers in the United States* (Westport, Conn.: Greenwood Press, 1980); Vera Laska, *Women in the Resistance and the Holocaust: The Voice of Emptiness* (Westport, Conn.: Greenwood Press, 1983); Marie-Madeleine Fourcade, *Noah's Ark* (New York: E. P. Dutton, 1974), originally published as *L'Arche de Noë* (Paris: Fayard, 1968); June A. Willenz, *Women Veterans: America's Forgotten Heroines* (New York: Continuum, 1983); K. J. Cottam, ed. and trans., *The Golden-Tressed Soldier* (Manhattan, Kansas: MA/AH Publishing, 1983); K. J. Cottam, *Soviet Airwomen in Combat in World War II* (Manhattan, Kansas: MA/AH Publishing, 1983); and Françoise Thébaud, *La femme au temps de la guerre de 14* (Paris: Stock, 1986).

systems of gender that construct and differentiate male and female activities and identities in accord with but not actually determined by biological sex. A gender system consists not merely of a set of social roles but also of a discourse that gives meaning to different roles within a binary structure. Moreover, although the fundamental distinction between masculine and feminine appears to be universal, the gender system takes a different form in each culture. Finally, gender systems are not fixed, but respond and contribute to social change, discursively assimilating new social phenomena and reconstituting the fundamental distinction between the genders.

To study women in wartime, then, a new historical perspective is called for, one in which women are studied in relation to men and as part of identifiable gender systems. This perspective avoids the pitfalls of isolationism, which stresses the uniqueness of women's experience and, because it examines that experience virtually in a vacuum, cannot always explain change in women's lives. The study of gender systems also avoids the problems of assimilationism, which, by emphasizing parallels between actions and achievements of women and men, obscures historical distinctions between the two. By insisting that feminine identities and roles—femininity itself—must always be analyzed as part of a system that also defines masculine ones, the study of gender moves women's history from the margins to the center of "mainstream" history. This shift entails nothing less than a rewriting of mainstream history.

Perhaps nowhere will this shift be more dramatic than in the study of war. As a first step, war must be understood as a *gendering* activity, one that ritually marks the gender of all members of a society, whether or not they are combatants. The implications of war for women and men are, then, linked in symbolic as well as social and economic systems. During total war, the discourse of militarism, with its stress on "masculine" qualities, permeates the whole fabric of society, touching both women and men.[11] In doing so, it draws upon preexisting definitions of gender at the same time that it restructures gender relations. When peace comes, messages of reintegration are expressed within a rhetoric of gender that establishes the postwar social assignments of men and women.

One of the main purposes of this book is to bring together essays that analyze the gender implications of wartime discourses. This type of analysis makes clear that, however necessary, it is insufficient to examine only the objective situation of women before, during, or after the war. Statistics of

11. This was true in all nations at war; cf. Wright, *Ordeal,* chap. 4; and Aron, *Century,* 86–92. See also Harold D. Lasswell, "The Garrison State," *American Journal of Sociology* 46, pt. 2 (1941), 455–68.

military participation or factory employment are only the beginning of the story. The analyst must also explain the social meanings attached to those activities and to the general condition of women through the discourses of all participants.

The discourses that give meaning to gender take many forms. In wartime, the most explicit and deliberate efforts to redefine masculinity and femininity have appeared in propaganda, the principal tool of governments seeking to mobilize people to assume unaccustomed roles. Many of these "official" definitions are echoed in the popular media, while letters, diaries, and snapshots describe personal reactions to sexual upheaval.[12] In "high" culture we find more complex and critical responses, both political and psychological, to the sudden transformation of relationships between women and men. In addition, a focus on the construction of gender through discourse reminds us that not only literature or film but also economic, social, and political relationships function as semiotic systems.

Analyzing discourse in all of these manifestations, the authors in this book show that total war has acted as a clarifying moment, one that has revealed systems of gender in flux and thus highlighted their workings. Emergency conditions either alter or reinforce existing notions of gender, the nation, and the family. These ideas are not, however, created anew, but grounded in previous social and cultural sources. Within this system, female dependency is almost always presented as "natural," as is the state of peace. War appears to be "unnatural," "abnormal"—but warranted, in part, by men's need to protect and defend their women and families.

Such tropes appear valid as long as both terms remain stable. But during the two world wars, the female term—women's situation—underwent radical change, thus destabilizing the tropic balance. In 1914–1918, women displayed their independence by taking over men's jobs and risking their lives as nurses and ambulance drivers at the front. By the Second World War they had gone into combat in the Soviet Union and joined resistance movements throughout Europe.[13] At the same time, the symbolic value of the homefront

12. For examples, see Martin Page, ed., *"Kiss Me Goodnight, Sergeant Major": The Songs and Ballads of World War II* (Gt. Britain: Granada, 1975); for analyses, see Paola di Cori, "Gender Categories and Women's Politics: Photographic Images of Italian Women during World War I," forthcoming in Italian; and Mary Cadogan and Patricia Craig, *Women and Children First* (London: Gollancz, 1978).

13. Cottam, *Golden-Tressed Soldier* and *Soviet Airwomen;* Mary E. Reed, "The Anti-Fascist Front of Women and the Communist Party in Croatia: Conflicts within the Resistance," in *Women in Eastern Europe and the Soviet Union,* ed. Tova Yedlin (New York: Praeger, 1980), 128–39; Laska, *Women in the Resistance;* Margaret L. Rossiter, *Women in the Resistance* (New York: Praeger,

as an inviolate zone had been eroded by the advent of Zeppelins, aerial bombing, guerrilla combat, and extended occupation.[14] As the feminine term threatened to break through, the old tropes of gender appeared outmoded. But new images of women and men quickly took their place.

The metaphor of a double helix evokes the paradoxical progress and regress that has characterized women's status and representation during the two world wars.[15] When the homefront is mobilized, women may be allowed to move "forward" in terms of employment or social policy,[16] yet the battlefront—preeminently a male domain—takes economic and cultural priority. Therefore, while women's objective situation does change, relationships of domination and subordination are retained through discourses that systematically designate unequal gender relations.

Despite the workings of the double helix, during the two wars the arbitrariness of gender designations stood briefly exposed. Seeing this, historians have asked why women failed to capitalize on wartime disruptions of gender norms in order to transform their position within society and increase their power.[17] The first war seemed to offer women even greater social opportunities than the second, for it shattered what remained of the stifling nineteenth-century consensus on the female role. In Italy, for example, the cultural hegemony of Mediterranean Catholicism had kept "respectable" women sequestered until wartime labor shortages drew them into munitions factories; for the first time, public visibility did not connote disrepute.[18] In many countries, the wars brought female suffrage in their wake.[19] But acquiring the vote or taking up

1986); and Margaret Weitz, "As I Was Then: Women in the French Resistance," *Contemporary French Civilization* 10, 1 (1986), 1–19.

14. Sandra Gilbert, "Soldier's Heart: Literary Men, Literary Women, and the Great War," this volume.

15. Margaret R. Higonnet and Patrice L.-R. Higonnet, "The Double Helix," this volume.

16. In 1941 Winston Churchill urged women to use the opportunities presented by the "technical apparatus of modern warfare" to move "towards the harder forms of service and nearer to the fighting line"; "Manpower and Womanpower," a speech to the House of Commons, December 2, 1941, in Winston Churchill, *Blood, Sweat and Tears* (New York: Putnam's, 1941), 310.

17. See for example "The Retreat to Patriotic Motherhood," in *Women, War and Revolution,* ed. Carol R. Berkin and Clara M. Lovett (New York: Holmes and Meier, 1980), 209–14.

18. Di Cori, "Gender Categories and Women's Politics." While Di Cori shows that visibility was a progressive step for Italian women during World War II, Maria Antonietta Macchiocchi points out the repressive effects on women of the superficially liberating rhetoric of Mussolini; "Female Sexuality in Fascist Ideology," *Feminist Review* 1 (1979), 67–82.

19. Women won the vote in the United States, Great Britain, Canada, Germany, Sweden, the Soviet Union, Latvia, Lithuania, Estonia, and the countries formed out of the former Austro-Hungarian empire after World War I, and in France and Italy after World War II.

new employment did not readily translate into social or political power, and women everywhere suffered the effects of postwar gender backlash. Most puzzling, no strong, mass-based feminist movements arose to preserve and extend women's wartime gains.

To explain the "lag" in the development of women's consciousness, we must take a broad view, looking not just at wartime changes themselves, but also at how they were discursively encoded, and how women, like men, drew upon existing cultural resources to make sense of their experiences.[20] With this in mind, the essays herein examine the content of wartime and postwar culture, political organizations, state policy, and labor markets to see how models and metaphors gave meaning to women's new activities in ways that limited their potential to transform gender relations.

These essays draw out the implications of earlier findings that, although wartime propaganda exhorted women to brave unfamiliar work, these appeals were contained within a nationalist and militarist discourse that reinforced patriarchal, organicist notions of gender relations. It stipulated that women's new roles were "only for the duration" and that wives and mothers must make heroic sacrifices "for the nation in its time of need."[21] Propaganda reminded female defense workers that they were not themselves—that is, not "natural"—but behaving temporarily *like men*. Industrial employment would not permanently endanger their femininity (Rosie the Riveter wears nail polish as she holds her riveting gun)—and neither could such employment be expected to last.

Although most of the combatant nations had experienced some form of feminist mobilization prior to both wars, the organic discourse of wartime patriotism, with its emphasis on national solidarity, discouraged expressions of women's rights and needs, labelling them selfish, divisive, or even treasonous. When a number of feminists turned to pacificism after World War I, their essentialist arguments ironically drew upon and reinforced the postwar emphasis on femininity and sexual difference.[22]

20. Here our analysis follows the model suggested by Leed and Fussell.

21. Leila Rupp shows the prevalence of this rhetoric in Germany and the United States during World War II in *Mobilizing Women for War* (Princeton: Princeton University Press, 1978), esp. chaps. 2, 5, 6; for the United States see also Maureen Honey, *Creating Rosie the Riveter: Class, Gender, and Propaganda during World War II* (Amherst: University of Massachusetts Press, 1984). Similar phrases may be found in the propaganda of almost all combatant nations in both wars; see Margaret Allen, "The Domestic Ideal and the Mobilization of Woman Power," *Women's Studies International Forum* 6 (1983), 401–12.

22. Elshtain, "Women as Mirror," 37–38; and Barbara Steinson, "The Mother Half of Humanity: American Women in the Peace and Preparedness Movements in World War I," in

The system of gender also shaped women's participation in the military. Serving in auxiliary roles such as clerks, nurses, or ambulance drivers, women did not threaten the sexual status quo, but, when British women sought admittance to the armed forces in World War I, they met with opposition on all sides.[23] During World War II, both the Soviet Union and resistance movements throughout Europe, prompted by egalitarian ideologies as well as desperate manpower shortages, mobilized women as combatants. They were, however, frequently segregated into all-female units or assigned missions that exploited gender characteristics. And, although they faced similar risks and displayed courage equal to that shown by men, they received less recognition.[24] Citations of women emphasized their anomalous status: one Soviet account, for example, describes the feat of a "golden-tressed soldier."[25] Thus postwar valedictories restored the gendered myth of war with its affirmation that men perform acts of bravery while women contribute to the national effort through domestic constancy.

Similarly, the discourse of wartime social policy worked to limit gender disruption and preserve families, particularly those affected by the long-term absence or death of male heads. When necessary, the state moved in to serve in loco patris. In the 1940s, for instance, while the Vichy regime subtly blamed French prisoners in German hands for the fall of France, its paternalistic policies with regard to the prisoners' wives were designed in part to ensure that men would be restored to their rightful positions within the family.[26] At the same time, when the British and American governments reluctantly consented to provide childcare for female defense workers, they stressed that it was strictly a wartime measure and not meant to become a permanent entitlement.[27]

Berkin and Lovett, eds., *Women, War and Revolution,* 259–84. By contrast, Linda Schott argues, in "The Woman's Peace Party and the Moral Basis for Women's Pacificism," *Frontiers* 3, 2 (1985), that the peace activists of the World War I period saw themselves as broadly humanist, not limited to affirming the values traditionally associated with femininity.

23. Jenny Gould, "Women's Military Services in First World War Britain," this volume.

24. Schwartz, "Redefining Resistance," this volume; Cottam, *Soviet Airwomen,* xiii; Weitz, "As I Was Then."

25. Yuliya Drunina, "The Golden-Tressed Soldier," in Cottam, *Golden-Tressed Soldier,* 192–97. In *Night Witches: The Untold Story of Soviet Women in Combat* (Novato, Calif.: Presidio, 1981), Bruce Myles reproduces this attitude; while sensationalizing and sentimentalizing Soviet women's contributions to the war ("it seemed the very stuff of romantic thrillers," p. viii), he fails to note that they received a disproportionately small number of commendations, or to criticize their neglect in Soviet military history.

26. Sarah Fishman, "Waiting for the Captive Sons of France," this volume.

27. Denise Riley, *War in the Nursery* (London: Virago, 1983), chap. 5; and Sonya Michel, "American Women and the Discourse of the Democratic Family," this volume.

Most extreme was the social policy of the Nazis, who were driven by the twin demands of preserving racial and sexual domination to adopt programs that proved irrational and prevented them from engaging in total war. So great was their commitment to promoting Aryan motherhood that they used the labor of immigrants—and eventually of slaves—to spare their own women the hardships of defense work. Although all adult females were required to register for employment, the orders were never applied consistently, so most middle- and upper-class women were able to avoid taking jobs, leaving working-class women to bear the major part of women's labor burden.[28] Ironically, the Nazis' unparalleled intervention in reproduction and family life undermined the power of individual men within their families—the very power the government had vowed to preserve.[29]

Postwar social policy once again linked motherhood to national security, but for the ends of demobilization. Although many historians agree that the two wars had an equalizing or democratizing effect on the societies of belligerent nations,[30] women and men benefited unequally. Most governments, stressing the need to reward and reintegrate veterans and restore family life, instituted pronatalist and redistributive policies, such as family allowances and subsidies for housing and education, while playing down women's demands for employment opportunities and equal pay, even though they had supported such principles during the war.

Because the wartime work of women constituted the most visible challenge to prewar gender assignments, the discourse governing women in the national economies is of critical interest. Both wars stepped up the pace of technological advance, accelerating the division of labor and creating a wider gap between skilled and unskilled jobs. In most countries wartime labor shortages allowed women to move into well-paid, skilled jobs. Yet attitudes toward female

28. Leila J. Rupp, "'I Don't Call that *Volksgemeinschaft*': Women, Class, and War in Nazi Germany," in Berkin and Lovett, eds., *Women, War and Revolution,* 37–53; Annemarie Tröger, "The Creation of a Female Assembly-Line Proletariat," in *When Biology Became Destiny: Women in Weimar and Nazi Germany,* ed. Renate Bridenthal, Atina Grossmann, and Marion Kaplan (New York: Monthly Review Press, 1984), 237–70.

29. Gisela Bock, "Racism and Sexism in Nazi Germany: Motherhood, Compulsory Sterilization, and the State," in Bridenthal et al., eds., *When Biology,* 271–96. Richard J. Evans makes the point that the Nazis violated the sanctity of the family, stressing the effect on women, but he does not consider the effect on men as well. See "German Women and the Triumph of Hitler," *Journal of Modern History* 48, 1 (March 1976), suppl., 17–29.

30. This is one aspect of the "war as revolution" thesis; see Wright, *Ordeal,* chap. 11; and Arthur Marwick, *Britain in the Century of Total War: War, Peace, and Social Change, 1900–1967* (Boston: Little, Brown, 1968), chap. 10; see also Richard M. Titmuss, "War and Social Policy," in *Essays on the Welfare State* (Boston: Beacon, 1969), 86.

workers prevented them from enjoying the full symbolic importance of their new positions. Women's representatives were barred from war labor boards or granted only nonvoting status. Trade unions readily organized women in order to maintain members' pay levels and influence over the production process, but their leadership remained heavily male-dominated.[31]

Both unions and management manipulated women's identification with motherhood. During the war, Denise Riley argues, women were "under-feminized," their extra responsibilities as housekeepers and mothers ignored when it came to assigning overtime or nightwork.[32] According to production managers, the chief problem of female employment was "absenteeism," a code word they used for a complex set of issues that neither they, the state, nor union officials were willing to confront. During reconversion, by contrast, motherhood became a privileged category. Exploiting pronatalist rhetoric, management unapologetically favored men in peacetime hiring. Unions made few objections, although in some cases a clear majority of their female members had chosen to continue working despite the propaganda.[33] In countries that experienced postwar prosperity, women were recruited into the expanding but low-paid clerical and service sectors. This work was deemed more suitable to mothers or potential mothers and also appeared to make use of women's "special" skills.[34] Thus women could only hope for substantial economic advance through their husbands' employment and via the family unit—not through their own work.[35] After the war, women's protests over lost jobs, inadequate pensions, or dismantled childcare centers were drowned by the choruses of concern over the adjustment problems of former soldiers.

In short, the double helix governed both wartime and postwar culture. As returning veterans "retreated" on the masculine strand of the helix, women too stepped back, thus maintaining the gender hierarchy. The combatant nations

31. See Ruth Milkman, "American Women and Industrial Unionism during World War II," this volume.

32. Denise Riley, "Some Peculiarities of Social Policy concerning Women in Wartime and Postwar Britain," this volume.

33. Nancy Gabin, "'They Have Placed a Penalty on Womanhood': The Protest Actions of Women Workers in Detroit-area UAW Locals, 1945–1947," *Feminist Studies* 8, 2 (Summer 1982), 373–98.

34. See Renate Bridenthal, "Something Old, Something New: Women between the Two World Wars," in *Becoming Visible: Women in European History,* ed. Renate Bridenthal and Claudia Koonz (Boston: Houghton Mifflin, 1977), 434–38; and Julie A. Matthaei, *An Economic History of Women in America* (New York: Schocken, 1982), chap. 11.

35. See Matthaei, *Economic History,* chap. 6; Susan Hartmann, *The Home Front and Beyond: American Women in the 1940s* (Boston: Twayne, 1982), 92–95; Elizabeth Wilson, *Only Halfway to Paradise: Women in Postwar Britain, 1945–1968* (London: Tavistock, 1980).

were concerned with the problems of the veterans' readjustment; civilians feared that men taught to hate and kill might resist the constraints imposed by peacetime society. (Ironically many former soldiers were aware that their much-vaunted masculine aggressiveness was little more than a facade.)[36] In this regard, the postwar discourse on gender operated on two levels. Typically, it glorified male heroism and praised feminine submissiveness, assuming women's willingness to subordinate their own needs and desires to those of their men.[37] These twin emphases upheld the myth of masculinity while attempting to balance it with an equally strong femininity, containing both within a newly eroticized and consumerist domestic unity.

In postwar rituals of commemoration women were generally ignored; when they were singled out for attention, it was often for their role in events that emphasized their sexual status. Women who had been victimized through rape, imprisonment, or execution were contrasted with those who had consorted with the enemy or been unfaithful to husbands and sweethearts. In both cases, their identities were encoded in a complex system of nationalist and gender politics: while their status was linked to that of their respective nations, it was also determined by gender.

Within this system, political alliances offered women no guarantees. The two world wars perpetuated the tradition that regarded women as "booty," no matter "whose" women they were. For example, Allied servicemen stationed in Britain aggressively pursued local women, whom they were as an army assigned to defend. The British response was more jocular resignation than indignation; the only problem with American GIs, so the saying went, was that they were "overpaid, oversexed, and over here."[38] A double standard was clearly at work here—the same standard that assumed that female victims of sexual assault were virtuous while women who actively sought relationships were immoral. Because the victimization of women revealed their defenselessness and thus emphasized the importance of the male protective role, it was generally treated with great sympathy. Female traitors, on the other hand, were excoriated, for they had dared to assert themselves, thus violating codes of gender as well as patriotism.

In contrast to both the victims and the traitors were the war brides, who were especially numerous in North America after World War II. Whether they

36. Leed, *No Man's Land,* 7.

37. Karin Hausen, "The German Nation's Obligations to the Heroes' Widows of World War I," this volume; Susan Hartmann, "Prescriptions for Penelope: Literature on Women's Obligations to Returning World War II Veterans," *Women's Studies* 5 (1978), 223–39.

38. Quoted in Calder, *People's War,* 310.

came from Axis or Allied nations, these women were warmly welcomed, no doubt because they were fulfilling conventional feminine roles, and also because their status demonstrated that at least some of the conquering heroes had behaved honorably toward foreign women. But the photographs of smiling women, many holding children, who lined the railings of arriving ships diverted attention from those who had been treated less honorably.[39]

Because public references to sexuality tended to gloss over male outrages while decrying female assertiveness, they may have had a more repressive effect on women than on men who were attempting to come to terms with tumultuous wartime emotions. Members of both sexes were equally susceptible to the loneliness, disorientation, and stark physical need that led to sexual encounters with strangers, political identities notwithstanding.[40] For both women and men, wartime separation often produced mutual suspicion and mistrust. Rigid public codes of legitimacy more readily excused male lapses than female ones; at the very least, they relegated women's wartime activities to the realm of the extraordinary and lauded a return to the status quo ante bellum.[41] Although disturbed by their experiences, women were reluctant to discuss their feelings directly. Sobered, perhaps guilty, they felt compelled to put their exhilarating experiences behind them.[42] But from about 1944 on, as Andrea Walsh has pointed out, female audiences flocked to "noir" films that allowed veiled expressions of jealousy and hostility through responses to gothic plots and psychological allusions.[43]

Thus, although wartime experiences no doubt affected women's consciousness and may have temporarily altered their identities, for many women the war years were perceived and remembered, both individually and collectively, through discourses that revived rather conventional gender relations.[44] In-

39. See Joyce Hibbert, ed., *The War Brides* (Toronto: Peter Martin Associates, 1978), and Peggy O'Hara, ed., *From Romance to Reality* (Cobalt, Ont.: Highway Book Shop, 1983).

40. Marguerite Duras explores the often incongruous or inappropriate erotic dimensions of her work in the Resistance in her fiction-memoir, *The War* (originally published as *La Douleur,* Paris: P.O.L., 1985), (New York: Pantheon, 1986); in Betty Miller's World War II novel about Britain, *On the Side of the Angels* (Great Britain: Robert Hale, 1945; rpt. London: Virago, 1985), an inarticulate servant mourns the death of a German pilot shot down over her village (chap. 10).

41. In Sloan Wilson's *The Man in the Gray Flannel Suit* (New York: Simon and Schuster, 1955), for example, when the protagonist confesses that he impregnated an Italian woman while stationed overseas, his wife not only forgives him but insists that he support the child.

42. See Gilbert, "Soldier's Heart."

43. Andrea Walsh, *Women's Film and Female Experience, 1940–1950* (New York: Praeger, 1984), chap. 5.

44. Dominique Veillon, "Résister au féminin," *Pénélope* (special issue, "Mêmoires de femmes") 12 (1985), 87–92; Annemarie Tröger, "German Women's Memories of World War II," this volume.

stead of allowing women to affirm their newfound independence, postwar notions of femininity in propaganda and the popular media were restrictive and frustrating. In this way potentially progressive social transformations culminated for many in what might be termed reaction formations.

But hegemonic, conventional definitions of gender were not all-pervasive. If popular culture insisted on the anchoring polarities of gender, the literature of war allowed more latitude for probing definitions of masculinity and femininity. Both male and female authors challenged prevailing myths about their sex. Yet, though modern scholars readily find oppositional discourses of gender in much of twentieth-century war literature, these messages had little political impact on their authors' contemporaries.

The reasons for this lack of effect were different for male and female writers. Men's writings passed directly into the canon of twentieth-century war literature, where the prevailing critical categories, resting on conventional definitions of gender, read sexual ambivalence as irony and cynicism. Women's wartime writings, on the other hand, passed into obscurity, and their exposés of gender myths were submerged. Only when feminist scholars began delving into the literary history of "minor" authors did many of these critical works by women come to light.

To understand why women's writings disappeared, we must look at the process by which the canon was established. The two world wars altered the literature of war in several important ways. The Great War, with its mass conscription of educated, nonprofessional soldiers, created a new phenomenon: the soldier-writer.[45] The authentic voice and the intensity of moral conflict to be found in the finest works of a poet like Wilfred Owen created a new set of touchstones for the literature of war; because those who gave voice to the experience of the trenches were so imbued with the classics, they became keepers of a new canon.[46] And despite the fact that their writings exposed the mythical quality of received notions of masculinity, they could not help creating fresh myths that were also identifiably masculine.

45. Some recent poetry anthologies include Brian Gardner, ed., *Up the Line to Death: The War Poets, 1914–1918* (London: Methuen, 1964), and *The Terrible Rain, The War Poets, 1939–1945* (London: Methuen, 1966); and Ian Hamilton, ed., *The Poetry of War, 1939–45* (London: Alan Ross, 1965). A classic short story collection is Ernest Hemingway, ed., *Men at War: The Best War Stories of All Times* (New York: Crown, 1944). For literary analysis of the canon, see Fussell, *The Great War;* Léon Riegel, *Guerre et littérature: Le bouleversement des consciences dans la littérature romanesque inspirée par la Grande Guerre* (Nancy: Editions Klincksieck, 1978); Vernon Scannell, *Not without Glory: Poets of the Second World War* (London: Woburn, 1976); and Peter G. Jones, *War and the Novelist: Appraising the American War Novel* (Columbia: University of Missouri Press, 1976).

46. Fussell, *The Great War,* chap. 9.

Wartime writing became significant not only in itself but in its impact on the rest of twentieth-century literature. Hemingway considered war to be "one of the major subjects . . . and those writers who had not seen it were always very jealous and tried to make it seem unimportant, or abnormal, or a disease as a subject, while, really, it was just something quite irreplaceable that they had missed."[47] By World War II, male writers were self-consciously seeking to perpetuate the canon of war literature, their major works unified by a tone of cynicism, black humor, and ironic detachment. While the settings and imagery varied, many shared the theme of male community, expressed through the device of multiple protagonists.

Given the privileged position of the literature of war, it is not surprising that in women's wartime writings we find some special variants on the anxiety of authorship that Sandra Gilbert and Susan Gubar have argued infects women's writing. Women, even during the Second World War, were rarely situated where they could create war poetry; nor did they belong to the exclusive fellowship of male poets to whom Brian Gardner dedicates his World War I anthology, *Up the Line to Death*.[48] Since the definition of war poetry privileges actual battlefront experience, women who are barred from combat can only participate in this literary mode at second hand. To evoke the experience of blood and muck, they may ventriloquize, using what Judith Kazantzis in her preface to *Scars upon My Heart* calls a "transferred voice." Unfortunately, they risk producing sentimental elegies for the "gallant multitudes" strewn like "snowflakes."[49] Indeed, many women writers verbalize precisely this dilemma of the "idle, useless mouth," as Cicely Hamilton puts it in her poem, "Non-Combatant."[50]

Even when women writers describe the wartime losses that they have suffered as women—as wives, mothers, and lovers—they are displaced, for the primary loss in war literature is inevitably death; mourning is secondary. The sense of helpless observation, palpable and most lyrical in poetry about nursing, oddly resembles the tone of prisoner-of-war poetry written during World War II.[51] The peculiar situation of women, however, is marked by their

47. Ernest Hemingway, *The Green Hills of Africa* (New York: Scribner's, 1935), 70.

48. Gardner, *Up the Line,* xx.

49. Margaret Postgate Cole, "The Falling Leaves," in *Scars upon My Heart: Women's Poetry and Verse of the First World War,* ed. Catherine Reilly (London: Virago, 1981), 21.

50. Ibid., 46.

51. See for example three poems written by Rudolph Leonhard, who was imprisoned at the concentration camp in Vernet, France, before being executed by the Nazis: "We Take a Walk," "The Last Days," and "Christmas Song," in *War Poems of the United Nations,* ed. Joy Davidman, (New York: Dial, 1943), 121–23.

implication as the motive of war: "How can I for such sacrifice atone?" asks Juliette de Bairacli-Levy's "Threnode for Young Soldiers Killed in Action" (1947).[52]

Here also we can observe differences between women's and men's experience of time, insofar as that division overlaps with the line between battle- and homefront. For the soldier, the battle collapses time, steals "the undone years" (Wilfred Owen), whereas for women who have lost those they love, "the long battle now against defeat" continues even when the war is over.[53]

The most powerful of women's writings about war rely on indirection, or writing "slant"; in some poems the only direct reference to battle occurs in the title. Again, there is a resemblance between women's writing and the devices of internal (and external) exile; French *contrabande* poetry written under German occupation is similarly alert to the uses and abuses of "la fausse parole."[54] Like the noir films analyzed by Andrea Walsh, women's writing about war uses indirect techniques to evoke the experience of gendered violence and other forbidden subjects.[55]

Women's removal from the ultimate sacrifice constrains their direct critiques of the wars supposedly waged on their behalf.[56] Much of the strength of men's literature of war derives from the tensions between patriotism and criticism. Siegfried Sassoon describes grotesquely how "clotted heads slept in the plastering slime"; others, like Isaac Rosenberg, explore their sense of guilt at the senseless slaughter or probe the psychology of power. In women's poetry, such creative tensions appear reflexively, turned back upon women themselves, as in Edith Sitwell's sharply etched image: "We are the dull blind carrion-flies that dance and batten."[57] Not until two decades after the Great War did Vera Brittain and Virginia Woolf feel free to criticize it without ambivalence.

If marginality made women hesitant to speak against war, no such compunctions prevented them from expressing their views of gender inequality, for this was something they experienced directly. Already in the first war we hear from Nora Bomford, "O, damn the shibboleth/Of sex![58] The most characteristic strategy of subversion is simply to invert gender roles, as Simone de Beauvoir

52. In *Chaos of the Night: Women's Poetry and Verse of the Second World War,* ed. Catherine Reilly (London: Virago, 1984), 8.

53. Vera Bax, "The Fallen," in Reilly, ed., *Chaos,* 14.

54. See Ian Higgins, ed., Introduction to *Anthology of Second World War French Poetry* (London: Methuen, 1982), 7–8.

55. Walsh, *Women's Film,* chap. 5.

56. Judith Kazantzis, Preface to Reilly, ed., *Scars,* xxi.

57. "The Dancers," ibid., 100.

58. "Drafts," ibid., 12.

does in *The Blood of Others*.[59] The hero, Jean, directs resistance operations from safety, while a female character, Hélène, risks and loses her life on a mission. De Beauvoir also questions the identification of masculinity with strategic planning and heroic sacrifice and femininity with the preservation of life and horror of shedding "the blood of others." In *History: A Novel,* Elsa Morante separates her heroine's narrative, focused on everyday experience, from masculine history; a list of political and military events precedes each chapter, throwing this gender division into sharp relief.[60] (This is an interesting reversal of Norman Mailer's technique in *The Naked and the Dead;* he flashes back to the homefront through his "Time Machine" sections, which are also set apart.)

It may be that female writers, because of their marginality, were more alert than their male counterparts to the systems of gender that were revealed in wartime. Yet only a handful of women—Woolf, Brittain, de Beauvoir—allowed their insights to lead them to overt feminism, either literary or political. In other writings, protest was more muted. Mollie Panter-Downes, for example, wrote about Britain during World War II with a certain nostalgia for the excitement of her country's collective striving, a curious detachment from its tragedies, and a genteel distress at the prospect of running a household without "those anonymous caps and aprons who lived out of sight and pulled the strings."[61] In her novel *One Fine Day,* the heroine Laura Marshall vaguely resents the demands of her husband, a returned veteran, but her rebellion takes the form of napping on a hillside when she should be home fixing his supper. Despite her inability to redirect her own life, Laura is optimistic about her daughter's future: "I want a good deal for Victoria, she thought . . . but not the same things that my mother wanted for me."[62] Writing in 1946, Panter-Downes was prescient: although the women who lived through the wars made few permanent gains, the momentary experience of sexual disruption granted them an ironic view of gender that they passed on to their daughters. Turned critical, the irony of one generation became the feminism of the next.

This book is not a comprehensive comparative study of the condition of all women touched by the two world wars. Nor is it an attempt simply to

59. Simone de Beauvoir, *The Blood of Others* (originally published as *Le sang des autres: Roman,* Paris: (Gallimard, 1946), trans. Yvonne Moyse and Roger Senhouse (London: Secker and Warburg, 1948).

60. Elsa Morante, *History: A Novel* (originally published as *La storia: Romanzo* (Turin: Einaudi, 1974), trans. William Weaver (New York: Knopf, 1977; rpt. New York: Avon, 1979).

61. Mollie Panter-Downes, *One Fine Day* (London: Hamish Hamilton, 1946; rpt. London: Virago, 1985), 19.

62. Ibid., 149.

document that "we were there." Rather, these essays are meant to serve as models for analyzing the wars as events of gender politics. They provide readings of a variety of wartime discourses ranging from the semiotics of the division of labor in defense industries to women's poetry and fiction, from the dominant to the oppositional. These readings are, by definition, resisting—that is, they refuse to accept the tacit categories the discourses enfold and attempt to enforce, but rather seek to expose systems of gender and analyze their inner workings. In this sense, the essays press toward the unavoidable conclusion that the deconstruction and reconstruction of gender was another battlefront in the two world wars.

PART ONE

Reconceptualizing the Two World Wars

JOAN W. SCOTT

Rewriting History

History has become an increasingly complicated project over the course of the past two decades. New research and new conceptualizations have called into question the idea of progress, which was once a central narrative theme; the emphasis on politics as the focus of that narrative; and the use of Western white man as the representative of a universal human subject. It is now almost impossible to define History, as did earlier generations of historians, as the story of man's progress toward political democracy. Instead, we increasingly think in terms of the changing forms of power, diverse groups of men and women, and many foci for historical experience.

These new ways of thinking have not been easily accepted or acknowledged. The profusion of histories has created a sense of fragmentation and confusion, characteristic perhaps of moments of profound intellectual transition. (Social history, with its seemingly endless proliferation of subjects, themes and topics, is often cited as a cause of this transition when in fact it merely exemplifies a larger epistemological shift.) It is not surprising that at such moments some seek to "reclaim a legacy" they feel is being lost, while others insist on the validity, even the primacy, of some new area of inquiry. It is also not surprising that debate has opened on narrative, the essential form of historical writing.[1] What is surprising is the resistance of so many historians—themselves students of change—to changes in the practice of their own discipline. But this resistance has positive effects: it reveals to those writing new histories the connections between professional politics and intellectual inquiry, and it underscores

1. Lawrence Stone, "The Revival of Narrative," *Past and Present* 85 (1979), 3–24; E. J. Hobsbawm, "The Revival of Narrative: Some Comments," *Past and Present* 86 (1980), 3–8; Philip Abrams, "History, Sociology, Historical Sociology," *Past and Present* 87 (1980), 3–16; Gordon Wood, "Star-Spangled History," *New York Review of Books* 29 (August 12, 1982).

the need to examine the impact of such histories on History as it has been traditionally written and understood.

Historians of women have long been conscious of the need to articulate their relationship to History. They have challenged the notion that women were non-actors by making visible those "hidden from history," and they have exposed the biases of a political history that omitted significant contributions by women. They have illuminated the historical importance of the areas of human experience beyond the narrow political arena, such as workplace, household, and family, and have shown how women figured in them. They have suggested as well that the watersheds of any age—war, revolution, economic crisis, religious reform—had different impacts on women and men. Most recently, they have begun to ask what their new information about women can tell us about events and processes that have traditionally preoccupied historians. This enterprise has involved major methodological and theoretical reformulations, especially analyses of symbolic representations and theories of language. In this process, historians of women have begun to articulate the ways gender might be used as a category of analysis, not only for direct study of the relationships between women and men, but also for a more complex understanding of politics, power, state policy and so on. This new understanding promises more than the integration of material about women into standard historical accounts (a problematic undertaking in any case); it has the potential to rewrite History itself.

Of course, the writing of women's history and the formulation of new concepts has been more diverse and less coherent than my description suggests. Opinions differ on how History should be rewritten and on the ultimate purpose of women's history. For some scholars, rewriting is inevitable once the terms of women's experience have been documented; for others, the exposure of the profound differences between women and men—the delineation of some inherent sexual difference—is the real aim of historical inquiry; for a third group (and I include myself in this group), there is a need to redefine the terms of traditional historical analysis. Such redefinition seems critical for two reasons. First, women's history will always remain separate, a subdepartment of History, unless its practitioners are able to point out its relationship to History or to the rewriting of History. Second, a separate women's history tends to confirm the notion that women belong in a separate sphere. This underscores, indeed legitimizes, the existing lines of sexual difference—and the inequality associated with them.

The essays in this book exemplify all three of these approaches. They do not always support one another's conclusions, but taken together they can be seen to develop a subtle and complicated picture of the economic, political, social, and cultural meanings of women's wartime experiences. Some deny that gender is a defining category of these experiences; others assume it to be the key to women's consciousness, motivation, behavior, and identity. Still others suggest the need to examine connections between political representations of women and women's behavior. All the essays address questions of women's history, women and war, and women in the specific contexts of the world wars. And they provide some of the material necessary for introducing gender into analyses of politics.

The need for this approach becomes evident when one looks at the limitations of existing interpretive frameworks for the subject of women and the world wars. The great wars of the twentieth century have typically been characterized as watersheds for women. The focus has been on women's experience, on the impact of war upon them, with evidence being presented to affirm or deny that war was a turning point for women. There are at least four variations on the watershed theme. The first hails the new opportunities that opened for women during the war: skilled, high-paying jobs in heavy industry; new positions in government bureaucracies, educational institutions, the armed forces, and on the front lines as ambulance drivers, medics, and *résistantes*. During the war, this argument continues, women were able to demonstrate their capabilities, skill, and power, and thus to challenge the irrational prejudices that had confined them to a separate sphere. Women proved they could be like men. For historian William Chafe, the changes for American women during World War II were irrevocable and fundamental, even if there was something of an ideological lag until the 1960s.[2] At that time, feminism initiated the change in attitudes required to make social ideas about women's roles and place match the behavior of the past twenty years. Dissenting, Leila Rupp argues that the power of ideology prevented real changes in women's status. American war propaganda appealed to notions of female service and self-sacrifice "for the duration," thus perpetuating cultural notions of female difference even in circumstances that should have challenged those notions.[3] Both sides in this debate see ideology as a powerful explanatory factor, yet neither sees as problematic its creation, change, or effects on behavior.

The second variation on the watershed theme stresses political rights and points to the irony of the fact that women (whose interest was presumably in

2. William H. Chafe, *The American Woman: Her Changing Social, Economic, and Political Role, 1920–1970* (New York: Oxford University Press, 1972).

3. Leila Rupp, *Mobilizing Women for War: German and American Propaganda, 1939–1945* (Princeton: Princeton University Press, 1978).

peace) received formal citizenship in England, the United States, and Germany after World War I; in Italy and France after World War II. In textbook renditions, women's "good behavior" during wartime assumes far greater significance than their organized suffrage struggles in the pre- and postwar periods. That good behavior, of course, was often the politicians' explanation of why they extended the right to vote to women (a far better justification in their eyes than appearing to give in to the militant tactics of the suffragists.) But other accounts of suffrage also deal with war and the nature of its social and political impact on the women's rights movement. And some major political histories—of British suffrage, for example—argue that women's cooperation with the war effort earned them support for the franchise and softened the negative attitude engendered by militant suffragists before 1914.[4] Those who argue that war did not have a major impact on women's rights minimize both the effects of war as compared to the ongoing suffrage campaigns and the effects of the vote on women. Without other legal, economic, and social changes, they insist, the public recognition of women as citizens was an essentially empty or symbolic gesture.[5] Both sides in this debate tend to view the vote as a political issue *about* women, as if politics could be compartmentalized according to the explicit object of its concern.

The third (minor) variation on the watershed theme presupposes a fundamental (or natural) female antipathy to war and documents women's leadership in peace movements and in life-saving and nurturing activities. In this view, war gave women the opportunity to articulate a feminist politics in opposition to the destructive ("masculine") impulses of the nations involved. The world wars were thus a turning point in feminist consciousness, a starting point for pacifist activities embodied in the early years of this century in the Women's International League for Peace and Freedom and leading in more recent times to Greenham Common and Seneca Falls. In Lynne Layton's essay "Vera Brittain's Testament(s)," this theme appears in somewhat different form. The war experience, she suggests, permitted Vera Brittain to eschew masculine ways of thinking and to achieve (inherent? appropriate? characteristically female?) feminine moral reasoning (as defined and described in the work of psychologist Carol Gilligan.) The opposing view is that female opponents of war were, in fact, very few. The vast majority of women lost sight of their presumably common interests as the political crisis united women and

4. See, for example, Constance Rover, *Women's Suffrage and Party Politics in Britain, 1866–1914* (London, 1967). It would be interesting to determine the extent to which these histories transmit uncritically politicians' rhetoric regarding the granting of female suffrage.

5. Steven Hause's "More Minerva than Mars," this volume, eloquently makes this case for France.

men around national concerns. If sexual difference persisted, it did not inform national mobilizations in support of war.[6] Indeed, if we take Yasmine Ergas' "Growing Up Banished" seriously, it becomes clear that in certain circumstances gender is far less central than race, ethnicity, or class in the construction of personal identity.

The fourth variation on the watershed theme discusses the long- and short-term impacts of war. Some historians insist that war initiated changes which ultimately revolutionized women's status. Although it took years to work out the details of the revolution, change began with the structures improvised or established during the war. Others see women's gains as temporary, "for the duration." They may have affected individual consciousnesses, but they had no lasting transformative impact. The sexual division of labor, unequal treatment of women, and obstacles to their economic, educational, and political advancement persisted despite the "proof" the war furnished of women's responsibility, capability, and skill. The elusive issue in this debate is the measure of improved status. What constitutes an improvement or revolution; how does one measure it; what indicators does one use?

Although research undertaken within the context of the watershed theme has yielded important information, the debates seem ultimately unresolvable. And, because they appear to speak primarily about women, their relevance to other historical inquiry is not immediately obvious, nor is the connection of this women's history to History. How can that connection be made? How can we use women's history to rewrite History? How might the history of the world wars change if women and gender figured in the story? How can information about women help us reconceptualize aspects of the wars' political history? By asking questions not about the impact of events on women but about the processes of politics, connections between economic policy and the meanings of social experience, cultural representations of gender and their presence in political discourse, we move the inquiry to new terrain. Questions about the representation of sexual difference can link women's history with political history, permitting historians to maintain a perspective that both makes women visible as historical actors, as subjects of the narrative, and offers new readings of the two world wars.

6. It should be obvious that, as in many historical disputes, this argument rests on a projection of current feminist debates onto historical materials. Here at least two points are at issue: whether women are essentially or naturally peace-loving because of their biological or cultural preoccupation with childbearing and -rearing *and* whether political appeals against militarism ought to speak to notions women are presumed to hold about themselves, whether or not these are "true." The first position assumes an inherent pacificism in women's nature; the second seeks to exploit cultural beliefs, asssuming that ideas about gender are less susceptible to change than ideas about politics and the military.

The questions I would ask begin with representations of gender. Was the gender system transformed or reproduced in the course of the extraordinary conditions generated by wartime? To answer this we must look at policies directed at women and at the construction of women's experience. How were mobilizations of women handled; what political processes were involved? What were the terms of appeal used to mobilize women? What were the connections among women's experiences at work and in public roles (which women? which roles?) and policy debates about appropriate activities for women? Who took what sides in the debates and what reasons did they offer for their positions? How, in Denise Riley's terms, was the "web of cross-reference," which included politics, social science, and social policy, formulated?[7]

To answer questions about the gender system, however, we must move beyond examination of the terms of women's experience per se to metaphoric uses of gender representation. Did nations express political goals in sexual terms? What meanings did sexual representations of war have for social and personal experience? Here it seems critical to analyze political discourse in the way Sandra Gilbert examines wartime literary production in terms of manliness and masculinity.[8] Indeed, the two kinds of text must be analyzed to expose their similar uses of sexual representation. Here Michelle Perrot's "The New Eve and the Old Adam," on antifeminism in pre-World War I France offers an important model of interpretation. She suggests that, long before hostilities commenced, the climate of opinion expressed national anxieties as a crisis of masculinity (brought on in part by heightened feminist activity during the last decades of the nineteenth century). The terms by which wartime efforts were defined and by which war itself was depicted existed before the war began. With this information in mind we can ask whether the war strengthened or relaxed cultural definitions of gender. How? In what terms? Was the process singular or varied? Who was affected and in what ways? Is there a politics of gender (that is, dispute about language, terminology, allocation of resources, the exercise of power, and the definition of the terms of relationship between the sexes) in the politics of war? The essays in this book begin to formulate some answers and point to areas of fruitful examination. By focusing on a variety of themes and details and by moving among different levels and kinds of analysis, we can extract from them a sense of the possible directions for a new History.

The first theme we might want to explore further is the coincidence of

7. Denise Riley, *War in the Nursery: Theories of the Child and the Mother* (London: Virago Press, 1983), 189

8. "Soldier's Heart: Literary Men, Literary Women, and the Great War," in this volume.

militarist and misogynist rhetoric. Michelle Perrot and Sandra Gilbert illustrate how political threats can be represented in terms of gender. Gender relationships are seen as timeless, unchanging, outside social and political systems. The turmoil of politics is then depicted as an overturning of the natural order: men are weak and impotent, while women are strong, ugly, domineering, taking over public life, abandoning husbands and children. War is the ultimate disorder, the disruption of all previously established relationships, or the outcome of earlier instability. War is represented as a sexual disorder; peace thus implies a return to "traditional" gender relationships, the familiar and natural order of families, men in public roles, women at home, and so on. Between the wars, the fascists' call for order and their promise of stability was also presented in terms of gender, as a restoration of established and commonly understood relationships between the sexes. In " 'This Is My Rifle, This Is My Gun,' " Susan Gubar shows that Nazi ideology articulated an ideal of virility which put women in subordinate and inferior positions. (Indeed, Gubar argues that the virulence of Nazi misogyny catalyzed the opposition of women writers.) The Nazis also expressed anti-Semitism in explicit gender terms. The Aryan, masculinized nation was defined in contrast to representations of effeminate, homosexual Jews. Those who were excluded and marginalized were also feminized, justifying their exclusion. How did these representations resonate in German and Jewish families? What alternative meanings of ethnic and male and female identity were created among Germans who resisted the Nazis and among Jews? What political appeals are inherent in these kinds of gender representation?

The second theme this book addresses is state policy, especially family welfare and pronatalist policy. An examination of the terms of the policy reveals not only the intentions of its proponents but also the way politics itself was represented. As states developed wartime or postwar policies for families, they appealed to the need to restore natural order. Thus Karin Hausen shows how the German state aimed at restoring "natural families" for war widows; Sonya Michel finds American social workers arguing for education and daycare as a way of bolstering mothers' natural ties to their children; and Denise Riley discusses post-World War II British pronatalism as a policy that enshrined motherhood as an inherent function of all women.[9] In all these cases political decisions were represented as protections of natural social relationships among family members, especially mothers and children. This kind of representation depicted social policy as outside politics—when in fact vast social and political

9. "The German Nation's Obligations to the Heroes' Widows of World War I"; "American Women and the Discourse of the Democratic Family in World War II"; "Some Peculiarities of Social Policy concerning Women in Wartime and Postwar Britain."

reorganizations were being attempted or implemented. Postwar stabilization efforts were also almost always attempts at reorganization; yet the political processes at work were obscured by discussing maternal and child welfare in terms of natural psychological and biological needs. Indeed, the political processes were hidden not only from contemporaries but also from historians, who accepted the terms of the discussion at face value and separated their treatments of social policy from the more "serious" politics of diplomacy and war. Since women tended to be the focus of social welfare policy, those who have attended to women's history are in a special position to reveal not only the politics of the welfare programs themselves but also their relationship to the "larger" issues of national politics.

A third theme addressed by this book is the power of ideological representation. Examinations of women's experiences in war, especially those based on oral histories, are remarkable for their emphasis on death and deprivation. They contrast dramatically with the official emphasis on heroism and valor aimed at mobilizing national support. Karin Hausen writes, "the silence surrounding the hard, gray, everyday realities of wartime and postwar life is part of the pathos of hero worship. The innumerable war monuments in the city squares block our view of the realities of war." She then quotes the president of the German Reichstag in 1918, and we can see in his words the transformation of suffering into heroism, and the silencing of the human experience of loss and grief by invocations to patriotism and the life of the fatherland. The dead soldiers become, in this speech, the children, property, and lifeblood of the nation.

> Heavy, too, the losses of human life demanded by the war. Many a woman's heart is consumed by grief at the death of her fallen husband and brother, many a father and mother's heart aches for the sons torn from them. We honor their pain and mourn with them, but the fatherland thanks them and is proud of so many heroic sons who have spilt their blood and laid down their lives in the World War we are fighting for our own existence.[10]

Women's experience, when contrasted with official pronouncements on the meaning of war, provides insight not only into the discrepancy between domestic, private history and official, national history, but also (and more important) a means of analyzing how and by whom national memory is constructed. The private-public distinction—families as compared to the nation, mothers needs versus the needs of the state, individual death as opposed to national survival—is critical in the formulation of nationalist or patriotic ideologies. To what extent these ideologies also rest on and reinscribe existing

10. Quoted in Hausen, "The German Nation's Obligations."

notions of gender relationships and the sexual division of labor remains an important—and as yet unstudied—question.

The state's silence on individual war experiences contrasts with its noisy pronatalism, especially after World War II. Positive attention to women and families is evident; indeed, analyses point to an "overfeminization" of the language of social policy in this period. Is there a connection between official silence on (or minimization of) misery and death and the loud discussions of maternal and child welfare? Instead of treating them separately can we view them as aspects of the same national politics? How? Tim Mason has written about the "reconciliatory function of the family in Nazi ideology"; does it have a similar function in postwar Western politics?[11] What can these questions reveal about the operations of political discourse, the appeal of ideological rhetoric, the connections among government policies, the perceptions and politics of two world wars?

Focusing on political discourse raises important methodological and theoretical issues. This book documents the diversity of experience of social and national groups. There are differences between women and men, Jewish and German women, different races and ethnic groups, dominant cultures and persecuted minorities. Yet my emphasis on the state, political discourse, cultural construction, and ideological representation suggests a uniformity not only in language but also in its impact. In fact, as Denise Riley suggests, we need to study the "lived effects of political language." We must find out how people interpreted and used the language of politics, how official pronouncements resonated with various publics, how people articulated their understandings of war and its consequences, how opposition was expressed and silenced, how these processes differed in various nations and groups. This involves more than a search for documentation whether in the form of texts or interviews. We cannot simply accept at face value the written records or people's memories; we cannot assume that women's experience lies outside officially constructed contexts, as a definably separate, "purer" commentary on politics. Instead we must read the evidence we accumulate for what it reveals about how people appropriate and use political discourse, how they are shaped by it and in turn redefine its meaning.

One finds gender in political discourse not only by reading women's texts. When women, children, or the family are the subject of policy debate or legislation, references to sexual difference abound. In addition, and perhaps most interesting, are the uses of gender in other kinds of political representations—ones that may not have anything to do with real women or the relations

11. "Women in Nazi Germany," *History Workshop* 1 (1976), 74–113; 2 (1976), 5–32.

between the sexes. Analyses of gender imagery in political rhetoric can reveal a good deal about the intentions of speakers, the appeal of such rhetoric, and the possible nature of its impacts. They will also reveal some of the ways gender systems are reproduced. Traditional historians of the great wars of the twentieth century may be more interested in the first kind of analysis; historians of women may be more interested in the second. The important point is that the concerns of political history and women's history can be joined around analyses of gender in political discourse. By examining how events are constructed in political discourse and how gender or sexual difference figures in those constructions, we can begin to reveal the connections between gender and politics. By examining women's history—female experience, actions, and expressions, as well as policies and legislation formulated for them—as a part of political history, and by asking how women's history figured in national and international politics, we gain new understanding of that politics. The question then becomes, not what was the impact of the wars on women, but what does the history of women reveal about the politics of war? Beyond that there is a whole series of questions about gender and politics that can be summed up in a question I asked earlier: Is there a politics of gender in the politics of war? And, what does one reveal about the other?

These are questions that are answered, at least in part, in this volume. They offer the possibility of a new understanding of the politics of the two world wars. There are, to be sure, limits to the ways these questions can be used to create new understanding; just as there are limits to the uses of gender as an analytic category and of women's history as a tool for rewriting History. These limits cannot be decided a priori, but only by hard thinking and careful sifting of empirical evidence. Which questions can and cannot be answered will be decided in the course of future research. In the meantime, the questions are worth asking, for in asking them we push the enterprise of women's history forward to an encounter with political history and to the rewriting of History that still needs to be done.

Writing more than fifty years ago, Virginia Woolf scanned the shelves for books that were not there, books that would write women into history. "It would be ambitious beyond my daring," she mused, "to suggest to the students of those famous colleges that they should rewrite history."[12] Women's history as the rewriting of History is still an ambitious undertaking, but it is no longer beyond our daring. Indeed, as the essays in this book indicate, it is now very much within our grasp.

12. *A Room of One's Own* (London, 1929), 68.

MARGARET R. HIGONNET
PATRICE L.-R. HIGONNET

The Double Helix

When is change not change? The social and economic roles of many women undergo rapid and radical transformation both at the onset of war and, in a symmetrically opposed direction, at its conclusion. For some observers, these advances and withdrawals are easily explained. Wartime changes are short-term variations. Historians like Alan Milward and Angus Calder argue that war does not cause social or economic phenomena but merely accentuates or hastens ongoing processes. The radical changes for women precipitated by war are understood to be mere interruptions of "normal" gender relations. The nation calls upon women to change their roles only "for the duration."

Yet, if we perceive the wartime changes in women's roles as a realignment of social territory that produces, however piecemeal or inadvertently, greater social equality, then the rapid retreat from those advances during the immediate postwar years seems puzzling. Even a brief exposure to new day-to-day experience may theoretically have revolutionary consequences for our acceptance of paradigms. We do find some evidence that women's experience of new roles made them reconsider the validity of conventional gender divisions of labor and arrive at a new self-perception. The British chief factory inspector reported in 1916 a "new self-confidence engendered in women," and the *New Statesman* found women to be "more alert, more critical of the conditions under which they work, more ready to take a stand against injustice than their pre-war selves." By 1915 the National Union of Women Workers had already held a conference to stress the importance of women's role in Britain's postwar reconstruction.[1] To be sure, some feminists have challenged the perception of

1. Arthur Marwick, *The Deluge: British Society and The First World War* (1965; repr. New York: Norton, 1970), 94, 97.

women's new wartime roles, particularly their military participation, as "advances." Still, we want to explore this evidence of change to reveal the interplay between individual experience and consciousness, as well as between our discourses and unformulated attitudes.

In both world wars many women gained economic independence and assumed familial authority; some of these women understood men's return to mean the loss of both. How can we relate this evidence of change in the gender consciousness of individual women to the postwar reconstruction of social "normalcy"? Two central themes in this book are the impermanence of wartime transformations in the social roles of women and women's failure to develop consciousness of themselves as a socially defined group. If wartime changes in women's material conditions and cultural image seem ephemeral in the short run, we must next ask what changes in women's social situation over the long run can be attributed to these wars.

The research gathered here focuses on the two major European wars of this century. We could argue that women have always suffered in wars and even participated in them: literature offers us Amazons and Camilla, Andromaque and Mother Courage; history may point to Joan of Arc and Florence Nightingale, to fighters as well as healers. But the participation of women both in a militarized industrial economy and in the regular army was first institutionalized in these two modern wars, which witnessed the "registration," "direction," and "conscription" of women.[2] The two world wars occasioned massive state intervention in all aspects of the economy and social structure. These wars not only devoured the social resources defined by GNP but mobilized resources previously uncounted or undervalued, including the labor of women. In the process, income was equalized, child mortality rates lowered, and attention focused on the "double burden" of married working women. In the twentieth century, mass mobilizations have helped expose ideology concerning women. Women have always been a concern of the state, but in these wars nations made explicit their paternalistic relationship to female citizens in startling ways, as Karin Hausen and Sarah Fishman reveal here.

One might have expected the world wars to catalyze a broad and durable

2. Cynthia Enloe has finely traced the complex evolution of women's relations to military organizations, which have both exploited and excluded women, in *Does Khaki Become You? The Militarization of Women's Lives* (London: Pluto, 1983). The United Kingdom, as Jenny Gould shows in "Women's Military Services in First World War Britain," established the WAAC in 1917 after an intense struggle; although the U.S. Army and Navy Nurse Corps did not acquire full military status until World War II, "yeomanettes" and "marinettes" who served in communications had military rank in the Great War. See Martin Binkin and Shirley J. Bach, *Women and the Military* (Washington, D.C.: Brookings Institution, 1977), 5.

transformation of social institutions as a response to cumulative change in consciousness about the meaning of gender. In the mid-nineteenth century, women had gained expanded educational opportunities and access to selected professions and occupations. While bourgeois culture had identified women with private, domestic activity, mythologizing their roles as arbiters of taste and first teachers of children, leading feminist thinkers like John Stuart Mill or Susan B. Anthony had taken cognizance of the evident disparity between the bourgeois cult of individualism and institutional restrictions on women's rights. Suffragist movements in turn gave women a certain public presence. In 1792 it took an exceptional writer like Mary Wollstonecraft to question cultural norms in her prophetic *Vindication of the Rights of Women*. Later, at Seneca Falls in 1848, Elizabeth Cady Stanton and Lucretia Mott met with like-minded radicals to call for equality. And by 1914, days before the outbreak of war, a large sector of the educated middle class was involved in the mass demonstration in Paris for suffrage. This gradually developed, broad base of support explains why feminists in several countries confidently predicted during the First World War that women's contribution to their nation's war effort would produce political gains. Many contemporary observers thought women's actual or quasi-military participation would finally "entitle" them to the vote.

War did bring short-term changes in women's specific tasks. And postwar constitutional changes gave women in many countries the vote (French and Italian women had to wait for a second war). But these political adjustments were not accompanied by the fundamental changes in the situation of women that had been anticipated. This failure challenges us to reconsider political models of "progress" that stress visible but isolated material changes. The evidence points to ideological mechanisms limiting the transformation of gender lines, as well as to the functions that gender plays in social, economic, and political discourse.

To demonstrate the rapidity and extent of the shift in the social roles of women in wartime, we can turn to nearly any of the essays presented here. The most obvious change was the dramatic increase in the number of women employed outside the home in munitions industries. On the face of it, many of these newly employed women appeared to be integrated into the work force: Ruth Milkman writes that the proportion of women in American unions rose from 9.4 percent in 1940 to 21.8 percent in 1944. As Steven Hause reminds us, the shift in employment is all the more critical because women moved from domestic services or feminized industries like textiles to masculine industries like the railways. As a corollary to the increased number of women in the workplace, we find the creation of public and industrial daycare facilities.

An equally prevalent leitmotiv in these essays, however, is the drastic swing *back* in the postwar periods. By 1921, the number of French women employed in industry was lower than it had been in 1906. After the close of the Second World War in 1945, the British labor government halved state grants to local authorities for nurseries, and the number of nurseries dropped by almost half in two years. The work of Dominique Veillon suggests that women subordinated and even repressed their memories of active participation in the French Resistance for two decades.[3] This backswing suggests that war is indeed a "gap." Were apparent wartime shifts in social roles deceptive? Steven Hause and Michelle Perrot trace the progress of women's rights after 1918 to events that took place before 1914. Political gains apparently due to women's war effort, like the vote, cannot be explained by a simple connection to war. Other factors must bear on the spotty and slow nature of postwar change. Indeed, as Jane Jenson points out, women's political gains in France masked the continued social and professional subordination of women to men, endorsed and enforced by the state.

To explain why the changes in women's activities during wartime did not improve their status, we can use the image of a double helix, with its structure of two intertwined strands. This image permits us to look at woman not in isolation but within a persistent system of gender relationships. The female strand on the helix is opposed to the male strand, and position on the female strand is subordinate to position on the male strand. The image of the double helix allows us to see that, although the roles of men and women vary greatly from culture to culture, their relationship is in some sense constant. If men gather and women fish, gathering will be thought more important than fishing; in another society where men fish and women gather, fishing will be more prestigious. The actual nature of the social activity is not as critical as the cultural perception of its relative value in a gender-linked structure of subordination.[4] The constancy of this systematic subordination is problematic for feminist theory; among its possible causes are biology, binary mental structures, or the sex-differentiated processes of identity formation. In general, this

3. "Elles étaient dans la Résistance," *Repères* 59 (1983), 9–12, and "L'Association Nationale des Anciennes Déportées et Internées de la Résistance," *Mémoire de la Seconde Guerre Mondiale* (Actes du Colloque de Metz, 6–8 Oct. 1983), ed. Alfred Wahl (Metz: CRHC de l'Université de Metz, 1984), 161–76.

4. Sherry B. Ortner, "Is Female to Male as Nature Is to Culture?" *Woman, Culture, and Society,* ed. Michelle Zimbalist Rosaldo and Louise Lamphere (Palo Alto: Stanford University Press, 1974), 67–87.

book is concerned with the social and ideological reproduction of the double helix, that is, with the resistance to change that obscures inquiry into causes.

In wartime, women have indeed taken on, massively and very quickly, roles previously reserved to men. But in a deeper sense the access to new roles is of no consequence. For example, nursing done by men in a hospital during peacetime may have been more prestigious than women's nursing of children at home; but masculine combat at the front was in turn more prestigious than feminine nursing outside the home or even at the front. In this social dance, the woman appears to have taken a step forward as the partners change places—but in fact he is still leading her. War alters the vocabulary of feminine dependence (as it moves women from the "home" to the "homefront"), and it may even improve the lives of some working women. In the long run, however, the dynamic of gender subordination remains as it was. After the war, the lines of gender can therefore be redrawn to conform to the prewar map of relations between men's and women's roles. Even when material conditions for women differ after the war, the fundamental devaluation of the tasks assigned to them remains.

The illusory nature of wartime change is underscored in many ways. First is the temporary nature of the industries involved: Rosie the Riveters riveted bombers and battleships, which were not needed for long, rather than I-beams for houses, in an industry that had existed before the war and would go on after it. At the same time, Steven Hause's evidence suggests that the reassignment of female labor disrupted and set back previously feminized industries.[5] Women were not in fact fully integrated into a gender-free labor force during the war. Rather, they were hired in certain sectors that were temporarily reclassified as appropriate for women. They were barred from highly skilled and supervisory positions and were, ostensibly because of the duress of war, given incomplete training and made to work without proper safety precautions.[6] Similarly, in

5. We could argue counterfactually, of course, that the realignment of industry already underway before the war would have led inevitably to the decay of feminized industries like textiles.

6. Milkman makes these points here and in her book, *The Dynamics of Job Segregation by Sex during World War II* (Champaign: University of Illinois Press, 1986). See also Karen Beck Skold, "'The Job He Left Behind': American Women in the Shipyards during World War II," *Women, War and Revolution,* ed. Carol R. Berkin and Clara M. Lovett (New York: Holmes and Meier, 1980). This valuable book points to the problems of change and consciousness that we pursue here. See also Penny Summerfield, *Women Workers in the Second World War: Production and Patriarchy in Conflict* (London: Croom Helm, 1984); Sheila Lichtman, *Women at Work, 1941–1945: Wartime Employment in the San Francisco Bay Area* (Ann Arbor, Mich.: University Microfilms, 1982); J. E. Trey, "Women in the War Economy: World War II," *Review of Radical Political Economics* 4 (1972), 41–57.

the military, women were generally treated as auxiliaries and reserves, assigned to "feminine" medical and communications duties or symbolically located at the rear of combat zones.

Second, the authorities were reluctant to institutionalize changing sex roles by creating nurseries, as Sonya Michel's research shows. Wartime daycare programs were opposed because of their potential link to a permanent reordering of the sexual division of labor. Nursery centers were few and far between. The very use of the term *centre* is revealing, according to Denise Riley, since a center is optional, but schools are a necessity. In England and to a certain extent elsewhere, bombing forced the evacuation of children, a painful response that incidentally solved their parents' daycare problem, but only for the short run.

Third, the intentions of state bureaucracies when they did encourage the establishment of nurseries must be probed. In times of war, women's productive capacity becomes more valuable than their role as a form of reproductive national property. But the size and health of the population, especially in Europe, remained central concerns, and the absence or death of male heads of households triggered quasi-paternal state intervention. Sonya Michel draws parallels between Depression and wartime daycare policies, showing that, when Rosie went to work and dropped her child off at a center, it was not her needs as a worker that were being considered. Instead, the short-run needs of the employer and the security of the nation's budding citizens engendered daycare arrangements that lasted only "for the duration." The paternalistic state, one might add, was taking care of its own needs for matériel.

Indeed, the carnage, the physical and mental cripples that the state accepted as part of the costs of war necessitated a continuing pronatalist policy that eventually put women back into the home and, in the opinion of many policymakers, eliminated the need for daycare centers. The reserved seats in the French Métro today neatly juxtapose *mutilés de guerre* and maternity. Karin Hausen and Sarah Fishman show that social services to war widows in Germany and the wives of Vichy POWs depended on the state's ideological formulation of its own paternalistic duties and demographic ambitions, a situation that constrained women as it protected them.

The issue of pronatalism produces evidence about women's situation in wartime that is consonant with the double helix thesis. The natural result of the separation of men and women during wartime, that is, the intensification of gender segregation, is a drop in the birth rate. (Occupied France in World War II, at least during the first years when food was not yet scarce, was the exception that proves the rule.) The human cost of war, however, intensifies demographic pressures. Military strategy and pronatalist policy, then, are two columns in a double-entry political accounting system. From this joint policy flows the wartime segregation of the sexes and the symbolic politicization of women's reproductive function. The nation addresses to its soldiers or prisoners of war a political discourse that is ironically obsessed with sexual reproduction. War strengthens the sense that women are property, as well as symbols of national victory. Women who consort with the enemy are stigmatized, humiliated, even executed, while soldiers' romantic interludes in enemy territory are idealized. Vichy politicians worried about the infidelities of POWs' wives on grounds not only of personal morals but also of political morale, for such acts constitute not only betrayal of the fighting man but of the fight itself.

Georges Bataille's study of *Death and Sensuality,* in which he explores the interpenetration of our cult of eroticism and our experience of violence, is relevant here.[7] As sexual acts become political, war itself is eroticized. To some extent, it is homoerotic. World War I addressed a "crisis of masculinity" in France, Germany, Britain; and in the latter case it clearly enhanced the male bonding fostered by the public school system.[8] When women entered the military one of the anxieties the commands faced was how to continue to foster male bonding in the face of conflicting sexual interests. World War II offered unrivaled opportunities for sadistic eroticism in the concentration camps, as testimony about guards, including women like Dorothea Binz or Hermine Braunsteiner, has taught us.

From another angle, we can see in the rhetoric and emblems of war a recurrent "representation of what would seem to be a political threat as if it were a sexual threat," and a corresponding stress on masculine control over women's generativity.[9] Rhetoric escalates from images of domestic woman to those of sexual woman. This possessive sexualization of woman in times of war is obvious at the individual level of soldiers' private fantasies and pinups, and it is more covert but more troubling in the public territories of propaganda, poetry, and philosophy, as in Expressionist drama or the work of Jünger and Spengler. The masculine struggle for geographic territory is motivated by the

7. Bataille, *Death and Sensuality* (New York: Walker, 1962).

8. Paul Fussell, *The Great War and Modern Memory* (New York, Oxford University Press, 1975). See also Michelle Perrot, "The New Eve and the Old Adam," this volume, on the masculinity crisis that helped prepare the war, and Klaus Theweleit's study of German soldiers' sexual fantasies, *Männerphantasien,* 2 vols. (Frankfurt/Main: Roter Stern, 1977–78).

9. Neil Hertz, "Medusa's Head: Male Hysteria under Political Pressure," *Representations* 4 (1983), 27 and Catherine Gallagher's amplifying response, ibid., 57.

symbol of a feminine nation populated by faithful women. For the aggressors, viewing military technology as masculine permits the domination and ordering of a nature and territory perceived as female. For nations on the defensive, the radical changes entailed in mobilization and demobilization may be symbolically limited by a rhetorical continuity that stresses the subordination of woman to the family. Thus a Eureka public service ad praising "Courage—Feminine Gender" shows a woman worker with her baby in her arms, looking forward to postwar "leisure" with a new vacuum cleaner. Anthropologists note that demobilization threatens to feminize the male population. This threat was dealt with by reemphasizing the dominant paternal role within the family, as well as by renewing a cult of such "virile" activities as violent sports.[10]

While the image of the double helix serves to point up the identification of woman with her culturally assigned subordinate position, it also points to the fact that, in a relationship dominated by man, woman is generally understood as Other.[11] When she performs a "masculine" function, it cannot easily be read. Thus French women in the Resistance, because German soldiers read them as women, often escaped detection when men could not. Indeed, the contribution of those women was, in the postwar period when awards were being made, unreadable for French politicians as well.

Viewed as Other, woman is indirectly the signifier for man, the signified. Lévi-Strauss writes that all societies have at least three "languages" or systems of communication: verbal messages, goods and services, and women.[12] From early childhood a woman learns to please, to reflect male desire; she mirrors man rather than speaking for herself. The functions of complementary performance and indirect communication strikingly mark women's roles in wartime. They assimilate new roles with astounding swiftness, possibly because of a sense that their identity is not bound up in the social roles they play. In their new assignments, women continue to provide social services of all kinds, remaining in a subordinate relationship to the other strand of the helix. In the

10. Richard Sipes, "War, Sports, and Aggression: An Empirical Test of Rival Theories," *American Anthropologist* 75 (February 1973), 64–86. Eric Leed rejects this "drive-discharge" thesis but argues that images and rhetoric (such as that of the "liminal" figure) function socially to mediate the transgressive experiences and return of the veteran. *No Man's Land: Combat and Identity in World War I* (Cambridge: Cambridge University Press, 1979).

11. Simone de Beauvoir, Introduction to *The Second Sex,* trans. H. M. Parshley (1952; repr. New York: Vintage, 1974), pp. xv–xxxiv.

12. Claude Lévi-Strauss, *Structural Anthropology* (New York: Doubleday/Anchor, 1967), 289. Lévi-Strauss qualifies this metaphor elsewhere in the same volume: "One should keep in mind that the processes by which phonemes and words have . . . become reduced to pure signs, will never lead to the same results in matters concerning women. For words do not speak while women do; as producers of signs, women can never be reduced to the status of symbols or tokens" (60).

grammar of social structure, women are "auxiliary" verbs; despite all substitutions, the syntax remains the same.

If women's linguistic function is only a metaphor for Lévi-Strauss, their wartime experience underlines their actual identification with communication skills in modern Western societies. Like Vera Laska's memoirs about her career as a courier on the Eastern front,[13] the work here on the French Resistance shows that women often served as liaison agents who coded, decoded and carried messages. We may see here women's sophistication in manipulating sign systems controlled by others. But their liaison functions also reflect women's exclusion from physical action. These complexities mean we must reflect again on discourse as the handmaiden of war. As historians, we must not simply reproduce the double helix. We must beware of interpreting women's involvement in the war simplistically through the image of the Other, a figure so often understood to be a passive victim without responsibility for constructing the relationship.

The double helix permits us to trace the continuity behind the wartime material changes in women's lives. That continuity lies in the subordination of women's new roles to those of men, in their symbolic function, and more generally in the integrative ideology through which their work is perceived. The dominant ideology of wartime for women remains nationalist. At union meetings where women's issues or their jobs were at stake, it turned out that women were just war workers who happened to be women. In the Resistance, Jewish women considered themselves to be *French* political agents. Steven Hause argues that World War I, with its nationalist pressures and paper shortages, silenced the French feminist movement. To stress difference, to pursue potentially disruptive, gender-specific goals, would constitute treachery. Similarly, as Yasmine Ergas shows, oppression of women as a racial group wipes out their sense of gender. Even if *within* social units women assume feminine roles, such as the provision of food for armed Resistance units or the performance of "light" industrial tasks at the factory, they must assume a stance of solidarity with the social unit when they face outward.

Ideological containment requires temporal containment and symbolic differentiation: women became mayors in France and mechanics in America, but only to fill interim *man*-power shortages. In the informality and confusion of civil wars and wars of national liberation, women do fight shoulder to shoulder

13. *Women in the Resistance and in the Holocaust: The Voices of Eyewitnesses,* ed. Vera Laska (Westport, Conn.: Greenwood Press, 1983).

with men, as Louise Michel did during the Paris Commune. Once their military presence is institutionalized, however, the picture is different. As Susan Gubar has noted, women in the American military wore skirts and buzzards, not eagles, on their buttons. Although they served in dangerous anti-aircraft batteries, female British volunteers were not considered to be in "direct combat" roles. Russian women in tank, machine-gun, and air crews made major contributions to the war effort, in both all-female and mixed units. In assessments of general strategy, however, their tasks were understood as subordinate: they offered airlifts to generals and carried out night raids in support of the primary fighting by a largely male army.[14] In the British military in World War I, Jenny Gould found, combat forces were redefined in order to retain a gender division of labor.

Postwar ideology changes in tone and terms but not in its fundamental message, as becomes clear in Maureen Honey's study of the collaboration between magazines and the U.S. government to facilitate both mobilization and demobilization: plots and characters were fed to the magazines in order to shape public conceptions of women's appropriate (but changing) role.[15] As opposed to the defensive statism of wartime rhetoric, postwar rhetoric appeals to a positive reconstruction of a former order, which is presented as "organic," a golden age of "natural" gender relations. These appeals struck resonant chords: married women who had juggled family and jobs, working long hours and then queuing for rations, or who had been separated not only from husband but from children too, welcomed a return to the traditional divisions of labor and the possibility of rebuilding a home that had been threatened or even shattered by years of bombardment. Some were glad to give up work on the night shift in heavy industry and return to more protected work in the tertiary sector. But we must be alert to the political as well as personal implications of the rhetoric. Jane Jenson comments on the continuity in political discourse from the Third Republic and Vichy, which made sure that

14. Kazimiera Janina Cottam, *Soviet Airwomen in Combat in World War II* (Manhattan, Kansas: Military Affairs, 1983); Binkin and Bach, *Women and the Military,* 124–25.

15. Maureen Honey, *Creating Rosie the Riveter: Class, Gender, and Propaganda during World War II* (Amherst: University of Massachusetts Press, 1984). The essays by Gilbert and Gubar in this volume touch on propaganda and popular discourse. There is also valuable material in Michele Shorer, "Roles and Images of Women in World War I Propaganda," *Politics and Society* 5 (1975), 469–86; Leila Rupp, *Mobilizing Women for War: German and American Propaganda, 1939–1945* (Princeton: Princeton University Press, 1978); Susan Hartmann, "Prescriptions for Penelope: Literature on Women's Obligations to Returning World War II Veterans," *Women's Studies* 5 (1978), 223–39; and Karen Anderson, *Wartime Women: Sex Roles, Family Relations, and the Status of Women during World War II* (Westport, Conn.: Greenwood Press, 1981).

no new rights for women, as women, were guaranteed in the process of consolidating social programs favorable to them. In the postwar period, the reconstitution of the nation required that society reintegrate returning soldiers. The high costs of war characteristically entail a conservative reaction, whether political or social. The social disorder engendered by World War II produced what Denise Riley has aptly described as overfeminization. After the Armistice, everyone stepped forward on the helix, that is to say backward.

Plus ça change, plus c'est la même chose has been the dominant historiographic position on war. Our stress on structural continuities, on the double helix, agrees with this view that war does not change but rather exacerbates the social and political order. Thus, the intensification of ideological structures in wartime propaganda and in defensive statist measures exposes the way gender functions as a parameter of political thought. At the same time, however, a study of war is truly productive for the study of women and social change, because war crystallizes contradictions between ideology and actual experience. Just as the military effort forced Nazi Germany to move peasants into factories, ironically undercutting the defense of *Blut und Boden,* it also threatened the identification of women with *Kinder, Kirche,* and *Küche.*[16] War exposes the relationship between women and the state, changes the material roles of women, and therefore necessarily redefines the relationship between the rhetoric of gender and the gender-specific assignment of tasks. It eventually makes possible a new consciousness of gender discourse as social construct.

Perhaps a new consciousness can, after all, be traced in the cultural palimpsest, as Sandra Gilbert and Susan Gubar show. Certain differences may be noted in the impact of the two world wars. The Great War was taken by contemporaries on either a political or a metaphysical plane ("the battle for civilization," "the war to end all wars"). It juxtaposed nationalist goals with religious values (the war as apocalypse, bloodshed as purification); the gap between these abstract ideals and the actual experience of trench warfare created a gap in understanding between those at the front, predominantly men, and those at home, especially women. This discontinuity of time spent "in parentheses" was felt by men like David Jones, but also by women who had served at the front, Vera Brittain for example. While the war challenged familiar values, it seems to have reinforced separate gender identities, cumulat-

16. Claudia Koonz, "Mothers in the Fatherland: Women in Nazi Germany," in *Becoming Visible: Women in European History,* ed. Renate Bridenthal and Claudia Koonz (Boston: Houghton Mifflin, 1977), 445–73.

ing class differences. Mass conscription in World War I may have "democratized" war, but the literature and propaganda of the period continued to depict the fallen men as hero-victims; such idealizing individualization corresponds to the tone of the poetry of the Great War, at once ironic and poignant. At the same time some women's writings celebrated a euphoric group experience of a middle-class Herland protected from the battlefront, capping the prewar rise of the New Woman. If we examine women's sense of their losses, we find that traditional "feminine" values and their subordination to men are reaffirmed. Even in those countries where the war brought the most terrible economic upheaval (inflation, food shortages, or even destruction of their homes), women perceived the cost of war primarily as emotional. The "gains" some women achieved through war affected their sense of individual potential and independence; but their losses, which held the public eye, involved their situation as dependents—lovers, mothers, or widows. In short, while the Great War in some sense inverted the relationship of men, trapped and sacrificed in the trenches, to women, on the homefront, it also reinscribed their differences and prepared the postwar misogynistic backlash that Gilbert describes.

World War II presents a very different picture, for various reasons. Marx noted that history as repetition loses its tragic force. The wretched, horrifying, and absurdist aspects of war become evident in the literature of the 1940s and 1950s, which often used black humor to express the loss of self forced upon those who experienced this war. As Thomas Pynchon and Paul Fussell have pointed out, pastoral homoeroticism yielded to cynical, aggressive, self-conscious horror, indeed to Norman Mailer's paradoxical attempt to retrieve human dignity through warmaking and obscenity. We may bear in mind the American Marines' slogan, reminiscent of Bluebeard, "If she's old enough to bleed, she's old enough to be butchered." Against such grotesquely erotic violence we must set the cool analyses of many intellectuals. Even before the war, women such as Mary Beard and Virginia Woolf recognized the misogyny inherent in militaristic discourse on both sides. Hitler's ideological offensive made observers aware that rival systems of discourse (fascism, communism, and liberalism) were at stake. A reaction against the abstract idealism of World War I may have led politicians in World War II to rely on a discourse of the state as family to personalize and domesticate the vast social upheaval of war. But disillusionment about the semi-religious patriotic militarism of World War I had prepared observers like Vera Brittain, André Gide, and Thomas Mann to examine war propaganda on both sides in World War II more objectively. (Ironically, this very awareness may have contributed to disbelief in the actual, tragic costs of that war.)

The two wars appear to have fostered different, perhaps cumulative aspects of women's consciousness and therefore to have engendered what may be seen as phases of feminism. Gilbert provocatively describes the experience of young British women during the Great War as a "festival of feminine misrule," a sort of matriarchy. And World War I fed a belief in feminist pacifism, symbolized by the International Women's Peace Congress held at the Hague in 1915. We can now see, of course, that the war also fostered women's conservative associations and their militarism (patriotic Englishwomen handed white feathers, suggesting cowardice, to civilian men they deemed "able-bodied").[17] Whereas middle-class women on the eve of World War I had been prepared for far-reaching political and social gains, on the eve of World War II, the Depression had limited the feminist movement. Gubar has noted that the ideological struggle in the 1930s and 1940s fostered in its first phase a feminist critique of the patriarchalism implicit in not only fascist but also liberal ideology. In 1938 Virginia Woolf described the repressive cult of family, which restricts women in education and the workplace, as a poisonous worm: "There we have in embryo the creature, Dictator as we call him when he is Italian or German, who believes that he has the right, whether given by God, Nature, sex or race is immaterial, to dictate to other human beings how they shall live; what they shall do." The woman who struggles for her job, for freedom and justice, is "fighting the Fascist or the Nazi" whether he speaks English or German.[18] Then, however, their new ideological awareness led some feminist thinkers to recognize the contradictions between their own aims of assimilationism and separatism. Leading feminists and other thinkers came to perceive relations between the sexes in terms not of structural complementarity but of estrangement.

The kinds of change in women's consciousness that these studies trace in the course of the two wars is undoubtedly limited. We must of course distinguish between the conscious and articulated arguments of an intellectual elite and the often half-conscious experience of the majority. Significantly, however, we see that many working women in the first World War had already gained confidence in their ability to do tasks different from those traditionally assigned to them. The political gains in some countries following the Great War in turn permitted the new institutional representation of women that distinguished their position in World War II. In this second phase, tokenism marked the

17. Barbara J. Steinson shows that the thesis of nurturant feminism is ambiguously linked to both pacifism and militarism in "'The Mother Half of Humanity': American Women in the Peace and Preparedness Movements in World War I," in Berkin and Lovett, eds., *Women, War and Revolution,* 259–84.

18. *Three Guineas* (San Diego: Harcourt Brace Jovanovich, 1966), 53.

anomalous process of change without change. Again, the majority of women whose working roles changed were already working women. Over 75 percent of American women war workers in ten key production areas did not wish to surrender their jobs to returning GIs.[19] Yet the sense of accomplishment, independence, and even liberation that some women experienced through their war work in both periods did not prevent their demobilization in order to make way for returning men. Women were not politically influential or well enough organized to preserve economic gains, much less to alter the terms of discourse. Indeed, one of the crucial factors seems to be the containment of women's organizations, as can be seen in the subordination of women's union committees to the union war boards.

This book strikingly points up the diversity of women's wartime experience, as actors and victims, as workers and widows. The victims of persecution, as Yasmine Ergas shows, differ from victims of bombardment. We are also reminded to distinguish between the experiences of young, single women and those of women caring for small children, since the same jobs affected their daily lives in radically different ways. If war seemed to many veterans a time of shared male experience, of male bonding, this seems significantly less true for women, who were in part divided by the private aspects of their experience during war, as well as by their postwar privatization. The homefront is feminized in the Great War, as Gilbert points out, but large disparities remain between women of differing status. In the Second World War, women separated from their children experienced particular stresses of mobilization; and those living under bombardment faced a challenge different from that to which those working in North America responded. Renate Bridenthal's study of German housewives' unions convincingly shows that women's politicization takes on many colors: the cult of domestic, feminine values may be militarist as well as pacifist. And D'Ann Campbell's book, *Women at War with America,* reminds us of the complexity and conflicts within individual women's experiences of war. This variety in women's wartime situation needs to be explored both at the national level and by comparative historians.[20] Furthermore, the

19. U.S. Women's Bureau, Bulletin No. 209, *Women Workers in Ten War Production Areas and Their Postwar Employment Plans* (1946), cited here by Ruth Milkman. This figure is significantly higher than Skold's, who writes that 50 percent of women in the Kaiser shipyards wanted to stay on their jobs at war's end, "'The Job He Left Behind,'" Berkin and Lovett, eds., *Women, War and Revolution,* 55–75. On demobilization, see Sheila Tobias and Lisa Anderson, *What Really Happened to Rosie the Riveter: Demobilization and the Female Labor Force* (New York: MSS Modular Publ., 1974).

20. Renate Bridenthal, "'Professional' Housewives: Stepsisters of the Women's Movement," in *When Biology Became Destiny: Women in Weimar and Nazi Germany,* ed. Renate Bridenthal, Atina Grossman, and Marion Kaplan (New York: Monthly Review Press, 1984), 153–73; this anthol-

experiences of male soldiers, which have been subsumed under umbrellas of patriotism, fraternity, and heroic suffering, may turn out to have been significantly different, for example, for Germans on the Russian front and Americans in the Pacific.

The diversity of women's (and men's) experiences brings us back to the simplifying function of most gender models. In order to break out of the double helix, we need to move beyond binary models of analysis. We need to hear the polyphony of historical experience, especially that of women. We must recognize the significant variations in women's situation along a life course. We need to unpack the confusion of woman with the nuclear family and to extend our awareness of the complex quasi-familial structures that also affect our lives—those of men as well as women. A study of war is useful for the reassessment of these difficulties in gender analysis, since it reveals the importance of the rhetoric through which women are perceived, by themselves as well as by others. War as a disruptive state of affairs makes it possible to rewrite political and economic rights and especially arrangements of gender. Yet, as we have seen, organicist familial rhetoric can alter subtly to contain potential disruptions. We need to recognize and challenge the images of gender and their function in social discourse.

Joan Scott has challenged historians to move beyond fresh empirical research about women ("herstory") or analyses of women's socio-economic conditions that subordinate the evidence to preexisting models. The problem, as she sees it, is to find a new way of writing history.

Certainly several of these studies permit us not only to reexamine the material evidence about women's condition in wartime but also to refine existing categories. The essay on women in the Resistance, for example, offers both fresh material and a reassessment of earlier models of political and military action. This topos forces us to look at not only full-time but also part-time involvement and domestic labor (a lesson broadly applicable to the study of capitalism). A study of the Resistance also forces us to consider not only parties or networks but also individual actions—even silence—as political. Other essays remind us that the family is not simply a biological unit but one fostered and manipulated by the state, which in wartime assumes the role of the father. Personal, social, and political categories merge.

The focus on women forces us to revise the hierarchy of received histo-

ogy also provides one model for a national study. D'Ann Campbell, *Women at War with America: Private Lives in a Patriotic Era* (Cambridge: Harvard University Press, 1984), stresses the diversity of women's wartime experiences.

riographical categories. More than other historical writing, studies of war have pivoted on "high politics" and on the evolution of what might be called, for want of a better term, public economic life, both primarily masculine preserves. The reliance of historians on official archives and the memoirs of leaders confirms this trend. If we pursue the situation of women in relation to war, *mentalités* take their place beside ideologies, and both tend to displace diplomatic and military historiography. An oral history of women not only reflects but corrects the mythologies of our past. Annemarie Tröger's essay on the metaphoric meaning of war recollections shows how political change, immobility, or inconsistencies can be understood in relation to the nature of discourse, where women as well as men play a critical role, rather than in terms of material or political continuities, where men obviously prevail.

Political historiography has tended to study the *impact* of war on women and thus to reinforce a view of women as passive objects. True, women can be words or objects that one group of men uses to deceive another. But by focusing on their role as victims, rather than as agents, scholars have tended to exculpate and extricate women from history. We suggest that the traditional view of women as passive victims of historical forces may be due in part to our categorical subordination of women's activities and culture to those of men, a particularly damaging instance of the double helix at work.

When war is understood as an ideological struggle rather than strictly a physical or diplomatic event, as Cynthia Enloe argued at the conference on women and war held at Harvard in 1984, we redefine its temporal limits. Women experience war over a different period from that which traditional history usually recognizes, a period which precedes and long outlasts formal hostilities. Masculinist history has stressed the sharply defined event of war; women's time more closely reflects Bergson's concept of *durée*. Military casualties have more often been recorded in statistics than in studies of the long-term psychological (and economic) effects of gassing or amputation. A feminist re-vision of the *time* in wartime can make the history of war more sensitive to the full range of experience of both men and women. What holds for historical time is also true for the historical space we record. We must move beyond the exceptional, marked event, which takes place on a specifically militarized front or in public and institutionally defined arenas, to include the private domain and the landscape of the mind.[21]

21. Already women's memoirs reveal the range of a wartime ecology and break down barriers between public and private, although not in a systematic, analytic fashion. See Dominique Veillon, "Résister au féminin," *Pénélope* 12 (1985), 87–92. Veillon's lecture on the oral history of World War II (given at the conference on oral history, sponsored by L'Institut d'Histoire du Temps Présent, Paris, June 20, 1986) analyzes the interplay of memory and social fictions.

If we attach more importance to cultural phenomena like symbolic language, we perceive history in a different way. Insofar as the Second World War was about ideology, we must study it as it was fought in the minds of men and women. Our chronology of the event shifts, as does our sense of general historical causation. Words and actions which in a previous historiography had seemed marginal now move to the center of the stage. So do social groups, like women, who had also been considered marginal. Walter Benjamin writes that the blows must be struck not at random, but with the left hand. The historians of women in war can also strike such blows, left-handed but precise and telling.

PART TWO

Sexual Identities in Conflict

MICHELLE PERROT

The New Eve and the Old Adam: Changes in French Women's Condition at the Turn of the Century

Translated by Helen Harden-Chenut

On the eve of the twentieth century, the image of the New Woman was widespread in Europe, from Vienna to London, from Munich and Heidelberg to Brussels and Paris. The image took root in new definitions of public and private spheres and sex roles, in a new vision of the couple, and in individualized love relationships, all of which were seen as markers of modern times.

This situation found expression within the particular social and cultural context of each country, but the French experience was especially conflictual. *L'Eve future (The Future Eve)* by Villiers de l'Isle Adam (1888) and *L'Eve nouvelle (The New Eve)* by Jules Dubois (1896) were celebrated by some as heralding the beginning of a new era in which women, finally recognized as persons in their own right, would acquire at last *les droits de l'homme* (man's rights/ human rights). The majority, however, rejected this new model with extreme violence that found expression in the abundant antifeminist literature and culminated in Marinetti's "Futurist Manifesto," published in 1909. Parallel to the affirmation of a new feminine identity, a "masculinity crisis" developed for which World War I eventually provided a heroic outlet. After the war, the celebration of the "death cult" in war monuments, elegiac poetry, and commemoration of the Armistice was accompanied by other virile portraits—the conqueror, the revolutionary, the manager—which served to put women back in their place, at the foot of altars erected to honor male heroes. We might say that war had a profoundly conservative, even retrogressive, effect on gender relations.

I will consider here some of the changes in the situation of women in France before the First World War, the resistance these changes encountered, and the developing male identity crisis. My focus is gender relations, not exclusively women's history. The study of symbolic relations between women and men before the war prepares us to understand women's wartime situation and the postwar backswing in gender relations.

CHANGES IN WOMEN'S CONDITION

In the decades before World War I urban women began to change their silhouettes: they cut their hair and wore shorter skirts, even divided skirts for bicycle riders. Hats called "skyscrapers" reached extraordinary heights. These liberated, sporting women, known as "American women," were a minority, but their attractive image, diffused by fashion magazines, had cultural prestige.

Another important change in women's situation concerned their work. In 1906 women represented nearly 38 percent of the French labor force (2.25 million of nearly 6 million workers), and 20 percent of married women worked—one of the highest proportions in Western Europe. The job distribution was rather traditional: 52 percent of working women were domestics or home workers, while only 25 percent were factory workers, 12 percent headed their own businesses, and 8 percent were clerical workers. Women did achieve several breakthroughs, particularly in the service sector. Department stores, a male sector up until the end of the Second Empire, were feminized by 1914, although men retained the administrative jobs as heads of departments, inspectors, and so on. In schools and hospitals (the public hospitals in Paris were secularized by this time) women were employed in jobs that were thought appropriate to their sex. The development of telephone and telegraph communication and the invention of the typewriter helped to transform the world of clerical workers. In a "rationalized" office, the old hierarchical system became gendered. Men became executives of all sorts while women took on jobs as stenographers and typists. One advertising slogan of the period proclaimed: "If you can't afford a dowry for your daughter, send her to the Pigier School."[1]

In the field of knowledge, women achieved a number of first performances. The first woman physician graduated in 1875. By 1900 there were thirty or so

1. On the feminization of certain professions, especially in the tertiary sector, see *Madame ou Mademoiselle? Itinéraires de la solitude féminine XVIII–XXe siècle,* ed. Arlette Farge and Christiane Klapisch (Paris: Montalba, 1984). "Femmes sans maris: Les employées des postes," by Pierette Pézerat and Danièle Poublan on women in the Post Office (PTT, pp. 117–62, is supplemented by Susan Bachrach's "The Feminization of the PTT in the Nineteenth Century," *Mouvement Social,* special issue, "Métiers des femmes," (forthcoming in 1987).

women doctors and by 1914 several hundred, including some working in hospitals as interns.[2] Ten or more women practiced law, and some worked as architects and journalists. At the turn of the century the competititve exam known as the *agrégation,* which led to a career in administration or teaching, was opened to women, and by 1907 there were three hundred women *agrégées* and an equal number of certified teachers.

It is striking that at this time women of middle-class origins, even those from the established, "bonne" bourgeoisie, manifested a desire to work. Most of the girls from Parisian lycées, when questioned about their intentions, indicated that they wanted to combine professional and family roles. Accordingly, women wanted better educations for themselves and for their daughters. This meant the *baccalauréat,* not the decorative but useless *brevet* that marked the end of primary schooling. From 1900 to 1914 about six hundred young women passed the *baccalauréat* each year. Eventually, in 1924, the state abolished separate secondary education for women, which was more oriented toward the domestic sciences of the future homemaker than toward professional training.

In civil rights, there were several breakthroughs in the patriarchal Napoleonic Code. In 1884 a law known as *la loi Naquet* reestablished the right to divorce; at the turn of the century, the number of divorce procedures instigated by women, especially on the grounds of cruelty, reached about fifteen thousand a year, and demands for *séparation de corps* numbered even higher.[3] In 1907 married working women obtained the right to retain full control over their own wages. And in 1912 the state reinstated the right to bring paternity suits *(la recherche de la paternité),* which had been forbidden since Napoleon I. Some small progress was also made toward women's gaining the right to vote.

2. Dominique Lorillot, "Les premières femmes médecins," 3d cycle thesis, Ecole des Hautes Etudes en Sciences Sociales, 1982; Véronique Leroux-Hugon, "Les infirmières de l'assistance publique de Paris (1880–1914)" (3d cycle thesis, Paris VII, 1983). See also Yvonne Knibiehler et al., *Cornettes et blouses blanches: Les infirmières dans la société française (1880–1980)* (Paris: Hachette, 1984).

3. Bernard Schnapper, "La séparation de corps de 1837 à 1914: Essai de sociologie juridique," *Revue Historique* 526 (April–June 1978), 453–67. Schnapper has shown that 80 percent of the requests for physical separation were made by women, and their justification was predominantly violence. Through this form of refusal, a new conception of marriage came to light: it was an institution "no longer exclusively dedicated to procreation but . . . to the blossoming of sentiment and sensuality for the couple." Joëlle Guillais-Maury similarly shows that the breakup was usually initiated by the women, and this subjected them to physical attacks. The similarity between these two sets of findings indicates that women no longer accepted their condition as beaten or tyrannized wives. J. Guillais-Maury, "Recherches sur le crime passionnel au 19ème siècle" (3d cycle thesis, Paris VII, 1984).

In 1898 women were authorized to vote for *les tribunaux de commerce*. They became eligible to vote and to run for the Conseil Supérieur du Travail in 1900 and for the Conseil des Prudhommes in 1907; a woman from the garment workers' union was immediately elected to this special work court.

Resistance was strongest in the world of high politics, despite ardent campaigns led by an active suffrage movement, more active perhaps than is customarily admitted. This movement was supported by such associations as the Union Française pour le Suffrage (which had ten thousand members in 1912), by newspapers like *L'Avant-Courrière,* and by petitions, demonstrations, refusal to pay taxes, and running women as candidates for public office. These campaigns gained credibility for the idea that women would vote. In 1914, *Le Journal* ran a referendum on women's suffrage and reported five hundred thousand votes in favor. The political Left, which previously had held itself aloof, was converted to women's suffrage: in 1914 Jean Jaurès openly favored giving women the vote. But the war halted this momentum. The procrastination of the 1920s and 1930s and the Senate's long resistance to proposals for women's suffrage illustrate how women's cause regressed during the interwar period. French women did not obtain the right to vote until 1945.

In these changes at the beginning of the century, although some are admittedly quite small, one can recognize a new type of woman who refused to be trapped in traditional feminine roles and who demanded equality. Some of these women went so far as to demand birth control and free sexuality. The neo-Malthusian movement, started by men, was strongly supported by radical feminists like Gabrielle Petit, Nelly Roussel, and Madeleine Pelletier, who headed difficult campaigns in favor of contraception. They urged women to "learn to become mothers only at your own will."[4] Working-class women, however, were not much involved in the birth-control movement and generally did not adopt contraception; instead, married women with several children relied more and more on abortion, proof of their intention to limit family size. Such refusal to accept unwanted births has been interpreted by Angus McLaren as a sign of popular feminism.[5]

This refusal to reproduce (*la grève des ventres*—"wombs on strike") was experienced as a threat and gave rise to indignation among demographers (Jacques Bertillon) and such moralists as Senator Bérenger and Emile Zola in his novel *Fécondité*.[6] The fact that women had access to *les funestes secrets,* "deadly secrets," seemed dangerous, especially when such knowledge was

4. Francis Ronsin, *La grève des ventres* (Paris: Aubier-Montaigne, 1980).

5. Angus MacLaren, *Sexuality and Social Order* (New York: Holmes and Meier, 1983).

6. Jacques Bertillon, *La dépopulation de la France* (Paris: Félix Alcan, 1911); Emile Zola, *Fécondité* (Paris, 1899): a surprising, anti-Malthusian novel.

accompanied by women's insistence that they had a right to the sexual pleasures that had been denied them for such a long time. (These expectations were influenced in France by Havelock Ellis, whose ideas were taken up by neo-Malthusians.) The question of women's sexual liberation lay at the heart of this troubled reaction. At the same time, several "Amazons," for the most part artists and intellectuals like Natalie C. Barney, Renée Vivien, Gertrude Stein and her friends, lived in Paris a quiet life of lesbian and creative love. Symbols of women's emancipation, such Amazons were not held directly responsible for the French "demographic crisis," but their "insolent" pleasures may have helped kindle public anxieties.

PROGRESS AND ITS LIMITS

These changes in women's outlook and image were due first of all to the activism of women themselves, to various forms of feminism, a sometimes divided but active movement since the 1890s. The associations and leagues, mutual societies and working women's unions together had a membership of several thousand by the end of 1914. Large congresses in 1900, 1907, and 1908 demonstrated feminists' capacity to organize their followers.[7] There were also a number of noteworthy publications, a press that published more than thirty titles between 1900 and 1914, and a great newspaper, *La Fronde,* headed by Marguerite Durand. All of these displayed the feminists' understanding of public relations and their sense of the political importance of the written word.

The feminist movement of this period was divided into three main streams. Christian feminism emphasized the maternal role and the social power and duties of women.[8] Secular feminism, represented by Marguerite Durand and *La Fronde,* demanded equal civil and political rights.[9] And radical feminism, more subversive, attacked patriarchy, spoke of the oppression of women's bodies, called for a new feminist education for girls, and even advocated militant celibacy (proponents included Arria Ly and Madeleine Pelletier).[10]

7. For the general history of feminism, see the recent work of Daniel Armogathe and Maïté Albistur, *Histoire du féminisme français* (Paris: Editions des Femmes, 1977); and Jean Rabaut, *Histoire des féminismes français* (Paris: Hachette, 1978). The forthcoming theses by Florence Rochefort and Laurence Klejman will advance knowledge in the field.

8. Anne-Marie Sohn, "Les femmes catholiques et la vie publique: L'exemple de la Ligue Patriotique des Françaises," in *Stratégie des femmes,* ed. Marie-Claire Pasquier (Paris: Editions Tierce, 1984).

9. Iréne Jami, "La fronde" (master's thesis, Paris I, 1980).

10. Madeleine Pelletier, *L'éducation féministe des filles et autres textes,* ed. Claude Maignien (Paris: Syros, 1979).

Women's achievements also owed a debt to the feminists' alliance with a fraction of men who out of necessity or conviction wanted to open the way for women to enter public life. Like their female counterparts, these men had varied goals. Several explained, "we need materialist wives," expressing their fear of the lasting ascendancy of the conservative Catholic Church over women, a fear that reflected both the common fact of women's education in convent schools and certain myths of the counterrevolutionary woman inherited from the past.[11] Other "new men" aspired to new relationships as friends, lovers, or sexual partners with intelligent and liberated women (see Villiers de l'Isle Adam, *The Future Eve*). Léon Blum argues on behalf of this vision of the couple in *Du mariage* (1907). But undoubtedly such men were a small minority.[12] Thus the proper limits of women's world became an object of political struggle not only between feminists and conservatives but among the proponents of feminism as well.

What is most striking for our purpose is not the changes in women's situation but their limits. First of all, only certain social milieux were involved. The changes affected essentially the urban middle class, in part for political and economic reasons (a relative proletarianization and the need for women to work). Rural society, on the other hand, tended to reproduce itself within a dominant patriarchal pattern in which women shared complementary roles, tasks, and spaces with men, according to the analysis of rural ethnologists like Martine Segalen and Yvonne Verdier.[13] It was perhaps within the working-class culture that the new image of women met with the strongest resistance. Married women's work outside the home was considered merely a source of supplementary income. Women's competition for jobs previously reserved for men was feared to be a major cause for lower wages.[14] Women were valued as housewives and their "investment" of time in children's education strengthened their role as mothers.[15] Working-class symbolism itself became more

11. The debate on the education of girls, latent throughout the nineteenth century, was revised in the Second Empire. In this context, Michelet's *La femme* (1860) was both innovative and paternalistic. See the works by Françoise Mayeur, *L'éducation des filles en France au 19ème siècle* (Paris: Hachette, 1979); *L'enseignement secondaire des jeunes filles sous la Troisième République* (Paris: Fondation Nationale des Sciences Politiques, 1977); Marie-Françoise Lévy, *Education familiale et éducation religieuse des filles sous le Second Empire* (Paris: Calmann-Lévy, 1984).

12. Laure Adler, *Secrets d'alcôve: Histoire du couple de 1830 à 1930* (Paris: Hachette, 1983).

13. Martine Segalen, *Mari et femme dans la société paysanne* (Paris: Flammarion, 1980); Yvonne Verdier, *Façons de dire, façons de faire* (Paris: Gallimard, 1979).

14. Michelle Perrot, "Eloge de la ménagère dans le mouvement ouvrier français au 19ème siècle," *Romantisme* 13–14 (October–December 1976), 105–21; "Le syndicalisme français et les femmes: Histoire d'un malentendu," *CFDT-Aujourd'hui* (March–April 1984).

15. Yvonne Knibiehler and Catherine Fouquet, *Histoire des mères du Moyen-Age à nos jours* (Paris: Montalba, 1980).

virile: feminine figures (whether allegories like Ceres or realistic representations of misery) were replaced by the more aggressive image of the worker, stripped to the waist, muscles flexed. He symbolized the male producer, key to the future.[16]

A more important limit was that these changes did not fundamentally alter women's subordinate and dependent relationship to men. In the family, factory, schools, hospitals, and on the street, men were still the masters. This was true in the public sphere, especially with regard to state policy, but it was also true in the home, where the father, even when absent, retained influence and symbolic authority.[17] It was in their role as mothers that women obtained new rights. Anne Martin-Fugier has shown that the model of the mother was transposed from the private to the public sphere: a woman teacher or nurse was seen primarily as a mother, and female professions exploited the image of feminine devotion and sacrifice.[18] Therefore, these changes were superficial, bringing about no revolution, either in legislation or in practice.[19]

Moreover, at the advent of the twentieth century, fear of women's sexual and economic liberation—perhaps an imaginary fear—gave rise to renewed antifeminism, expressed as a masculinity crisis. This crisis was complex in both its aspects, neither of which should be neglected. In part, it was a sharp reaction to the perceived menace the New Woman posed to the traditional equilibrium of public and private roles. The intrusion of women into the public sphere seemed threatening. Women intellectuals were perceived to be particularly dangerous, as were women of the leisured class who sought to use their leisure not for social representation of their family's success ("vicarious leisure" in Thorstein Veblen's term) but for the pursuit of individual pleasure. These women were the main targets of antifeminist literature.

More positively, the crisis of masculinity marked an awakening consciousness of what it meant to be a man. In the context of developing individualism,

16. Eric Hobsbawm, "Sexe, vêtements et politique," *Actes de la Recherche en Sciences Sociales* 23 (1978), 2–19.

17. Although the father figures prominently in nineteenth-century literature, there are relatively few historical studies of the father in the nineteenth-century family.

18. Anne Martin-Fugier, *La bourgeoise: femme au temps de Paul Bourget* (Paris: Grasset, 1983).

19. Several recent biographies bear testimony to this: [Marthe de Montbourg], *Marthe* (Paris: Seuil, 1982), trans. Donald M. Frame (San Diego: Harcourt Brace Jovanovich, 1984); and Louise Vanderwielen, *Lise du plat pays* (Lille: Presses Universitaires de Lille, 1983), a remarkable autobiographical novel. See also recent historical studies by James McMillan, *Housewife or Harlot: The Place of Women in French Society, 1870–1940* (Brighton: Harvester, 1981), who insists on the conservatism of French feminism and the lack of change in women's situation; and Bonnie G. Smith, *Ladies of the Leisure Class: The Bourgeoises of Northern France in the Nineteenth Century* (Princeton: Princeton University Press, 1981), who analyzes women's withdrawal into private life and the home in the second half of the nineteenth and the beginning of the twentieth century.

men became aware of their sexual difference, their physical and moral specificity. Hence the intense tone of adolescence in this period, expressed in such "novels of apprenticeship" as Roger Martin du Gard's *Le Lieutenant-colonel de Maumort*. This autobiographical fragment vividly evokes an adolescence lived at the end of the nineteenth century.[20] The development of a culture of homosexuality also bears witness to the awakening of men. All these aspects of masculinity deserve to be studied for their own sake—men should write the history of their sexuality, just as women are writing ours today.[21]

This crisis in the relationship of masculinity to femininity was only secondarily related to the transformation in economic structures, although women's increasing presence in the labor force was not insignificant. In France, women's access to jobs was facilitated by the drop in the birth rate and by their adaptability, due to their unacknowledged skills, which made them competitive with other unskilled labor.

Although political and cultural factors seem most important in the crisis of masculinity and the rise of the New Woman, we should also acknowledge the role of scientific factors. In the middle of the nineteenth century the discovery of ovulation showed that women play an active part in procreation and are not simply receptacles, as had been believed for thousands of years. Neo-Malthusian propaganda in favor of birth control invoked this discovery to underline the responsibility of women themselves. But in all likelihood this momentous discovery only gradually penetrated into people's awareness and modified representations of the relationships between the sexes.

ANTIFEMINISM AND THE MASCULINITY CRISIS

If these changes in scientific knowledge were slow to reach the masses, can we speak of a general crisis in male-female relationships? At first, the crisis was considered to be "all in the head." But in the realm of sexual identity, minority reactions, considered as premonitory signs, must be taken seriously. The questioning of sexual roles is no small affair. In periods of social tension, society tends to seek out scapegoats—in this case women. Furthermore, men themselves suffered from the system which they helped to create, for example, from the overinvestment of cultural power in maternity.

20. Roger Martin du Gard, *Le Lieutenant-colonel de Maumort*, ed. André Daspre (Paris: Gallimard, 1983).

21. Miguel Rodriguez is writing a thesis on the consciousness of masculinity at the beginning of the twentieth century in France. On masculinity in England, see Jeffrey Weeks, *Sexuality and Its Discontents: Meanings, Myths and Modern Sexualities* (London: Routledge and Kegan Paul, 1985).

The masculinity crisis found positive expression in the affirmation of virile values, physical, cultural, and moral. We see the development of sports, the praise of athletic figures, the new stadium gods who displayed their beautiful muscular bodies before women spectators. New types of novels appeared—notably detective stories and science fiction—in opposition to serialized sentimental novels that focused on families, abandoned children, or quarrels over inheritances. In spite of prohibitive measures and attempts at medical intervention, a homosexual culture of virile friendships, love relationships, and male sociability developed.

On the negative side, an overabundant antifeminist literature appeared. It was not an entirely new phenomenon. Popular literature, like the *Bibliothèque bleue series,* was full of antifeminism.[22] Anne-Lise Maugue shows the intensity and density of these attitudes in novels, plays, and essays of the time, pieces written mostly by men, but also occasionally by women such as Marcelle Tinayre and Colette Yver, whose novels *Princesses de science* and *Les cervelines* attack women intellectuals. The themes of antifeminist literature include men's anguish at being deprived of power, pleasure, and the female body—their experience of being evicted by this new competition not only from the public sphere but even from the home, where dominating mothers displace the father. Georges Darien, an anarchist, antifeminist, and anti-Semite as well, spoke of this fear of the mother, which was later taken up by François Mauriac *(Génitrix)* and André Breton. These men denounced the social and domestic power of women (as did Georges Deherme in *Le pouvoir social des femmes,* 1912)—perceived as an occult, diffuse, and secret power for which men are mere playthings. For these authors, loss of virility is a sign and cause of the social degeneracy and decadence thought to be prevalent during the period. The political left and right joined in denouncing this decadence. Zola, in such resolutely antifeminist novels as *Travail* and *Fécondité,* rejoined Maurice Barrès and Octave Mirbeau, an anarchist sympathizer. This literature even received the approval of official institutions: in 1905 Théodore Joran was awarded a prize by the Académie Française for his book of essays, *Le mensonge du féminisme.* However, a distinction must be made between radical antifeminists such as Albert Cim, C. Vogt, and Barrès, partisans at least verbally of a heavy-handed treatment that included beating women and even killing the more liberated ones (a lot of whom die in their novels!), and the liberals, novelists

22. Arlette Farge, *Le miroir des femmes* (Paris: Montalba, 1982), esp. her introduction, "L'homme et la femme: Un conflit qui traverse la *Bibliothèque bleue.*"

23. Anne-Lise Maugue, "La littérature antiféministe en France, 1871–1914" (3d cycle thesis, Paris III, 1983).

such as Anatole France or Emile Faguet, more conscious that women's roles must undergo a necessary evolution. Faguet comforts himself with the reflection that custom lags behind the law.

The art of this period also bears the mark of antifeminist obsession. Claude Quiguer sees "Modern style" as an art that mobilizes against women's liberation.[24] However, Futurism goes even further in its revolt against women and its exaltation of virility. As Marinetti wrote in his famous manifesto (published in *Le Figaro* on February 20, 1909), "We want to glorify war—the only cleansing act of the world—militarism, patriotism, the destructive act of the anarchists, beautiful ideas which kill, and contempt of women. We want to destroy museums, libraries, to combat moralism, feminism and all such opportunistic and utilitarian acts of cowardice."[25]

Marinetti did not realize how right he was. We can hypothesize, in fact, that the Great War, far from liberating women, contributed to putting them back in their place—and putting men in theirs. It seems that the moral effects of the war helped to consolidate traditional values and gender relationships. The destruction of feminism, the strengthening of the image of woman as mother, the glorification of feminine and masculine myths all seemed to go together. The turn of the century was a time of prodigious invention and novelty which raised significant questions about the social organization of gender—but this questioning was soon silenced by the war.[26]

24. Claude Quiguer, *Femmes et machines de 1900: Lecture d'une obsession Modern Style* (Paris: Klincksieck, 1979), shows that the fear of modernity inspires a return to nature and to woman's face.

25. Fanette Roche-Pézard, *L'aventure futuriste (1908–1916), Ecole Française de Rome* (Paris: de Boccard, 1983), attributes important developments to the antifeminism of the Futurists and to the case of Valentine de Saint-Point, the only woman Futurist.

26. I have sketched my first reaction in an essay, "Sur le front des sexes: Un Combat douteux," *Vingtième Siècle* 3 (July–September 1984), 69–76.

ELAINE SHOWALTER

Rivers and Sassoon: The Inscription of Male Gender Anxieties

On July 23, 1917, 2d Lt. Siegfried Sassoon arrived at Craiglockhart War Hospital near Edinburgh to be treated for war neurosis by Royal Army Military Corps psychiatrist Capt. William H. R. Rivers. Their three-month-long therapeutic relationship, intensified by the urgency of the war, exerted a powerful influence on each man's life and ideas. The record of this encounter is one of the best sources we have for studying the inscription of male gender anxieties during the war, anxieties that manifested themselves in the body language of neurotic symptoms and in the structures of writing, both memoir and psychiatric text.

"Dottyville," as the hospital was called by Sassoon and his friends Robert Graves and Lt. Wilfred Owen, also a patient, was a former hydropathic hotel for the nervous or alcoholic rich, which boasted extensive facilities for gardening, tennis, swimming, and other games. Yet Sassoon—who had been ordered by a military review board to undergo medical treatment after he published his famous pacifist denunciation of the war, "A Soldier's Declaration," in May 1917—was apprehensive. "After all," he wrote, "a mad-house would be only a few degrees less grim than a prison, and I was still inclined to regard myself in the role of a 'ripe man of martyrdom.'"[1] But he had heard that there was something unusual about Rivers, a professor at Cambridge who had made a distinguished reputation for himself as an anthropologist and clinical psychologist. One of the first in England to support Freud's work, after the war he became a pioneer member of the British Psychoanalytic Society. "Rivers was evidently some kind of great man," Sassoon wrote in his war memoir, *Sherston's*

1. Siegfried Sassoon, *Sherston's Progress* (New York: Doubleday, Doran, 1936), 3.

Progress. He looked forward to meeting him, and from the first five minutes of their conversation, he felt reassured: "There was never any doubt about my liking him. He made me feel safe at once and seemed to know all about me."[2]

In order to understand the transactions between Rivers and Sassoon, we must first look at the phenomenon of war neurosis or, to use the term invented by military physicians, shell shock. Although he did not seem to have any unusual physical or behavioral symptoms, the stresses and concerns that motivated Sassoon to publish his open letter of protest against the war could easily be seen as part of the larger syndrome of shell shock to which army doctors and administrators had gradually become accustomed. The Great War was the first large-scale military operation in which mental breakdown played a signficant role. This was so, historians have suggested, because of the high degree of impersonality, tension, passivity, and uncertainty trench warfare produced. As Eric Leed explains, "neurosis was a psychic effect not of war in general but of industrialized war in particular . . . the neuroses of war were the direct product of the increasingly alienated relationship of the combatant to the means of destruction."[3] In a study of neurosis in the air corps, Rivers had discovered that the "quantity of neurotic symptoms correlated not with the intensity of battle, the length of an individual's service, or his emotional predisposition, but with the degree of his immobility."[4] Rivers concluded that a man's most rational response to anxiety is some kind of manipulative activity, through which he acquires a sense of himself "as an autonomous actor in a world of instrumentalities."[5] When technological warfare deprived men of their sense of agency, they lost their natural defenses against fear and regressed toward neurosis, magic, or superstition.

The diagnosis of shell shock encompassed a wide range of physical and emotional symptoms, strikingly differentiated by class and rank. In soldiers, symptoms tended overwhelmingly to be physical: paralyses, limps, blindness, deafness, mutism (the most common symptom), contractures of a limb, or vomiting; in officers, symptoms tended toward the emotional: nightmares, insomnia, fatigue, dizziness, disorientation, and anxiety attacks. Sexual impotence was widespread in all ranks, so that the sexual wounds that Sandra Gilbert has noted as a major trope of postwar writing had their source in symbolic disorders of powerlessness.

Shell shock has also developed a unique mythology in the literature of the

2. Ibid., 3–4.

3. Eric Leed, *No Man's Land: Combat and Identity in World War I* (Cambridge: Cambridge University Press, 1979), 164.

4. Ibid., 183.

5. Ibid.

war. The historian Martin Stone, for example, sees it as the "tragic motif of the death of the Victorian Spirit" and suggests that "the shell-shocked soldier has taken on something of a Romantic guise, like his 19th century counterpart, the tubercular artist."[6] In a psychiatric context, however, shell shock can be seen as the first large-scale epidemic of male hysteria. Doctors had long been aware that hysteria could appear in men, but they were not prepared for the enormous numbers of men who developed hysterical symptoms during the war. By 1916 shell-shock cases accounted for as many as 40 percent of the casualties in the combat zones. By 1918, there were over twenty army hospitals for shell-shock patients in the United Kingdom. And, by the end of the war, eighty thousand cases had passed through army medical facilities. One-seventh of all discharges for disability were for nervous disorders.[7]

This parade of emotionally incapacitated men was in itself a shocking contrast to the heroic visions and masculinist fantasies that had preceded it in the British Victorian imagination. The poetic image of the Great War was one of strong, unreflective masculinity, embodied in the square, solid figure of General Haig, prepared by the poems of Kipling and the male adventure stories of G. R. Henty and Rider Haggard. For officers in particular, the cultural pressures to conform to these British ideals of stoic and plucky masculinity were extreme. As Paul Fussell notes in his glossary of the romantic vocabulary of war literature in which this generation was steeped, "not to complain" is to be "manly."[8] A brochure of *Instructions for the Training of Platoons for Offensive Action* (1917) describes how the platoon commander should gain the confidence of his men. He must be "well turned out, punctual, and cheery, even in adverse circumstances," look "after his men's comfort before his own and never spare himself," "enforce strict discipline," and be "blood-thirsty and forever thinking how to kill the enemy."[9] Legends circulated of officers who went over the top kicking a football as they charged the enemy trenches. In fact, the rate of war neurosis was four times higher among officers than among enlisted men.[10]

6. Martin Stone, "Shellshock and the Psychologists," in *The Anatomy of Madness,* ed. W. F. Bynum, Roy Porter, and Michael Shepherd (London: Tavistock, 1985), 2:242–271.

7. For a fuller discussion of the impact and treatment of shell shock, see Elaine Showalter, *The Female Malady: Women, Madness, and English Culture* (New York: Pantheon, 1985), chap. 7, "Male Hysteria: W. H. R. Rivers and the Lessons of Shell Shock."

8. Paul Fussell, *The Great War and Modern Memory* (New York: Oxford University Press, 1975), 22.

9. Reprinted in Paul Fussell, *Siegfried Sassoon's Long Journey* (New York: Oxford University Press, 1983), 30.

10. Thomas W. Salmon, *The Care and Treatment of Mental Diseases and War Neuroses ("Shell Shock") in the British Army* (New York: War Work Committee of the National Committee for Mental Hygiene, 1917), 13, 29.

Initially, army personnel tried to assimilate the evidence of shell shock into the moral, military, and medical categories they had established before the war. Some tried to excuse it as a physical injury to the central nervous system caused by proximity to an exploding shell. When faced with a hysterical soldier displaying unmanly emotions—such as a private who cried so continuously that he could not handle his rifle—they diagnosed his case as "excessive action of the lachrymal glands" and blamed it on organic causes. Many senior army officers, on the other hand, believed that shell-shock cases were either madmen who should be committed or cowards and malingerers who should be shot.[11]

But gradually most military psychologists and medical personnel came to agree that the real cause of shell shock was the emotional disturbance produced by warfare itself, by chronic conditions of fear, tension, horror, disgust, and grief; and war neurosis was "an escape from an intolerable situation," a compromise negotiated by the psyche between the instinct of self-preservation and the inhibition against deception or flight, which were "rendered impossible by ideals of duty, patriotism, and honor."[12] Placed in intolerable and unprecedented circumstances of fear and stress, deprived of their sense of control, and expected to react with outmoded and unnatural "courage," thousands of men reacted instead with the symptoms of hysteria; soldiers lost their voices and spoke through their bodies. For some, the experience of combat and loss may have brought to the surface powerful and disturbing feelings of love for other men. For most, however, the anguish of shell shock included more general but intense anxieties about masculinity, fears of acting effeminate, even a refusal to continue the bluff of male behavior. If it was the essence of manliness not to complain, then shell shock was the body language of masculine complaint, a disguised male protest, not only against the war, but against the concept of manliness itself. Epidemic female hysteria in late Victorian England had been a form of protest against a patriarchial society that enforced confinement to a narrowly defined femininity; epidemic male hysteria in World War I was a protest against the politicians, generals, and psychiatrists.

"The real source of wonder," wrote Thomas Salmon, was not that neurosis "should play such an important part in military life, but that so many men should find a satisfactory adjustment without its intervention." In *Shell-Shock and Its Lessons* an important book by military doctors G. Elliot Smith and T. H. Pear published toward the end of the war, the authors explained that the long-term repression of feeling that led to shell-shock symptoms in combat was only

11. See H. C. Marr, *Psychoses of the War* (London: Henry Froude, 1919), 60–73.
12. Salmon, *Care and Treatment,* 88.

an exaggeration of male sex-role expectations in civilian life. "The suppression of fear and other strong emotions is not demanded only of men in the trenches," they wrote, "it is constantly expected in ordinary society."[13]

There were two major ways of treating shell shock during the war, both intended to get men back to the trenches as fast as possible. The treatments were differentiated according to rank. Shell-shocked soldiers, on the one hand, were treated with the hostility and contempt that had been accorded hysterical women before the war. Not only in England, but in all European countries, they were subjected to forms of disciplinary treatment, quick cures, shaming, and physical retraining, frequently involving painful electrical shocks to the afflicted parts of their bodies. These were in fact semi-tortures designed to make the hysterical symptom more unpleasant to maintain than the threat of death at the front.[14] Officers, however, were regarded as harder to treat and usually given various kinds of psychotherapy.

Sassoon's therapy raises some interesting specific problems, because he did not think he was suffering from shell shock at all. His assignment to a war hospital rather than a court-martial had been engineered by the desperate efforts of Robert Graves and others to save him from the consequences of his pacifist outburst. Yet there were reasons why Sassoon's late-blooming pacificism could be officially understood and categorized as a form of war neurosis. His letter declaring the war a "deliberately prolonged . . . war of aggression and conquest" seemed like a bizarre aberration from one whose daredevil valor in combat had earned him the nickname Mad Jack and won him the Military Cross. In London, recovering from a war wound in the spring of 1917, he had had hallucinations of corpses on the pavement and fantasies of assassinating General Haig. And some shell-shock experts would have regarded Sassoon as a likely candidate for mental breakdown according to a theory that "strange first names" were symptomatic of latent family degeneracy.[15]

Rivers diagnosed Sassoon's case as a "very strong anti-war complex" and set about curing it through psychoanalytic techniques. In his therapeutic practice, Rivers relied on what he called *autognosis,* or self-understanding, which involved discussion of traumatic experiences; and reeducation, in which the "patient is led to understand how his newly acquired knowledge of himself may be utilized . . . and how to turn energy, morbidly directed, into more

13. Ibid., 31; G. Elliot Smith and T. H. Pear, *Shell-Shock and Its Lessons* (London: Longmans Green, 1917), 7.

14. See Leed, *No Man's Land,* 170–76; and Showalter, *The Female Malady,* 176–78.

15. E. C. Southard, *Shell-Shock and Other Neuro-Psychiatric Problems* (Boston: W. M. Leonard, 1919), 60.

healthy channels."[16] In Sassoon's case, this meant Rivers embarked on a delicate and subtle intensification of his fears that pacifism was unmanly and cowardly, a process heightened by Sassoon's strong admiration, respect, and affection for Rivers and by the Craiglockhart regime. In contrast to the passive rest cures favored in this period for hysterical or neurasthenic women of Sassoon's class (such as Virginia Woolf), military doctors felt that intense activity was essential for the restoration of male self-esteem. Sassoon was urged to resume a life of energetic masculine endeavor at Craiglockhart. Unlike the nervous women of the generation, who were forbidden by male psychiatrists to write or work, Sassoon was encouraged to take up a vigorous program of sports, was provided with a room of his own so that he could write undisturbed, and even had a hospital newspaper, *The Hydra,* edited by Wilfred Owen, in which to publish his poems.

In lengthy conversations three times a week, Rivers and Sassoon talked not only about Sassoon's life and war experiences but also about European politics, German military history, and the dangers of a premature peace. This talking cure was intended to make Sassoon feel uneasy about the gaps in his information and to emphasize the contrast between his emotional, and thus feminine, attitude toward the war and Rivers' rational, masculine, Cambridge don's view of it. At the same time, Sassoon found himself in the company of "nurses and nervous wrecks" and men who had "done their bit in France" crying like children. He was anxious to assert his superiority to his fellow officers: "Sometimes I had an uncomfortable notion that none of them respected one another; it was as though there were a tacit understanding that we were all failures, and this made me want to reassure myself that I wasn't the same as the others."[17]

By October, Sassoon was overwhelmed with guilt about his exile from the troops, about betraying the men who had fought with him, and about making a convenient separate peace that served to shorten the war for him. These anxieties were expressed in nightmares about the war, described in such poems of the period as "Sick Leave":

When I'm asleep, dreaming and lulled and warm—
They come, the homeless ones, the noiseless dead
. . . .
Out of the gloom they gather about my bed.

16. W. H. R. Rivers, "Psycho-therapeutics," in *Encyclopedia of Religion and Ethics,* ed. James Hastings (Edinburgh: T. & T. Clark, 1918), 10:440.

17. Sassoon, *Sherston's Progress,* 14.

They whisper to my heart; their thoughts are mine.
"Why are you here with all your watches ended?
. . . .
In bitter safety I awake unfriended;
And while the dawn begins with slashing rain
I think of the Battalion in the mud.
"When are you going out to them again?
Are they not still your brothers through our blood?"[18]

In November, acceding to Rivers' diagnosis that he had been sick and giving up his antiwar complex, Sassoon was cleared by a medical board, became once more, as he says, an "officer and a gentleman," and went back to the front. Some historians have argued that there was really something neurotic in Sassoon that craved death, loved the war, and derived a drug-like satisfaction from facing danger.[19] But this view seems mistaken to me. Without psychiatric intervention, Sassoon might have stuck to his pacifist principles. Rivers was the agent of a military establishment which had to frame his rebellion as a nervous breakdown and which found it more practical to isolate him in a mental hospital then to let him reach a political and public audience that might have supported his resistance.

Ironically, Rivers was as changed by their discussions as Sassoon was. He began to have antiwar dreams brought on by what Sassoon had told him. In his posthumous book, *Conflict and Dream* (1922), Rivers explored the psychoanalytic issues of fear, anxiety, and sexual repression which had come out of his work with Sassoon and other patients at Craiglockhart. In a series of brilliant hypotheses, he also began to apply to female hysteria some of the ideas about gender anxiety that he had developed in his study of male hysteria.[20]

Yet the covert intention of Rivers' therapeutic practice had been the reinscription of male gender anxieties in someone who had spoken against the war, and we can see his enormous and lasting success in Sassoon's postwar literary career. As Paul Fussell has pointed out, Sassoon devoted virtually all of his life after the war to an obsessive "re-visiting of the war" and his life before the war, "plowing and re-plowing" his experiences in a series of six memoirs. He was one for whom, as Fussell says, "remembering the war became something like a life work."[21] Sassoon described himself as motivated by a "queer craving to revisit the past and give the modern world the slip."[22] He seemed to

18. Sassoon, *Counter-Attack and Other Poems* (New York: E. P. Dutton, 1918), 43.
19. Robert Wohl, *The Generation of 1914* (Cambridge: Harvard University Press, 1979), 100.
20. Rivers, *Instinct and the Unconscious* (Cambridge: Cambridge University Press, 1922), 136.
21. Fussell, *The Great War,* 92.
22. Sassoon, *The Old Century and Seven More Years* (London, 1938), 140, quoted in ibid.

be continuing the process of autognosis in which he had been trained by Rivers, conducting a kind of self-psychoanalysis the object of which was to justify his life as a man. George Sherston, the autobiographical hero of the war trilogy that comprises *Memoirs of a Fox-Hunting Man, Memoirs of an Infantry Officer,* and *Sherston's Progress,* is a simplified and macho version of what Sassoon called his "outdoor self," not a poet, but rather the manly participant in hunting and combat.[23]

Rivers is installed in the memoirs, in Sassoon's diaries, and in his autobiography *Siegfried's Journey* as a father figure, conscience, or, we might also say, superego. He appears for the first time in *Sherston's Progress*. The first section of the book is named for him, and he is the only character given his real name. As Sassoon declares, "[my] definite approach to mental maturity began with my contact with the mind of Rivers," and in his writings Sassoon continues to use Rivers as the measure of mature masculine wisdom. When, at the end of *Sherston's Progress,* he describes his convalescence from yet another war wound, it is Rivers who comes to see him and to set him straight: "His presence was a refutation of wrongheadedness. I knew then that I had been very lonely while I was at the War; I knew that I had a lot to learn, and that he was the only man who could help me."[24]

The note struck here, of loneliness and dependence, is one of many which hint at the homoerotic element in Sassoon's feeling for Rivers. Fussell suggests that Rivers was the embodiment of the male "dream friend" who had been the companion of Sassoon's boyhood fantasies.[25] Rivers, who was fifty-three when he met Sassoon, was unmarried; he derived his greatest emotional satisfaction from his role as the teacher, mentor, and therapist of troubled young men. His colleague and student Charles Myers was one of many acquaintances who observed that through his psychiatric work in the war Rivers was able to release many of his long-repressed nurturant feelings, and thus "became . . . a far happier man."[26] When Rivers died suddenly in 1922, Sassoon was emotionally devastated. In a poem called "Revisitation," he imagined himself haunted by Rivers' ghost, "selfless and ardent . . . whom I am powerless to repay."[27]

23. For a detailed analysis of Sassoon's trilogy, see Fussell, *The Great War,* 90–105.

24. *Sherston's Progress,* 245.

25. Fussell, *The Great War,* 101.

26. See Richard Slobodin, *W. H. R. Rivers* (New York: Columbia University Press, 1978), 58–59, for the changes in Rivers' personality after the war.

27. "Revisitation," in Sassoon, *Diaries, 1920–1922,* ed. Rupert Hart-Davis (London and Boston: Faber and Faber, 1981), 164.

In his diary for March 26, 1921, Sassoon recorded his ambition to write the great English novel about homosexuality, "another *Madame Bovary* dealing with sexual inversion" which would be "free from any propagandistic feeling . . . as natural as life itself."[28] Although he never wrote such a novel, one might argue that the trilogy of war memoirs is Sassoon's disguised epic of homosexual feeling. The romantic homosexual subtext of his memoirs, the chronicle of "a wholly masculine way of life," is one of the indirect forms through which he addresses questions of masculinity, which paradoxically can only *be* indirectly expressed since "to think about masculinity," as Peter Schwenger notes, "is to become less masculine oneself."[29]

However indirectly, the psychiatric discourse of shell shock and the literary discourse of war memoirs opened up a significant discussion of masculinity that had been avoided by previous generations. Feminist interpretations of hysteria in women have helped us decode physical symptoms, psychotherapeutic exchanges, and literary texts as the representations of feminine conflict, conflict over the meaning of femininity within a particular historical context. Yet the meaning and representation of masculinity have been accepted as unproblematic. By applying feminist methods and insights to the symptoms, therapies, and texts of male hysteria, we may begin to understand that issues of gender and sexual difference are as crucial to understanding the history of masculine experience as they have been in shaping the history of women.

28. Ibid., 53.

29. Peter Schwenger, *Phallic Critiques: Masculinity and Twentieth-Century Literature* (London: Routledge and Kegan Paul, 1984).

LYNNE LAYTON

Vera Brittain's Testament(s)

When attempting to make sense of women and war, to study the personal quirks and the ambivalence of the individual may seem to obscure rather than clarify events. But case histories have an important place in history, for they permit us to focus on the gradual processes of questioning and commitment and can thus correct our tendency to simplify and modernize the historically varied manifestations of a movement such as feminism. Vera Brittain's struggle with war offers particularly rich insights into the process by which one woman reached feminist and pacifist positions.

Vera Brittain (1893–1970), a feminist, socialist, writer, and pacifist,[1] wrote in many genres, always addressing the most devastating experience of her life: World War I. The disparity between her later autobiographies, in which she sought a consistent self-representation, and the more ambivalent writings of the war period itself sheds light on the difficult process of coming to pacifism, which most studies of Brittain ignore.[2] Brittain is often represented as a born pacifist. In her later, retrospective works, she encouraged that interpretation by

1. Brittain's novels and autobiographies have recently been reissued in England by Virago Press. See also Carolyn G. Heilbrun's introductions to the reissued U.S. editions of the autobiographies (Seaview Books), as well as articles by Dale Spender, "The Whole Duty of Woman: Vera Brittain," in *Women of Ideas (And What Men Have Done to Them)* (London: Ark, 1983), 627–39; Muriel Mellown, "Vera Brittain: Feminist in a New Age (1893–1970)," in *Feminist Theorists: Three Centuries of Key Women Thinkers,* ed. Dale Spender (New York: Pantheon, 1983), 314–33; and Muriel Mellown, "Reflections on Feminism and Pacifism in the Novels of Vera Brittain," *Tulsa Studies in Women's Literature* 2 (Fall 1983), 215–28.

2. One exception is Marvin Rintala, who argues similarly for the value of the case study in "Chronicler of a Generation: Vera Brittain's Testament," *Journal of Political and Military Sociology* 12 (Spring 1984), 23–35. He focuses, as do I, on the personalized nature of Brittain's writing, but he concludes that she is not representative of her generation of women and that she was neither a socialist nor a feminist.

promulgating her essentialist notions of natural female pacifism.[3] But her diaries and letters of 1914–18 show that she was torn between patriotism and pacifism. Brittain later thought it imperative that pacifists understand the attraction that war holds for youth; in her early writings, her youthful ambivalence and the language in which it is expressed point to a complex relation between women and war. Not until war touched her personally did she begin a painful rebellion against the patriarchal values that had dominated her prewar life.

When war broke out in 1914, Brittain was just within reach of a feminist dream: to go to Oxford. Just after her acceptance by Somerville College in April, 1914, Brittain again met Roland Leighton, a friend of her younger brother Edward. By August, Brittain's excitement over Oxford had as much to do with the fact that Roland would also be attending as with her long-held ambition to become a writer. But when war was declared in August, her father, who had opposed her application, again proclaimed that he would not allow her to go.

Brittain's diary of 1913 and 1914 reveals the reactions of a young woman who met continual resistance to and social disapproval of her individualistic ambitions. Although she was a professed agnostic, she sought the spiritual meaning of life[4] and longed for some cause or person worthy of her devotion (*CY*, 75–76). She wanted to become a famous writer or leader of men (*CY*, 61, 64) and to help the poor and weak, teaching them to strive and achieve (*CY*, 29, 57). She was in sympathy with socialism, but elitism always marked her discussion of the masses. Likewise, although she more than once professed a dislike for women (*CY*, 324), she considered herself a feminist (*CY*, 35). In her diary Brittain repeatedly identified with Lyndall, the feminist protagonist of Olive Schreiner's *Story of an African Farm*, because of her idealistic ambitions: "I want to love! I want something great and pure to lift me to itself! . . . I am so cold, so hard, so hard; will no one help me?"[5]

Brittain's prewar values explain her susceptibility to wartime propaganda. The diary records the annoyance of this self-declared "nonmilitarist" with her father's antiwar sentiments and captures the way an articulate, upper-middle-class twenty-one-year-old reacted to war: "To-day has been far too exciting to

3. See her "Women and War," in *Lady into Woman: A History of Women from Victoria to Elizabeth II* (London: A. Dakers, 1953), 200.

4. Vera Brittain, *Chronicle of Youth: The War Diary, 1913–1917,* ed. Alan Bishop with Terry Smart (New York: William Morrow, 1982), 61, 71. Hereafter referred to in the text as *CY;* when important, the date of the entry is included before the page number.

5. Olive Schreiner, *Story of an African Farm* (1883, repr. London: Ernest Benn, 1951), 229.

enable me to feel at all like sleep—in fact it is one of the most thrilling I have ever lived through. . . . That which has been so long anticipated by some & scoffed at by others has come to pass at last—Armageddon in Europe! . . . The great fear now is that our bungling Government will declare England's neutrality." (*CY,* 8/13/14, 84). The young Brittain here exhibits the naive idealism that she later realized had been both the virtue and the fatal weakness of her generation.

Brittain's idealistic seeking is a normal facet of identity formation in adolescents;[6] as she wrote in *Testament of Youth,* her 1933 autobiography, states exploit this idealism in formulating their war propaganda:

> The causes of war are always falsely represented; its honour is dishonest and its glory meretricious, but the challenge to spiritual endurance, the intense sharpening of all the senses, the vitalising consciousness of common peril for a common end, remain to allure those boys and girls who have just reached the age when love and friendship and adventure call more persistently than at any later time.[7]

Like Roland, who could not wait to be called to the front, she worshipped and pursued "heroism in the abstract" (*CY,* 156).

Brittain's excitement about the war also reflected her boredom and stifled aspirations. Like many English and European men, she hoped that war would change the order of things and put an end to a long period of stagnation (*CY,* 3/21/15, 163). The feeling of uselessness, passivity, her relegation to the female sidelines of anxious waiting, poisoned Brittain's year at Oxford. At first committed to a life of the mind "above the strife of nations" (*CY,* 163, 170), she increasingly felt impotent by contrast to the new masculine model of military action and suffering. Roland told her that the delay in his being posted to the front made him feel effeminate. Thus both men and women experienced the inability to participate in war as impotence and equated it with being female.

Yet, after the very first report of losses, Brittain drew back from an unequivocal endorsement of war. The tension between her horror at wasted lives and her need for a noble cause lasted throughout the war. Her letters express her ambivalence even more clearly than does the diary. As early as October 1, 1914, she wrote to Roland, who would not acknowledge the negative side of war until he was in the trenches, "I always call myself a non-militarist, yet the

6. See, for example, the developmental theory of Erik H. Erikson, *Identity: Youth and Crisis* (New York: Norton, 1968).

7. Vera Brittain, *Testament of Youth* (New York: Macmillan, 1934), 291–92. Hereafter referred to as *TY.*

raging of those elemental forces fascinates me, horribly but powerfully, as it does you. You find beauty in it too; certainly war seems to bring out all that is noble in human nature, but against that you can say that it brings out all the barbarous too."[8] Brittain's letter and her description of Roland's view suggest that intellectual adolescents may sexualize war as raging "elemental forces" and the "intense sharpening of all the senses." Thus aestheticized, war seemed the culmination of Brittain's brand of spiritual humanism. Ironically, Brittain went on in the same letter to rank the sheer masculine activity of war above any moral value it might have: "But whether it is noble or barbarous I am quite sure that had I been a boy I should have gone off to take part in it long ago; indeed I have wasted many moments regretting that I am a girl. Women get all the dreariness of war and none of its exhilaration. . . . The fact that circumstances are abnormal is not consolation for being unable to take active part in them." There is an element of conscious theatricality in Brittain's desire to play a masculine role. Letters from the trenches, she wrote her brother, "made me wish desperately that I were a man and could train myself to play that 'Great Game with Death—' I wish it were *my* obvious duty to 'go and live in a ditch,' as Roland called it" (February 19, 1916).

Brittain attempted to fight her sense of impotence by imitating the conditions under which she imagined that Roland lived—an example of her persistent identification with the men in her life. When Somerville buildings were evacuated to make way for the army, Brittain was "joyful to be told that the sacrifice of one's comfort and convenience is of use" (April 11, 1915). She longed to suffer, not only because it made her feel more like one of the boys but also because it encouraged the growth of the soul: "[College is] for me at least too soft a job—even though one suffers more in a fairly inactive existence than in the other sort. I want physical endurance; I should welcome the most wearying kinds of bodily toil" (April 25, 1915). Most chilling is Brittain's imitation of Roland's new militaristic mode of discourse. Reporting to Roland "the latest news from my side of the war," she referred to the order to evacuate Somerville as the "Principal's official communiqué." Further, she wrote, "I am to be—I had almost said 'billeted'—in rooms at a place called Micklem Hall" (April 11, 1915). She used military language even to describe her feelings: "It is extraordinary how one's sorrows don't come singly. I thought there was enough to bear before; one feels hedged about by whole battalions of distresses" (April 29, 1915).

8. Vera Brittain to Roland Leighton, October 14, 1914, unpublished letter, William Ready Division of Archives and Research Collections, McMaster University Library, Hamilton, Canada. Subsequent references to Brittain's unpublished correspondence will be cited by date in the text.

Even after Roland's death, Brittain found it difficult to weigh her non-militarism against the patriotic propaganda in favor of war:

> Tah says He [Roland] always used to say that our one hope of salvation as a nation lay in a Great War, and if He had said this to me I should certainly have agreed with Him. I do condemn War in theory most strongly . . . but there are some things worse than even War, and I believe even wholesale murder to be preferable to atrophy and effeteness. It is better to do active harm and definite wrong than to drift and make no effort in any direction. . . . And when the War in question is a War *on* War, all the usual objections are changed into the opposite commendations. (January 24, 1916)

This emphasis on activity for activity's sake is reminiscent of futurist manifestos and distortions of Nietzsche. Brittain silenced her own pacifist questioning with the slogan that called World War I "a war on war."

As the war went on, she increasingly turned to patriotic and religious discourse: "Next Sunday is Easter-Day. I think perhaps one may celebrate even more than one could last year, the Resurrection of England—an England purged of much pettiness through the closeness of her acquaintance in these days with Life and Death" (April 19, 1916). Here Brittain endows England with her own experience—it was actually she who faced life and death in her work as a nurse and who wished to be saved from the pettiness of prewar Buxton. She uses religious discourse to translate her personal suffering into a higher reality of resurrection. Thus she gives herself hope for a life after Roland and attempts to quell her increasingly grave doubts about whether the war is worthwhile. Whereas the discourse Brittain used to express her prowar sentiments is abstract, suffusing religion and an adolescent sensuousness into patriotism, her antiwar discourse is much more immediate and personal. When Brittain descended from the clouds of "noble causes," she faced an earth of wasted lives.

At the end of the year at Oxford, Brittain decided to become a full-time nurse. This enabled her to emulate Roland, particularly by sharing his physical discomforts (*TY,* 166, 246–47), and to care for him "by proxy" (*CY,* 215; *TY,* 166). But, early on, Brittain was disillusioned by the lack of spirituality in nursing: "'There is no provision,' I told Roland in one of my earliest letters from Camberwell, 'for any interests besides one's supposed interest in one's work. Of course I hate it. There is something so starved and dry about hospital nurses—as if they had to force all the warmth out of themselves before they could be really good nurses'" (*TY,* 211). She took comfort in comparing her work to Roland's, but she never really felt that her war work was as important as that of the men in her life.

Brittain was also motivated to nurse by her desire to be more active and to challenge her fears of her own cowardice; as she wrote in "Folly's Vineyard"

(1918, unpublished), nursing was the least safe thing that women could do.[9] Finally, she hoped to help those who she knew were suffering as much as she. She wrote to Roland: "Suffering myself makes me want nothing so much as to do all I can to alleviate the sufferings of other people. The terrible things you mention and describe fill me . . . with a sort of infinite pity I have never felt before. I don't know whether it is you or sorrow that has aroused this softer feeling–perhaps both" (April 25, 1915). Brittain's suffering eventually led her not only to empathize with working women, who do involuntarily all their lives the kind of hard labor she voluntarily chose to do in wartime (*TY,* 174), but with the wives, lovers, and mothers of the enemy—and finally with the enemies themselves.

In her final autobiography, *Testament of Experience,* Brittain cited the empathy she learned during her duty in a German ward in France as one of the great turning points of her life.[10] The importance of this experience is evident in her creative writings of the period. Her poem "The German Ward" (1917) captures the absurdity of patching up the Germans after the Allies had blown them apart.[11] And in *Folly's Vineyard* the narrator says of the heroine, a nurse modeled closely on Brittain herself, "the more Sybil pitied them, the more acutely she felt the tragedy of War. It seemed to her that she and they alike were victims, broken by the desire for domination of that military caste which had plunged Europe into disaster."

Brittain's individualism and her tendency to personalize the war countered her patriotic abstractions and fostered her antiwar sentiments. Even before she began nursing in London, she repudiated Roland's sensuous, aesthetic rhetoric:

> The more I think of this War, the more terribly incongruous seems to me the contrast between the immense importance of the individual, and calm ruthlessness with which hundreds of individuals are mown down at once by an impersonal gun. Postal Service, ASC, RAMC, Taxes, Hospitals, etc.—all perfectly organised simply to afford the greatest facility to the Science of Death—in its noble work of interrupting and nullifying all the other sciences that make for life. . . . Public opinion has made it a high and lofty virtue for us women to countenance the departure of such as these and you to regions where they will probably be slaughtered in a brutally degrading fashion in which we would never allow animals to be slaughtered. This, I suppose is "the something elemental, something beautiful" that you find in War! To the saner mind it

9. Vera Brittain, "Folly's Vineyard," MS, 1918, in William Ready Division, McMaster University.

10. Vera Brittain, *Testament of Experience* (1957, repr. New York: Seaview Books, 1981), 470–71. Hereafter referred to as *TE.*

11. *Poems of the War and After* (London: Victor Gollancz, 1934), 34–36, hereafter referred to as *PWA.*

seems more like a reason for shutting up half the nation in a criminal lunatic asylum. (October 10, 1915)

In a letter written the very next day, however, she apologized to Roland, explaining that her outburst was motivated by Edward's impending departure for the front—that is, by personal attachment.

By 1917, Brittain no longer apologized to her male correspondents for her personalization of the war: "The longer the War goes on, the more one's concern in the whole immense business seems to centre itself upon the few beings still left that one cares about, and the less upon the general issues of the struggle" (April 17, 1917). We do not see such a personalization of war by the men with whom she had been intimate.

Brittain came close to quitting nursing after Roland's death, when she realized that she had been doing it only for him and actually hated the work (*TY,* 246–47). But she felt it was her duty to Roland and to the country to continue. When Edward died in June, 1918, she again wished to quit the detested labor of nursing, but again chose to continue—not for any patriotic or abstract purpose, but to be worthy of those she had loved who had died. By the end of the war, Brittain realized that nursing had saved her from utter despair over personal loss. In her poem "Hospital Sanctuary" (1918), she wrote that what kept her going were not patriotic platitudes but the people who were dependent on her care. In "Epitaph on My Days in Hospital" (1919), she used religious discourse to express salvation through caring, but her language celebrates humanity, not England (*PWA,* 57).

When the war ended, Brittain was in a state of "numb disillusion" (*TY,* 458). Of her feelings on Armistice Day, she wrote, "all those with whom I had really been intimate were gone; not one remained to share with me the heights and the depths of my memories" (*TY,* 462–63). Thus cut off from a past, it was difficult for her to imagine a future. For lack of an alternative, she returned to Oxford, determined to gain an understanding of what had happened to her generation. In a section of *Testament of Youth* entitled "Survivors Not Wanted," she discussed the difficulty of resuming a normal life. Unlike a returning soldier, she was not given thanks or special care; her four years of nursing were purposefully ignored.

During her years at Oxford, Brittain struggled against overwhelming feelings of personal discontinuity. The sense that she had lived two lives, one before the war and one after, never really left her. As early as May, 1915, she reported feeling like a different person, centuries older (*CY,* 189). Metaphors of premature aging crowd her diaries and letters; the heroines in nearly all of her fictional work suffer the same discontinuity as a result of their World War I losses.

By the time she wrote *Testament of Youth* in 1933, Brittain saw the war effort as an utter waste and recalled feeling in 1918 that only "piping for peace" could give meaning to her own survival. In 1922, she volunteered as a lecturer for the League of Nations. Her early postwar fiction, however, belies her later self-presentation as a woman unambivalently antiwar. Her works of the early 1920s still try to justify her sacrifice of years and loves to war.

In *Not without Honour* (1924), Brittain dealt with her conflict by splitting herself between two heroines, Christine Merivale and Virginia Dennison. At Oxford in the beginning of the war, Christine, whose background is similar to Brittain's, comes under the influence of a pacifist teacher. Adopting his views, she argues against patriotic Virginia's desire to do "something useful": "*I* don't see how you're going to get away from what he says about the preservation of Learning and Literature and Art. It won't be much use anybody winning the war unless there's some Beauty and Joy left for those who inherit the victory."[12] Patriotism does battle with Truth and Beauty. And, as in Brittain's life in 1914–15, not pacifism but patriotism born of personal concerns gets the last word. At the end of the year, Virginia goes to nurse not only for her fiancé but for the thousands who have fiancés at the front (*NWH,* 295). Christine, disgusted by the jingoism all around her, takes refuge in the "real, solid work" that she is doing at Oxford, until she learns that a pre-Oxford mentor and love has been killed at Gallipoli. In his dying letter, he expresses his belief that Christine will play her role in this war fought for the sake of eternal peace. Christine then realizes that she must do war work or there may be no civilization left to carry on. Thus, like Virginia, she redeems Brittain's choice, drawing on the same idealist discourse that had carried the younger Brittain into war: "She saw that the dramatic surroundings of a great deed or a great ideal were the necessary response to human nature's need for the interpretation of Truth into symbols" (*NWH,* 314). Christine actually experiences this as a religious revelation, and her return to Christianity foreshadows Brittain's return to religion in the 1930s and 1940s. Although Brittain wrote about women's decisions to do war work, she attributed their motivation to personal relationships with men and formulated it in patriarchal nationalist or Christian terms. Even the alternate pacifist ideal is articulated by a male character.

Similarly, *The Dark Tide* (1923), which begins at Oxford at the end of the

12. Vera Brittain, *Not without Honour* (London: Grant Richards, 1924), 294. Hereafter referred to as *NWH.*

war, pairs protagonists to deal with Brittain's major postwar conflict: the hostility between women who had served in the war and those who had not. Virginia Dennison, like Brittain, has worked and suffered many losses in the war; when she returns to Oxford at war's end she is aloof, haughty, isolated, and resentful of the frivolity of the other young women, particularly that of her rival, Daphne Lethbridge, whose war work entailed no risks. She feels that it was her work and that of others like her that "saved the country and their wretched little academic careers from complete chaos."[13] One of her woman professors, Pat O'Neill, who had stayed at Oxford during the war, points out that Virginia is being uncharitable: "It was the women here who kept the nucleus of a University and made it easy for the men who were left, and other people, like you, to come back and take up their work again" (*DT,* 53). But Virginia never really recovers from her sense of discontinuity. As she states toward the end of the novel, "It's one's future, not one's past, that they really hide—those graves in France" (*DT,* 204).

Work and her friendship with Winifred Holtby, a writer and feminist whom Brittain met at Oxford after the war, had been critical for Brittain in facing the future, and in *The Dark Tide* these themes are linked both to Virginia and to Daphne, who in the course of the novel suffers enough to make her worthy of Virginia's friendship. Pat, Brittain's spokesperson in *The Dark Tide,* makes it clear that only work can heal the discontinuities caused by personal loss and suffering. Encouraging Daphne's decision to write, Pat says, "You see, when everything else is gone, there's always work. I don't think anyone ever realizes how much work can mean until the other things *are* gone." Daphne replies, "It's the only thing no one else can take away from you whatever happens, isn't it?" (*DT,* 267–68).

When Brittain published *Testament of Youth* in 1933, she saw that yet another war was imminent. Her purpose was twofold: to write about how women had experienced the war (*TE,* 77), and to warn the adolescent generation of 1933 not to be so easily fooled as hers had been. In this antiwar manifesto, she described her own life from 1900 to 1925 in an attempt to show how she and her contemporaries had been duped by English propaganda into laying down their lives.

In *Honourable Estate* (1936), Brittain wasted no words justifying World War I or extolling heroism. The heroine's brother Richard sought death in battle apparently because he feared public disclosure of his homosexual rela-

13. Vera Brittain, *The Dark Tide* (1923; repr. New York: Macmillan, 1936), 51. Hereafter referred to as *DT.*

tionship with a fellow soldier. Although Ruth Alleyndene is appalled by militarism, she volunteers to nurse when she hears of her brother's death. When she then loses her first love, Eugene, she seeks death by doing relief work among famine and disease victims in postwar Russia. Only Denis Rutherston, her future husband, persuades her to return to England to work for a new order, "the struggle for peace through rationality."[14] Yet Denis himself had entered the war because he had no desire to live. Through Ruth's politics (she becomes a Labour M.P.) and pacifism, Brittain speaks against the deceptive power of militarist rhetoric. Thus Ruth decries the beauty of the cemetery as a lie that increases "the illusion born afresh with each generation that war is an instrument of honour, a road to glory!" (*HE,* 498–99).

Honourable Estate is much more outspokenly feminist and pacifist than Brittain's works of the 1920s. The subtitle, *A Novel of Transition,* suggests its theme of changing opportunities for women between 1894 and 1930. The novel expresses Brittain's belief that the war only hastened what the patient work of suffragists like Denis' mother had set in motion (*HE,* 460).[15] But the narrator does argue that the war changed women's roles more than did the attainment of the vote. For example, when Ruth tells her parents she wishes to quit school and nurse, they do not oppose her and the narrator says, "neither they nor she recognised this unopposed exercise of initiative as the typical first stage of a transition period which would change the women of Ruth's generation more rapidly and profoundly than they could ever have been changed by the mere use of the vote" (*HE,* 321).

The novel also offers a partial critique of the moral standard that demanded sexual purity of women. Ruth makes love with Eugene once before he goes to the front. She makes the proposal but Brittain couches her desire in a rhetoric of self-sacrifice: Ruth wants Eugene to know the whole of love before he dies (*HE,* 397). Ruth avoids pregnancy but finally is sorry that she did not have Eugene's baby. Echoing Brittain's assertion in *Testament of Youth* that she

14. Vera Brittain, *Honourable Estate: A Novel of Transition* (New York: Macmillan, 1936), 451, hereafter referred to as *HE.* Denis, who supports Ruth's independence and whose values she shares, is based on Brittain's husband, G. E. Catlin.

15. Similarly, in "Women and War," Brittain states: "War may shatter the structure of society and with it many obsolete patterns. It may accelerate, and in Britain did accelerate, processes set in motion by other historic forces long before its outbreak. But it did not create those progressive forces, and usually appeared to be hostile to them owing to the anti-social and anti-biological policies to which it led.

"Wartime improvements in the position of women have seldom been due to any new realisation of woman's dignity and needs; they originate in the selfishness of States seeking additional workers for temporary and unconstructive ends." *Lady into Woman,* 195.

became more comfortable with sexuality through nursing and that the war gave women more liberty to be alone in the company of men (*TY,* 166, 177), the novel claims the war put an end to the double standard. Unlike her 1915 diary, however, where Brittain noted and tried to justify her physical desire for Roland, the 1936 novel implies that the pleasures of sex are for the man, the baby for the woman.

In *Honourable Estate,* Brittain developed a semi-religious discourse of sacrifice and suffering to express her feminism and pacifism. Janet Rutherston speaks in religious terms of the great 1913 suffragist demonstration that honored feminist Emily Wilding Davison's self-sacrifice to the cause: "that solemn tribute paid by religious devotees to an impersonal end that was dearer to them than life!" (*HE,* 138). The book's final chapter, covering the years 1926–30, is headed by an epigraph attributed to the historian Louisa Creighton: "So long as one bears one's life in one's own hands, the burden is intolerable. It is only by seeing that life as part of a universal life that peace is found" (*HE,* 502). Whereas Brittain's adolescent idol, Olive Schreiner, had urged redemption through individual suffering, Brittain now seemed to believe in political and religious causes that transcend the individual, such as feminism and pacifism.

Although Brittain was an active pacifist in 1933, she became a revolutionary pacifist through her encounter in 1936 with Canon Dick Sheppard, head of the Peace Pledge Union. Brittain suddenly realized that she had been working with peace organizations that were "politically respectable because they were ultimately prepared to compromise with war" (*TE,* 168). Henceforth, citing the Sermon on the Mount, she opposed love to power (*TE,* 169–72).[16] Although the love she refers to is an abstract love of humanity, it is perhaps not too far-fetched to trace her ideological position back to her love for Roland.[17]

In 1937, Brittain took a neutral position on Spain. But it was her Christian pacifism in World War II that brought upon her the public disapproval she had feared. Although, as she later discovered, she had been on a Gestapo hit list, the British government viewed her biweekly "Letter to Peace Lovers," which had almost two thousand subscribers at its peak, as pro-Nazi heresy, and they refused to allow her to lecture in America. Brittain opposed the view that the

16. The interpretation that follows draws on Brittain's fiction and her autobiography of the years 1925–50, *Testament of Experience.* The reader should be advised that an analysis of the letters and diaries of this period might reveal the same kind of discrepancies in self-representation that we saw in the years 1914–25.

17. Rintala argues that Brittain's turn to Sheppard's form of pacifism was directly linked to her father's suicide and Winifred Holtby's death. "Chronicler of a Generation," 30.

only war aim was the destruction of Hitler. In 1939, she wrote to Chamberlain and asked that Britain refrain from bombing civilian women and children. During the war, she helped arrange the large-scale emigration of British children, cared for victims of civilian bombings, and worked to exempt food from the British blockade, so that it could reach the children, mothers, and invalids of the German-occupied continent.

Her book *England's Hour* (1941), about civilian life in England during the war, was quite unpopular, not least because she ended it with a plea to forgive the enemy, the legacy of her World War I nursing experience (*TE,* 274). *Seed of Chaos,* her pamphlet against obliteration bombing, which was first published in America in 1944, was rejected by the public and journalists because it emphasized the spiritual consequences of bombing, not only for the victims, but for those who inflicted the suffering (*TE,* 331–32, 328).

Brittain's faith in a "spiritual imperative," which is evident even in the diaries of 1913–14 but which she claimed was destroyed by World War I, became an absolute certainty on V.E. Day, "when the innate goodness of the men and women waiting patiently in Whitehall had shown me that God lived, but only with their cooperation could carry out His purpose" (*TE,* 471). Toward the end of *Testament of Experience,* she described the last of those "creative experiences" that shaped her pacifism, an open-air religious service that combined the scriptures of four world religions. Of this service, which followed a conference in India on Ghandian principles of nonviolent means of achieving peace, she wrote: "I had long known that there were many roads to Jerusalem but now this truth came alive for me, and I saw that the Christian revelation was only a small part of the evidence accumulated . . . by the great religions of mankind that God exists" (*TE,* 471). Thus was her pacifism finally consciously reconciled with her religious urgings.

After the war, Brittain lectured for the Women's International League and was a delegate to their 1946 conference in Luxembourg. Although she was wont to express belief in an essential female pacifism, she reported that, of the delegates to the conference, all women, one half pleaded for international reconciliation and one half for revenge (*TE,* 412). In *Honourable Estate,* Brittain had endorsed Olive Schreiner's argument that, if women had political power, they would never let their children, whom they bear in anguish, go to war (*HE,* 565). In "Women and War," she agreed with feminists who argue that "war violates a profound biological urge in women" (*HE,* 200). We can trace this sentiment all the way back to 1915, even though at the same time as she professed it she was urging her parents to let Edward enlist. But in her novel *Born 1925* (London: Macmillan, 1948) the mouthpiece for her Christian pacifism is not a woman but a man, Robert Carbury, modeled on Dick Sheppard, who attributes all the evils of the world—including poverty and hunger—to war. Unlike *Testament of Youth* and the earlier novels, neither *Testament of Experience* nor *Born 1925* speaks for women; they speak for humanity.[18]

In tracing Brittain's struggle with war from 1914 to 1950, we discover not a straight line to pacifism or feminism but a series of backward and forward movements. If we attempt to understand Brittain's ambivalence and the discourse that expressed it, we may uncover a relation between women and war. Brittain's prowar sentiments and her desire to be active in the war seem part of her professed desire to be a man. Although Brittain had declared herself a feminist as early as 1913, almost all of her role models during her adolescence and young adulthood were men.[19] She borrowed her abstract rhetoric of patriotism and heroism from male friends and the male establishment. More than once, she cursed having been born a woman and more than once she showed a lack of respect for women.[20] And more than once she wished Roland might be wounded so that she could nurse him and gain the sense of importance and usefulness that was only accorded men.

But it was love for Roland and the victims she nursed that finally brought Brittain into touch with her suppressed female identity. If we believe Carol Gilligan and others, who have argued that women, unlike men, see relationship as an essential part of self-development,[21] then we might say that Brittain's personalization of the war, which eventually vanquished her tendency to prowar abstraction, involved a shift from male to female identification. She began nursing out of love for Roland and compassion for other women with sons and lovers at the front. Through love and nursing, she learned empathy, even with those who daily endangered the life of her loved ones. Before the war, all her intimates were men; afterward she found friendship with a woman, Winifred Holtby.

18. Mellown points out that Brittain's turn to "salvation through humiliation" produced a temporary decline in her concern for feminism. "Reflections on Feminism and Pacifism," 220.

19. There are a few exceptions: Brittain identified with a woman teacher at St. Monica's, a woman in Buxton, and a woman don at Oxford, but, until she met Winifred Holtby, she never really had a female friend whom she respected as much as her male friends.

20. A few months after Roland's death, Brittain wrote in her diary: "Oh! I know! It was happiness, not sorrow, that softened me; I had bitterness enough in my nature before. I didn't need suffering to soften me. I needed joy. I never loved my fellow-men—or fellow-women, rather, for I like most men—in large quantities. And now I like them even less" (*CY*, 3/23/16, 324).

21. Carol Gilligan, *In a Different Voice* (Cambridge: Harvard University Press, 1982); and Jean Baker Miller, *Toward a New Psychology of Women* (Boston: Beacon Press, 1976).

Brittain's road to pacifism was inextricably intertwined with the passage from abstraction to relationship, which included the shift from a self-concerned to an empathic feminism. The final form of her pacifism was buttressed by a Christian rhetoric not much less abstract than her previous patriotic rhetoric. But, of the two voices with which she spoke, it was the voice embedded in relationship and then universalized that had the last word, the word for peace.

YASMINE ERGAS

Growing up Banished: A Reading of Anne Frank and Etty Hillesum

Memories help us live. Oddly, they need not be our own, seared as they are into the lives of those who were not there. Wars, for example: long after the bombing has stopped and the shell-shocked cities have been reconstructed, children learn to remember scenes of devastation they never witnessed. Persecution, too: age-old fears come to haunt generations born and bred in safety. Partly experienced and partly borrowed, memories are selective—mental notebooks we keep to honor the past, but equally to keep track of ourselves. "*Remember what it was to be me:* that is always the point," Joan Didion said of her jottings, and the same could well be said of what we choose to recall.[1]

Diaries serve a double function, reminding both author and reader of a past self. Anne Frank and Etty Hillesum tracked their personal routes along transitory moments, and we in turn trace in their diaries the signposts to the present. Although the differences between then and now, between them and us, are enormous, these diaries still feed the memories of many today.

An Interrupted Life and *The Diary of a Young Girl* bear witness to life as it was lived in parallel to the Nazi concentration camps.[2] They are not "camp" stories, permeated by the horrors of Auschwitz or Dachau. Instead, they tell of the attempt to maintain or construct normalcy in a rapidly bestializing civil society.

1. Joan Didion, *Slouching towards Bethlehem* (New York: Washington Square Press, 1981), 139.

2. Etty Hillesum, *An Interrupted Life* (New York: Pantheon Books, 1983). Henceforth abbreviated to EH, with page references in the text. Anne Frank, *The Diary of a Young Girl* (New York: Pocket Books, 1953). Hereafter referred to as AF.

From them we learn of persecution and war as they once intertwined with the processes of growing up female and Jewish.

What do they tell us? Synopses of such works are always difficult. For portrayals of the authors, let me refer you to the texts themselves. My intent is to unravel something of what they say about developing identities in the context of genocide. The diaries talk of maintaining individuality, forging personalities, coming to terms with femininity when persecution straitjackets its victims into a racial identity intended to be all-encompassing and all-defining. Although Anne Frank and Etty Hillesum repeatedly attempt to fashion and review their ways of being women, gender ultimately recedes to second place. As Nazism casts them, they must cast themselves: first and foremost as Jews.

These diaries speak, then, of the intersection of war and persecution. War is not for everyone the same. For persecuted groups, its contours are dictated by banishment. Their men and boys do not defend their countries at the front; they are not the nation's warriors. Their women and girls do not courageously nurse the wounded in battle, send their beloveds patriotic messages sealed with state approval, or otherwise join the country's effort. They may escape, resist, or submit. But they must always confront the condition of having been singled out—in this case, for annihilation.

Both young women, relatively affluent, of cultured milieux, and trapped in German-occupied Holland, Etty and Anne recorded the passages that led from individual lives to a collective fate. Etty Hillesum began writing first, at the age of twenty-seven. Her diaries, abridged by her Dutch publisher, were written between March, 1941, and October, 1942. The book also includes a few letters written later, up until her deportation on September 7, 1943. When Anne Frank started her diary on June 14, 1942, Etty was close to ending her own. And by the time the Frank household was deported—on August 4, 1944—Etty has been dead in Auschwitz, eight months.

Their styles are very different. Anne receives a diary for her thirteenth birthday. Within a week the diary has acquired a name, Kitty, and been properly introduced, via Anne's descriptions, to the entire family. Kitty is Anne's confidante in a friendship initiated in freedom and continued in the cloistered captivity of the *Achterhuis* or Secret Annexe where the family, together with a colleague of Otto Frank's, Mr. Van Daan, his wife, and their adolescent son, Peter, find refuge.[3] (Some time after going into hiding, they

3. Anne Frank portrays Kitty's character in a short story written in hiding: see *Anne Frank's Tales from the Secret Annexe* (New York: Pocket Books, 1983), 11–14. Hereafter referred to as AF: *Tales*.

invited Albert Dussel, a dentist of late middle age, to join them.) Notwithstanding occasional doubts, Anne possesses the "instinct for reality" that is the hallmark of a diary keeper.[4] Everyday life is not too prosaic to be carefully recorded. She chronicles its details, patterning the day's events into a coherent narrative. The narrative is its own point, although it also often serves as the springboard for moral reflections, laying the foundations of *Selbstbildung,* of construction of the self or of self-improvement.

Etty hardly ever reports a day's events and never provides an introduction to her cast of characters. Like a diver going off the deep end, she plunges in with "Here goes, then" (EH, 1). A series of reflections follows, written at all times of day and night. Etty is not addressing a paper standin for a best friend as she records impressions and feelings in a nervous reworking of her spiritual and moral self. Her diaries are written in the mode of annotations designed to evoke a full range of associations rather than to record each day's passing. "That may seem rather clumsily put, but I know what I mean," she comments after a particularly elliptical entry, making the point of her writing clear (EH, 119).

A variety of factors must have contributed to the two women's divergent approaches. The one conjures up her alter ego as an imaginary penpal, while the other seeks to fathom and reorder her innermost self. For Etty, turning inward is painful: "So many inhibitions," she remarks at the outset, "so much fear of letting go, of allowing things to pour out of me, and yet that is what I must do if I am ever to give my life a reasonable and satisfactory purpose. It is like the final, liberating scream that always sticks bashfully in your throat when you make love" (EH, 1). For Anne, the diary is an immediate source of joy: "Now I must stop. Bye-bye, we're going to be great pals!" she ends her first entry (AF, 1).

Despite their differences, Anne and Etty share a propensity to harp on the limitations inherent in women's attitudes toward men and to set themselves on routes of less fettered freedom. For Anne, the captive community in which she lives provides the models from whom she fully intends to differ: her mother, Mrs. Van Daan, even her much-admired sister. The pettiness of their concerns strikes her, as does the triviality of their accomplishments. "If God lets me live," she exclaims in April, 1944, "I shall attain more than Mummy has ever done, I shall not remain insignificant" (AF, 187). A few days earlier she remarked in a similar vein: "I want to get on; I can't imagine that I would have to lead the same sort of life as Mummy and Mrs. Van Daan and all the women

4. Didion, *Slouching towards Bethlehem,* 135–44.

who do their work and are forgotten" (AF, 177). The road to significance leads, Anne thinks, through working "in the world and for mankind"; the road to life after death, she hopes, can be paved by writing (AF, 187, 177). Femininity rarely threatens these aspirations: there are no obvious traces of female fear of success.[5] Just before scorning her mother's "insignificance," Anne affirms confidence in herself. "I know what I want, I have a goal, an opinion, I have a religion and love. Let me be myself and then I am satisfied. I know that I'm a woman, a woman with inward strength and plenty of courage" (AF, 187).

Like Anne, Etty is impatient with the conventional bonds of womanhood. While also referring critically to her mother, she frequently proffers general comments on the "not at all simple . . . role of women," whose marks she recognizes in herself—unlike Anne (EH, 27). Passing "a beautiful, well-groomed, wholly feminine, albeit dull woman, I completely lose my poise. Then I feel that my intellect, my struggle, my suffering, are oppressive, ugly, unwomanly; then I, too, want to be beautiful and dull, a desirable plaything for a man" (EH, 27). This desiring to be desired Etty dismisses as "only a primitive instinct" (EH, 27). Reflecting on traditional feminine conditioning, she looks forward to an "essential emancipation of women." "We still have to be born as human beings, that is the great task that lies before us" (EH, 27–28).

This want of emancipation notwithstanding, Etty's lifestyle seems largely unhampered by patriarchal constraints. Her reviewers often cite as indicators of her sexual liberty her dual involvement with her mentor, Speier, and Papa Han, her kindly and elderly landlord; and her entries allude to several earlier experiences. She pursued her psychological and spiritual liberation in tandem with her studies. Having already earned a degree in law at the University of Amsterdam, she enrolled in the Faculty of Slavonic Languages before turning to psychology. She lived in Papa Han's house with four friends, in an arrangement similar to that often found around university campuses today. The way to free femininity may have been arduous and uncharted, but it was open. So it appeared, at least, as described by Anne and Etty, upper-middle-class girls of "enlightened" and cultured backgrounds. But, while the future of women revealed avenues of possibility, that of the Jews appeared increasingly walled in by political foreclosures.

Branded as a special enemy in occupied lands, the Jews were sharply set off

5. Nonetheless, describing Kitty, who "wants to work in a factory, like those jolly chattering girls she sees passing by the window," Anne does say, "Kitty's mother always says that a girl doesn't get a husband if she's too clever, and that, Kitty thinks, would be just awful" (AF: *Tales,* 13).

from their societies. As the racial laws were strengthened, demarcations became more rigid. Race prevailed as the ordering societal criterion. Yet Etty had been keeping a diary for six months before she talked of herself as a Jew, and even then the mention is more metaphorical than factual. On walking through south Amsterdam, she wrote, "I felt like an old Jew, wrapped up in a cloud. No doubt that's recorded somewhere in our mythology: a Jew moving along, wrapped up in a cloud" (EH, 35). Over the course of many months, however, her Jewishness impinges on her sense of self at an accelerating pace, finally becoming the implicit referent when she says *we*. For Etty, "Jew"—once a seemingly marginal connotation—had been transformed into the ineluctable answer to the question "who am I?" In July, 1942, she wrote: "What is at stake is our impending destruction and annihilation, we can have no more illusions about that. They are out to destroy us completely, we must accept that and go on from there" (EH, 130).

A fortnight earlier, Anne had introduced herself to the as yet unnamed Kitty. "Sketching in the brief story of my life," a sentence and a half sufficed for the family's vital statistics: her parents' ages at marriage, the births of her elder sister, Margot, and of herself (AF, 3). Immediately she launched into a description of their lives, "as we are Jewish." Friday evening dinners or Passover festivities do not ensue. Of the forty-five lines that Anne dedicates to this presentation, thirty are devoted to the Nazi racial laws and their repercussions. "As we are Jewish," Anne explains, the Franks had left Germany in 1933. But the rest of the family stayed behind, "so life was filled with anxiety" (AF, 3). With the arrival of the Germans in Holland, "the sufferings of us Jews really began. Anti-Jewish decrees followed each other in quick succession," and she lists them (AF, 3). To be a Jew, a persecuted Jew, is an essential component of Anne's sense of self: it prescribes the coordinates by which she locates herself in the world.

Anne chafes against the racial yoke represented by the yellow star. "Surely the time will come when we are people again, and not just Jews," she writes well into 1944, longing not for the obliteration of Jewish identity but for the restoration of individuality (AF, 186). Etty invokes that time too, in a letter from Westerbrok.[6] "The outside world probably thinks of us as a grey, uniform, suffering mass of Jews, and knows nothing of the gulfs and abysses

6. Westerbrok was a "transit camp" in the east Netherlands to which Jews were deported before being sent to other camps. For histories of the Netherlands during the Second World War focusing on policies toward the Jews, see J. Presser, *The Destruction of the Dutch Jews* (New York: E. P. Dutton, 1969); and Helen Fein, *Accounting for Genocide: National Responses and Jewish Victimization during the Holocaust* (New York: Free Press, 1979), 262–89.

and subtle differences that exist between us. They could never hope to understand" (EH, 218). To understand, that is, how differences persist notwithstanding the iron rule of racial caste.[7]

Collective identities imply common destinies. As the Nazi persecution intensified, the futures Anne and Etty envisaged changed. In April, 1942, Etty could anticipate the day when, chancing upon an anemone preserved in the pages of her diary, she would remember Speier's fifty-fifth birthday.[8] Looking back upon this happy moment of her youth, she would then be, Etty foresaw, a matron who had attained a clearly imagined moment of the future. That future represented a personal development woven from the idiosyncratic yearnings of an aspiring writer endowed with intense spiritualist tendencies and strong passions. "I am sure," she wrote in the early summer, "that one day I shall go to the East" (EH, 116). But within a matter of weeks the prospect of walking through Japanese landscapes had faded. The future was reduced to the question of survival or death as persecution crystallized the awareness that reordered experience, the anticipation of imminent mass murder. On "July 3, 1942, Friday evening, 8:30" she describes the rupture that has sundered her life's apparent continuities. "Yes, I am still at the same desk, but it seems to me that I am going to have to draw a line under everything and continue in a different tone" (EH, 130). "Every day I shall put my papers in order and every day I shall say farewell" (EH, 140).

Anne undergoes a similar transition. In the summer of 1944 the young girl who "did so want to grow into a real young woman" (AF, 125) senses her impending doom and recalls her obligations. "I must uphold my ideals, for perhaps the time will come when I shall be able to carry them out," she reminds herself, having stared disaster in the face. "I see the world gradually being turned into a wilderness. I hear the ever approaching thunder, which will destroy us too, I can feel the suffering of millions and yet, if I look up into the heavens, I think that it will all come right" (AF, 237). Months earlier, she had equated the time when it would "all come right" with survival and testimony. In April she had written: "If we bear all this suffering and if there are still Jews left, when it is over, then Jews instead of being doomed will be held up as an

7. The Nazis did differentiate. Etty's parents, for instance, fruitlessly hoped to be admitted to Barneveld, a temporary refuge for the privileged. Even at the camps particular powers and protection were given to some: kapos, entertainers, physicians, technicians. Ultimately, however, these distinctions only articulated and bolstered the general category of "Jew."

8. Speier, a Jewish psychochirologist, had moved to Amsterdam from Germany. Etty began as his patient, worked temporarily as his secretary, and remained devoted to him until his death. He, however, was engaged to a young woman in London, and, although emotionally involved with Etty, remained "faithful to her [his fiancée] above everthing else" (EH,170).

example" (AF, 186). Distinguishing herself from Margot, who wished to be a midwife in Palestine, Anne dreamed that May of a year in Paris and one in London, learning languages and studying the history of art, seeing "beautiful dresses" and "doing all kinds of exciting things" (AF, 206). Hopes of an individual, lighthearted future remained, hostage of an uncertain collective fate.

The leaden quality of that fate contrasted sharply with the possibilities feminine identity seemed to hold in store. Reading Anne and Etty it seems, however, that persecution provided a greater impetus to searches that stretched Jewish spirituality than to social experiments that yielded transformative models of femininity. Bound to a hunted community at once racial and religious, Anne and Etty seek the transcendental meaning that can endow their lives with reason, value, and significance. In a novel written in hiding, Anne grapples with the divisiveness of race. The tale of Cady—who appears in many ways indistinguishable from her narrator—breaks off in grief when the heroine's friend Mary is deported. " 'Mary, forgive me, come back.' Cady no longer knew what to say or think. For this misery she saw so clearly before her eyes there were no words . . . she saw a troop of armed brutes . . . and in among them, helpless and alone, Mary, Mary who was the same as she was" (AF, *Tales,* 96).

Anne's fiction echoes her diary. On November 26, 1943, she dreamed of her deported school friend, Lies. Lies's imploring gaze mesmerized Anne, now anguished and incapable of offering help, wracked by grief and an emotion we term today "survivor's guilt."[9] Like Anne in her dream, Cady ranks among the privileged. But between them there is an important distinction: Cady is a Christian. As Anne's double on the other side of the racial divide, she incarnates a pedagogy of the persecuted. A Christian emphasizing anti-Semitism's savagery, she epitomizes the moral stance Anne must have recognized in the Christian friends on whose unfaltering loyalty the Secret Annexe depended. Anne became conscious of the growing precariousness of such a stance when the news of spreading, virulent Dutch anti-Semitism reached the family's refuge. Insisting that "one must always look at things from both sides," she tried to explain to Kitty the alleged behavior of those Jews who, by betraying resistance secrets or otherwise acting wrongly, had incurred the wrath of the Germans on the Netherlands (AF, 214–15). Anne did look at things from

9. For a succinct discussion of survivor's guilt, see Robert J. Lifton, "The Concept of the Survivor," in *Survivors, Victims, and Perpetrators: Essays on the Nazi Holocaust,* ed. Joel E. Dimsdale (New York: Hemisphere, 1980), 113–26.

both sides, through Cady: as a Jew taking on the persona of a Christian and as a Christian seeing herself in the person of a Jew.[10]

Strikingly, in this only fictional piece to mention Jews, Anne does not clearly identify as one herself. Here the *Tales* and the *Diary* differ: with the exception of Cady's story, Anne refrains from literary forays into the matter of her own race. But, although no one ever utters a *kiddush,* religiosity surfaces throughout fables and short stories animated by Anne's psychological twins: fairies, elves, bears, and little girls. Belief in God repeatedly issues from their voyages in search of self. "In the field, amid the flowers, beneath the darkening sky, Krista is content. Gone is fatigue . . . the little girl dreams and thinks only of the bliss of having, each day, this short while alone with God and nature" (AF, *Tales,* 41). The first-person protagonist of "Fear" comes to a similar conclusion. Having fled her city home in the midst of violent bombings, she finally rests in the countryside. Later, when war is over, fear appears as "a sickness for which there is only one remedy . . . look at nature and see that God is much closer than most people think" (AF, *Tales,* 47). Locked into the Secret Annexe, Anne could not indulge longings for nature and personal space. The claustrophobic world of confinement forced the quest for meaning—and identity—inward.

Exploring spirituality introspectively and untrammeled by religious observance, Anne developed beliefs at most loosely related to Judaism. Embracing practices and systems of signification proper to Christianity, Etty even more evidently strained the limits of her received religion. The morning of Good Friday, 1942, she recounts having knelt in prayer and recalls the bathroom's "rough coconut matting" (EH, 89). Hesitantly, she confesses to success, for the struggle to bow down in prayer has long engaged her and is central to the allegory she has been weaving, the tale of "the girl who could not kneel" (EH, 40ff). In October of that year she equates kneeling with prayer. Her story, she says, is strange: "the girl who could not kneel. Or its variation: the girl who could not pray" (EH, 194). Like her practices, her beliefs assume Christian tonalities. "I have broken my body like bread and shared it out among men. And why not, they were hungry and had gone without for so long," the last diary entry notes before her sacrificial closing words: "We should be willing to

10. Pleading for understanding toward individual Germans, Etty insisted that they were also suffering. Of "that kosher German soldier with his bag of carrots and cauliflowers at the kiosk" who had told her friend Lies that "she reminded him of the late rabbi's daughter whom he had nursed on her deathbed for days and nights on end," Etty says: "I knew at once: I shall have to pray for this German soldier . . . German soldiers suffer as well. There are no frontiers between suffering people, and we must pray for them all" (EH,132–33).

act as balm for all wounds" (EH, 195). The Christian hues of her faith notwithstanding, Etty never disavows Judaism, nor does she dwell on its potential conflicts with her spiritual trajectory. On the contrary, referring to her love for Speier she exclaimed at the end of April, 1942, "I am so glad that he is a Jew and I a Jewess" (EH, 107).

While the grip of racial Jewishness tightened, its hold as an organized religion weakened. Practice was largely impossible. The Franks, who took a menorah into hiding, complemented Chanukah candle-lightings with Christmas celebrations. Perhaps privileged Dutch and German Jews like Etty or Anne were already too distant from the Jewish religious tradition to perpetuate it in such trying conditions and on their own. And yet, Anne's father oversaw her nightly prayers. Many factors must have fashioned their spiritualities. Certainly, persecuted Jews found innumerable solutions to the question all were asking: "God Almighty, what are You doing to us?" The words escaped Etty in Westerbrok (EH, 211).

Somehow, every Jew had to find an answer. And every answer found remained that of a Jew. No matter how apostate individual Jews' beliefs, the Nazi persecution had established the supremacy of descent over faith in the definition of the Jewish community.[11] For all her spiritual trespassing into Christian domains, Etty, like Anne, stayed within that community. In the practical activity of evolving beliefs, with untold others they explored possible religiosities of the unobservant Jew.

By contrast, persecution provided Anne and Etty with few opportunities for the practical remodeling of their identities as women.[12] Where soldiers are drawn from populations neatly cleaved along lines of gender, age, and health, when war leads ablebodied men to battle and leaves all others at home, persecuted groups are promiscuously amassed into communities of fear. Nazi anti-Semitism did not emancipate Jewish women. Slave labor cannot be equated with enlistment for factory jobs or other patriotic—and remunerative—tasks. For Jewish women, barriers affecting labor-force participation were not lifted. They were not called upon to occupy posts men left vacant. They were not integrated into labor organizations. They did not axiomatically

11. Anti-Semitic persecutions have not always been based on race: the Spanish Inquisition, for instance, focused on beliefs. At that time, as the history of the Marranos shows, conversion provided an escape.

12. Jewish women active in the Resistance or imprisoned in concentration camps were probably confronted with more need and occasion to alter radically their gender roles. The changes in gender roles and the "gains" experienced by some women during wartime are discussed by Sandra Gilbert, Ruth Milkman, Sonya Michel, and Margaret Higonnet and Patrice Higonnet.

gain special powers over their households, head communities and families, bring in vital wages, reorganize living arrangements, support dependents. They were not awarded childcare services, nutrition programs, widows' pensions. They were not extolled by ideologies that elevated their status while catalyzing their support.[13] In their struggles to survive extermination, Jewish women often found themselves alone, responsible for the shelter of others, or otherwise pivotal to collective moral and material economies. Nazism undid the patriarchal family as it ripped apart the fabric of Jewish life. But gender roles were not systematically rewoven by women darning the holes that men's absences opened. War befits women, some have argued, pitching bellicose Minervas and triumphant Nikes against romantic portrayals of pacifist Geas. At a minimum, they claim, war has benefited women in the twentieth century and in the West. Yet neither economically nor socially nor politically did the Nazi war reallocate power to Jewish women.

Persecution brought Etty a new job as a clerical employee of the Jewish Council, with its attendant emotional responsibilities toward the deportees with whom she worked and lived at Westerbrok. Lowly as her position may have been in the Council's hierarchy, it conferred petty powers and offered her temporary security. But it also tainted her with the guilt of collaboration and of that, too, she was sporadically aware. Before entering into this Nazi-created employment, Etty had worked, earned money, and overseen her own living arrangements. As a woman, under Nazism, she never gained; as a Jew, she only lost.

Anne lost too. Like others in hiding or attempting escape, the Franks lived within a drastically narrowed circle of social relations. Here familial or quasi-familial bonds strengthened into clandestine enclaves of solidarity. With everyone's safety at the mercy of the others' fealty and sense of responsibility, a general flattening of social status ensued. The Secret Annexe housed an extended ménage that partially reshuffled gender roles. Otto Frank and Mr. Van Daan peeled potatoes alongside their wives: testimony more to the loss of their external, head-of-the-household functions than to their wives' elevation. However, many other tasks retained their conventional gender markings. Protection, for example, remained a manly duty.[14] Peeling potatoes and

13. On the ideological mobilization of women in the second world war, see Leila J. Rupp, *Mobilizing Women for War: German and American Propaganda, 1939–1945* (Princeton: Princeton University Press, 1978).

14. The permanence of conventional gender roles is clear in Anne's description of the Annexe's response to an attempted burglary (AF:180–81).

protecting the household need not clash, and in the Annexe clandestine life restricted role-playing and the potential for role conflict.

In this context of limited activity, there were few occasions for Anne to realize her emancipatory desires. Her diary and short stories provided writing practice, an informal apprenticeship for the career she wished to undertake. Lessons, from math to shorthand, broadened the scope of her abilities. Her mother proved a source of frustration and rivalry, her father of affection, Mrs. Van Daan of contempt, and Albert Dussel of irritation. With Peter, the Van Daans' adolescent son, she navigated through a sentimental journey clouded by parental disapproval. Yet all these elements spurring Anne's development pale by comparison to her world before confinement or even to the war-ridden world of her non-Jewish peers. Stripped of every right, amid the debris of their decimated milieux, Anne and Etty were killed. Women, but most of all Jews, on every possible count for them Nazism and war entailed losing.[15]

As the persecuted resist the progressive diminishment of self, they struggle against the temporal scansions that are imposed upon them. They do not walk in step with the drumbeat of battles and bombs. For persecution proceeds at its own pace, and the persecuted are mobilized not to the call of the nation but to the cumulation of special prohibitions and obligations.[16] Some, like Anne and her family, meticulously plan for invasion. For over a year, the Franks stocked food, clothes, and furniture in the Secret Annexe. Or, like Etty, they tenaciously cling to everyday life. "I cannot take in how beautiful the jasmine is," she wrote on July 1, 1942, "but there is no need to. It is enough simply to believe in miracles in the 20th century. And I do, even though the lice will be eating me up in Poland before long" (EH, 128). Others join the Resistance, engaging their oppressors in armed struggle. No matter which stance they take, persecution, more than war, orders their public experience.

Persecution imposes its measure on personal time, too. Anne divided life into before, during, and after hiding. Memory reigned over "before." Routines provided a modicum of activity to make time pass in the present. Her passion for Peter, like the radio broadcasts announcing the war's events, anticipated a

15. It should be clear, however, that war itself did not necessarily carry negative connotations. Thus once Holland had been taken over by the Germans, the Allies' victory was, of course, eagerly awaited.

16. Persecution marches in uneasy synchrony with war. The Wehrmacht complained bitterly that extermination policies drained the German military effort. See Saul Friedlander, *Reflections of Nazism: An Essay on Kitsch and Death* (New York: Harper and Row, 1984), 123–24. For a synthetic discussion of the economic, administrative, and psychological obstacles the Nazis had to overcome in implementing their extermination policies, see Raul Hilberg, "The Nature of the Process," in Dimsdale, ed., *Survivors,* 5–54.

time to come "after." Ultimately, writing for both Etty and Anne bridged the time of persecution and that which followed, transforming their diaries from tools of authorial apprenticeship into testimonials to the present and instruments of its transcendence. Etty kept her diary to remain her "own witness, marking well everything that happens in this world" (EH, 33). She was determined to "know this century of ours inside and out" and describe it (EH, 37). Finally, her diary condensed her aspirations, the legacy she bequeathed in fulfillment of a promise made in the summer of 1942, when she vowed: "When I have survived it all, I shall write stories about these times that will be like faint brush strokes against the great wordless background of God, Life, Death, Suffering, and Eternity" (EH,146). Anne, too, planned a testimonial, hoping "to publish a book entitled *Het Achterhuis* after the war"—the book her diary became.

Tales of persecution are crucial to the European memory of World War II. It is a memory periodically fanned by the celebrations of antifascist resistances (where they existed), national holidays, the capture or escape of a Nazi war criminal. And by a few, enduring testimonies. Such testimonies are provided by the *Diary of Anne Frank* and Etty Hillesum's *An Interrupted Life*. Like many memoirs of war, they bespeak a remote "other" path to, or through, adulthood: one produced by fragments of past normalities as they shatter into conflict and loss. But, unlike war literature at large, these memoirs evoke the specific horrors of anti-Semitic persecution four decades ago. Their protagonists have become emblematic of the journey through banishment and exile that so frequently ended in death. Their words resonate today, and not simply because they left lessons about our possible tomorrows. Rather, they resonate because we remember, and what we remember colors who we are.

PART THREE

Wartime Politics and the Construction of Gender

STEVEN C. HAUSE

More Minerva than Mars: The French Women's Rights Campaign and the First World War

During the First World War, French feminists believed that the end of hostilities would bring legislative attention to the rights of women. The foremost feminist newspaper, *La Française,* proclaimed that women were "almost certain" to win important new rights as soon as the Chamber of Deputies could devote time to them. The leaders of the French Union for Women's Suffrage (UFSF) scorned the cautious "almost": their report to the 1916 congress of the UFSF stated that women would vote at the end of the war.[1]

There were good reasons for this optimism. By midwar there were palpable differences in the role of French women. They had entered the economy in greater numbers and new capacities; they had obtained legal rights previously withheld. Attitudes about appropriate roles for women had apparently shifted, producing a new climate of opinion in which women could anticipate equality. Women were even serving as mayors of some villages and sitting on municipal councils—a situation scarcely plausible a decade earlier. "In three years," wrote

This essay draws on two previously published works: "Women Who Rallied to the Tricolor: The Effects of World War I on the French Women's Suffrage Movement," *Proceedings of the Western Society for French History* 6 (1979), 371–81; Steven C. Hause (with Anne R. Kenney), *Women's Suffrage and Social Politics in the French Third Republic* (Princeton: Princeton University Press, 1984). The author wishes to thank the Department of History, the Center for International Studies, and the Office of Research Administration at the University of Missouri, St. Louis, for their financial assistance in this research.

1. *La Française,* March 16, 1918. Notes to this chapter have been restricted to identifying sources for direct quotations and data. Sources for this study are listed more extensively in "Women Who Rallied to the Tricolor" and *Women's Suffrage and Social Politics,* as well as by James F. McMillan, who first advanced these arguments in his dissertation, "The Effects of the First World War on the Social Condition of Women in France" (D. Phil. thesis, Oxford University, 1977), and in *Housewife or Harlot: The Place of Women in French Society, 1870–1940* (New York: St. Martin's, 1981).

one sympathetic author at the end of the war, "women realized more progress than in fifty years of struggle."[2] Women were also contributing directly to the war effort; without their labor in the munitions industry, the army could not long have continued to fight. Feminists, therefore, simply could not believe that, on the morrow of the victory that women had helped to win, a grateful nation would refuse their claims.

They were doubly mistaken. Women did not obtain equality after the war, and the actual improvement in their situation during the war was much smaller than it appeared. Instead, the altered roles of French women can be better understood through the vivid image proposed by the Higonnets: a social double helix in which male and female strands change positions as they coil around their axis but maintain an essentially constant relationship even as their positions alter. French women did not win great improvements in their position due to the First World War; on the contrary, the war was actually a setback to feminist efforts to break out of the fixed relationships of the social helix.

Feminist aspirations had been clearly articulated in France in the generation before the war. Liberal-republican feminist leagues had been established by Léon Richer and Maria Deraismes at the very beginning of the Third Republic. Their movement remained small (less than a thousand participants) until the turn of the century. Then, stimulated by a series of feminist congresses (in 1896 and especially in 1900), a strong feminist daily newspaper (Marguerite Durand's *La Fronde,* founded in 1897), and a reformist coalition of feminine and feminist groups (the National Council of French Women or CNFF, formed in 1901), the women's rights movement grew rapidly. In 1914 it numbered over twenty-five thousand adherents. This movement was essentially a bourgeois, urban, republican, and non-Catholic phenomenon. It was estranged from a much larger Catholic women's movement (over five hundred thousand members in 1914) on its right, which opposed most feminist reforms; on the feminist left, there was only occasional cooperation with the smaller but more militant socialist women's movement which resisted many feminist objectives, such as the vote, as bourgeois palliatives intended to prevent true social revolution.

The position of women under the Third Republic was so dramatically inferior that feminists had a long list of *revendications,* and two dozen different organizations emphasized different priorities. The resolutions of the feminist

2. Léon Abensour, *Histoire générale du féminisme: Des origines à nos jours* (1921, repr. Geneva: Slatkine, 1979), 310.

congress at Paris in 1908 and the program of Durand's campaign during the 1910 parliamentary elections reveal this range: the opening of all schools and careers to women, with equal pay for equal work; the abolition of paternal authority within marriage and the family in favor of equal rights (for example, the right to be a guardian); drastic revision of the Civil Code to end the treatment of adult women as minors and to permit them full civil rights (for example, the right to serve on juries); further social legislation to emancipate women (for example, easier divorce and state aid in childcare); the elimination of the double standard in the criminal code and the corresponding abolition of all paternalistic legislation. This translated into hundreds of specific targets. At the 1908 congress, French feminists agreed that the best way to obtain these changes was to concentrate upon winning political rights first and then to use the vote to force attention to their interests. Thus, the years before the war witnessed frequent suffragist activities.

French feminists were confident in 1914. Within a few weeks, they organized a "poll" (sponsored by *Le Journal*) in which over five hundred thousand women called for the vote; formed a feminist federation to unite all suffragist groups; and then staged the first mass demonstration in the history of French feminism (the Condorcet demonstration), which put more than five thousand marchers into the streets of Paris. The leaders of the UFSF and the CNFF were certain that their policy of calm advocacy and close cooperation with their parliamentary supporters (led by Ferdinand Buisson) would soon succeed. Cécile Brunschwicg, the secretary-general of the UFSF, was so confident that she informed the twelve thousand members of the union that they would vote in the municipal elections of 1916. The world war prevented this, but feminists felt sure that they were winning more supporters through their war efforts.

The fallacy of that wartime optimism can be seen by examining the context in which changes seemed to have occurred. A review of the participation of women in the war economy, the new rights they won during the war, and the social attitudes that supposedly changed will show that French women had not come far from the feminist campaigns of 1908–14. Looking at the women's suffrage campaign in more detail will illustrate how the war was actually a setback to feminist efforts to achieve their foremost goal.

The most difficult argument to assess about the war and the position of women in France concerns attitudes. A strong case can be stated to show that attitudes about the public role of women changed, that new behavior was socially acceptable. By necessity, women had acquired a freedom of action that would not have been entirely respectable in the antediluvian world of 1914. Women had to go out unchaperoned, had to work alongside men, had to live alone on their own wages. Thousands of nurses and clerical workers in the masculine world of warfare, business, and government plus tens of thousands of female factory workers had to affect attitudes. Women alone on the streets in 1917 were a common sight; in 1900, the *police des moeurs* might have detained them. The world in which Hubertine Auclert (the founder of the women's suffrage campaign) had once been denied a hotel room while traveling to visit her family, on the argument that no respectable young woman would seek such lodgings, was gone. A freedom, born of necessity, could even be seen in the clothing that women wore, which was shorter, looser, more practical.

Such obvious changes attracted a lot of comment at the time. Célestin Bouglé, a Sorbonne sociologist, asserted at the end of the war, "a hundred thousand of the surviving barriers to women fell at a single blow."[3] Such judgments belong in a Pantheon for optimists. The war probably did adjust some public attitudes, but one must also ask if this new mood was far-reaching or long-lasting. Many of the changes were temporary, enduring only as long as the unusual circumstances that produced them. It is more accurate to see the war as only one factor in a longer and slower evolution of attitudes than as a momentous change. Did millions of veterans return from the front having thrown off their traditional prejudices? Could any society with deeply ingrained feelings about the nature of the family and women's position within it suddenly embrace the concept of the autonomous, emancipated woman? Is it not a more probable human reaction, after so great a tragedy, to seek to revive the status quo ante bellum—to "return to normalcy," in the language of the 1920s?

To modulate the claim of dramatic new *mentalités,* one might recall the image of the double helix. Women occupied new positions on the social axis, and public attitudes accepted this as necessary. But did this constitute a fundamental alteration in the relationship between the sexes? If one examines masculine attitudes and the masculine agenda at the end of the war, this seems highly unlikely. Many other issues inundated the woman question on that agenda—issues that politicians, pressure groups, and journalists considered more urgent. The list was staggering. Economic matters included the reconstruction of the war zone, the resettlement of refugees, the reparations and war-debt problems, the transformation of production to peacetime manufacture, the demobilization and economic reintegration of hundreds of thousands of veterans, widespread labor unrest, and the stabilization of supply and prices.

3. Célestin Bouglé, *De la sociologie à l'action sociale: Pacifisme, féminisme, coopération* (Paris: PUF, 1923), 109.

Diplomatic matters included the general issues of security against Germany, the negotiation and application of the Versailles Treaty, troubled relations with wartime allies, exceptionally complicated financial diplomacy, and the international politics of anti-Bolshevism.

Some women, such as Louise Bodin (the editor of *La Voix des Femmes*), saw this political agenda as adding up to a new basis of antifeminism. She was not far from the mark. Where did it show traces of the supposed new attitude about women? Where did it address the woman question at all? If one probes, it is there; but it resembles a conservative backlash instead of feminist-egalitarian reform. Economic and diplomatic issues were important matters, upon which ministers might build their reputation or risk their portfolios. Women's rights, on the other hand, were secondary matters which might be examined in calmer times. The Chamber of Deputies did propose women's suffrage, but it did not become law. Instead, the successful masculine agenda expected women to step aside from their wartime roles and let men return to important business. This reaction, of course, incorporated praise for women for their service to the *patrie;* it then expressed pleasure that victory allowed women to resume their roles in the home. Indeed, the greatest pressure for legislation affecting women derived not from new attitudes but from a desire to enforce their traditional prewar roles. This was expressed in terms of great concern about the "depopulation" of France. The rebuilding of the economy and of national security demanded motherhood, not emancipation; the woman question was inscribed on the agenda under the heading of pronatalism, not feminism. Thus, in addressing Joan Scott's exhortation to develop gender as a category of analysis, it might be interesting to start with Arno Mayer's work on counterrevolution and add the French social agenda as profoundly opposed to the feminist revolution.

Shifting the focus to the economic and legal victories of French women during the First World War, there are many more reasons to doubt that the war years constituted a climacteric. Much of the progress was illusory, many of the changes evanescent. Women mobilized to serve in an extraordinary situation found themselves demobilized rapidly in the postwar rush back to normalcy. The poilu returned to his job, his wartime replacement to her home. For what did we endure such suffering, veterans might have asked, if not for the preservation of prewar France? Both the economic and the legal gains of women fell to such attitudes. To be sure, some important changes endured and others followed the war. This, however, must in part be attributed to gradual trends in France. The steady growth of an educated class of women, for example, would have brought alterations in occupations and attitudes, war or no. At the very least, the war could not have produced change without the simultaneous existence of such trends. Furthermore, attributing to the war an altered position of women slights the work of the prewar feminist movement.

The medical profession provides a good illustration of the situation for middle-class women. It is hardly surprising that women physicians obtained wider acceptance during four years of fighting when casualty rates averaged over 1,000 per diem. The important fact is not that the French public accepted *doctoresses* as replacements, that women received appointments at new levels; it would have been stunning had they not. Rather it is the gradual entrance of women into medicine during the previous forty years and the efforts of feminists to open the profession to them. The trend that led to 357 female medical students being enrolled at Paris in 1912 is more important than the emergency use of women doctors, many of whom were deprived of their positions after the armistice. A woman (Dr. Long-Landry) had become the head of a clinic in 1911; that others followed her during the war only to be demoted afterwards hardly marks a turning point in women's rights.

The situation of working-class women was equally deceptive. Before the war, the state railways employed 6,000 women (85 percent of them as barrier guards); 57,000 worked for the railroads by 1918. Similarly, the Paris Métro went from employing 124 women workers to 3,037. The Ministry of Posts had been the second largest source of state jobs for women (18,000 in 1911) yet still had to replace over 20,000 men who were drafted. The Ministry of Education, which already employed 71,000 women (96 percent of them in primary education), had to open 30,000 positions (chiefly in secondary education) due to conscription. Banks, businesses, and government alike desperately needed to replace men on clerical and secretarial staffs. The greatest need, of course, occurred in the munitions factories, where women workers numbered 15,000 by 1915 and increased to 684,000 in 1917.[4]

Such illustrations are deceptive because they convey misleading impressions about the extent and nature of what was changing. This is partly due to inadequate data—the government did not conduct the quinquennial census scheduled for 1916. But it is chiefly a result of misreading the evidence that does exist. First of all, many women sought jobs less as a matter of patriotism or feminism than of simple survival. Any woman who had been dependent on the wages of a working man was immediately in trouble if that man was drafted.

4. Prewar data from the survey by Senator Gervais, published in *Le Matin,* January 9, 1911, and reprinted in Ferdinand Buisson, *Le vote des femmes* (Paris: Dunot-Pinat, 1911). Conscription and female replacement data from Alain Decaux, *Histoire des françaises,* 2 vols. (Paris: Perrin, 1972), 2:983. Munitions data from Léon Abensour, *Le probléme féministe: Un cas d'aspiration collective vers l'égalité* (Paris: Radot, 1927).

The government provided the wives of mobilized men with a daily allotment of one franc, twenty-five centimes; dependent mothers, sisters, or lovers received nothing. Second, if one views the situation of women as the war unfolded, rather than from the end of the war, the story of working women is very different. At the beginning of the war, a broad range of businesses closed or were curtailed. In 1914–15, the chief effect of the war was to drive women out of work. Female unemployment reached enormous proportions—61 percent of those in textiles and 67 percent in the garment industries were put out of work.[5]

The employment of French women during World War I must therefore first be understood as a process of redistribution of the labor force, based as much on women's need to survive as on governmental policy. According to Clemenceau's secretary, half a million women entered the industrial work force during the war. That total, however, is far smaller than the number of women who found work in munitions alone. What was happening was the arrival of women from other sectors of the economy, women left unemployed, and women in straitened circumstances. The war took women from domestic services or traditionally feminized segments of the economy, such as textiles, and put them in wartime jobs as replacements for men. Viewed in one way, the war enabled working-class women to find new kinds of work and acquire new skills, just as it permitted middle-class women to capitalize on their previous training. But, from a different perspective one can see that these women found jobs that would disappear or be reclaimed by veterans after the war, while leaving prewar jobs they could not hope to recover.

French women, whether they came from other occupations or entered the labor force for the first time, did not retain their wartime jobs. According to census data (see table "Women in the Work Force"), there were 8.6 million women in the *population active* in 1921, compared to only 7.7 million in 1911. The number of working women declined, however, reaching 7.8 million by 1926—meaning that women actually constituted a smaller percentage of the national labor force in 1926 than they had in 1911. Furthermore, when one considers only industrial occupations, the number of women employed in 1921 was already lower than it had been in 1906! By 1926, women accounted for only 28.6 percent of industrial workers, whereas they had held 34.3 percent of the jobs in 1906. The sharp decline occurred despite the fact that 1.4 million men had died during the war.

Postwar governments and employers obviously made a tremendous effort to

5. Arthur Fontaine, *French Industry during the War* (New Haven: Yale University Press, 1926), 43–45, 406.

Women in the Work Force, 1906–26

	French work force (in millions)			Agricultural work force			Industrial work force			Women in the work force[1]		
Census year	Total	Women	% Women	Total	Women	% Women	Total	Women	% Women	Total	% Indus.	% Agric.
1906	20.7	7.7	37.2	8.8	3.3	37.5	6.1	2.1	34.4	7.7	27.3	42.9
1911	20.9	7.7	36.8	8.6	3.2	37.2	—[2]	—	—	7.7	—	41.6
1916[3]	—	—	—	—	—	—	—	—	—	—	—	—
1921	21.7	8.6	39.6	9.0	4.0	44.4	6.3	2.0	31.7	8.6	23.3	46.5
1926	21.4	7.8	36.4	8.1	3.4	42.0	7.0	2.0	28.6	7.8	28.6	43.6

1. Percentages of women in the work force total 100% with the addition of women in fishing and services.

2. The 1911 census combined industrial work force figures with services.

3. There was no census in 1916.

Source: J.-C. Toutain, *La population de la France de 1700 à 1959* (Paris, 1963), tables 58–59, pp. 162–63.

hire demobilized soldiers and to send working women back to the home. Justice for veterans completely overshadowed justice for women in public policy. Veterans' organizations soon grew to immense proportions (the associations of *mutilés* alone counted 345,000 members in 1926), dwarfing women's rights leagues (the UFSF reached 100,000 members in 1928). And the Chamber of Deputies elected in 1919 included so many veterans that it was labeled "the horizon blue chamber" after the color of army uniforms. The government acknowledged the problem of displacing women workers by paying a bonus to those who lost their jobs to returning soldiers. One wonders if this bonus was intended primarily to aid the stricken or to encourage women to return to the home. For it was to the household that most demobilized women went. The textile industry had accounted for 85 percent of the prewar industrial employment of women; but employment there declined by 13 percent (for women) between 1906 and 1921 and 17 percent between 1906 and 1926. Nor did women return to domestic service; female employment there declined from 781,000 (1906) to 698,000 (1921), and then to 688,000 (1926). Only in the agricultural sector did the effect of the war endure for a decade. There, women constituted a much larger share of workers in 1921 and 1926 than in 1911. But this reflected the number of war deaths among the peasantry and hardly represented a great turning point in the economic history of French women.[6]

6. Data from Toutain, *La population de la France,* tables 73, 83.

Similar doubts appear when one examines the legal and political rights that French women obtained during the war. It is true that the extraordinary wartime circumstances resulted in a few cases of women performing the functions of mayors and adjunct-mayors or sitting on municipal councils. Special wartime agencies, such as the Comités d'Action Agricole established in each rural commune in 1916, made provisions for women's suffrage. Women also obtained release in 1915 from some provisions of the Civil Code, permitting them certain rights previously limited to men. After July 3, 1915, for example, mothers could exercise the paternal authority defined by the code. In March, 1917, the Senate finally gave women the right to become legal guardians, accepting a bill that had passed the chamber several years before the war. French feminists had worked for this right for over twenty years, and they were understandably pleased with their victory.

A closer look shows how meager were these legal victories. The few instances where women held political office were in desperate circumstances, usually rural communes denuded of educated males. In most cases, the commune turned to the local *institutrice* to study and sign documents. Her powers were strictly limited and her career expectancy clearly understood to be short. In cases where women sat on municipal councils, they were explicitly nonvoting members. The right to vote for agricultural *comités,* restricted from the beginning, ended with the war. The law of 1915 providing paternal authority to women was also valid only for the duration of hostilities, only in urgent cases, and only with individual judicial approval. It was necessary for the orderly continuation of business and was adopted as such, not as a feminist landmark. And it was no improvement over the same temporary rights that the Government of National Defense had granted women in December, 1870. As a detailed legal thesis demonstrated in 1919, the war government had only extended the rights of women during the "nonpresence" of the men in whom those rights actually reposed. The return of the army meant the disappearance of such rights.

French women certainly won some permanent rights during World War I. The only major right that survived the war, however, was that of guardianship. That was important, but it scarcely made 1914–18 a period of feminist legislative triumph to overshadow the prewar years. The liberal republicans of the 1880s, for example, reinstituted divorce in France and expanded educational opportunities for women. The post-Dreyfus radicals (hardly the best friends of the women's movement) managed more significant feminist reforms in a few months in 1907 than all of the war governments combined: the Married Women's Earnings Law (the *loi Schmahl*) and the right of working women to vote for and serve as trade-dispute arbitrators (the *conseils des prud'hommes*). Thus, viewing wartime legislation in a longer context greatly diminishes its importance.

Of course, it is also necessary to consider women's legislation after the war to determine whether the war prompted subsequent change. What legislation did the *chambre horizon bleu* produce to alter the position of women in France? One tremendously important law of July, 1920, forbidding the mere advocacy of abortion or birth control. Yes, French politicians had learned from the war—learned that a neo-Malthusian menace cost France more sons than the Germans did. Depopulation begat pronatalism. Hence, any form of encouragement, even private, to abort a pregnancy, was cause for a fine of 100–3,000 francs plus imprisonment for six months to three years; if the crime were circulating birth control information, the punishment might reach 5,000 francs. The living symbol of this policy toward women was Dr. Madeleine Pelletier, the most revolutionary prewar feminist. She died in a mental asylum because a judge ruled that she was unfit to stand trial for performing abortions.

The First World War also set back the feminist campaign to alter the relations of the sexes. This becomes clear by an examination of the effect of the war on the women's suffrage campaign. The war truncated a political movement that had apparently reached its takeoff stage in 1914 but could not recover so well in 1919. The hiatus of suffrage activities during the sacred union marked the passing of a generation in French feminism; the postwar campaign was missing a large number of leaders, organizations, and periodicals. Much of the disbanded movement could not be reconstituted in time to participate in the debate of 1919–22. Those who returned to suffragism often did so with less single-mindedness, as their wartime interests now took more of their time. Some social problems affecting suffragism, notably depopulation, were exacerbated by the war, demanding a more vigorous feminist response but simultaneously driving away potential support. The success of the Russian Revolution of 1917 also weakened French suffragism. Communism siphoned off some activists from the suffragist left, fragmented the women's movement anew, and led to a "red scare" against the advocates of any egalitarian reform. As already noted, the war buried women's rights under a host of other problems to which politicians accorded primacy, such as economic reovery and the diplomacy of French security. These problems created a national mood in which the foremost desire seemed to be a return to the halcyon days of a lost *belle époque* rather than the further transformation of French society. In response, many feminists became more conservative, both in what and how they asked. Ironically, French suffragists were simultaneously overconfident, believing that the government would reward them for their contributions during the war. All of this added up to a suffrage campaign weaker in 1919–22 than it had been in 1908–14.

When five thousand suffragists had assembled in the Tuileries Gardens and marched to the Left Bank in July, 1914, their goal had seemed in sight. Women's suffrage had been inscribed on the agenda of the Chamber of Deputies for the first time and suffragists held pledges of support from nearly 49 percent of the deputies. Brunschwicg was not alone in believing that women would vote in the elections of 1916. Then the war truncated the suffrage campaign at its apogee. Within days of the Condorcet demonstration, French suffragists wholeheartedly supported their government in its war effort. The movement had always been deeply republican and committed to cooperation with its friends in Parliament. When Premier Viviani (a lifetime feminist) called on feminists to rally to the war effort, they did not hesitate. Nor did the socialist women's movement, which followed the lead of the SFIO; when Jules Guesde entered the sacred union, so did the Groupe des Femmes Socialistes. With no apparent hesitation, the women's movement abandoned its pacifism and its efforts to win the vote. Periodicals disappeared, congresses were cancelled, lectures and demonstrations no longer scheduled. Instead, feminists sought ways to participate in the war—through the Red Cross, through organizations to aid refugees, through the recruitment of women to replace men called to the colors. "We will claim our rights," they proclaimed, "when the triumph of Right is assured."[7] Only late in the war did suffragism reappear in France, and by then much of the movement was missing. Many of the small organizations and their leaders were lost and never managed to regroup as effective bodies. The deaths of both Hubertine Auclert and Eliska Vincent removed the two oldest militants from activism. Jeanne Oddo-Deflou survived the war, but her society did not: she lost most of her family and her income during the hostilities; poor and demoralized, she retired to a *maison de retraite*. The collapse of the small shares on which she lived reduced Mme. Remember to penury; she survived by selling flowers on the streets. Arria Ly, totally disillusioned, left France for permanent exile. Nelly Roussel became seriously ill in 1918 and died in 1922 without being able again to devote her full energies to feminism. And the wartime suspension of activity meant that no young leaders were available to take over the activities of these women.

Along with leaders and organizations, the war took a terrible toll of feminist publications. The costs of paper and manual labor increased dramatically,

7. *Le Droit des Femmes,* June 15, 1915.

forcing some publications to fold and others to curtail sharply their size or frequency. The largest feminist newspaper, *La Française,* was forced from weekly to monthly publication in 1919, at which rate it was difficult to be the *journal officiel* of feminism. Smaller publications were hurt more. *L'Action Féministe* cut its format by half. *La Voix des Femmes* continued to appear only when Louise Bodin's husband absorbed its losses. Mme. Remember slowly lost *Le Féminisme Intégral:* it appeared irregularly during the war and became a quarterly in 1917, suffering until "exorbitant costs" forced her to convert it to a short-lived pamphlet series. Pelletier had not published *La Suffragiste* during the war but tried to revive it in 1919. It soon folded. She later explained to Arria Ly: "printers are extravagantly expensive; they want six hundred francs for what I formerly paid fifty. Impossible!" The same crisis afflicted the Parisian daily press, of course; even *Le Radical* shrank to a two-page paper in 1919. This also hurt the suffragist cause. Old supporters almost disappeared: *L'Action* lost 95 percent of its circulation between March 1912 and November 1917; *La Petite République,* 87 percent. And smaller newspapers found that it was easy to cut out items submitted by feminist societies.[8]

Other parts of the suffrage movement, especially provincial organizations, suffered from their patriotic disbandment and were only slowly reestablished. Local commissariats of the police and several prefectures surveyed feminist efforts to rebuild provincial suffragism in 1918; several reported to the *Sûreté générale,* as the prefect of the Loire did, that a few militants were trying but having no success. While the larger chapters of the UFSF had continued to meet during the war, smaller groups disappeared completely. Some of these groups were still not active in 1920, when the union claimed twelve fewer branches than in 1914. The war also impeded suffragist activity by drawing away supporters to nonsuffrage enterprises. Individuals who had ceased their campaign in 1914 chose to continue the interests that had taken their time in 1914–17 rather than taking up the suffrage cause again; social feminism thus consumed more of the efforts by suffragists in 1918 than it had in 1914. The UFSF, for example, never returned to its statutory concentration solely upon the vote. Pacifists who had chosen patriotism in 1914 now felt conscience-bound to give some of their time to the League of Nations. Marguerite de Witt-Schlumberger (the president of the UFSF), for example, presided over a Union Féminine pour la Société des Nations.

The most important instance of this diffusion of suffragist activity was the

8. Quotations from Madeleine Pelletier to Arria Ly, June 6, 1921, Bouglé Collection, Bibliothèque Historique de la Ville de Paris; data from Dossier Tirage des Journaux, F^7 12843, Archives Nationales.

response to the question of depopulation. Conservative opponents of women's suffrage found the birth rate a forceful argument against any change in the position of women: more than ever, women owed France motherhood. "France has more need of children than electors," ran a typical article of 1919—"The fate of France, its existence, depends on the family."[9] The suffragist response to this situation combined a sincere agreement that patriotic women must be mothers and a feminist argument that women could still contribute more to France if enfranchised. Whatever their perspective, all feminists had to devote more attention to such issues after the war.

Among the many French national concerns of 1918–19 that obscured feminism, one had an especially strong impact on the women's movement: the repercussions of the Russian Revolution. The response to Bolshevism enlarged the disagreements between bourgeois feminists and socialist women, driving each group away from conciliation. Furthermore, many militant suffragists defected to Communism during the revolutionary enthusiasm of 1917–21: the feminist left lost Pelletier, Séverine, Roussel, Caroline Kauffmann, Marianne Rauze, Hélène Brion, and Anne Léal for varying periods. Pelletier was so enraptured that she undertook a trip to Russia to contemplate permanent residence there. The rump organization of Solidarité left Paris for Montreuil where it became a nonfeminist association of proletarian women. French revolutionary socialism, and later French Communism, did not receive this influx of former suffragists by adopting their program. Communist women felt, as Louise Saumoneau had taught, that political emancipation within bourgeois society was a sham. Republican socialists such as Maria Vérone attacked Bolshevism as a threat to both their suffragism and their republicanism, but this was insufficient to spare feminism another ill effect of the Russian Revolution: the ensuing wave of anti-Communism. Fearful conservatives had little difficulty in connecting the feminist threat to the family and to traditional French society with an international Communist conspiracy, especially when so many prominent feminists became Communists. Hence, police surveillance increased and government cooperation decreased.

The reaction of the authorities was no small difficulty for French suffragists. For years, the hostility of the government had meant police harrassment and the occasional use of force, as Auclert had found in the Civil Code protest of 1904. But the Condorcet demonstration of 1914 had convinced French feminists that attitudes had shifted. Premier Viviani had supported that demonstration and his government had facilitated it; feminists even found the

9. *Action Sociale de la Femme*, April 1919.

police courteous. Their patriotic participation in the war effort redoubled the conviction of these women that they could rely upon the cooperation of the government. It was a considerable shock, therefore, to discover in 1919 that they were again considered subversives. When suffragists sought to resume public efforts to win the vote, the government blocked many of their meetings and almost all projected demonstrations. By decrees of 1914, France had been governed under a state of siege, and civil liberties were sharply curtailed. As the armistice did not lead to the immediate rescinding of these restrictions, suffragists were at the mercy of the government for their campaign. Neither the cabinet, the prefects, nor the police were in a merciful mood. Their greatest anxieties concerned labor agitation, pacifism, and Bolshevism rather than feminism per se, but they found sufficient correlation between feminist organizations and these activities to justify the continued curtailment of women's demonstrations.

One final, and ironic, result of the war must be noted. While it may seem contradictory in view of the preceding evidence, French suffragists left the war with an astonishing overconfidence. They perceived many of the problems discussed here, but they underestimated them. The women who were optimistic in 1914 believed as an article of faith in 1919 that they would participate in the next elections. When peace came, the UFSF even participated in discussions about dissolving the International Woman's Suffrage Alliance because it was no longer needed. Some suffragists were so confident that they devoted their time to teaching women about the political process rather than lobbying for enfranchisement. Could French politicians possibly refuse? Valentine Thomson asked this of the readers of *La Vie Féminine* in 1919. "For my part, I cannot believe it," she answered.[10] This overconfidence produced a postwar suffrage campaign that was notably weaker than the prewar effort. Even when restrictions were eased, suffragists staged no demonstrations comparable to those of 1914—no poll of five hundred thousand, no march of five thousand.

French suffragists might have profited from a reading of the history of the women's movement in the United States; Elizabeth Cady Stanton and Susan B. Anthony had similarly suspended their suffrage campaign during the Civil War and formed a National Woman's Loyal League in support of the union. The victors acknowledged the contributions of women by refusing to include them in the constitutional amendment that enfranchised emancipated male slaves. This lesson went unnoted in 1919; French suffragists understandably chose a comparison to the postwar adoption of women's suffrage in

10. *La Vie Féminine,* June 1, 1919.

Britain and America. And, when the Chamber of Deputies actually voted in favor of women's suffrage, feminists were positive that they had made the right choice. But they were mistaken. The French Senate easily blocked women's suffrage throughout the interwar years. Rather than gaining strength due to the First World War, French suffragism had suffered a severe setback.

When women's suffrage in France was proclaimed by Charles de Gaulle in 1944, the myth that modern wars emancipated women received another boost. But the history of French women exposes the myth for what it is. The liberation of French women has taken place only over *la longue durée*. The First World War was certainly an important episode in that evolution, but not a climacteric for women, the gift of Mars. The ancient argument of attributing change *tam Marte quam Minerva* must be inverted: changes over *la longue durée* owe more to the accumulated wisdom of Minerva and the hard work of those who applied it.

JENNY GOULD

Women's Military Services in First World War Britain

The Women's Army Auxiliary Corps of the British Army, set up in 1917, was one of a number of innovations introduced by concerned civilian and military authorities to help solve the persistent problem of providing sufficient manpower for the army. The story of its formation is one of confusion: schemes, conflicting interests, power struggles and lack of communication between government departments, rivalry among women—all before the corps was even established. Once it was born, of course, it faced the inevitable problems that attended the introduction of women (other than nurses) into the military services.

The Daily Express, expounding on the theme of "The Woman as Soldier" shortly before the official announcement of the formation of the WAAC, proclaimed,

> [The war has] brought into being many different aspects of women as worker, organiser, and general helper, but the greatest innovation of all is the woman soldier, recognised by the military authorities, uniformed, living in camps beside the men, under the same conditions as to food and lodging, and working day in, day out, under strict discipline. . . . There is not the smallest doubt that, had it been suggested that women should undertake work of this kind during the first months of the war, there would have been a great outcry, and the busybodies would have shaken their wise heads and said it was asking the impossible.[1]

Before August, 1914, neither military nor civilian authorities in Britain had given serious thought to the question of how women might best be organized if war broke out. If the army ever considered women collectively before the First World War, it saw them as belonging to one of three main groups: nurses,

1. *Daily Express*, February 21, 1917, 4.

potential carriers of venereal disease (therefore a threat to army organization and manpower), and wives of soldiers—that is, women "on the married strength."[2] None of these categories provoked the kind of discussion that might lead to a radical change in the relationship of women to the military establishment. The latter two especially encouraged the view that women were at best a nuisance, at worst a serious threat.

If political or military authorities had ever considered whether women could play a role (other than nursing) in the military activities of the nation before the First World War, such consideration would have been possible only within the context of Home Defence policy as it developed in this period. For example, the Territorial and Reserves Force, set up in 1907 by Richard Haldane, Liberal secretary of state for war, was designed to defend Britain against invasion. There were, as in the regular army, many noncombatant jobs available for Territorial Force volunteers. Haldane's vision was of "a nation truly in arms" with a military structure supported at local level by associations promoting training and drill, at schools, in cadet corps and rifle clubs.[3] But women had no part to play in Haldane's nation; he did not consider including them in the new force. An opportunity for women to help prepare for their country's defense came only in 1910, with the establishment of Voluntary Aid Detachments (VADs). These were to be a technical reserve of the Territorial Force Medical Service for mobilization in case of invasion, and they were intended for home defense, to provide voluntary aid to the sick and wounded.[4]

A few other organizations set up in the first decade of the twentieth century offered women a chance to prepare for voluntary war work. In 1907 the First Aid Nursing Yeomanry (FANY) was founded, with the aim of training its members as nurses on horseback to ride out from field hospitals to the battlefield. The Women's Convoy Corps, founded by Mabel St. Clair Stobart in 1907, also trained women to provide service in wartime.[5] Mrs. Stobart founded her organization in order to allow women to demonstrate that they

2. The number of men allowed to join the Married Establishment of the army was limited; those to whom permission was granted were referred to as being on the "married strength."

3. R. B. Haldane, "The 4th Memorandum," April 25, 1906, quoted in Edward Spiers, *The Army and Society, 1815–1914* (London: Longmans, 1980), 275.

4. The VAD scheme was devised by Sir Alfred Keogh, director general of army medical services at the War Office.

5. Mabel St. Clair Stobart, *War and Women—From Experience in the Balkans and Elsewhere* (London: G. Bell, 1913); David Mitchell, *Women on the Warpath: The Story of the Women of the First World War* (London: Jonathan Cape, 1966), 150–60; Monica Krippner, *The Quality of Mercy: Women at War, Serbia 1915–1918* (Newton Abbot, Eng.: David and Charles, 1980), 19–22.

were capable of taking a real share in national defense. On returning to England from the Transvaal in 1907, she discovered that everyone was talking about two great dangers supposedly threatening England: the invasion of England by Germany, and the possibility that parliamentary franchise might be granted to women. She believed that the juxtaposition of these two problems offered women a perfect opportunity: what better way of demonstrating women's capability in sharing the government of the country than by showing that they could contribute to the national defence? The Women's Convoy Corps was officially accepted as a VAD in 1910 and registered with the British Cross Service at the War Office.

These individual efforts to organize women to play a part in the defense of the nation were of interest only to a minority, however. In the first years of their existence, when the threat of war was less apparent, those who joined the VADs were often ridiculed, and the whole scheme was frequently regarded as a "fashionable fad."[6] The activities of the suffrage societies, and especially the militant Women's Social and Political Union (WSPU), run by Emmeline and Christabel Pankhurst, drew far more public attention than the small groups of women who marched to camp in Swanage, dressed in "a very service-like blue-grey uniform," carrying "haversacks and water-bottles."[7] When war broke out, the only military sphere in which women were accepted was their traditional role of caring for the sick and wounded.

At 7:00 P.M. on Tuesday, August 4, 1914, Great Britain formally declared war against Germany. The response of thousands of women paralleled that of thousands of men: according to reports in the press, military preparations were accompanied by scenes of remarkable enthusiasm. Newspapers were filled with requests for women to help in different ways, and voluntary societies sprang up overnight. Hundreds of women enthusiastically volunteered to care for the sick and wounded. The head of a local hospital which had asked for a few volunteer nurses was reported as saying, "if Kitchener had asked for half a million women, he would have been oversubscribed by first post."[8]

Although women's support for the war effort was widely approved, the idea

6. Katharine Furse, "War Work and Its Lessons," MS, Bristol University, Furse Collection, Ref. 196/9/A1. Dame Katharine Furse (1875–1952) was appointed the first director of Women's Royal Naval Service in November, 1917. She had joined the VAD when the organization first formed, and in April, 1916 was invited to head the Women's VAD in England, Wales, and Ulster.

7. *Red Cross and Ambulance News,* 1910, describing the Women's Convoy Corps, quoted in Mitchell, *Women on the Warpath,* 152.

8. *The Daily Mail,* September 5, 1914.

that women might play roles other than those of nurse, fundraiser, knitter, or canteen organizer was not popular. This resistance was rooted in conventional attitudes about women's roles and was expressed most vehemently by those who also opposed women's suffrage. The "physical force" argument was frequently used by antisuffragists in the years before the First World War. It was based on the assumption that in the last resort all government rests upon physical force, thus political power must rest with men, the physically stronger sex. The *Anti-Suffrage Review* was packed with examples of such sentiments: "Man votes, then, first as a male being and potential defender of person and property"; "we still have to maintain that the full power of citizenship cannot be given to a sex which is by nature debarred from fulfilling some of the crucial duties of citizenship—enforcement of law, of treaties, and of national rights, national defence, and all the rougher work of Empire."[9] It was a circular argument: women could not have the vote because they could not fight; they could not fight because they were women.

Moreover, even though suffrage supporters frequently attacked this prejudice,[10] they did not necessarily see a place for women within the military services. A handbook put out by the Men's League (an organization of men who favored women's suffrage) rejected the physical force argument, insisting that the most important question was whether Britain would actually lose military strength if women had the vote. Their handbook claimed this would not be the case.[11] Describing as nonsense the argument that women should not take a share in decisions to send men to the battlefield because they were not fighters themselves, the author nevertheless concluded that it was probably "not desirable that women should enter the Army and the Navy; they might not add to the usefulness of the forces; it would certainly remove them from their natural sphere."[12]

The idea of women performing military service—with the implication that eventually they might be required to take part in battle—was both disturbing and offensive to many people for a variety of reasons. Some simply believed that fighting was a man's job and should remain so. Others feared that women

9. *The Anti-Suffrage Review,* May 1909, 1; John Massie, Report of Deputation to Prime Minister Mr Asquith, June 21, 1910, in *The Anti-Suffrage Review,* July 1910, 5.

10. For example, Arabella Shore, "The Present Aspect of Women's Suffrage Considered," pamphlet, 1877; Laurence Houseman, "Articles of Faith in the Freedom of Women," 1910; A. Maude Royden, ed., "Physical Force and Democracy," National Union of Women's Suffrage Societies, April 1912.

11. J. Malcolm Mitchell, "The Physical Force Objection," in *The Men's League, Handbook on Women's Suffrage* (The Men's League for Women's Suffrage, 1913), 128.

12. Ibid., 130.

could not cope with the reality of war at the front. Some asked, if women go off to fight and are killed in the same numbers as men, who will rebuild (repeople) society afterward? And, if men were not fighting for women and children at home, for whom were they fighting? During the First World War, people—especially women—worried about the moral consequences of allowing women to become part of the military forces and live in close proximity to men. Finally, considerable disapproval was expressed during the First World War of women who were seen to be "aping" men.[13]

The Marchioness of Londonderry, founder of the Women's Legion,[14] described a meeting at Mansion House in London in December, 1914, held after she had been asked to become colonel-in-chief of the Women's Volunteer Reserve, an offshoot of the Women's Emergency Corps.[15] She accepted, despite her dislike of the military-sounding title (which she thought "a mistake and misleading"), because she was excited by the enthusiasm of many of the women involved and she had ambitions of altering the direction of the organization.[16] At the Mansion House meeting, she reassured the audience that they had no plans to create "a militant force of warlike Amazons"; rather, their object was to organize the women of the country to release men for active service.

According to Lady Londonderry, at the end of 1914 people were still so prejudiced against the concept of women working outside their accepted occupations of nursing, sewing, or cooking that immediately after the Mansion House meeting insulting letters complaining of women "masquerading as" or "aping" men began to appear in the papers. Lady Londonderry disapproved of this development but admitted that some of the women in the reserve provoked such reports: "We had to contend with a Section of 'She-Men' who wished to be armed to the teeth and who would have looked quite absurd had they had their way."[17] She claimed that, as reports of these "male-

13. According to the Marchioness of Londonderry, this term was a favorite abuse of women during the First World War. Marchioness of Londonderry, *Retrospect* (London: Frederick Muller, 1938), 112.

14. The Women's Legion was founded in July, 1915, with voluntary organizers and paid workers. It was comprised of several sections, the best known of which were the Military Cookery Section and the Motor Transport Section. The women of these two sections were the first to be accepted by the War Office to work directly with the Army.

15. The Women's Emergency Corps was one of the first women's organizations set up at the outbreak of war. Differences of opinion on the most appropriate direction women's war work should take were quickly apparent, and in September, 1914, a break-away group, the Women's Volunteer Force, was formed. Its intention was to protect women, children, the sick, and the old in the event of a German invasion. *The Times,* September 4, 1914.

16. The Marchioness of Londonderry, *Retrospect,* 111.

17. Ibid., 112–13.

females" spread, she took to task some of "these martial spirits of the Women's Volunteer Reserve." She recognized that "their intentions were of the best—it was a hard and cruel fate that had created them women"; but she was convinced that, if the movement were to grow, the Women's Volunteer Reserve would have to be organized on a less military basis.

Many people were highly suspicious of the militaristic tendencies they claimed to observe among some sections of the female population. Typical of the criticism was a letter by an anonymous woman to the editor of *The Morning Post* that asked if there were "not some regulation forbidding that the King's Uniform be worn in such a manner as to bring it into contempt?" Two days earlier, the writer had watched a show that had included four women dressed in khaki shirts, ties, and tunics:

> These women wore short skirts it is true, as a concession to their sex; they had either cropped their hair or had managed so to hide it under their khaki felt hats that at first sight the younger women looked exactly like men. It is well known that clothes exercise an enormous influence on the mind, and that women will be dignified or frivolous, sporting or artistic, according to the type of clothes they wear. . . . I noticed that these women assumed mannish attitudes, stood with legs apart while they smote their riding whips, and looked like self-conscious and not very attractive boys.
>
> Near these ridiculous "poseuses" stood the real thing—a British Officer in mufti. He had lost his left arm and right leg. . . . [S]urely if these women had a spark of shame left they should have blushed to be seen wearing a parody of the uniform which this officer and thousands like him have made a symbol of honour and glory by their deeds. I do not know the corps to which these ladies belong, but if they cannot become nurses or ward maids in hospital, let them put on sunbonnets and print frocks and go and make hay or pick fruit or make jam, or do the thousand and one things that women can do to help. But, for heaven's sake, don't let them ride and march about the country making themselves and, what is more important, the King's uniform, ridiculous.[18]

This letter sparked off a correspondence that continued for days. "Another Woman" attacked the "ridiculous masquerades of women in khaki" which were "an unhappy by-product of the War" and asked, "[w]hat are we to think of the taste, let alone the humour, of the self-appointed 'colonels' and 'captains' who are capable of such a display at so grave and terrible a time?"[19] Lady Isabel Margesson defended the maligned women and praised the practice of wearing uniforms, which the war had shown was so useful "in stimulating true patriotism."[20] Uniforms were increasingly seen as visible sign of service and efficiency—in the north of France women were not allowed to do war work unless they wore a uniform. Margesson asked,—"is nursing to be the women's only

18. Letter to the Editor from "A Woman", *The Morning Post,* July 16, 1915.
19. Letter to the Editor from "Another Woman," *The Morning Post,* July 19, 1915.
20. Letter to the Editor from Isabel Hampden Margesson, *The Morning Post,* July 19, 1915.

expression of patriotism and the nurses' uniform the only one of value?" The originator of the correspondence wrote in again, pointing out that she objected not to women wearing nurses' uniforms but to women wearing soldiers' uniforms. Women "never can be soldiers, and all the drill and marching in the world will never make soldiers of them. Therefore I consider that military training is entirely unsuited to the female sex and a sheer waste of time, and that uniform only makes them ridiculous."[21]

Violet Markham, a strong supporter of the antisuffrage movement until 1912 who played a prominent part in discussions about women's work during the war, joined the debate to explain what she believed was the point of the objection to the use of khaki by women. Drill and discipline were always useful, and no one minded the use of a distinctive uniform or dress by women enrolled for various services. But the use of khaki and the adoption of military titles by the leaders of these movements struck "a wrong and jarring note." Services in connection with hospitals and canteen work were useful, of course, "but hardly give women a claim to assume the uniforms and titles of men who have fallen on the blood-stained field of Flanders or in the trenches at Gallipoli. These things have become the symbols of death and sacrifice. They should not be parodied by feminine guards of honour at concerts or entertainments. . . . [T]he use of Khaki by women is primarily a question of taste."[22]

If letters to newspapers reflect popular prejudices, then hostility towards women's militaristic enthusiasm decreased in the last two years of the war—or at least such sentiments were not expressed so freely. Yet there remained throughout the war a conflict between those who believed that, even though women might do useful war work, they should eschew a military image; and those who believed, for a variety of reasons, that women's corps should be modelled closely on their male equivalents. Disapproval of displays of "masculinity" or "militarism" by women is most readily explained within the context of the prewar struggle for women's suffrage. Despite evidence of a new rationality among suffrage supporters, exhibited since the outbreak of war, masculine behavior by women remained unsettling. During the war it was complicated by the fact that even women who could in no sense be described as militant suffragists were displaying a frightening determination to "ape" men. They were not demanding the vote; they simply wished to participate fully in the war. But such behavior could only stimulate the old antisuffrage prejudices.

21. Letter to the Editor from "A Woman," *The Morning Post,* July 21, 1915.
22. Letter to the Editor from Violet Markham, *The Morning Post,* July 22, 1915.

Antisuffragists had often accused the militant suffragettes of masculine behavior, and such accusations were meant as wholehearted condemnation. But, confusingly, *masculine* as applied to women's behavior was not always a term of abuse—especially during the war, when it was often considered the highest praise to say of a woman that she had "behaved like a man." Whether applauded or decried, expressions of masculinity in women were undoubtedly regarded as a challenge to the status quo: women saw masculine women as both a threat to and a criticism of their own femininity and personal security; and such women clearly challenged the political, social, and economic preeminence of men.

There was another less tangible dimension to the hostility toward militarism in women. During the First World War people drew links, either consciously or unconsciously, between displays of militarism and masculine women, feminism, and lesbianism. The feminism-lesbianism connection had been set out by Edward Carpenter, who claimed that many women who became feminists were not normal: their maternal instincts were weak; they were mannish in temperament; they did not represent their sex.[23] This association of lesbianism with feminism (and with masculinity and militarism in women) must have affected both relationships between women and the public's view of such relationships. Lillian Faderman comments that "openly expressed love between women for the most part ceased to be possible after World War I. Women's changed status and the new medical knowledge cast such affection in a new light."[24]

Women who displayed "symptoms" of lesbianism (an inclination to dress up in masculine clothes, to drill, and to shoot) were considered not only distasteful but abnormal and in need of medical help. Any attacks on them were thus fully justified. Women in military organizations were a target for those who held such views, and it was not uncommon during the First World War for women who joined the military services to be regarded as peculiar at least, if not downright immoral. Such attitudes are illustrated by the disturbing story of the downfall of Violet Douglas-Pennant, the commandant of the Women's Royal Air Force in 1918. She was haunted for years by a belief that she had been sacked because of other women's accusations that she had engaged in immoral acts with young women in the Air Force.

23. Edward Carpenter, *Love's Coming of Age,* 7th ed. (1911), quoted in Lillian Faderman, *Surpassing the Love of Men: Romantic Friendship and Love between Women from the Renaissance to the Present* (New York: Morrow, 1981), 337.

24. Faderman found plenty of evidence of "female same-sex love" after the First World War, but it was "almost invariably accompanied by a new outlaw status." *Surpassing the Love of Men,* 20.

Despite these objections, the idea of an official Women's Army—a uniformed corps of women, with officers, ranks, regulations, and drills, who could be sent to France as an auxiliary force—can be seen as a natural development in the evolution of the policy of "dilution," which sought to employ female labor in areas previously reserved for skilled men.[25] Despite what was happening in industry, and the work of the Women's Legion from 1915 on,[26] army officials did not seriously consider using women on a large scale until the second half of 1916. Undoubtedly the crucial factor in persuading those in authority to set up a women's corps was the continuing manpower shortage. It was a simple and obvious calculation: if women replaced men wherever possible, more men would be available to fight. The Manpower Distribution Board was set up to resolve departments' conflicting claims. In its Third Report to the War Committee, after hearing evidence from numerous sources, it recommended that the Army Council consider "a suggestion made by Mrs. Charles Furse, Commandant of the V.A.D., for the establishment of a trained corps of volunteer women, under women officers and in uniform, for employment in substitution for men on various subsidiary army services."[27]

The Army Council recognized that, if the War Office were to convince the Manpower Distribution Board that its own claims for men should be met, it had to be seen as doing its best with its existing force. The crisis of manpower and the conflict between different departments in late 1916 provoked complaints by both Ministry of Munitions and the Board of Trade against the War Office. They suggested that the Manpower Board make sure that men fit for active and general service were not being used for tasks which could be performed by older men "or even by women," both at home and in France.[28] There was also a complaint that the proportion of combatants to noncombatants in the army was ludicrously low.[29] All this suggests that, if the army could have gotten all the men it wanted without having to organize women, it probably would not have bothered to form the Women's Army Auxiliary

25. "Dilution" was debated from the early days of the war. Despite opposition, by the beginning of 1916 it was generally accepted as official policy. See Winston Churchill, January 7, 1915, Paper 201B, Public Record Office Cabinet Papers (PRO CAB), 4/6 "Report on Increased Employment during the War," October 1916, London School of Economics, Beveridge Papers IV/9.

26. The women of the Cookery Section of the Women's Legion were the first officially employed with the army, from August 3, 1915. *War Service Legion and Women's Legion, 1915–1918,* Imperial War Museum, Women's Section (IWM WS), Army 1¹/11, p. 11.

27. This recommendation was based on one of numerous schemes drawn up over the previous months by Katharine Furse.

28. Montagu, "Notes on 3rd Report of Man-Power Distribution Board," November 18, 1916, PRO CAB 17/156.

29. Ibid.

Corps. In the circumstances, however, a women's corps seemed a small price to pay to ensure the success of their claims for more manpower.

The formation of an official women's military corps within the army was also seen as a way of giving women what they wanted while at the same time retaining the control over them that many War Office officials believed was necessary. By the end of 1916 women such as Katharine Furse, Violet Markham, and Frances Durham were most concerned with the state of women's war work.[30] They believed that large numbers of women were not usefully employed, that the lack of coordination among existing socieities had led to a considerable amount of overlap, confusion, and waste of effort, and that more effective organization was needed. They called for a central committee to organize and control women's labor for public service of the state. It was to be independent of any existing government department though in close cooperation with the War Office, authorized to enroll women applicants for a State Service and to arrange for their training, placing, and control. The committee was envisioned as a small body consisting of a majority of women whose principal function would be to organize a group of women for full-time national service.[31] There were differences of opinion about the nature of the proposed women's organization—Violet Markham, for example, believed that "the fallacious analogies current at the moment of an 'army of women' mobilised alongside an army of men" should be discarded, while Katharine Furse wanted an organization of women, based and run on military lines, to work with the army, and she felt that "gentle-women who are considered suitable to act as officers should be given Commissions as in the Army."[32] Despite these differences, on one issue at least there was no conflict: women themselves must be given the power to control women.[33]

The desire of these women, who had been working for years for the war effort, to have control of organizations of women was in direct conflict with the view of the Adjutant General Nevil Macready, under whose auspices the first official Women's Army Corps in Britain was established. After the publica-

30. Frances H. Durham was a civil servant who worked in both the Board of Trade and the Employment Department of the Department of Labour and took an active part in discussions about women's war work.

31. *Report of Women's Service Committee,* December 16, 1916, PRO Home Office (HO) 185/258.

32. Violet Markham, "Notes on Organization of Women Power," Committee on Women's Service, Circulated Paper No. 3, December 1, 1916, PRO HO185/258; Katharine Furse, Committee on Women's Service, Circulated Paper No. 1, November 24, 1916, PRO HO185/258.

33. See, for example, Katharine Furse, "Memorandum of Women Power," November 4, 1916, LSE Markham 4/11; Violet Markham to ? (unknown), December 7, 1916, LSE Markham 4/11.

tion in January 1917 of a report ordered by the Army Council, which discussed favorably and in some detail the desirability of employing women in France outside the battle areas, Macready was forced to alter his previous, rather limited conception of the scheme for employment of women in the army.[34] But he continued to insist that women "should be part and parcel of the Army, and entirely distinct from any outside organisation. . . . If we once admit outside interference, jealousy will be created among the various organisations, and I feel sure there will be no peace."[35] He could see no objection to the ladies who had experience in outside organizations "being consulted in the first instance, before the scheme is launched in order that we may have the benefit of their advice, but I strongly urge that the War Office Organization should be entirely free of them." Lord Derby, the secretary of state for war, agreed about "resisting any outside interference whatsoever," though he was most anxious "not to give outside associations of women an opportunity for agitation." [36] A number of women were thus invited to attend various conferences preliminary to the establishment of the Women's Army Auxiliary Corps, but it is difficult to conclude that either the adjutant general or the secretary of state for war attached much importance to the ideas and opinions of the women they invited. Mrs. Chalmers Watson, the sister of Sir Auckland Geddes (then director of recruiting at the War Office), who was appointed the first head of the WAAC, described one meeting as not a consultation with women at all but rather a presentation of what had already been decided upon.[37]

The women's branch within the Adjutant General's Department of the War Office, called AG XI, was officially inaugurated on February 19, 1917,[38] and the first public announcement of the Women's Army Corps appeared the following day in the *Daily Express*.[39] The paper advanced the view that allowing women to work in noncombatant occupations in France was "a proof that

34. Report by Lt. General H. M. Lawson, C.B., "On the Number and Physical Categories of Men Employed out of the Fighting Area in France," para. 32, "Employment of Women," January 16, 1917, IWM WS Army 3³/2.

35. Minute, January 24, 1917, Adjutant General Nevil Macready to Lord Derby, Secretary of State for War, IWM WS Army 3⁶/3.

36. Ibid. (Note typed at bottom of memo, dated January 25, 1917.)

37. Interview with Mrs. Chalmers Watson in Edinburgh, June 9, 1918, IWM WS Army 3¹²/5. See also Women's Conference, Draft Minutes, February 6, 1917, IWM WS Army 3⁹/6. Her opinion was probably correct: a "Communique to Press" had been drawn up by February 1, some days before the meeting, that summarized terms and conditions of services with the armies in France and listed classes of employment and rates of pay. Dept. F6, War Office, to director of financial services, Minute 1, February 1, 1917, PRO WO32/5250.

38. Directorate of Organization, History 1914–1918, PRO WO162/6.

39. *Daily Express*, February 20, 1917.

the Government is determined to make the mobilisation of the nation a reality and not a pretence. The new invitation to woman is an acknowledgement that she is indispensable, and this acknowledgement must have a far-reaching effect on the social and political changes that will follow after the War."[40] Once the principle of an official women's army corps had been approved, it was only a matter of time before two other women's services were set up: the Women's Royal Naval Service at the end of 1917, and the Women's Royal Air Force on April 1, 1918.

Even after two world wars in which women served in women's corps, prejudices remain. The old physical force argument reappeared in the House of Commons Standing Committee debate on the British Nationality Bill as late as February, 1981, when Enoch Powell claimed that nationality should be transferred only through men, because "[n]ationality, in the last resort, is tested by fighting. A man's nationality is the nation for which he will fight. His nationality is the expression of his ultimate allegiance. . . . [W]hether we like it or not . . . at the heart of nationality there lies a commitment to defence—the defence of a society, to the defence of a territory—a commitment which, in the last resort, must be sealed by physical force and by personal self-sacrifice."[41] Powell insisted that women have no part to play in this test of nationality. One of the essential differentiations of function between men and women, he claimed, is that between fighting, on the one hand, and the creation and preservation of life, on the other. The two sexes are deeply differentiated in accordance with those functions; the "differentiation of specialisation corresponds with the human sexes—with man and woman." Powell's "whether we like it or not" suggests that he is expressing what he regards as a "natural," if not a written, law. Despite evidence to the contrary, the widely held belief, stated explicitly by the anthropologist Lionel Tiger, remains: that "almost universally war is an all-male enterprise."[42]

40. Ibid., 4.

41. Enoch Powell, Ulster Unionist M.P. for South Down, in parliamentary debate: House of Commons, Official Report, Standing Committee F, British Nationality Bill, 3rd Sitting, February 17, 1981. (HMSO London, 1981, cols. 110, 113, 114).

42. Lionel Tiger, *Men in Groups* (London: Thomas Nelson, 1969), 80.

KARIN HAUSEN

The German Nation's Obligations to the Heroes' Widows of World War I

Writing the social and economic history of the Weimar Republic "from below" has usually meant digging no deeper than the normal situation of the lower classes. But beneath that level there was yet another social group whose history has been forgotten—the victims of World War I, among them millions of women and children, the families of soldiers who died in the war.[1] Their story requires two narrative tracks: one tracing how they were discovered and dealt with as a "problem group" in society, and another showing how, under conditions of public support and social control, they faced crises in their private lives.

German war widows, especially those with children, paid the costs of World War I in installments of their daily lives. They were "war victims," along with disabled veterans and their wives and the mothers and fathers of fallen sons.

1. Only recently has this situation been changed by the new book of Robert Weldon Whalen, *Bitter Wounds: German Victims of the Great War, 1914–1939* (Ithaca: Cornell University Press, 1984); and Michael Geyer's important article, "Ein Vorbote des Wohlfahrtsstaates, die Kriegsopferversorgung im Frankreich nach dem ersten Weltkrieg," *Geschichte und Gesellschaft* 9 (1983), 230–77, which concentrates on the disabled soldiers. But the subject of war widows is omitted, for example, in such studies as J. Kocka, *Klassengesellschaft im Krieg: Deutsche Sozialgeschichte 1914–1918,* Göttingen, 1973, repr. 1978); and G. Mai, *Kriegswirtschaft und Arbeiterbewegung in Württemburg, 1914–1918* (Stuttgart, 1983); as well as in more detailed case studies such as K.-D. Schwarz, *Weltkrieg und Revolution in Nürnburg* (Stuttgart, 1971); and V. Ullrich, *Die Hamburger Arbeiterbewegung vom Vorabend des Ersten Weltkrieges bis zur Revolution 1918/19* (Hamburg, 1976). Literature on women and war, such as U. v. Gersdorff, *Frauen im Kriegsdienst, 1914–1918* (Stuttgart, 1969); and C. Boyd, "*Nationaler Frauendienst:* German Middle-Class Women in Service to the Fatherland, 1914–1918" (Ph.D. diss., University of Georgia, 1979), does not take account of daily life problems. See the forthcoming Ph.D. dissertation by U. Daniel (University of Bielefeld) on the social history of the German homefront.

The war victims' pensions secured only a bare subsistence for most. Inflation, initiated by the war and increasing until late 1923, hit those dependent upon pensions particularly hard. If they wanted to earn a much-needed supplementary income, they faced as a group meager chances in a labor market already stretched by high unemployment.

When the publications of wartime and postwar social agencies are combed, they yield up testimony of these women and their sufferings, such as the following, written by a forty-six-year-old German woman in 1930:

> In August, 1914, after five years of happy marriage, my husband was called up for military service. He left me behind with three children, aged one, two, and three years. In September, 1916, he was wounded and in December sent back home to work for three months. On March 17, 1917, he died from his war injuries. At that time I was ten weeks pregnant. . . . The oldest boy started school at Easter. I had to go on poor relief for six months because [my husband's] war injury was being investigated. I received sixteen marks support weekly and the rent money. The money was already greatly devalued and covered only the bare necessities. Clothing or other purchases were out of the question. . . . On September 24 my last boy was born, a child who never knew his father. On September 26, my second day in childbed, I was informed that the pension had been approved. . . . Thus I could . . . support my children myself and do home work on the side. . . . I stayed up working many nights while others slept and when morning came returned exhausted to my household duties.

The widow goes on to recount the fates of three of her sons, who, lacking the funds for university education, had learned trades and then faced long periods of unemployment with only minimal relief. The youngest son, then thirteen, was still in school.

> Because of the war I had to work to the point of exhaustion in order to supplement my meager pension. Thus, in 1923, after long sacrifice and much work, I had to drop everything and take care of myself. After a five-week illness at home [complete nervous breakdown, the effects of cold, undernourishment, and severe anemia], I had to go into the hospital for complete rest and then to a sanitarium.
>
> When the children were small I always hoped things would get better when they were older and were earning money. . . . For the last two years I have not been able to earn anything because my household makes demands on me different from those it made when the children were younger. Besides, I am forty-six years old and I do not have much strength left after a life of so much worry and labor.[2]

Sixteen years of wartime and postwar history as it was lived by one woman: she finally lost even the hope that her situation might improve when her children grew up. The world economic crisis left only the grim prospect of

2. H. Hurwitz-Stranz, *Kriegerwitwen gestalten ihr Schicksal: Lebenskämpfe deutscher Kriegerwitwen nach eigenen Darstellungen* (Berlin, 1931), 85–88.

continuing poverty and loneliness in old age. Other widows surveyed in 1930 echoed her lament: "The great inflation was the most terrible time for the dependents of the war dead. The state can never redress what we and our children had to suffer through the total devaluation of our pensions." Another recalls, "I remember that my pension for two weeks once bought only four pounds of bread. I was forced to send my youngest out begging in the neighborhood so that the others could take some bread to work." And a third: "Many times we went to bed hungry. I still remember how the widows and orphans thronged the local war relief office."[3] For these women and their families, wartime conditions did not end with the armistice but persisted for decades afterward.

According to the first published figures of 1922, of the 13.25 million German men called up for military service, 1.69 million had died. Later estimates placed the number of people who had died in or as a result of the war at 2.4 million.[4] Of these men, nearly half were twenty-five or younger when they met "a hero's death," and nearly a third were married. In 1924 the government recognized the right to support of approximately 1.6 million financial dependents of the men killed in the war. These included 371,795 widows, 1,031,409 orphans and half-orphans, 113,607 widowed mothers, 17,580 widowed fathers, and 62,734 parents as couples.[5] The total number of women widowed by the war must have been about 600,000, but by 1924 approximately one third of them had apparently remarried and become ineligible for widows' pensions. In the period that followed, the number of widows eligible for pensions scarcely changed, remaining at around 362,190 in 1930. Of the 364,950 widows still receiving pensions in 1924, 88.9 percent were between thirty and fifty years old. Some 286,624 of them supported 594,843 children under eighteen who were still eligible for dependents' allowances. Nearly one third of the widows had one child, 24.9 percent had two children, 13.8 percent had three, and 9.3 percent had four or more children to support.[6]

3. Ibid., 58, 78–79, 86.

4. Figures may be found in *Wirtschaft and Statistik* 2, (1922), 385–87, 487; E. Kirsten, E. W. Buchholz, and W. Köllmann, *Raum und Bevölkerung in der Weltgeschichte,* pt. 3 (Würzburg, 1955) 296. The 1.69 million mortalities break down as follows: 241,343 soldiers in 1914; 434,034 in 1915; 340,468 in 1916; 281,905 in 1917; 379,777 in 1918; and 14,314 in 1919.

5. *Wirtschaft und Statistik* 5 (1925) 28–30; *Reichsarbeitsblatt* (1925), no. 4. unofficial part. pp. 64–73; ibid. (1926), no. 24, unofficial part, pp. 424–29; and *Deutschlands Kriegsbeschädigte, Kriegshinterbliebene und sonstige Versorgungsberechtigte. Stand Oktober von 1924. Bearbeitet im Reichsarbeitsministerium nach Zahlung der Statistischen Reichsamts* (n.p., n.d).

6. Hurwitz-Stranz, *Kriegerwitwen gestalten ihr Schicksal,* 133–34.

In order to assess the magnitude of these figures, it should be added that the German Empire in 1925 had a total population of 62.4 million, and that 2.8 million widows and 182,536 divorced women lived alongside 12.7 million married women. There were thus two widows for every nine married women, as opposed to only two widowers for every twenty-nine married men.[7] Among the nation's widows, the 400,000 war widows stood out because they were younger and had smaller children and better pensions than the others.

In the prewar society of the German Empire, families without "breadwinners," children without the "strong hand" of a father, and women without the "moral support" of a husband would have been seen as anomalies when measured and judged against the norm of an orderly family life. But this society would have paid less attention to the poor but honest widow or abandoned wife supported and supervised by a poor relief fund than to the unwed mother whose baby, not least out of pronatalist considerations, was to be given better physical and moral chances of survival. World War I, with its mass slaughter of husbands and fathers, blurred the previously clear border between socially marginal groups and an established, norm-setting majority with "orderly" family circumstances. To remedy this perceived threat to German family life, social leaders proposed war welfare for all soldiers' families.

War widows and orphans became a new client group in this welfare program on April 16, 1915, when a conference on "Social Welfare for War Widows and Orphans" opened at the Reichstag in Berlin with these words: "Every day the German soldier faces his enemy and looks death in the eye, but today it is our duty to remove his heaviest care, that for his wife and child. In this conference we are to suggest the ways and means to absolve the German people's debt of gratitude and to do justice to those left behind by our fallen soldiers."[8]

The "soldier's cares" and the "debt of gratitude," not the hard living conditions of widows and children, served as the rationale for a conference whose first task was to grapple with the fact that the misery of those left behind by the

7. *Statistik des Deutschen Reichs* 401 (Berlin, 1930), 174–75.

8. See *Soziale Fürsorge für Kriegerwitwen und Kriegerwaisen, Allgemeine Deutsche Tagung einberufen vom Deutschen Verein für Armenpflege und Wohltätigkeit am 16. und 17. April 1915, im Plenarsitzungssaal des Reichstags in Berlin: Stenographische Berichte über die Verhandlungen* (München, 1915), 2.

The sources for my essay are primarily printed publications of the Soziale Kriegshinterbliebenenfürsorge. For the larger context of social policy and welfare in Germany, see R. Landwehr and R. Baron, *Geschichte der Sozialarbeit: Hauptlinien ihrer Entwicklung im 19. und 20. Jahrhundert* (Weinheim, 1983); L. Preller, *Sozialpolitik in der Weimarer Republik* (1949, repr. Kronberg/Th., 1978); G. A. Ritter, *Sozialversicherung in Deutschland und England: Entstehung und Grundzüge im Vergleich* (München, 1983); and F. Tennstedt, *Sozialgeschichte der Sozialpolitik in Deutschland* (Göttingen, 1981).

war had been little considered during the mobilization of the homefront. Initiated by the German Federation for Poor Relief and Charity (Deutscher Verein für Armenpflege and Wohltätigkeit), the central organization of private, communal, and regional poor relief associations, the conference attracted over thirteen hundred representatives of all levels of government, the churches, old age insurance institutions, federations and societies, as well as individuals from all over Germany and Austria. All parties, denominations, classes, and interest groups, men and women, were represented. Only the war widows themselves were nowhere to be seen. No shrill or discordant notes disturbed the display of harmonious national unity that characterized the two-day conference.

In the papers and discussions, war widows appeared as a social problem first of all because the prewar law on allowances for military casualties' dependents regulated pensions solely on the basis of military service grades, without differentiating according to the social position of the fallen. This problem was intensified because the war widows' plight assigned them two contradictory sets of responsibilities: those of mother and breadwinner. It was considered especially important to protect the now fatherless children from neglect. Providing for children in homes for war orphans was suggested but rejected. According to one of the conferees, "[i]t is true that when the father dies, the family loses its head, the strong hand of the educator, and the breadwinner, but, on the other hand, the child needs the love, care, and work of its mother if she can somehow fulfill the duties of feeding and education."[9] So the question of waged work for widows with several small children became central to the discussion.

Was it true that "the problem of employment and motherhood, of employment and housework, could not be solved,"[10] even by emergency action, or did the war open opportunities for far-reaching innovations? All the conferees agreed that children must remain with their mothers, but it was the feminists who, as an extension of their prewar discussions, came forward with a provocative solution. They did not fall back on homework as the best way to combine family and workplace. Instead they maintained that paid employment must no longer be measured solely against male work patterns. It would be necessary to find "time arrangements and workloads which would not interfere with the maternal role."[11] Gertrud Hanna, the secretary for women workers in the socialist labor unions, argued even more decisively: "[a]s long as housework is

9. *Soziale Fürsorge,* 15.
10. Ibid., 53.
11. Ibid., 56.

still based upon the individual households, and as long as there are no major changes in child care, the household economy and children, especially the smaller children, must remain in the hands of the housewife and mother." She considered it appropriate to guarantee the economic situation of mothers with small children because "the higher compensation for such mothers is nothing more than their compensation for the work they perform for the public good in caring for and educating their children. This work deserves compensation as much as any other occupation."[12]

Kaethe Gaebel, known for her activities in home-work reform, argued that paying "capable" mothers for raising their own children, just as foster mothers were paid, would create an "inner recognition that the occupation of mother is a public service performed in the national interest."[13] Finally, Helene Simon, who later organized welfare offices for dependents of fallen soldiers, carried the radical wages-for-housework argument a step further to include unwed mothers.

In their discussion the conferees covered all the central issues and problems of widows' paid employment: that women would be divided between their work as mothers and as wage-earners, that they could fail to advance professionally, that widows because of drawing an additional income from pensions could dangerously depress wages, and that the jobs suitable for widows in the civil and municipal service might later be needed for long-service noncommissioned officers or disabled veterans.

This discussion on widows as mothers and motherhood as a profession deserving compensation reveals the gender ambiguities of wartime society. The conferees were aware that, because men's patriotic engagement at the front rendered precarious public and private male dominance at home, they had to tread carefully on men's vested interests. In the discourse of the conference, the concern over male prerogatives was reflected in the contrast between a vigorous emphasis on the desirability of the presence of the father and breadwinner, and the simultaneous consideration of ways to organize the social replacement of these fathers, whose absence was now both real and, in case of the war widows, permanent. In this context Helene Simon skillfully combined both sides of the contemporary understanding of war widows and orphans. She couched her remarks in the pathos of the patriotic front:

War widows must not be forced to take outside employment. It is our most sacred duty to the fallen soldier, so proud of his home and of being able to free his wife from the burden of wage work, to allow her to devote herself completely to maintaining his

12. Ibid., 61.
13. Ibid., 125.

home and children. . . . We are not asking for alms or supplementary pensions, but rather for payment for work performed, sufficient to redeem all the moral and economic, national and individual value of the mother's professional achievement.[14]

Essential elements of future family policy were foreshadowed in these discussions. The children's allowance came after 1933, with the significant revision that it was not paid as part of the mother's income but rather as a supplement to the breadwinner's.

Until the Reichstag conference, relief for dependents of men killed in or dead as a result of the war had been regulated by the 1907 Military Casualties' Dependents' Law (*Militärhinterbliebenengesetz*), which proved insufficient to handle the results of the mass mobilization practiced for the first time in World War I.[15] The law determined the size of pensions solely on the basis of military rank, allowing for no consideration of social situations or local differences. Widows of enlisted men, who made up 98 percent of the casualties, received a monthly pension of 33.33 marks plus 14 marks for each child. It was already apparent in 1914 that the pension payments were inadequate, even for minimum subsistence, for a widow with one to three children in a large city or industrial region. Despite repeated intervention, a thorough legal revision of relief for families of fallen soldiers was rejected during the war, prompting charitable organizations to call for the conference as a means of drawing attention to the dire situation of these dependents.

In the period that followed, some temporary—and insufficient—measures were taken under the direction of the Ministry of War in an attempt to prevent downward mobility. A decree of August 14, 1915, authorized payment of a hardship compensation based upon the prewar wages of the deceased. The total income of fatherless families was not to exceed 75 percent of the dead man's prewar income, with a ceiling of 3,000 marks a year. Because it was intended to maintain status rather than to aid the impoverished, however, the decree *excluded* families whose prewar income was less than 1,500 marks for enlisted men and 1,700 marks for noncommissioned officers.

14. Ibid., 29–30. For the prewar discussion, see B. Greven-Aschoff, *Die bürgerliche Frauenbewegung in Deutschland, 1894–1933* (Göttingen, 1981), 62–69; I. Stoehr, "'Organisierte Mütterlichkeit': Zur Politik der deutschen Frauenbewegung um 1900," in K. Hausen, ed., *Frauen suchen ihre Geschichte* (München, 1982), 221–49.

15. Critical comments in *Soziale Praxis* 25 (1916), 346–50; *Soziale Kriegshinterbliebenenfürsorge* (cited hereafter as *SKHF*) (1917), 118–20. The following statements are based on *Denkschrift des Reichsarbeitsministeriums betr. die bisherigen Aufwendungen für Kriegshinterbliebene vom 16. Oktober 1916,* in *Stenographische Berichte der Verhandlungen des Deutschen Reichstags,* vol. 339, Aktenstück 1281, 1276–80. It should be added that, in spite of the famous Bismarckian social insurance programs in place in prewar Germany, most working-class widows had no claim to a pension.

With the accelerating inflation rate the financial situation of those drawing pensions worsened even in comparison to that of military families. Out of consideration for the mood at the front, relief to families of living soldiers was raised twice during 1916, but pensions for dependents of fallen soldiers remained the same, and demands for an inflation supplement for them were also rejected. Welfare agencies protested repeatedly against this ruling, arguing that "discontent" and "bitterness" would surely result if a woman were confronted with not only the report of her husband's death but also a significant loss of income. Women living in Berlin who received 67.50 marks a month as a soldier's wife collected only 47.33 marks as a widow. Even if some widows received an additional orphan's allowance under the Imperial Insurance Law of 1911, their financial situation nevertheless declined because upon their husband's death they lost both their municipal rent allowance and the support frequently offered by former employers of soldiers.[16]

Not until April, 1917, were needy soldiers' widows and children eligible for a rent supplement. The decree of November 26, 1917, stipulated that the additional allowances could be paid as continuous support without an upper limit, in order to equalize the incomes of families of living and dead soldiers. A few cities had already undertaken such an adjustment out of their own funds. In 1916, for example, Cologne began paying widows 42 marks in addition to their widows' pensions, plus 16.50 marks per child.[17] Even though by the end of 1917 the purchasing power of the mark had sunk to half its prewar strength, the policy remained "to approve revocable allowances and equalization benefits only in case where the present family income was below 75 percent or in some cases 100 percent of the prewar level."[18]

A general increase in dependents' allowances did not come until June, 1918. War widows received an additional 8 marks, and each child under sixteen received 3 marks, without having to demonstrate need. In light of rapidly rising prices, a one-time inflation supplement of 50 percent of dependents' monthly payments was approved on January 22, 1919. Not until June 1, 1919, were dependents with a right to claim relief awarded a continuous inflation supplement of 40 percent of their monthly pensions. This regulation followed

16. *SKHF* (1917), 21, 38, 57, 76; *SKHF* (1918), 34.

17. See *Zur Theorie und Praxis der Kriegshinterbliebenenfürsorge (Schriften des Arbeitsausschusses der Kriegerwitwen- und Waisenfürsorge,* ed. im *Auftrage des Hauptausschusses,* n. 3) (Berlin, 1916), 32 (cited hereafter as *Theorie und Praxis*).

18. *SKHF* (1917), 143; estimates of inflation rates in Kocka, *Klassengesellschaft,* 17, *SKHF* (1919), 40–41 noted critically that the well-organized disabled veterans received a one-time inflation supplement of 100 percent on December 31, 1918, while the widows got only 50 percent on January 22, 1919.

large national demonstrations by disabled veterans and dependent families in April, 1919. Further inflation supplements followed until May 12, 1920, when, as a long-overdue amendment to the Military Casualties' Dependents' Law, the National Relief Law (*Reichsversorgungsgesetz*) was passed. This bill took account of all grievances voiced during the war and, for the first time in German social legislation, considered child maintenance in calculating widows' pensions. Even this recalculation of pensions had to be constantly revised under conditions of galloping inflation.

During the entire period of the war and the immediate postwar years, the pensions of fallen soldiers' families were insufficient for even the most urgent necessities.[19] Families with small children in particular remained dependent upon donations of clothing and shoes. Worst placed of all were those who were ineligible for relief for one of several reasons: the cause of death was not considered a result of military service, the man was missing, or he had committed suicide at the front.

The Germans' enthusiasm for the war stimulated the development of numerous charitable activities alongside the state's dependents' relief programs. The Mutual Insurance Funds for the 1914 War, founded in 1914 to provide a kind of reinsurance for men whose patriotism had led to irresponsibility toward their families, were quickly frustrated by lack of financing. Some professional organizations and businesses started to sponsor the education of members' or employees' war orphans. Public old age disability insurance institutions made honorary, one-time payments (called *Ehrenbeihilfen* or *Dankes-und-Ehrengaben*) to the widows and orphans of insurance policy holders.[20] On December 18, 1916, the National League for the Sponsorship of War Orphans (Reichsverband für Kriegspatenschaften) was founded with much pomp at the Reichstag. Under the patronage of the Prussian Ministry of War, it served propaganda purposes rather than effectively aiding dependents. In the opinion of its initiators, "the undertaking of sponsorship of war orphans is to express our feelings of gratitude to the soldiers who have given their lives for the fatherland. The sponsors will fulfill the testament of the fallen men by seeing that their children are raised to be capable people, sound in mind and body. Any German man or woman who possesses the appropriate personality and character traits can sponsor a war orphan."[21]

19. For the development of pensions and allowances and the total amount paid by the Reich, see *Reichstag*, vol. 339, 1277–78.

20. Information in *Soziale Praxis* 23 (1913–14), 1325, 1353; *SKHF* (1918), 4; *Soziale Praxis* 24 (1914–15), 202.

21. Speech at the foundation, quoted in *Soziale Praxis* 26 (1916), 258.

Only the National Foundation for Dependents of Fallen Soldiers (Nationalstiftung für die Hinterbliebenen der im Kriege Gefallenen), founded in 1914 under the chairmanship of the Prussian minister of the interior, achieved nationwide significance.[22] Its purpose was to organize a broad-based relief system for the families of soldiers that would supplement the legal pension program through individualized support and thus prevent the downward social mobility of dependents. The foundation's capital was drawn from donations. The main support came from organizations such as the The War Contribution of Grateful German Women (*Kriegsspende Deutscher Frauendank 1915*), a collection campaign run jointly by all the larger women's organizations, and from industry. In 1916 the Krupp Foundation joined the National Foundation with 20 million marks. From 1916 to the end of 1918, the foundation spent a total of 20.25 million marks on dependents' relief. It also began to provide more than merely financial aid—its state, provincial, and local offices became points of departure for institutionalized social welfare programs for dependents of military casualties.

To return to the development which had its beginning in the Reichstag conference of April, 1915: this conference strove to institutionalize a unified approach to social relief for dependents of military casualties on a municipal and local level, and to develop a central organization to coordinate local interests on the national level. To this end, a Central Committee for War Widows' and Orphans' Welfare was formed at the conference, with fifty-six men and fifteen women as members. In June, 1915, a working committee was formed by a smaller group of men and women well known for their involvement in various charity, social welfare, and social reform organizations.[23] In an effort to promote the installation of an efficient, uniform national system of welfare, they publicized the problems and attempted solutions of individual communities and made important suggestions for uniform procedures and organization. In 1918 the Central Committee merged with the National Foundation.[24]

As welfare provisions and regulations became more elaborate, more complex bureaucratic machinery was needed to put them into effect. For example, applications for the "revocable supplements" paid in addition to dependents' pensions required individual investigation and approval. At first the police performed this task, but by 1916 the Prussian government was beginning to

22. For the following see SKHF (1916), 4; *SKHF* (1917), 19, 76–77, 92; *Reichstag*, vol. 339, 1279.

23. *Theorie und Praxis*, 6–29.

24. *SKHF* (1918), 15–20, 29.

turn it over to welfare agencies with official connections, and eventually communal agencies were established for this purpose.[25] By the end of 1917 there were at least five thousand official dependents' welfare offices in the Reich, including those organized by government authorities, committees of the National Foundation, and other relief agencies.[26] The institutionalization of dependents' welfare was intended to be permanent. A regulation of February 8, 1919, finally organized social welfare for disabled veterans and dependents of military casualities on a uniform national basis.

During the war, the progressive interconnection of all dependents' relief activities and the centralization of all relevant information in one local office was considered advantageous because it allowed an overview of support activities and thus ensured "the most just and efficient distribution of relief possible."[27] The integration of various communal, church, and private relief agencies into a more centralized local welfare system under state control may have opened the way for more efficient aid, but at the same time it installed the preconditions for greater social control. To be sure, bureaucratic procedures varied from one agency to another. In some places war widows had files at the local dependents' welfare office even before they sought help. In others, files were not requested until the widow came to seek aid. But all offices wanted to have as much information as possible about "their" clients.

At times, the welfare offices' detailed investigation of the circumstances of those seeking advice and aid imitated the style of the police. In 1916, when the director of the welfare agency for war widows and orphans in Gleiwitz found that few clients were visiting the office, he determined to summon several widows at a time for appearances. Female assistants interviewed the clients and also had "the task of visiting the women at home, checking the circumstances they found there against the application, and making an extensive report on the questionnaire."[28] This extreme example illustrates not only the process of social control but also the division of labor by gender that pervaded welfare offices. Agencies also sought to influence their clients' behavior. A report from the city of Recklinghausen noted: "The 'dutiful' housewives were rewarded with special donations, clothing collections, and so on. As a result even the negligent ones began to place more importance on their households and made efforts to keep their homes clean."[29]

25. *Theorie und Praxis,* 102–13; *SKHF* (1917), 9.
26. *SKHF* (1918), 17.
27. *SKHF* (1917), 9.
28. *Theorie und Praxis,* 41.
29. Ibid., 58.

As in prewar time, social control and social relief went together, even for war widows, whose legal claim to pensions did not guarantee them an existence. But the practical aid offered by the welfare offices might have been quite essential for their clients. They assisted widows in applying for pension supplements or establishing their eligibility for public social insurance funds. If a widow needed help to arrange rent payment, pay off debts on furniture, or procure moving allowances, a temporary advisor could be appointed. Indigent families received food, clothing, and fuel grants as well as health care, sanitarium care, medical treatment allowances, and medication. Occupational counseling and employment were also provided. For widows with small children who had to earn money, agencies proposed childcare arrangements with relatives, provided home work, and in some cases arranged for education grants to help unite motherhood and wage work.

The efficient but probably also very costly welfare bureaucracy undertook investigations into welfare cases and maintained documents with the same enthusiasm that it brought to individual problems. In general the welfare agencies seem to have offered effective aid in the period immediately following the husband's death. At the same time, they clearly invaded their clients' privacy, claiming the right to unlimited observation of their living conditions, and freely engaging in surveillance, manipulation, and control.

It is difficult, but not impossible, to go beyond the intentions and actions of relief bureaucrats and get to the widows and orphans themselves. One can find descriptions of particularly striking cases, such as the story of Mrs. B. from Berlin, who was accustomed to her husband's monthly income of 400–500 marks and had to survive after his death on a pension of 69 marks along with her children, two and three years old. There is also the case of a sickly forty-three-year-old woman with a fifteen-year-old daughter, whose monthly income slid from 300–400 marks in peacetime to 51 marks during her husband's military service and then to 47.33 marks after his death. We can see the dramatic effects of the economic emergency in the case of a family with three children whose father was discharged from the military service in September 1914 with tuberculosis. He could not work and received only unemployment relief of 5 marks a month until his death in May, 1915. From then until October, 1916, the welfare office helped his wife in her eventually successful fight for a war widow's pension.[30]

The welfare offices also attempted to gather statistics to describe the war

30. Ibid., 10, and *Die Frau* 24 (December 1916), 137–38.

widows under their care. The figures suggest that in general widows seeking help at the local welfare offices were almost all (95 percent) younger than forty, half of them under thirty. All but 12 percent had children to support; 31 percent had one child, 27 percent had two, 15 percent three and 15 percent four or more. Over half the children were six or under. During the war, the number of widows who performed wage work varied from place to place and from year to year. A report on 1,900 widows in Hamburg for the end of 1917, a time of labor shortage, revealed that before marriage 78 percent of the women had been employed, but only 5 percent continued working for wages after marriage. As widows, 52 percent of them were again earning money—as unskilled workers (20.8 percent), house servants (19 percent), skilled workers (18.6 percent), white-collar workers (13 percent), civil service employees (12 percent), by running businesses (7.4 percent) and renting rooms (4.6 percent), and through other occupations (4.6 percent). In Mönchen-Gladbach only 41 percent of 220 widows had taken up paid employment by mid-1916, although 89 percent had worked for wages before marriage. In Hagen, 77.5 percent of the widows had held jobs before marriage, 64 percent of them as servants, but in mid-1916 only 46 percent were working for wages. The percentage of employed widows in Berlin-Schöneberg, 88.8 in mid-1915, was very high in comparison. Some 95 percent had had work experience before marrying, 57.4 percent as servants. As widows, 29 percent were daily cleaners in the households of others and 29 percent did home work, that is, work on the lowest end of the pay scale.[31]

Information on the widows' husbands reveals just how much their incomes plummeted during the war. Ninety-eight percent of them had died as enlisted men or at most noncommissioned officers. One-third had been unskilled workers in civilian life. Skilled workers and master craftsmen, at 45 percent, represented the largest group. Before the war more than 80 percent had earned a monthly income of more than 100 marks; with entrance into military service, this had shrunk to a minimum. In Berlin, 174 households consisting of war widows with children were surveyed by the relief office in mid-1915.[32] Their incomes, composed of war relief, communal supplement, rent supplement, and in some cases support from the husband's employer, followed a sharp downward course (see table).

31. Information on Charlottenburg, Schöneberg, Berlin, and Worms in *Aus der Praxis der Kriegshinterbliebenenfürsorge* (*Schriften des Arbeitsausschusses,* n. 2) (Berlin, 1916); on Bochum, Hagen, Frankfurt, and Mönchen-Gladbach in *Theorie und Praxis;* on Hamburg in *SKHF* (1918), 100; on Landkreis Recklinghausen in *SKHF* (1919), 8.

32. *Hinterbliebenenfürsorge: Mitteilungen aus der Zentrale für Privatfürsorge e.V. in Berlin, August, 1915* (Berlin, 1915), 44–46.

Monthly Income of Prewar, Soldiers', and War Widows' Households

	Prewar	Soldiers'	Widows' (mid-1915)
0–100 marks	6.3%	78.7%	78.1%
101–150 marks	65.5	15.5	17.8
151–200 marks	21.3	3.4	2.3
201–300 marks	6.3	2.3	1.7
301+ marks	0.6	—	—

The longer the war continued, the more difficult it became for women to cope with radical reductions of the household budget. Wartime conditions, inflation that halved the value of the mark, shortages—above all of clothing and shoes—and the constant need to pay black-market prices for essential foods destroyed families' living standards. As early as mid-1915, the Berlin Center for Private Relief noted that, of the 500 war widows who had applied to them, 252 were ill. Alongside internal and lung ailments (63.5 percent of illnesses), 92 women were found to be suffering from nervous and physical exhaustion (36.5 percent of illnesses). Eleven women were pregnant.[33] The widows' health must have worsened rapidly with the immiserization of war.

When it became clear that upon her husband's death the old standard of living was gone forever, impossible economic problems accumulated for the widow. Her apartment was often too expensive, and it became increasingly difficult to find lodgers. The rent allowances provided to soldiers' wives by the municipal authorities were unavailable to widows. Back rent mounted while the woman looked for a smaller, affordable apartment. Many families were still burdened with installment payments on items purchased before the war, especially furniture, and furniture dealers used all possible means to retrieve the outstanding payments. The situation was even more critical if the husband had borrowed money to set himself up in a trade or small shop and the widow was not in a position to carry on the business. Selling the business was difficult and often entailed heavy losses.

According to all reports the transition period was particularly crucial. The despondent widow, often ill and weakened, found her life encircled by debts, her choices restricted by small children, and her possibilities for returning to wage work limited. In this situation she might get help from relatives or neighbors or find her way to the welfare office, which could solve or at least alleviate some of her overwhelming problems with donations or personal

33. Ibid., 41.

advice and aid. Given the magnitude of their problems and the relative dearth of resources, it is astonishing that so many women and their families were able to survive the descent into extreme poverty and eventually to learn to cope with their new condition.

The silence surrounding the hard, gray, everyday realities of wartime and postwar life is part of the pathos of hero worship. The innumerable war monuments in the city squares block our view of the realities of war for these women. Instead, women are portrayed as pietas, suffering for the glory of their heroic sons. The president of the German Reichstag expressed this mode of commemoration at the opening of the third wartime session on December 2, 1918:

> Heavy, too, the losses of human life demanded by the war. Many a woman's heart is consumed by grief at the death of her fallen husband and brother, many a father's and mother's heart aches for the sons torn from them. We honor their pain and mourn with them, but the fatherland thanks them and is proud of so many heroic sons who have spilt their blood and laid down their lives in the World War we are fighting for our own existence.[34]

Such lofty words provided little comfort for the hungry, homeless, and insecure widows whose anxieties about their own welfare and that of their children would linger for years to come. But the discourse of public commemoration could not simultaneously maintain the mythos of male heroism and also acknowledge women's real, if mundane, hardships. Instead, the widows were silenced, their testimony locked away in bureaucratic files.

34. *Reichstag*, vol. 306, 14.

PAULA SCHWARTZ

Redefining Resistance: Women's Activism in Wartime France

Le risque est le même pour tous. Celui qui lance [la bombe] et celui qui ne [la] lance pas."
—Dora, in Albert Camus, Les Justes

The Second World War, the occupation of France, and the Vichy regime created conditions favorable to the increased participation of women in French political life. Women of all political persuasions performed a variety of tasks in the underground movements, networks, and groups which mushroomed during the period. Present throughout the Resistance movement from positions of leadership to the base, women ran missions, collected intelligence, printed and distributed clandestine newspapers, smuggled arms and ammunition, staged demonstrations, and committed sabotage alongside men.

Although women's presence in and contribution to the Resistance was stressed after the war, scholarly treatment of the subject and studies of the Resistance that satisfactorily integrate women are relatively rare.[1] Only recently has a new consciousness begun to emerge on the part of Resistance historians and even women resisters themselves.[2] Several factors account for

This essay is based in large part on research funded by a 1977–78 ITT International Fellowship to France. All archives are located in Paris unless otherwise noted.

1. The most comprehensive volume is a collection of speeches made at the Sorbonne in 1975: Union des Femmes Françaises, comp., *Les femmes dans la Résistance,* (Paris: Editions du Rocher, 1977). See also Ania Francos, *Il était des femmes dans la Résistance . . .* (Paris: Editions Stock, 1978); and Marie-Claude Coudert, *Elles la résistance* (Paris: Messidor, 1983). The best effort at integrating an analysis of women resisters is Jacqueline Sainclivier, "Sociologie de la Résistance: Quelques aspects méthodologiques et leur application en Ille-et-Vilaine," *Revue d'Histoire de la Deuxième Guerre Mondiale* 117 (January 1980).

2. Henri Noguères, *La vie des résistants de l'armistice à la libération* (Paris: Hachette, 1984); Dominique Veillon, "Résister au féminin," *Pénélope* 12 (Spring 1985). The specificity of women's experience is illustrated in the memoirs of Lucie Aubrac, who traces her activism over the course of

this, but the major obstacle to date has been a conceptual one. The omission of women from Resistance scholarship is rooted in the very idea of what constitutes "resistance" in the first place. The result has been what the French call *occultation,* or the eclipse of a subject in literature and collective memory. This conceptual problem has obscured the roles of several actors.[3] However, it particularly excludes the contributions of many women because of the nature and form of their participation.

The French Resistance was not an operation conducted by a few, but a system of action supported by many. It was a series of small, nearly imperceptible elements which formed a larger construct. The actions of women clearly reflect this structure. Some women were full-time activists who left behind their everyday lives to live in total clandestinity. These resisters, or *illégals* in the terminology of the period, operated under new identities: they assumed false names, left schools, jobs, and families, changed residences in order to go underground. Many more women, however, contributed to this political movement by extending their roles as housewifes or mothers or by turning their workplace activities to other purposes. Called *légals* or *sédentaires,* these activists remained in place and operated "above ground" on a full- or part-time basis. Both types of resistance were formally prohibited by the Vichy and German authorities.

But prevailing notions of resistance have tended to obscure women's contributions by orienting research away from participants who did not occupy leadership positions or distinguish themselves in some extraordinary way. Due to the obvious material difficulties of reconstructing the more elusive aspects of a clandestine movement, scholars have studied the Resistance by way of its organizational components—the parties, groups, and networks. However, many resisters, especially women, rendered services without ever taking part in a group. Thus, women are not present in group-based studies that consider only full-time activists or official members. This other kind of activist has been lost from view, despite the fact that the existence of such rear-guard popular support is precisely what is purported to have given the Resistance a "mass" character. Definitions of resistance that emphasize combat also tend to exclude women, since few bore arms, although many provided the infrastructure that made combat possible. The social service organizations administered and

---

the nine months from the conception to the birth of her second child. See *Ils partiront dans l'ivresse* (Paris: Seuil, 1984).

3. For the double *occultation* of Jewish women resisters, see Rita Thalmann, "Une lacune de l'historiographie"; and Sabine Zeitoun, "'Résistance active,' 'Résistance passive,' un faux débat," in Association pour la Recherche sur l'Histoire Contemporaine des Juifs, comp., *Les juifs dans la résistance et la libération* (Paris: Editions du Scribe, 1985).

staffed exclusively by women have rarely been considered resistance groups per se, although their aims were political as well as humanitarian. Finally, many of the women who met traditional criteria of resistance activism operated within organizations linked to the French Communist party. Their contribution has been neglected outside party circles because the Communists' role in the French Resistance remains hotly controversial.

The war and occupation opened a range of new possibilities for political activism by politicizing the traditional role of women within the family. Family relationships proved especially important in mobilizing women, because resisters were primarily recruited through family and socioprofessional channels—a process which reproduced within the Resistance movement the prewar division of labor at home and in the workplace. Yet, even women who held supporting roles, who took other resisters into their homes and fed, clothed, and protected them, performed political acts and made political choices. Thus a revised notion of resistance is needed, one that can account for the new forms of political participation that arose in the social and political setting of occupied France. This essay points to the limits of the prevailing notions of resistance and suggests how they might be expanded to incorporate activities performed by those we should also think of as resisters.

Resistance is habitually equated with actual combat, evoking the image of the partisan fighters in the maquis, the French Forces of the Interior (FFI), which were organized late in the war to consolidate the combat units of various groups and the street fighters at the barricades during the Liberation. While few today would consider this a sufficiently broad definition of participation, it has crept into some primary source material of the period. For example, a document listing the membership of a maquis group reveals that only men in fighting or command positions were counted as full-fledged members. The three women associated with the group, whose activities have not been recorded and about whom we thus know nothing, are mentioned under a separate rubric, as "nonenlisted but active members."[4] Thus, strict adherence to a military definition of resistance made women's contribution invisible. They were less likely to have participated in combat and more likely to have engaged in the many nonconventional forms of resistance that gave the movement its highly original character, especially in the beginning.

Records and dossiers compiled on the recipients of awards also constitute a

4. Série 72 AJ, Archives Nationales. J. Sainclivier speculates that an underrepresentation of women in her data may derive from the slant of her sources, records of those who applied for recognition as a *"Combattant Volontaire de la Résistance,"* qualifications for which emphasized combat and extended to victims of repression who were not necessarily resisters at all. "Sociologie de la Résistance, . ." 34, 42.

rich source of information about individual activists, but the definition of resistance used to distribute laurels after the war omitted many, including women. The *Compagnon de la Libération,* the highest honor awarded a French citizen for resistance activities, was given to 1,059 individuals, of whom only 6 were women.[5] This does not accurately reflect the relative proportions of men to women resisters. It does, however, reveal a definition of resistance based on membership in a group affiliated with General de Gaulle.[6]

Women formed a complex web of support that sustained small groups of combatants. Provision of support allowed many women to resist without going underground or becoming a full-time member of an official group. During the occupation, ordinary peacetime professions became vehicles for activities subversive to the regime. A corps of teachers, concierges, clerks, and nurses resisted by exploiting the resources available to them on the job. Their contributions were scaled to their resources, but, because of the materials and opportunities to which they had access, they helped sustain a small army of clandestine activists.

As mentioned above, people were often recruited to resistance work—although not necessarily to organizational membership—through socioprofessional relationships.[7] Heavily feminized professions such as elementary school teaching, secretarial work, domestic service, the post office, and civil service posts in mayors' and prefects' offices offered unique opportunities for resistance work that the organized networks tapped. Sometimes a "connection"—a complicitous clerk working in some branch of the administration—could provide food tickets and "real" false identity papers bearing all the seals of officialdom to those underground.[8] Rare paper and printing equipment were procured by office workers for the manufacture of illegal handbills and newspapers. Secretaries typed stencils at night for the clandestine press. In this way, women with access to resources at work formed a network—acting as

5. Chancellerie de l'Ordre de la Libération.

6. The system of awards and compensation has been sharply criticized by some former resisters on the left, who maintain that official recognition for services rendered during the war took different forms for different groups: distinguished Gaullists received the lion's share of military and civilian honors, while the heroes on the left got streets named after them.

7. H. R. Kedward, *Resistance in Vichy France: A Study of Ideas and Motivations in the Southern Zone, 1940–42* (Oxford: Oxford University Press, 1978). Françoise Leclère analyzes group membership on the basis of socioprofessional affiliations—such contacts were a primary means of recruitment and often determined what duties a resister would perform: "La composition d'un réseau: 'Zéro France,'" *Revue d'Histoire de la Deuxième Guerre Mondiale* 61 (January 1966).

8. In contemporary jargon, "false" identification papers were forgeries fabricated by the Resistance. "Real" false identity papers were issued to resisters under pseudonyms, or *noms de guerre,* by civil servants.

individuals or in concert with a group—that supported and reinforced the efforts of those in hiding.

The importance of such work-related activities carried out by women is exemplified by the concierge.[9] Because of their constant presence in the building, concierges could be a source of information and valued accomplices. Many helped resisters by warning them of police inquiries, giving false information to pursuers, and providing living quarters and space for rendezvous. Henriette Labarbe hid several partisans in the underground tunnels of her building during the battle for the liberation of Paris;[10] others performed such activities on a regular basis throughout the occupation. The disposition of the concierge could be an important factor in the choice of hideouts for resistance activists, but those who provided such assistance were not considered resisters in their own right.[11]

These contributions have been acknowledged by women who were full-time resisters themselves and who depended upon the aid of such supporters. Cécile Goldet, a nurse attached to the maquis of the Vercors, remembers the support of various women who aided others as opportunities presented themselves. She cites the example of a nun who transmitted documents, supplies, and messages under her voluminous habit and a prostitute who provided a safe refuge for the hunted.[12] Yvonne Zellner, a former resister and member of the Communist party, has also called for the recognition of women whose quiet assistance facilitated the actions of others, even if they did not undertake action of the same nature upon themselves. She cites the case of her neighbor, a woman who did not necessarily share Zellner's political views but who was willing to take her young children at irregular and suspicious hours without asking questions. As Yvonne Zellner remembers it, an unspoken understanding passed between them. She feels sure that her neighbor suspected the reasons for her sudden and prolonged absences from home, which Zellner claimed were "to do the marketing," although she usually returned hours later empty-handed. By Zellner's own acknowledgement, the distribution of clandestine propaganda and the organizational work that she did in her early

9. In France most apartment and office buildings are tended by concierges who live on the premises and provide service and upkeep in exchange for housing. The concierge often serves as a security guard, taking note of those who enter and leave.

10. "Une parisienne sauva sept combattants," *Front National* 24 (September 1944).

11. In a panel discussion, Germaine Tillion invoked the concierge as exemplary of the forgotten resister and hoped a new generation of Resistance historians would take note of the "little" resisters at the base. Centre Pompidou, Paris, May 29, 1980.

12. Interview, Paris, December 21, 1974.

resistance years were possible thanks alone to the witting assistance of her silent neighbor.[13]

Partisan fighters in the bush, most of whom were men, also required an immense support apparatus. The survival of maquis groups in the countryside depended on support from the neighboring population. Tucked away in the woods or mountains, these resisters were supplied with food, information and equipment by those in the open. Sympathetic peasants provided homegrown produce, bases for the sick and wounded, or stopping points for resisters in transit. Some maquis groups had "godmothers" or "guardian angels" to whom they were attached on a formal or informal basis. One woman, nicknamed "Mother of the Maquis" by those in her charge, lent maternal comforts, provided food and good humor, and tooled homemade armbands and a flag for the group out of parachute cloth. A store of arms and ammunition lay buried in her garden under a bed of leeks, and her young children made deliveries to the *maquisards* who lived in the woods. She procured false papers for each fighter, calling on "patriotic civil servants" for aid or made false papers herself. Her story is told in a testimonial from "her boys":

> We want all to know the patriotic courage of this fifty-year-old woman . . . this "Mother of the Maquis" whom we loved so dearly in our saddest hours. She knew so well how to comfort us and nothing inconvenienced her. At all hours we went to her house; it was a little like finding our own long-lost homes. She overlooked nothing: "Have you eaten? No? Take pot-luck, my boys!" And she went to her stash of wine, of chocolate and preserves, or of potatoes and beans and fruit which she bought in large quantities to give us. . . . Good wine . . . we knew to appreciate this wine, for we had only bread and potatoes for the hard days ahead. How often we were fortunate to have what Mother had given us; a good drink raises the spirits and warms the body. . . . We owe much to our Mother of the Maquis; we owe her everything, maybe even our lives. . . . Here is a great Frenchwoman who in her little sphere knew how to do her duty. She knew how to show courage and sacrifice and intelligence and daring, but above all . . . a big heart.[14]

It is hardly surprising that the social services necessary to support full-time clandestine activists became the exclusive domain of women. The Service Social, a section unique to Combat, a large and well-developed resistance group, was staffed wholly by women members. In fact, most women who

13. Interview, Ivry, April 6, 1978. When Zellner went undergound, her mother cared for her children for the duration and throughout her prison and concentration camp terms.

14. "Hommage à la Mère du Maquis avant notre départ pour le front," Archives, Bibliothèque Marquerite Durand. For the similar case of Madame Lucette, see the scrapbook "Ceux du Maquis," Institut Charles de Gaulle. The story of Cathérine, "Mother of the Patriots," is recounted in the testimony of Jean Guyomarch, Musée de la Résistance, Ivry.

occupied leadership positions in Combat were representatives of this branch, which provided food, lodging, communications, false papers, and other essentials for group members. An analysis of the membership of several large resistance formations reveals that most women participants were liaison agents, social service personnel, or had other supporting roles, which suggests the existence of a gender division of labor within some resistance groups.[15] Although the support structure of most resistance groups was generally less formal than Combat's, it always existed in some form because it was critical to the groups' survival.

The tasks assumed by women in the Resistance were often extensions of traditional feminine roles in the home and workplace, as we have seen. They involved not only the provision of necessary support services to underground activists but also the care of needy families. Independent social service organizations were created to aid political prisoners and their families, Jews, and children whose parents had been arrested or killed. Sometimes these groups had contacts on the inside which enabled them to establish illicit communications between prisoners and families. One such group, the Comité des Oeuvres Sociales de la Résistance, was founded to care for the families of resisters and other victims of repression, but it also provided liaison services and funnelled intelligence to the Resistance.[16]

From these cases we can see that many women comprised, in the words of one resister, the "ground floor of the French underground."[17] While the involvement of these people was essential to the functioning of a larger operation, it was often not fully credited by the state, the national community, or postwar historians. But their implication in the "crimes" was complete. Indeed, it is significant that the German and Vichy authorities employed the expanded definition of resistance for which this essay argues. Decrees formulating sanctions against resisters did not distinguish degrees of involvement and responsibility of those implicated in so-called "terrorist" acts. A public notice of September 22, 1941, posted in cafes, in subways, and on the streets, warned that those who lent support of any kind to parachutists and other

15. Marie Granet and Henri Michel, *Combat: Histoire d'un mouvement de Résistance de juillet 1940 à juillet 1943* (Paris: Presses Universitaires de France, 1957); Madeleine Baudoin, *Histoire des Groupes-Francs (M.U.R.) des Bouches-du-Rhône de septembre 1943 à la Libération* (Paris: Presses Universitaires de France, 1963); and Dominique Veillon, *Franc-Tireur: Un journal clandestin, un mouvement de Résistance, 1940–1944* (Paris: Flammarion, 1977).

16. Interview with Thérèse Blaison, Paris, France, December 7, 1977; dossier of Marie-Hélène Lefaucheux, Bibliothèque Marguerite Durand.

17. Henriette Bidouze in an interview by Marianne Milhaud, in "Les Femmes dans la Résistance," *Heures Claires* 130 (October 1975), 31.

enemy agents could expect severe sanctions. This decree explicitly defined support as "giving direct or indirect assistance to members of enemy air crews dropped by parachute or forced landings; promoting their escape, hiding them, or lending assistance in any way whatsoever."[18] Men would be shot on the spot and, in a special provision, women would be deported to concentration camps in Germany. The gender distinction that operated here in the repression against resisters appears to show some leniency toward women. But the "benefits" applied only to those who escaped the camps with their lives. Resisters who were killed outright were spared the agony of those who suffered slow deaths in the filth, degradation, and disease of the camps.[19]

Such sanctions were aimed at the extensive infrastructure necessary to support resistance groups receiving aid from the Allies abroad. They applied equally to those who supported the maquis fighters in the countryside and others, often women, who used their homes to form networks of safe refuge for resisters in cities and towns.[20] The possible consequences of support to resistance activists show that such support was deemed very much a part of a threatening opposition that the authorities were willing to repress even at the expense of further alienation of the population.[21] The severity of such measures reflects an assessment of the value of popular support from the perspective of those to whom it posed a threat.

The use of restrictive notions of resistance also derives from political schisms which date from the internal struggles of the Resistance itself and which continue even now to exert an enormous influence on French political discourse. Historians of the Resistance have focused heavily on Gaullist formations, leaving the operations mounted by the French Communist party to

18. *Avis à la population,* September 22, 1941. For the role of women in escape lines for Allied soldiers and others, see Margaret L. Rossiter, *Women in the Resistance* (New York: Praeger, 1986).

19. Interview with Marie-Claude Vaillant-Couturier, June 15, 1984. A former French Communist deputy, Vaillant-Couturier is a survivor of Auschwitz and Ravensbrück. A later warning offers rewards to those who provide information leading to the capture of enemy agents or servicemen and reiterates the death penalty, this time without gender distinction—for those persons guilty of "hiding, giving shelter or aid of any kind to persons belonging to enemy armed forces, notably members of airplane crews, enemy parachutists, or enemy agents." *Avis,* 1944.

20. Special courts (the infamous *Section Spéciale*) were created by the Vichy government in 1941 to prosecute acts of "terrorism, anarchism, or social and national subversion," and anyone who knowingly assisted the perpetrators by providing "the instruments of [their] crime, means of correspondence, housing, transportation, food tickets, foodstuffs, or shelter." *Avis* 25 (June 1943).

21. Lucienne Reynal, a delegate of the social services organization *Assistance Française,* was arrested by the Gestapo because the "Germans considered that by helping the families of those who had been shot or deported, [Reynal] strengthened the Resistance and was . . . particularly dangerous": "Les tortures dans les prisons de femmes," Bibliothèque Marguerite Durand.

party historians. As a result, mainstream histories have neglected the important role that the party played in the mobilization of women, especially housewives, in broad-based neighborhood groups formed to protest living conditions and to rouse public opinion through petitions, strikes, and demonstrations—all forms of political activity that were anything but encouraged by the Gaullist leadership.

One way Communist organizers mobilized women was by appealing to them as mothers and housewives. The *comités populaires féminins* were neighborhood-based groups in Paris and other urban centers that aimed to inform and mobilize women via a clandestine women's press. Bulletins and newspapers such as *La Voix des Femmes* discussed grave consumer problems, the difficulties of providing for children and relatives, and the living conditions of husbands and sons taken prisoner of war, linking these popular household concerns to their political origins. The famous women's demonstrations in the Parisian market streets, the rue de Buci and the rue Daguerre, were styled by *comité* organizers after the women's bread march of 1789.[22] Madeleine Marzin, the diminutive schoolteacher who was arrested for leading the Buci demonstration, was probably the first woman condemned to death for political action against Vichy. Later these local groups were combined to form the *Union des Femmes Françaises,* an organization founded primarily by Communists but which appealed to and recruited women of different political opinions.

Expanding the customary notion of resistance to include the cases described here not only draws women into a more global picture of the struggle against fascism but also provides new insights into the specificity of women's role in the many forms of activity that came to be considered resistance in a formal sense. A revised and expanded concept of resistance makes provision for the real possibilities of political activism for women in accordance with their responsibilities as family members and their resources as housewives and workers.

We have seen how many women did participate, in a variety of ways, in the movement. Yet, obviously, the decision to participate—even once—was a difficult one to make. While many women were drawn in by family connections, these same relationships also often set limits on how and when they could participate. Since early forms of resistance originated among people who knew and trusted one another, families became natural recruiting centers and were particularly important in mobilizing women not employed outside the

22. Interview with Josette Dumeix, Paris, June 5, 1978. Dumeix assumed the leadership of these groups upon the arrest of her predecessor, Danielle Casanova.

home. Often women were drawn into the movement by lending protection and assistance to parents, husbands, and children. Resistance tasks were frequently shared among members of a single family. The prominent resistance households headed by Louis and Simone Martin-Chauffier, Pierre and Gilberte Brossolette, and Raymond and Lucie Aubrac are cases in point.[23] Male resisters often recruited their wives to serve as liaison agents and to receive other resisters at home during their absence.[24] The wife of one resister takes herself as an example of women who were brought into the Resistance by supporting the engagement of their husbands. One thing led to another: "a small step, a bit of help, and [wives] became accomplices."[25]

As a result, joining the Resistance was not only a personal decision but one with implications for family and friends.[26] Since repression against resisters was severe, it is small wonder that many women were reluctant to take risks which could place families or dependents in jeopardy. This was especially true for those who found themselves single heads of households in the absence of men taken prisoner of war or away from home for other reasons.[27] The arrest of the remaining parent could leave small children utterly without care or resources. Despite these risks, some mothers, like Yvonne Zellner, assumed full-time commitments. This often meant placing children with grandparents or other relatives. Once reunited in peacetime, some families and couples were unable to mend the break created by forced separation during the war.

Clandestine activities thus placed a great strain on the family, as parents and children were sometimes separated for years at a time. The Rabaté family provides a good example. Maria Rabaté's husband was already in prison when she was asked by the French Communist party to organize women against Vichy in different parts of France. Her work could take place only on a fully

23. Simone Martin-Chauffier, *A bientôt quand même* (Paris: Calmann-Lévy, 1976); Gilberte Brossolette, *Il s'appelait Pierre Brossolette* (Paris: Albin Michel, 1976); Lucie Aubrac, *Ils partiront*.

24. Leclère, "La composition d'un réseau," 79.

25. Testimony of M. and Mme. Jean Le Nedellec, June 16, 1950, Musée de la Résistance, Ivry.

26. Resistance activities often meant severing ties with friends and family to spare them the risks one took upon oneself. Renelde Bériot was a young woman who printed clandestine flyers, transported arms, and secured illegal food tickets for her colleagues in the French Communist party. Her retired parents were arrested in her stead after she imprudently sent them a letter through a friend. Testimony of Renelde Bériot Floridan, August 2, 1974, Musée de la Résistance, Ivry.

27. The war created a gender imbalance that was felt in many households. Members of the then-banned French Communist party, many of them men, were in prison or in hiding, where other resisters soon joined them. One and a half million French men had been taken prisoner of war; others left their families to join de Gaulle's Free French in London. Finally, the *Service de Travail Obligatoire* (STO), created in 1943, sent some French men to work in German factories and prompted others to go into hiding.

clandestine basis because the Rabatés were well-known members of the party leadership in the interwar years and particularly vulnerable once the party had been outlawed. Maria Rabaté left home and placed her two young children, then six and nine, with her seventy-five-year-old mother. Her only contact with them took the form of nonsensical letters sent to her mother's house addressed to her long-deceased great-grandmother. The use of her great-grandmother's name was a code that only her mother could read. "In this way," Rabaté explains, "my children knew at least that I was still alive."[28]

Family obligations had a more inhibiting effect on the full-time clandestine activism of women than of men, who were frequently also husbands and fathers. Women with minimal family responsibilities had a freedom of movement that enhanced their suitability for underground work, which accounts for the large representation of young, single, and childless women in the resistance. These women were more likely to share tasks on an equal basis with men, without regard to gender differentiation. An example is the teenage Madeleine Riffaud, whose military prowess earned her the command of a group of male partisans.[29] Those more fully inserted in the feminine condition—mothers, wives, and other women with adult obligations to others—were less mobile as a rule. But this did not prevent them from resisting in the home by serving as "letterboxes," safehouse keepers, or transmitters of intelligence.[30] Finally, for mothers like Maria Rabaté who had childcare alternatives, a full-time clandestine existence was possible, albeit at great cost.

The "women's work" of the Resistance is exemplified by the liaison agent, a particularly arduous job that required great mobility and physical endurance. A liaison agent operating in the provinces traveled sizable distances on a regular basis, risking searches and identity checks by the French police and the Germans. Though cities offered greater anonymity to her urban counterpart, frequent contacts and missions in densely populated areas were extremely dangerous. The ubiquitous liaison agents played a key role in the movement; Charles de Gaulle called them the infrastructure of the French Resistance.[31] Most liaison agents were women, because they could circulate more easily than men and were less subject to searches.[32] Many women activists, at one time or

28. Interview, Saint-Cloud, October 6, 1984.

29. Testimony of Madeleine Riffaud, July 4, 1946, Archives Nationales.

30. Letterboxes *(boîtes à lettres)* were people who received mail and messages for resisters who had no fixed residence. They were crucial links in the underground networks.

31. Quoted by Janine Jugeau, "'Les agents de liaison': Infrastructure de la Résistance," in *Les femmes dans la résistance,* 94.

32. André Tollet, a leader of the French Communist party during the war, preferred women to men for liaison work for these very reasons. Interview, Ivry, May 10, 1978.

another and often in conjunction with other duties, served as liaison agents between the resistance leadership and the rank and file, among different sections of the same resistance network, or among affiliated networks and movements.[33]

The rigorous, even monastic lifestyle demanded of Nicole Lambert-Philippot, a seventeen-year-old liaison agent for the Communist party, shows why taking to the underground was not a realistic option for all women. Her supervisor prepared her for a life of sacrifice to which she was previously unaccustomed. She was warned that upon going underground she could no longer maintain her own identity and would have to take an assumed name. This, in turn, would deprive her of the meager food allotment to which she was entitled under her real name. She could have no fixed residence; instead of a comfortable heated home she would dwell in a series of austere but safe *planques* (hideouts). Communication with her family and friends was to be severed completely; her father, also a resister, above all had to remain ignorant of her whereabouts. The party could provide her with small amounts of money for food but only at irregular intervals. Clothing, transportation, and other expenses had to be reduced to a minimum. Entertainment in any form, even small gatherings with friends, was out of the question. Cold, hunger, and solitude were conditions that came with the territory. Finally, "coquetry" in any form that could attract attention to her person was expressly forbidden. Here Nicole Lambert-Philippot comments, "I had at that time beautiful, long hair that everyone admired, which I had to sacrifice. . . . I was to become a soldier without uniform, mobilized twenty-four hours a day."[34]

I have called here for a new and broadened definition of resistance, one that would recognize the role of women in the large popular movement. Because of the form and nature of their activities, women's contributions often remained invisible, even to themselves. While their existing roles in the family and at work enabled women to provide essential support, these same roles also prevented women from undertaking the same types of "public," and especially combat, actions that men did. However, their risks were as great and no doubt reflected a similar level of political commitment to national goals.

If prevailing notions of resistance must be expanded, where then, are the limits? Are innocent victims of political repression and one-time or occasional supporters to be considered resisters in their own way? It is not so much the aim here to establish such parameters, which may in fact be different for each

33. "A nos amies, 'camarades de liaison,'" February 1944, Musée de la Résistance, Ivry.
34. Testimony of Nicole Lambert-Philippot, n.d., Musée de la Résistance, Ivry.

national or individual case, but only to relax restrictive notions that thus far give a very partial view of the big picture. An expanded definition of resistance can account for the new forms of participation that gave political expression to women's traditional roles. Exceptional new conditions served to politicize some French women for the first time—and in their very households. For others, of course, resistance activity was a natural continuation of political work begun before the war in the antifascist and pacifist leagues, political parties, trade unions, relief organizations for the Spanish Civil War, and the like.[35] Ironically, by undertaking such forms of participation in wartime, these women had assumed the burden of citizenship before they were accorded the rights and privileges that full citizenship affords: the right to vote and hold public office and the right to full equality before the law.

35. For further discussion of this and other issues raised in this essay, see Paula Schwartz, "Precedents for Politics: Prewar Activism in Women of the French Resistance" (M.A. thesis, Columbia University, 1981).

SONYA MICHEL

American Women and the Discourse of the Democratic Family in World War II

During World War II the United States, like many of its allies and enemies, sponsored public childcare programs for working mothers. Although wartime nurseries and after-school programs were beset with practical problems, they provided essential services that enabled many women with small children to enter defense industries. Yet, despite their success, most of the centers were shut down immediately after V-J Day on the grounds that they had been established only to help the war effort and were not intended to become a permanent entitlement for working women. No alternative rationale for public childcare was found until the 1960s, when Project Head Start was inaugurated to provide "compensatory education" for disadvantaged children.

The wartime policy must be seen as a product of the political and social ideological climate in which it was developed. While politicians and certain government officials objected to group care simply because they believed it was a mother's duty to look after her own children, much of the impetus for blocking permanent programs came from leaders in certain professions concerned with the family—social work, psychology, psychiatry, and, to a lesser extent, parent and early childhood education—whose reasoning was more complex and less overtly patriarchal. Together, these leaders both inside and outside government considered women and the family in the terms of what I call the discourse of the democratic family. In this system of meaning, the family was regarded as a key link in the nation's defenses and women were deemed essential to the family's survival and stability. This discourse not only reinforced traditional views of women's role but also invested the family with major political significance, thus making it more difficult for women to challenge the social division of labor without appearing to be virtually treasonous. Although the discourse became less intensely patriotic in the postwar period, vestiges of the connection between nation and family remained, confounding women's attempts to redefine their roles.[1]

THE FAMILY AND DEFENSE

The major themes of this discourse were first articulated at the White House Conference on Children in a Democracy held in January, 1940. President Franklin Roosevelt told the assembled conferees: "A succession of world events has shown us that our democracy must be strengthened at every point of strain or weakness. All Americans want this country to be a place where children can live in safety and grow in understanding of the part they are going to play in the future of our American nation."[2] Because children were an essential element of a democratic society, Roosevelt continued, their physical, intellectual, emotional, and moral development was a concern for the entire nation. Other conferees (who included family professionals and government officials from across the country) pointed out that "home and family are the first condition of life for the child." The family could, therefore, be "the threshold of democracy, . . . a school for democratic life."[3]

Beginning in the early twentieth century, sociologists and other students of American family life claimed that a decline of patriarchal authority was creating a more democratic family structure. Children looked increasingly to their peers for guidance, while "the wife . . . finds herself quite the equal of her husband in the family circle, if not the superior."[4] According to most American sociologists, as fathers' familial authority grew weaker, that of mothers increased. By the late 1920s, women were considered chiefly responsible for children's development and the smooth functioning of family relationships, so it was to them, either explicitly or implicitly, that most childrearing literature, marital advice, and parent education programs were addressed.[5] Family professionals

1. See Elaine Tyler May, "Explosive Issues: Sex, Women and the Bomb in Post-war America" (unpublished paper, Program in American Studies, University of Minnesota).

2. U.S. Department of Labor, Children's Bureau, *Proceedings of the White House Conference on Children in a Democracy,* Children's Bureau Publication No. 266 (Washington, D.C.: Government Printing Office, 1940), 70.

3. "General Report Adopted by the Conference," in ibid., 10.

4. Ernest Mowrer, *The Family* (Chicago: University of Chicago Press, 1932), 275.

5. Sociologist Chiara Saraceno points out that when such literature addresses "parents," it is mothers who are really meant; see her "Shifts in Public and Private Boundaries: Women as Mothers and Service Workers in Italian Daycare," *Feminist Studies* 10, 1 (Spring 1984), 10–11.

continued to adhere to these role definitions even during the Depression, when male unemployment drove many mothers into the labor force. One sociologist observed that, in this situation, "families organized along democratic lines allowing for some flexibility in authority patterns and family member roles [adapted] better than families organized along patriarchal lines," but, she implied, maternal employment should be regarded merely as a temporary expedient.[6] For sociologists, democracy within the family was never meant to imply wider social equality for women.

Public policy during the Depression upheld the ideal of the conventional family with a wage-earning father and housekeeping mother. The federal government, through its Works Progress Administration (WPA), established nurseries exclusively to serve the children of the unemployed—their purpose, in the words of WPA chief Harry Hopkins, to combat "the physical and mental handicaps being imposed upon young children by conditions incidental to our current economic and social difficulties."[7] It was clear that the program was not intended to accommodate the needs of working mothers. Daily sessions lasted only from about 9:00 A.M. until mid-afternoon, the period early childhood experts deemed optimal for the attention span and stamina of the very young. Mothers were expected not only to follow closely their children's progress in the nurseries but also to participate in parallel classes in parent education. If they or their husbands found employment, their children were no longer eligible for the program.

Nevertheless, the WPA programs represented a new level of government intervention into family life; they supplemented, rather than merely replacing, services previously provided privately by women in their own homes. By reaching a broad segment of the population and demonstrating the value of early childhood education, the WPA helped make nursery schools seem a normal part of American childhood. The nurseries did not, however, disrupt the sexual division of labor but rather reinforced it by redefining women's maternal responsibilities.[8]

6. Katherine DuPre Lumpkin, *Family: A Study of Member Roles* (Chapel Hill: University of North Carolina Press, 1933), 169.

7. Quoted in Christine Heinig, "The Emergency Nursery Schools and the Wartime Child Care Centers, 1933–1946," in *Living History Interviews,* bk. 3, *Reaching Large Numbers of Children,* ed. James L. Hymes (Carmel, Calif.: Hacienda Press, 1979), 9.

8. One study noted that it was primarily mothers who attended parent education classes and answered questionnaires about WPA nurseries; see William R. Clark, *Emergency Education: A Social Study of the W.P.A. Education Project in Rhode Island* (Washington, D.C.: Catholic University of America Press, 1940), 99.

THE CRISIS OF THE DEMOCRATIC FAMILY

With the prospect of war looming in the early 1940s, the idea of the democratic family took on new importance, its mode shifting from descriptive to prescriptive. If democratic families had done best in the Depression, they probably also had the best chance for survival in a war. Not only could the family serve as a school for democracy, it must positively be helped to do so. Family professionals attending the 1940 White House conference urged that parent education programs be extended to help bring about family relationships of a "democratic quality."

But even as the White House conferees were calling for measures to encourage the development of democratic families, other family experts were expressing concern that the trend had gone too far, that the emphasis on individual rights and wishes had attenuated family solidarity and jeopardized its stability. They noted that, while the prosperity of the immediate prewar period had prompted a rise in marriage rates, it had also stimulated an increase in the number of divorces.[9] Moreover, because of women's increasing importance within the family, their social and psychological influence had grown out of all proportion. One journalist claimed that twenty-five years of "feminization" had left Western nations with soft and degenerate cultures, their military strength depleted, their youth unprepared to fight.[10] Prominent psychiatrists pointed to the dangers of "maternal overprotectiveness" and "smother love," which not only prevented children from developing properly but also left a moral vacuum in the core of family life.[11]

Concurrent with their diagnoses of maternal overprotection, many of these family professionals also cautioned parents about the dangers of maternal deprivation.[12] While at first glance they appear to be contradicting themselves, upon further examination, the internal consistency of their warnings becomes apparent. They believed that a mother's presence in her child's life was

9. William Fielding Ogburn, "Marriages, Births, and Divorces," in *The American Family in World War II,* ed. Ray Abrams, *The Annals of the American Academy of Political and Social Science* 229 (Philadelphia, 1943), 20–29.

10. Roy Helton, "The Inner Threat: Our Own Softness," *Harpers Magazine* 181 (September 1940), 338.

11. On overprotection, see David M. Levy, "Maternal Overprotection," *Psychiatry* 2 (1939); Philip Wylie, *Generation of Vipers* (1942; repr. New York: Holt, Rinehart and Winston, 1955); and Leo Kanner, *In Defense of Mothers* (New York: Dodd, Mead, 1941); on the moral vacuum, see Doris Drucker, "Authority for Our Children," *Harpers* 182 (February 1941), 279.

12. See Kanner, *In Defense of Mothers;* and Arnold Gesell and Catherine Amatruda, *Developmental Diagnosis* (New York: Harper and Brothers, 1941), chap. 16.

all-important but doubted that every woman was capable of determining how, or with what intensity, she should interact with her child. As disinterested professionals they could help women calibrate the amount and control the flow of affection to their offspring. While allowing women a certain amount of autonomy to play out their assigned role in the family, the professionals would be watching and coaching from the wings. They seemed to envision inscribing a permanent place for themselves in the family picture.

The anticipation of wartime social disruption added a tone of urgency to warnings of both maternal deprivation and maternal overprotectiveness. Professionals feared that war might exacerbate both of these tendencies. With fathers absent, mothers could easily become overinvolved with their children, while working mothers might well neglect their offspring and deprive them of much-needed attention. Experts put new force behind their warnings by evoking the experience of British children who had been separated from their parents during the mass evacuations from urban bombing targets to presumably safe areas in the countryside. Both the popular press and professional journals were filled with reports claiming that the psychological effects of the evacuations may have been more harmful than the Blitz itself.[13] American donors to the Foster Parents' Plan for War Children received a newsletter in which Anna Freud and her associate Dorothy Burlingham described the children they cared for in London's Hampstead Residential Nursery.[14] Their studies concluded that parental—and especially maternal—deprivation resulted in a range of psychopathologies in children.

Anna Wolf, head of the Child Study Association of America, referred to these studies in her popular manual for parents, *Our Children Face War* (1942). Wolf did not dwell on the fact that, from the very beginning of the war, the Hampstead nursery had taken only "problem" children—those who could not adapt to their foster homes and, as the war continued, orphans. She also failed to emphasize the differences between a child's experience in an institution and in the bosom of his or her family—even one in which the mother was employed. Conflating the two, she drew broad conclusions from the Freud-Burlingham studies and translated them into prescriptions for the general public:

13. See, for example, Winifred Holmes, "A British Mother to American Mothers," *Parents' Magazine* 17, 4 (April 1942), 26–28.

14. The nursery was supported largely by American contributors. Freud's and Burlingham's reports were later compiled and published as *Infants without Families: The Case for and against Residential Nurseries* (New York: International Universities Press, 1944).

A child's mental and emotional well-being depends upon his parents' ability to remain emotionally integrated. When the parents, and especially in the case of young children, the mother, can face danger, the child almost without exception feels secure and contented. . . . For a young child's world is bounded on all sides by his mother. So long as she offers him herself unchanged, he will feel safe. When she leaves him, no matter how well cared for he may be by others, he is likely to become anxious and upset.[15]

Wolf's implication here was that American parents' failure to follow her advice would have devastating effects on children.

Reports from Germany also fueled concern about maternal deprivation. As early as the mid-1930s, observers began pointing out the inconsistency between the Nazis' emphasis on increasing the marriage and birth rates and preserving family life (the infamous *Kinder, Kirche, Küche*)—all to the greater glory of the state—and the harsh conditions of women's employment. Clifford Kirkpatrick, a University of Minnesota sociologist who had spent a sabbatical in Germany, reported that "thousands of German mothers stand at the machine for long hours at miserable wages and bear children to be neglected or to be cared for by relatives and day nurseries. Under such conditions, the scant contact of the exhausted mother with her children is not the joyous relation idealized in National Socialist propaganda." Nazi leaders, he concluded, were not "willing to pay the price of a complete restoration of the wife-and-mother role in the patriarchal family."[16]

OFFICIAL RESPONSES

American leaders, in contrast to the Nazis, seemed prepared to pay the price of maintaining traditional family structure—at least as long as the war effort could afford it. Paul McNutt, chairman of the War Manpower Commission (which excluded women—even members of its own advisory board—from its deliberations), stated in a 1942 directive: "No women responsible for the care of young children should be encouraged or compelled to seek employment which deprives their children of essential care until all other sources of supply are exhausted."[17] Official pronouncements drew on and simultaneously reinforced conventional views of the family. Brigadier-General Lewis B. Hershey, director of Selective Services, assured the American public that he had admonished local draft boards "almost prayerfully to consider the necessity for

15. Anna W. M. Wolf, *Our Children Face War* (Boston: Houghton Mifflin, 1942), 96.

16. Clifford Kirkpatrick, *Nazi Germany: Its Women and Family Life* (Indianapolis: Bobbs-Merrill, 1938), 288.

17. *Employment Security Review* (October 1942), 1.

maintenance of the family unit in the national interest—to remember the harm that may result from separating a father from his child, a husband from his wife."[18] In a similar vein, Paul McNutt intoned: "The first responsibility of women with young children in war and in peace is to give suitable care in their own homes to their children."[19]

By reaffirming the importance of women's maternal role, this discourse of national priorities had several effects. First, it served to *overfeminize* women—that is, to define them as mothers to the exclusion of any other role, such as worker, which was regarded as unfeminine or even masculine.[20] Second, it served to "demasculinize" or "refeminize" the culture as a whole. Although social critics of the late 1930s decried the feminization of American society, by the early 1940s they began to fear that total military mobilization and production would tilt the culture dangerously toward the masculine side. Official recognition of the significance of home and family reassured the American public that the society had not lost its grip on the essential values of civilization. Women *as mothers* were charged with perpetuating the culture that men were fighting for; abandoning this role in wartime would not only upset the gender balance but undermine the very core of American society.

Public officials—both women and men—stressed the importance of motherhood. While some historians have chosen to attribute the attitudes of prominent men to conventional sexist ideology,[21] such an interpretation cannot account for the women's views. As serious professionals, female government officials and leaders in the field of social welfare might have been expected to espouse, at least unconsciously, certain fundamental feminist views, for example, the ability and right of women to work outside the home. Such views should in turn have made them sympathetic to all women, including those with small children, who sought to take up defense work, and predisposed them to support programs to help working mothers.

But such was not the case. For example, the Children's Bureau, an agency headed and run almost entirely by women, was the branch of government most likely to concern itself with childcare. But the bureau equivocated on the issue

18. Lewis B. Hershey, "The Impact of the Draft on the American Family," in Sidonie Matsner Gruenberg, ed., *The Family in a World at War* (New York: Child Study Association of America, 1942), 111.

19. Quoted in Susan B. Anthony II, *Out of the Kitchen and into the War: Women's Winning Role in the Nation's Drama* (New York: Stephen Daye, 1943), 130.

20. The term *overfeminize* is Denise Riley's; see "Some Peculiarities of Social Policy concerning Women, in Wartime and Postwar Britain," this volume.

21. See, for example, Howard Dratch, "The Politics of Child Care in the 1940s," *Science and Society* 38, 2 (Summer 1974), 172.

throughout most of the war. One might speculate that bureau officials and other female leaders in social services lacked sympathy for the concerns of mothers because most of them were single and childless. But accidents of biography alone cannot explain their position. To be sure, women like Katherine Lenroot and Dr. Martha Eliot of the Children's Bureau and Abigail Eliot, a leader of the early childhood movement, were unmarried—but this appeared to have been their choice. They belonged to a generation of women educated in the 1910s and early 1920s who believed that marriage and career were incompatible. In their eyes, women were fully qualified to pursue careers, but if they decided to marry they must relinquish their work outside the home and accept the responsibilities of motherhood.[22]

This generation of women carried these ideals over into their work. As child welfare professionals, they pursued policies such as widows' pensions aimed at keeping mothers and children together; if a mother had to work, they preferred placing a child in a foster home rather than a day nursery, since the former provided a more "homelike" atmosphere. Thus, for these women, professionalism—a lifetime of training, practice, and associations—predominated over any inclination toward a kind of "natural" feminism or generalized support for all female endeavor. Even early childhood education specialists, who emphasized the benefits children would gain from nurseries, conceived of them primarily as a service to children, not to parents or working mothers.

The wartime policies of the Children's Bureau clearly illustrate the workings of professional child welfare ideology. In 1941, under the leadership of Dr. Eliot, the bureau initiated a program of Emergency Maternity and Infant Care (EMIC) for the wives and children of lower-ranking servicemen. Eventually instituted in 1943, the program was intended to raise servicemen's morale by relieving their anxiety over the health of their pregnant wives and young families. By 1946, it had paid for the hospital births of over one million babies.[23] Although the image of "babies and soldiers" initially caused legislative and bureaucratic hurdles to crumble in EMIC's path (Congress ultimately appropriated $140 million for the program), its success was due mainly to the fact that the Children's Bureau supported it wholeheartedly, for its goals were

22. See Ellen C. Lagemann, *A Generation of Women: Education in the Lives of Progressive Reformers* (Cambridge: Harvard University Press, 1979), 136–37, 152–53; also Nancy Pottishman Weiss, "The Children's Bureau: A Case Study in Women's Networks," paper presented at the Fifth Berkshire Conference on the History of Women, Bryn Mawr College, 1979.

23. "Interviews with Martha May Eliot, M.D., December, 1973, through May, 1974," Schlesinger-Rockefeller Oral History Project, Jeannette B. Cheek, interviewer, 104–18; and Susan M. Hartmann, *The Home Front and Beyond: American Women in the 1940s* (Boston: Twayne, 1982), 175–76.

consonant with the bureau's longtime concern with maternal-child health and welfare.

Yet, while pushing an essentially pronatalist program for new mothers, the bureau equivocated in its support of programs for those who had chosen to take defense jobs. Along with the Office of Education, it found itself in conflict with the WPA and its successor agency, the Federal Works Agency (FWA), over the supervision of wartime nurseries. In 1941, the bureau called a conference on the problem of childcare for working mothers. While numerous private sector professionals urged the government to take the initiative in setting up childcare programs, Katherine Lenroot, the chief of Children's Bureau, affirmed the principle that "mothers who remain at home to provide care for children are providing an essential patriotic service in the defense program."[24] By contrast, WPA officials attending the conference accepted the idea that expanding their emergency childcare centers was probably the most efficient way to meet wartime needs.[25]

Immediately after the conference, the Children's Bureau proposed to the WPA that the two agencies establish a joint program of wartime childcare, but WPA officials refused the offer.[26] Throughout the war, the WPA and the FWA remained at loggerheads with the Children's Bureau over the issue of childcare. At stake was the question of how childcare would be conceived—that is, which discourse would control it. The FWA regarded daycare centers as a means of providing early education to many children who might not otherwise enjoy its benefits. The Children's Bureau, by contrast, insisted that daycare fell under the rubric of child welfare services and, as such, must be used to prevent family disintegration under the stresses of war.

In 1943, the U.S. Senate held hearings on the Thomas Bill, which would have displaced the FWA by shifting administration of childcare programs to the state level and according the Children's Bureau power of approval over grants-in-aid. Dr. Eliot, then assistant bureau chief, testified:

> The Children's Bureau has constantly taken the position that mothers of young children, especially those under two years of age, should not leave home to enter war jobs or related jobs.
>
> The fact is, however, that increasing numbers of such women *are* working. There is, therefore, need to develop plans to extend supervision over many children now cared

24. *Proceedings of Conference on Day Care of Children of Working Mothers,* Children's Bureau Bulletin No. 281 (Washington, D.C.: Government Printing Office, 1942), 74.

25. Ibid., 39–43.

26. Eleanor F. Straub, "Government Policy toward Civilian Women during World War II" (Ph.D. diss., Emory University, 1973), 270ff.

for by neighbors or in homes selected by mothers without advice of trained workers; also a large number [of mothers] who have made no plan will seek individual advice as to the community resources for care and the best way to provide it.[27]

The bureau, according to Eliot, was enthusiastic about the bill's provisions for "information and advisory services" which, among other things, would offer mothers "the opportunity to discuss the particular needs of their child and to decide whether the mother can be employed without undue hardship and danger to the child." In supporting the bill, the Children's Bureau revealed that it had not actually changed its views, but it seemed to have accepted the fact of maternal employment and was now seeking closer control over the services required by working women.

Despite the strong support of the Children's Bureau and the Office of Education, the Thomas Bill died in committee in the summer of 1943. Shortly thereafter, however, the interested parties—at the urging of the president himself—reached a compromise: the Office of Education and Children's Bureau would continue to review proposals for children's programs, but the FWA would have final approval of all projects.[28] Under the terms of the Lanham Act, passed in 1941, the federal government could finance construction of facilities, but parents would have to pay fees for services.

PRIVATE SECTOR INITIATIVES

With the defeat of the Thomas Bill and the subsequent bureaucratic compromise, it appeared that the proponents of educational benefits had prevailed against those who insisted that nurseries serve the goals of child welfare. But neither the Children's Bureau nor the Office of Education remained silent during the remainder of the war. In addition, they found strong support for their views from private sector social workers who remained independent of government but who, because of their strategic locations in both national organizations and community agencies throughout the country, could influence policy at the local level.

Umbrella groups such as the Child Welfare League of America (CWLA) and the Family Welfare Association of America (FWAA) lobbied persistently for funds to support counseling for mothers seeking to admit their children to Lanham nurseries; when no federal money was forthcoming, private agencies

27. Testimony of Martha Eliot, M.D., U.S. Congress, Senate Committee on Education and Labor, *Wartime Care and Protection of Children of Employed Mothers,* Hearings on S. 876 and S. 1130, 78th Cong., 1st sess., June 8, 1943, 31 (hereafter cited as *Thomas Bill Hearings*).

28. Straub, *Government Policy,* 280.

"loaned" employees to daycare centers in their communities. Some social workers were so convinced of the value of their intervention that they even established evening counseling hours to reach mothers who were already employed.[29]

The counselors took their cues from specialists appearing in professional journals and addressing conferences. As their public pronouncements reveal, the CWLA and FWAA shifted their position on childcare slightly from unequivocal opposition at the outset of the war to grudging tolerance by 1945. The National Committee for Mental Hygiene was more adamantly opposed. Psychiatrist George Gardner, one of their major spokespersons, warned: "All schools of psychology and psychiatry agree . . . [on] the extreme importance of maintaining a stable family unit at all costs, and this applies particularly to the stability of the mother and her presence in the home. To my mind the last person to be employed in defense industry is the mother of children who are not yet old enough to supervise themselves."[30]

In practice, these concerns were often translated into suspicious attitudes toward women applying for daycare. One social worker advised interviewers to ascertain whether parents weren't "confusing the value of an additional income with other values in family living. . . . Are they trying to substitute day care for children when they need the services of a family agency?"[31] If a mother succeeded in running the gauntlet and actually placing her child in daycare, she was still subject to the social worker's wisdom. As one specialist put it, "[p]arents need continuous help and support with problems that arise after placement. The day nursery is not only a program for the growth of children, but one for the growth of parents, too. This is the reason why a case worker is a normal and imperative part of the day nursery."[32] Acting on this professional wisdom, counselors and social workers across the nation, many of them scantily trained volunteers, took it upon themselves to intervene between daycare centers and the mothers who sought their services. Not surprisingly, working mothers were not always receptive to caseworkers' ministrations. A 1943 study of forty-six applicants to a Baltimore family agency found that about half of them rejected offers of counseling altogether, most because they

29. See Della Shapiro, "Trends in Mississippi-Rocky Mt. Region," *Highlights* 3, 10 (January 1943), 156.

30. George Gardner, "Child Behavior in a Nation at War," *Mental Hygiene* 27, 3 (July 1943), 366.

31. Dorothy Hutchinson, "Spotlight on Day Nurseries," *The Day Nursery* 3 (April 1942), 15.

32. Gerald H. J. Pearson, "Co-operation between the Day Nursery Worker and the Psychiatrist," *The Family* 22 (January 1942), 310.

"wanted to use the agency for the purpose of receiving immediate and business-like direction in the matter of effecting a specific type of child-care plan" (which the agency, in most cases, refused to provide).[33]

Thus, while government officials like Martha Eliot called for public programs to prevent anarchy in the childcare field, social workers in the private sector looked for pathology in the parents and children who patronized childcare centers. They were not, however, really at odds; both insisted on the need for expert intervention in the family. Journalists contributed to the general mood of alarm with reports of child neglect on the part of "parents and even grandparents who could not resist the temptation to earn bonanza salaries,"[34] and youth experts predicted unprecedented rates of juvenile delinquency (mostly male) and promiscuity (female).[35] Public expressions of official anxiety simply added to the widespread (and also expert-provoked) popular belief that the democratic family was in crisis. And all fingers pointed to maternal employment as one of the chief causes of its disintegration.

THE FEMINIST CHALLENGE

Although these messages nearly monopolized both popular and professional media, constituting the dominant discourse of the wartime period, feminists provided a dissenting voice. But, because they were situated at the margins of the political process, their impact tended to be negligible. For example, in July, 1942, Representative Peggy Norton convinced Congress to grant funds to transform two thousand WPA nurseries scheduled for closing into nurseries for the children of defense workers, but less than a year later over one fourth of the centers had lost their funding because they did not fall within "war-impact areas."[36] Norton was one of the few women in the House of Representatives at the time and found few allies—male or female—for her position elsewhere in Washington.

She did, however, make an alliance with the Congress of Women's Auxiliaries of the CIO. The labor unions were potentially the most significant locus for gathering feminist forces, given the large numbers of women industrial workers and the paucity of feminist organizations and activities that survived

33. Barbara Gray, "Child Care Problems of Forty-six Working Mothers," (M.A. thesis, Smith College School of Social Work, 1943), 50.

34. Agnes Meyer, *Out of These Roots* (Boston: Little, Brown, 1953), 221.

35. Karen Anderson, *Wartime Women: Sex Roles, Family Relations, and the Status of Women during World War II* (Westport, Conn.: Greenwood Press, 1981), 103–11.

36. Dratch, "Politics of Child Care," 175.

the 1930s. But women unionists had their own problems. They faced opposition not only from the federal government, but also within the ranks of labor.[37] Male unionists were more likely to sabotage than to support women's causes because they believed men's jobs would be threatened if women became a permanent presence within the industrial work force.[38] The National Women's Trade Union League supported working women's demands for child care, but with little effect, since it was no longer the vibrant middle-class/working-class coalition it had been two decades earlier.[39]

Nevertheless, union women raised their voices whenever possible. At the Thomas Bill hearings, Eleanor Fowler, head of the Congress of Women's Auxiliaries, made a patriotic pitch: "[t]he establishment of child-care centers [would] enable women to make their maximum contribution to the defense of our country." More pragmatically, Catherine Gelles of the United Auto Workers–CIO pointed out, "[t]he fact that the Government allowances to wives of men in the armed forces are utterly inadequate means that thousands of wives of draftees will have to get jobs." Further, as she and other witnesses noted, without public subsidies, fees for childcare would take about half of women's wages, even including overtime. "We believe it is incumbent upon the Federal Government to take the main burden of seeing to it that child-care needs are met," Fowler concluded.[40]

Historian Susan Hartmann has identified an important difference in the approaches of "elite" and working-class women: "[while] elite women . . . often addressed the issue [of childcare] in terms of child neglect [and, I would add, family pathology], union women consistently emphasized working mothers' anxiety over the security of their children and defended child-care programs as essential for both 'the welfare of the child and the peace of mind of the mother.' "[41] Despite the commonsense appeal of their message and the fact

37. See Lois Scharf, *To Work and to Wed: Female Employment, Feminism, and the Great Depression* (Westport, Conn.: Greenwood Press, 1980), esp. chap. 3; Ruth Milkman, "Redefining 'Women's Work': The Sexual Division of Labor in the Auto Industry during World War II," *Feminist Studies* 8, 2 (Summer 1982), 365; and Milkman, "American Women and Industrial Unionism during World War II," this volume.

38. See Milkman, "American Women"; for the continuation of male opposition in the postwar period, see Nancy Gabin, " 'They Have Placed a Penalty on Womanhood': The Protest Actions of Women Workers in Detroit-area UAW Locals, 1945–1947," *Feminist Studies* 8, 2 (Summer 1982), 373–98.

39. See Susan Hartmann, "Women's Organizations during World War II: The Interaction of Class, Race, and Feminism," in *Woman's Being, Woman's Place: Female Identity and Vocation in American History,* ed. Mary Kelley (Boston: G. K. Hall, 1980).

40. Testimony of Eleanor Fowler, *Thomas Bill Hearings,* 106; testimony of Catherine Gelles, ibid., 91.

41. Hartmann, *Home Front,* 147.

that they arguably spoke for millions of women, working-class women's organizations were no match for professionals in the family and children's fields. Not only were the latter better organized, with greater access to political channels and the media, but they had the strategic advantage of being already well entrenched within the very services working women sought to make more responsive to their needs. Thus, although social service leaders in Washington suffered a defeat on the Thomas Bill, the existence of national networks ensured that professionals in the field who shared their views would continue to control access to and delivery of childcare at the local level.

Although reports of the mishaps or tragedies befalling "latchkey children" periodically scandalized the public, they did not lead to widespread demands for more and better daycare, but instead fed prophesies of family disintegration. Because the dominant discourse linked the family, nurtured by a full-time mother, to democracy, most Americans simply yearned more avidly for the time when the war would end and women would be returned to their proper place.[42] The war provided ideologues with new arguments articulated in the language of psychopathology: Americans (as well as the British) could no longer think of separating mothers and children without being reminded of war orphans languishing in their nurseries—clean, well-fed, but emotionally deprived. For American women, the legacy of World War II was not a set of permanent social entitlements, but instead a cluster of new social and psychological family responsibilities.

42. John Morton Blum, *"V" Was for Victory: Politics and American Culture during World War II* (New York: Harcourt Brace Jovanovich, 1976), chap. 2.

RUTH MILKMAN

American Women and Industrial Unionism during World War II

World War II not only drew American women into industry in massive numbers but also brought them into the organized labor movement. Female union membership nearly quadrupled during the war years, and unprecedented numbers of women became labor activists and leaders.[1] Moreover, unions, especially those affiliated with the Congress of Industrial Relations (CIO), became the primary vehicle through which women pursued gender equality in the workplace during the 1940s. For, while organized feminism was at its nadir during the war, the industrial unions were at the peak of their strength and had good reasons of their own to encourage women's participation.

The war created a unique opportunity for women to mobilize within the labor movement. The rise of the CIO in the late 1930s had already greatly expanded the potential of unionism for women, in comparison to the craft-oriented American Federation of Labor (AFL). The old trade union conception of women as secondary workers in need of special protection began to be supplanted by a new vision emphasizing nondiscrimination and equality. But the CIO organizing drives of the 1930s concentrated on industries in which men predominated. Women were included in the unionizing efforts insofar as they were employed in basic manufacturing, but there was minimal attention to their particular concerns as women. That changed virtually overnight with the economic mobilization for war, as women workers poured into the very industries the CIO drives had targeted in the prewar period.

Once within the unions, women fought sex discrimination in industry and

This article is adapted from chapter 6 of Ruth Milkman, *Gender at Work: The Dynamics of Job Segregation by Sex during World War II* (Champaign: University of Illinois Press, 1987).

1. Gladys Dickason, "Women in Labor Unions," *Annals of the American Academy of Political and Social Science* 251 (May 1947), 71.

in the labor movement and defined a range of women's issues. In this chapter, I sketch the history of women's wartime activity in the United Auto Workers (UAW) and the United Electrical Workers (UE), both of which had more women members during the war than any other union in the United States. Both gave careful attention to women's concerns and encouraged female leadership to a far greater extent than most other unions. However, such activity was defined in terms of its contribution to strengthening the labor movement as a whole. Although working to eliminate economic inequality fit comfortably within this framework, efforts to assert the interests of women as a special group were unacceptable in the industrial union context. Indeed, the only viable political ideology through which women unionists could pursue their interests as women was one of working-class unity. There was no political space for feminism or any other specifically woman-centered ideology within the labor movement. Nor was there any autonomous source of power for women workers outside the union structures. Thus, while a women's movement did emerge within the CIO during the 1940s, the preexisting framework of unionism set limits on its ideological and organizational scope.

THE GROWTH OF FEMALE UNION MEMBERSHIP

The wartime economic mobilization generated enormous growth in union membership. The proportion of the U.S. workforce that was unionized grew from 12.7 to 22.2 percent between 1940 and 1944. Growth in unionization of women was even more dramatic. The number of women union members rose from eight hundred thousand (9.4 percent of all union members) in 1940 to three million (21.8 percent) in 1944.[2] In the auto and electrical unions, both female and total membership grew especially rapidly, reflecting the centrality of these industries to the war economy. In 1939, there were forty thousand women in the UAW, about 10 percent of total membership; by 1945, women comprised 28 percent of what had become the nation's first union with over a million members. Similarly, while 15 percent of the UE's members were female at the beginning of 1942; by 1944, when it was the third largest CIO union, women were 40 percent of its seven hundred thousand members. In 1945, the UAW and the UE each had over a quarter of a million women members.[3]

2. Ibid.; Leo Troy, *Trade Union Membership, 1897–1962* (New York: National Bureau of Economic Research, Occasional Paper 92, 1965), 1–2.

3. Report of the UAW Fair Practices Department for 1946–47, p. 8, in Walter Reuther Collection, Wayne State University Archives of Labor History and Urban Affairs [hereafter WSU Archives], Box 21, Folder: "Fair Practices Dept., 1946–47". R. J. Thomas, "Report to the

These dramatic strides in women's union membership were due partly to new organizing but also to the "maintenance-of-membership" clauses in many wartime union contracts. The maintenance-of-membership formula, which emerged from a series of War Labor Board decisions in the mobilization period, stipulated that workers employed in a plant covered by a union contract would automatically become dues-paying union members and remain so until they left their jobs or the contract came up for renewal. Since few workers made use of the "escape clause" that allowed new union members (or old members under a new contract) to withdraw from the union during the first fifteen days of their employment under the contract, maintenance of membership in practice was similar to a union shop.[4] Many of the women who became union members during the war thus did so automatically, as a by-product of their employment in the unionized sector of the economy, and not because of any special efforts to attract them.

Whether through new recruitment drives or through expansion of employment in organized firms covered by maintenance-of-membership or other forms of union security, during the war the CIO unions not only grew but also gained new stability. Nevertheless, the war years presented the unions with a major challenge: to win the allegiance of their new constituents, many of whom had no past experience of either industrial work or unionism. Women made up by far the largest group among these new workers. Even in the UE, which always had many women in its ranks, over half of the wartime female membership had not worked in the electrical industry before the war. And, at the UAW-organized Willow Run bomber plant outside Detroit, 89 percent of the women (and 40 percent of the men) had never been union members before the war.[5]

New war workers often had an anti-union bias, particularly those from the less industrialized regions of the country. Seasoned unionists understandably harbored some resentment toward these women, blacks, Okies, and other new workers who effortlessly reaped the rewards of the CIO's past struggles. This

---

Union," *UAW-CIO Ammunition* 1 (October 1943), 8; "Women Take Posts as Union Leaders," *New York Times,* February 5, 1943; *Officers' Report* to the UE's 1944 Convention, 59; U.S. Department of Labor, Women's Bureau, *Women Union Leaders Speak,* April 18–19, 1945 (mimeo), 32.

4. Joel Seidman, *American Labor from Defense to Reconversion* (Chicago: University of Chicago Press, 1953), 91–108; Nelson Lichtenstein, *Labor's War at Home: The CIO in World War II* (New York: Cambridge University Press, 1982), 78–81.

5. "Women in Trade Unions during the War Period," 3, in Records of the U.S. Women's Bureau, National Archives, RG 86 [hereafter USWB], Box 1352; "Work and Wage Experience of Willow Run Workers," *Monthly Labor Review* 61 (December 1945), 1084.

was particularly true in the auto industry, in which women had been a tiny minority of the prewar workforce. "The women in our plant have never belonged to a union before," one local UAW president noted in 1944. "They have walked into the best wages in the area—the best conditions. They never had to struggle for this."[6] At the same time, in both the UAW and the UE, the leadership developed in the 1930s was decimated by the war mobilization, as male unionists left for the armed forces in vast numbers. So while maintenance-of-membership and other union security arrangements preserved the unions in a formal sense, the radical change in the composition of the membership wrought by the war nevertheless threatened the substance of unionism. Under these conditions, the CIO unions had a tremendous incentive to integrate women and other new war workers as fully as possible into their activities and organizational structures.

NEW OPPORTUNITIES FOR WOMEN IN THE CIO

As their numbers grew, women showed growing confidence as rank-and-file activists in the factories. "The women have learned . . . to organize, learned to make their power and influence felt," the Army Air Corps Labor Relations Office in Detroit reported to the War Department in 1943. "They have also learned how to improve their working conditions by fair means as well as what we who are responsible for war production consider unfair. . . . We have had in several vital facilities slow-downs that were traced to women."[7]

The evidence concerning women's participation in wartime strikes is fragmentary, but it appears that, like men, they stopped work over a wide range of issues. In 1944, of the workers participating in recorded work stoppages, 19 percent were female. Wartime strikes sometimes involved issues of particular concern to women, such as clothing regulations, but more often the issues were not sex-specific, and most of the strikes in which women participated also involved men. Thirty-nine percent of the recorded strikes in 1944 involved workers of both sexes, while less than 2 percent were exclusively made up of women.[8] Nevertheless, these strikes gave women valuable experience in shop-

6. Lichtenstein, *Labor's War,* 73, 101, 111–12; Questionnaire response from Wade H. Edwards, UAW Local 674, survey of locals, May–August 1944, in UAW War Policy Division—Women's Bureau Collection, WSU Archives, Series I, Box 5, Folder 5–11.

7. *Report of Conference on Women in War Industries,* March 11–12, 1943, 14, in USWB, Box 1533, Folder: "U.S. Conferences (Miscellaneous Reports)."

8. Ruth S. Coles, "Strikes and Lockouts in 1944," *Monthly Labor Review* 60 (May 1945), 965.

floor struggles, complementing the influence they simultaneously accrued within the formal union structures.

The industrial unions actively sought to educate women war workers and to win their allegiance. Both the UE and the UAW hired female staff in larger numbers during the war than ever before, and they also encouraged rank-and-file women to seek leadership posts, particularly at the local level. Both unions developed educational programs on women's issues and offered women a greater voice within their administrative structures. These creative activities reflected the fact that the war had made women's loyalty necessary to the unions. As UE President Albert Fitzgerald put it in the spring of 1942, "[t]here are thousands and thousands of women being introduced into our industries. . . . If we do not encourage women to come into the organization, think what this will mean. After the war, you will have a group of unorganized women working in the factories taking your jobs and your living away from you."[9] The electrical workers' union subsequently undertook a range of efforts to enhance women's participation and leadership.

Indeed, no union amassed a more impressive wartime record than the UE in increasing women's representation in both appointed and elected union staff positions. In September, 1943, top UE officials urged, "more women must be added to the staff, and the upgrading of women members of the staff must be given careful consideration and encouragement."[10] The number of women in appointed staff positions had already increased dramatically. In February, 1943, women made up 17 percent of the UE's national staff members, as opposed to 2 percent a year earlier. By the end of 1944, Ruth Young had become the first woman on the UE Executive Board, and more than a third of the union's full-time organizers were women. Their representation among elected UE officials also increased. In 1944, 18 women were local presidents and 33 were vice-presidents; in less powerful positions such as shop stewards, business agents, and local secretaries, women were even more numerous.[11] The number of women elected as delegates to the UE's national conventions also rose. In 1941, there were 25 women delegates, comprising 6.3 percent of the total; 104 women delegates made up 13.3 percent of the total by 1944.[12]

9. "Minutes of Conference of District #3," March 14, 1942, 15, in Records of UE District 3, UE Archives, File Folder 115.

10. *Proceedings of UE Convention,* 1943, 92.

11. "Women Take Posts as Union Leaders"; Labor Research Association, *Labor Fact Book* 7 (1945), 71; *Proceedings of UE Convention,* 1944, 110.

12. Computed from Credentials Committee reports in the *Proceedings of UE Convention,* 1941, 1944.

The UE's impressive record in increasing women's leadership was partly due to the fact that it had always had many women members and expected to retain women after the war as well. The considerable influence of the Communist party within the UE also contributed to the rapid rise in women's representation in staff positions. In any case, the results of the electrical workers' union's efforts to promote women's leadership were unmatched. Other unions, however, especially the UAW, also took more interest than ever before in recruiting women into leadership roles during the war.

"Sisters, I know we men have made some mistakes, dealing with you as you entered our industry and our union," implored UAW President R. J. Thomas in 1944. "[But] we want, we need more women leaders."[13] A 1944 UAW survey found that 60 percent of the union locals responding had women on their executive boards, and 73 percent had at least one female shop steward. Thirty-seven percent of the locals had women on their bargaining or negotiating committees.[14] Comparable data on local leadership in earlier years are not available, but the parallel increase in women's representation among delegates to the annual UAW conventions suggests the magnitude of the wartime changes. In 1940, only 8 of the elected delegates were women, about 1.5 percent of the total. Six years later, there were 73 female delegates, nearly a tenfold increase—although women still made up only 4 percent of the total.[15]

The incorporation of women into union leadership was motivated largely by fear of the consequences of neglecting them, but it was also facilitated by the conscription of male unionists into the military. "Day by day we are losing more of our staff members, organizers, local union officers, to the armed services of this country," UE president Fitzgerald noted in 1943. "Unless we develop the proper leadership, unless we encourage women to take an active part in the affairs of our organization, the men of this union are going to find themselves in a position where the structure of the union will be weakened."[16] The military draft created a leadership vacuum, which, together with the phenomenal wartime growth in union membership, eased the entry of workers of both sexes into union leadership posts. "During the war, a lot of the men had gone in service. . . . So places opened up. We got women on the staff," Ruth Young (Jandreau) recalls. "I don't think it was as much doing the right thing as it was having no choice. You couldn't get a draft deferment if you left the war

13. R. J. Thomas, "Your Rights and Your Responsibilities," *Women Work—Women Vote,* Special suppl. ed. of *UAW-CIO Ammunition* 2 (August 1944), 28.

14. "Sister Sue Says," *UAW-CIO Ammunition* 2 (December 1944), 21.

15. Computed from delegate roll calls in *Proceedings of the UAW Convention,* 1940, 1946.

16. *Proceedings of UE Convention,* 1943, 228.

plant. . . . They were better off keeping the guy in the shop and using him on lost time."[17] Florence Peterson, who later became a UAW International representative, also recalls the unusual opportunities available to women under these conditions:

> Many of the people who came to work at Irwin Pederson in war time, the women especially—and this was almost all women—had never been in a shop before. . . . It was more or less this kind of group with the exception of about three of us. . . . So I wasn't afraid to speak up. I was furious that they were asking us to work without lights. So I climbed all over the foreman when he came through. When he walked away after promising to do something, the group all turned to me and said, "You're our new shop steward." . . . So, I really kind of started at the top there. Only during war time could this have happened. Normally, you go to work in a plant and you work awhile before you get elected even to shop steward or to a committee.[18]

In addition to increasing the number of women leaders, the unions made special efforts to integrate the female rank and file into their organizations through educational programs. Both the UE and the UAW set up several women's conferences and both published pamphlets and other educational materials especially for women. The UAW Education Department's magazine, *Ammunition,* which began publication in early 1943, carried many feature articles about women workers as well as a regular column addressed to women, "Sister Sue Says." In August, 1944, a special supplemental edition of the magazine appeared, entitled *Women Work—Women Vote.* The UAW also issued pamphlets with special appeals to women like, "Sister, You Need the Union! . . . And the Union Needs You." The UE too began issuing special women's pamphlets during the war. The *UE News* carried a weekly column by Ruth Young, "Work and Play," and frequently dealt with women's concerns in regular news articles as well. The electrical union also ran special schools during the war to train women in leadership skills.[19]

17. Interview with Ruth Young Jandreau by Ruth Milkman and Meredith Tax, Schenectady, N.Y., August 29, 1985. Lost time is time spent on union business, for which a worker is paid by the company.

18. Oral History of Florence Peterson, *The Twentieth Century Trade Union Woman: Vehicle for Social Change,* Oral History Project of the Program on Women and Work, Institute of Labor and Industrial Relations, University of Michigan and Wayne State University (1978), 17. (Copy in WSU Archives.)

19. The UAW held special women's conferences in 1942 (transcript in UAW War Policy Division—Victor Reuther Collection, WSU Archives, Box 2, Folder: "Conferences") and 1944 (report in UAW War Policy Division—Victor Reuther Collection, WSU Archives, Box 27, Folder: "War Policy Women's Bureau Nov. 1944–Jan. 1945"). On the UE's many women's conferences, see wartime issues of the *UE News.* Educational publications include: *UAW-CIO Ammunition;* pamphlets in the UAW War Policy Division—Women's Bureau Collection, WSU

There were also efforts to incorporate women into the unions' organizational structures. In February, 1944, the UAW established a Women's Department within its War Policy Division, which made policy proclamations on women's issues and served in an advisory capacity to the union's Executive Board. In the UE there was no women's department, but Ruth Young became the first woman member of the Executive Board in 1944. (In contrast, the UAW's board remained an all-male preserve until the 1960s.) Significantly, Young joined the board not "as a woman" but as a unionist in her own right. She had worked closely with the union's top leaders for many years, and she gained the Executive Board post by virtue of her elected position as the second ranking officer of the union's huge District 4 (New York and New Jersey). Although she focused increasingly on women's issues during the war, her power in the UE was based on a much broader contribution. As she put it, "I was never viewed as a woman. . . . I represented the union. . . . Really what started happening [during the war] was that the union would send me places, and once I got there I represented the whole union, even though they may have asked for a woman or the union felt it was a good idea."[20]

Although women gained power during the war in both the UE and the UAW, in neither union was their influence commensurate with their representation in the membership. And, in both unions, female leadership was concentrated at the lower levels. A study of unions in the Midwest, including both UE and UAW locals, found that, of the eighty-one locals surveyed, only four had women presidents. Women held a variety of other union offices, but most were of minor importance, such as recording secretary, financial secretary, or trustee.[21] In some locals, the traditional social activities of the women's auxiliaries became the focus of women war workers' participation in the union, as in a Columbus, Ohio, UAW local, where "the men had allowed the women union members to cook and serve them a dinner after a big meeting."[22] Even in the UE, there was a sexual division of labor among the union staff. In the locals, women were overrepresented in sex-stereotyped roles, such as clerical

Archives, Box 5, Folder 5–15; PA Series, UE Archives. On the UE leadership schools see *UE News* 4, January 31, 1942, and March 28, 1942; *Proceedings of UE Convention,* 1942, 28, 205; Ruth Young to Mary Anderson, March 10, 1942, in USWB, Box 865; "Leadership Education," p. 3f of "Preliminary Report—District 6 Membership Activities Report," in Records of UE District 6, UE Archives, File Folder 148; and leaflet, "Announcing Women Leaders Training School," in Records of UE District 6, UE Archives, File Folder 180.

20. Interview with Ruth Young Jandreau.

21. "Survey of Women in Labor Unions in a Mid-West War Industry Area," n.d., and accompanying summary sheet, "Women's Participation in Union Affairs," in USWB, Box 899.

22. Elizabeth Hawes, *Hurry Up, Please, Its Time* (New York: Reynal and Hitchcock, 1946), 42.

functions and on social committees, and women field organizers were hired exclusively to work in plants where the majority of workers were female.[23] At the 1942 convention, Ruth Wellman complained that women "have been rather discouraged and shoved into positions as recording secretaries or perhaps social activities or maybe house committees to clean the windows."[24]

The limits on women's power in the unions were partly due to men's hostility. The UAW Women's Department's 1944 survey of local union policies toward women found that men's attitudes were, at best, ambivalent. "We men have not got used to women in [the] plant yet we try to give them equal rights [but] we don't understand women's problems too well," acknowledged Howard Pearson of Local 646. And James Burswald of Local 329 frankly stated, "Our first interest is in interesting male members in Union activity since women very likely will not be employed in our shop after the war."[25] Similarly, in 1943, UE organizer Marie Reed reported that "the girls [women activists] felt that the attitude of the men toward women . . . was not good. . . . [They] felt, therefore, that they had no place or a very small place in the war effort, and in the union."[26]

At the upper levels, too, there was resistance to women among male UAW leaders. "The policies of the UAW were always very good," recalled Mildred Jeffrey, who headed the union's Women's Department from its founding in 1944 until 1948. "Getting them implemented was another story."[27] Grievances that came to the Women's Department had to be referred to the powerful UAW regional directors, who were supposed to resolve the issue with the local union. As Florence Peterson recalled:

> The only recourse for the Women's Department was to bring the case back and attempt to get the people who had already made this decision [that is, the decision that had led women in the local to complain to the Women's Department in the first place] to reverse themselves. Considering that the only power the Women's Department had was the power of moral persuasion, a reversal did not often take place. It was an impossible situation.[28]

There were other obstacles to women's advancement in the wartime unions as well. Culturally, organized labor was alien territory for many women. Even

23. Nina Pillard, "Perspectives of Difference: UE Women in Leadership during the 1940s" (M.A. thesis, Yale University, 1983), 26–27.

24. *Proceedings of the UE Convention,* 1942, 205.

25. UAW War Policy Division—Women's Bureau Collection, WSU Archives, Series I, Box 5, File Folders 5–10.

26. Marie J. Reed to James J. Matles, January 21, 1943, in Records of UE District 6, UE Archives, File Folder 65.

27. Oral History of Mildred Jeffrey, *The Twentieth Century Trade Union Woman,* 50.

28. Oral History of Florence Peterson, 46.

more than the factory, the union was a traditionally male world. "The trouble with the women," delegate Mary Catherine Eddy suggested at the UE's 1943 convention, is that "they have never participated in the running of our country. And the sole problem . . . is giving the women . . . the feeling of confidence to carry on, to do away with the feeling that, 'Oh, Tom Jones is a man, he can do it better than I can.' "[29] Compounding this difficulty were the practical obstacles women had to overcome to become active unionists. Family responsibilities, especially, competed with paid work and unionism for women's time and energy. This was hardly a new problem, but it was greatly intensified in wartime, when an unprecedented number of married women had entered the labor force, working hours were longer than ever, transportation was often a problem, and rationing made shopping more difficult. As the U.S. Women's Bureau reported, there was "literally no extra time for [women] to even attend union meetings. They do not therefore get a very clear understanding of the union program."[30]

Both the UE and the UAW developed special programs to help women solve these problems. District 4 of the UE (New York) hired social workers to staff a Union Personal Service Department to assist members with childcare and other "personal and family problems." The UAW set up a union counseling program inside the factories, which offered advice about social services as well as personal counseling.[31] These services were valuable to the women they reached, and they made it possible for some to become active unionists who otherwise could not have. But these innovative programs were never adequate to the enormous need, and family responsibilities remained a critical obstacle to women's union involvement throughout the 1940s.

For many women war workers, simply gaining access to "men's jobs" had brought such a huge increase in wages that the traditional economic appeals of unionism fell flat. As Irene Young pointed out at a 1944 UAW conference:

> When you went to these new women who were getting top wages of $1.00 or $1.50 an hour for running machines, you just couldn't tell them if they didn't join a union, if they

29. *Proceedings of the UE Convention,* 1943, 226–27.

30. "Women in Trade Unions during the War Period," 6.

31. Ruth Young to Women Staff Members, May 20, 1943, in Records of UE District 4, UE Archives, File Folder 93; "A Personal Service Plan for UE Locals," *UE News,* 6, February 19, 1944; *Proceedings of the UE Convention,* 1943, 222; *Proceedings, First Annual Educational Conference,* UAW, Chicago, February 25–27, 1944, 94; "UAW Proposals for Union Counseling System," n.d., UAW War Policy Division—Women's Bureau Collection, WSU Archives, Box 4, Folder 9; "UAW-CIO Union Counseling System," n.d., UAW War Policy Division—Women's Bureau Collection, WSU Archives, Box 27, Folder: "War Policy—Women's Bureau," October 1942–October 1944.

didn't stay in the union, they weren't going to get a wage increase, because to these women they were getting more money than they ever heard of in all their life.

As to working conditions, if these women had ever worked at all before, they had worked, most of them, in laundries, restaurants, and things like that, where the conditions had always been lousy, and when they come into a plant where the union has been in control for five or six years, it is like a paradise to them.[32]

This was less true in electrical manufacturing, where many women had been employed before the war and had witnessed firsthand the economic improvements brought by unionization. But, even in the UE, the majority of the women had entered industry during the war.[33] And, in both industries, women experienced upward mobility in the 1940s because of the economic mobilization rather than union efforts, so many women were indifferent to unionism.

Despite these difficulties, the war situation led to the emergence of a substantial women's movement within the CIO during the 1940s. But its composition was shaped by the impediments to women's union participation just discussed. Older women, especially those with prewar industrial and union experience, were particularly likely to become involved. Those whose children were grown had more time for union work, and older women were also more likely to understand the gains that had accompanied unionization in the prewar years. Younger women from union families (especially the wives and sisters of union men in the military) were also disproportionately represented among female union activists.[34] Finally, leftists made up a large proportion of the wartime CIO's women leaders and militants.

The women's movement in the CIO in the 1940s was constricted, not only by the external problems that limited the number and types of women who could be active in it, but also by the internal organizational structure and attitude of the unions. On the one hand, the labor movement was the only available vehicle in this period for the active pursuit of women workers' interests, in the absence of any autonomous women's organization or mass feminist consciousness. On the other hand, since the unions were continuing organizations with their own needs, internal structures, and ideologies, there were constraints on the ways women were allowed to contribute and on how issues could be defined.

32. *Proceedings, First Annual Educational Conference,* 92–93.
33. "Women in Trade Unions during the War Period," 3.
34. Ibid., 6; Hawes, *Hurry Up, Please,* 40.

THE LIMITS OF UNIONISM FOR WOMEN

The definition of women's issues in the wartime CIO was shaped by two contradictory notions. The efforts to recruit women into union leadership and the educational and social service programs developed especially for them implicitly acknowledged that women were in some respects different from men and had their own needs. Yet, at the same time, women who became active members and leaders found that they could not recast the organization and ideology of unionism so as better to respond to women's concerns. Women were welcomed into the labor movement—but only on the terms previously defined by men. There was space for "exceptional women" like Ruth Young; there was little or none for a female perspective that might question the basic structure or ideology of unionism.

Unions were, after all, workers' organizations first and foremost. Their primary purpose was to unite their members in order to extract concessions from employers—always a difficult task. In this organizational setting, any effort to demarcate the special interests of a subgroup was likely to be interpreted as divisive and threatening by union leaders. This severely restricted the political space in which female union activists interested in mobilizing women could operate. They continually had to reassure male union leaders of their loyalty even as they sought to win broad support for the view that women were a group with distinct interests.[35]

The repeated insistence by female unionists that they were not seeking special treatment of any kind for women, either in the union or in industry, must be understood in this context. "We would make a mistake if we were to say we want special privileges because we are women," warned Ruth Young at a UE conference in 1942. "We don't have that right. We have to prove that we are equal to the tasks that face us." The vision articulated by women unionists of female workers' struggles was thus circumscribed by a politics of class interest, defined within the traditional framework of industrial unionism. "We are not fighting just for women," Ruth Wellman told the 1942 UE convention. "We are fighting to preserve all the standards that this Union has built up."[36]

35. See Alice Kessler-Harris, "Problems of Coalition Building: Women and Trade Unions in the 1920s," in *Women, Work, and Protest: A Century of U.S. Women's Labor History*, ed. Ruth Milkman (Boston: Routledge and Kegan Paul, 1985), 110–38.

36. "Minutes of the Women to Win the War Conference," UE District Council No. 7, Columbus, Ohio, December 12, 1942, 4, copy in USWB, Box 865; *Proceedings of the UE Convention*, 1942, 205.

The same position prevailed in the UAW. At its 1944 Women's Conference, the alternatives were clearly squared off when Florence Walton suggested that women should enjoy preferential seniority rights akin to those the union offered veterans. "If we're going to get special provisions for others," she asked, "why not make special provisions for women and Negroes?" This position, written up as a "favoritism" amendment to a conference resolution on seniority, was rejected overwhelmingly by the female UAW delegates. The resolution they passed instead explicitly opposed any form of special treatment for women. "The more than 300,000 women in the automobile and allied industries represented at this conference do not want special considerations or privilege," it read. "We thoroughly endorse and stand back of the seniority system which has been built up in plants under the UAW's jurisdiction."[37]

In practice, women union activists found that they could not function effectively unless they accepted the worldview of their male counterparts. That worldview did offer some avenues for mobilizing in support of gender equality. Indeed, the idea that unions should strive for unity among workers and equal treatment for all (which had led to women's inclusion in the CIO in the first place) became the basis for building opposition to sex discrimination in the 1940s. However, the scope of such struggles was restricted to efforts that served the interests of all union members. In effect, women could pursue their gender interests only when they coincided with the interests of the working class as a whole.

In most instances, the class and gender interests of women workers were not in conflict. Thus women were often able to mobilize effectively within the unions to secure equal treatment. They enjoyed considerable success in struggles for equal pay for equal work during the war, as well as for nondiscriminatory seniority systems and other gender-blind employment practices. Significantly, the extent to which discrimination was eliminated in these areas varied directly with the extent of women's activism and representation in union leadership. Thus a 1945 study found that, while separate seniority lists for women were written into only one-fifth of the local union contracts surveyed, in plants where no women were on the bargaining, grievance, or shop committees, three-fourths of the contracts provided for separate seniority lists.[38]

37. "150 Delegates Discuss Labor Problems Here," *Michigan Chronicle*, December 16, 1944, in UAW Research Department Collection, WSU Archives, Box 32, Folder: "Women and the Labor Movement 1943–4, 1 of 2"; "National UAW Women Spurn 'Special Favors,'" *Detroit Free Press*, December 10, 1944, in UAW Public Relations Collection, WSU Archives, Box 14, Folder: "Women."

38. "Seniority Status of Women in Unions in War Plants," U.S. Women's Bureau pamphlet, Union Series, no. 1 (1945).

The wartime struggles against sex discrimination in pay and seniority systems benefited women workers both as workers and as women. But if the gender and class interests of women workers generally coincided, this was not the case for men. Although ending discrimination was in their class interest, as a gender male workers might stand to lose from it. This presented a serious problem for, despite the wartime growth of female union membership, men were still in the majority, and they exercised power on a scale disproportionate even to their large numbers. Under such conditions, the task of women union activists was to persuade male union members to put their class interests ahead of their gender interests if the two were in conflict. Women, therefore, not only had to suppress their own gender consciousness, but also had to suppress effectively gender consciousness among men.

Although this was frequently accomplished during the war, in its aftermath uniting men and women along class lines became far more difficult. The uncertainty as to whether women would retain their foothold in "men's jobs" during the postwar demobilization brought the gender and class interests of men into potentially explosive conflict. For, if women workers' interests lay unambiguously in the defense of their wartime gains, their male coworkers had two contradictory interests. As a gender, their interests would best be served by a reconstruction of the prewar sexual division of labor. But if they defined their interests in terms of class, male workers would have to support nondiscrimination and the equitable allocation of postwar jobs according to seniority.

The outcome of the process through which this dilemma was resolved depended on many factors—especially on the historical structure of the sexual division of labor in each industrial setting.[39] Women's wartime mobilization in the unions was a necessary but insufficient condition for successful resistance to management's efforts to restore the prewar sexual division of labor. Such successes were the exception rather than the rule, and women's issues receded into the background once again after the war. The brief period when women's leadership and attention to women's issues flourished in the labor movement was the product of special, temporary wartime conditions. When "normalcy" was reestablished, women's leadership was no longer so important for maintaining the unions' strength, and was quickly eroded. The wartime experience, positive as it was, underscores the limitations built into the ideology and organizational structure of American trade unionism—limitations which have yet to be overcome.

39. See Ruth Milkman, *Gender at Work: The Dynamics of Job Segregation by Sex during World War II* (Champaign: University of Illinois Press, 1987).

SARAH FISHMAN

Waiting for the Captive Sons of France: Prisoner of War Wives, 1940–1945

"Never have so many men fallen into the hands of the enemy in so short a time," claimed Yves Durand in his study of French captivity during the Second World War.[1] The situation was extraordinary. Compared to the 563,000 French prisoners taken during the entire First World War, in 1940 the French government estimated that there were 1.6 million French men in captivity in Germany. This figure represented about 4 percent of the French population, a vital 4 percent, since the geographical and occupational distribution of these men, aged twenty to forty, matched closely that of the French workforce as a whole. Of the prisoners, 57 percent were married and 39 percent had children. Thus Durand concluded that captivity was an experience that touched the heart of French society; more than a military question, it was a "great social phenomenon."

Captivity shaped the lives not only of the men who underwent it but also of their wives and children. So far there have been no comprehensive studies of the latter group, though, according to Durand's figures, 790,000 prisoners left wives, 616,200 of them with children, to fend for themselves in France.[2] The impact of their experience was ambiguous. As the recent historiography of women in other countries indicates, wartime economic and social changes did not necessarily lead to a permanent transformation in the status of women in

1. The data and quotations in this paragraph are taken from Yves Durand, *La captivité des prisonniers de guerre français 1939–1945* (Paris: Fédération Nationale des Combattants Prisonniers de Guerre—Combattants d'Algérie, Tunisie, Maroc, 1980), 20–28.

2. This figure is confirmed by a 1942 French government estimate that, of the remaining 1.35 million POWs in Germany, 760,000 were married. Archives Nationales, F60 558.

society. France during World War II, even though some prisoners' wives lived for up to five years without their husbands, was no exception. These women coped with external forces pulling them in opposite directions and with equally contradictory internal conflicts. In their husbands' absence, they were compelled to take on new responsibilities and master unconventional roles to survive. These new roles upset the traditional family patterns that they and the rest of French society espoused. I explore here the contradictions faced by the prisoners' wives, as well as some of the ways they resolved their conflicts.

The most pressing external exigency for prisoners' wives was economic; wartime France was in dire straits. German requisitions left severe shortages of basic necessities such as food, clothing, and fuel. A complicated and time-consuming rationing system and long lines at every shop created difficulties even for families that remained intact and especially intensified the hardships for single parents. Although shortages and rationing affected homefronts everywhere, they were more severe in France than in any other Western country except Italy.[3] The military allowances paid by the government to prisoners' families failed to keep up with the cost of living, especially in urban areas.[4] Wives of prisoners were also under pressure to send their husbands the two packages a month they were allowed, since the food and clothing provided by the Germans was insufficient.[5]

Work outside the home was the only solution for many wives, but for those with children it created as many problems as it solved. Many women had to move in with their parents to survive. Parents or in-laws often helped reduce the burden of housework and childcare, though relying on them could create problems. One woman reported, "I am very satisfied with it. It's easier to bear

3. Robert Paxton, *Vichy France* (New York: W. W. Norton, 1972), 281. Germany only experienced hardship toward the end of the war, and its policy stipulated that occupied countries have a lower standard of living than Germany (310, 360). For example, in France the official meat ration in 1942 was 20 grams a day (less than an ounce), compared to the prewar consumption of 111 grams a day, and caloric intake dropped to 1,200 a day. See Henri Amouroux, *La vie des français sous l'occupation* (Paris: Librairie Arthème Fayard, 1961), 143, 146.

4. Prisoners of war, under the Geneva Convention, remain mobilized soldiers. For officers, a complex system of pay depending on rank, years of service, and martial status existed. Officers and NCOs could have one-half to three-quarters of their military pay sent to their wives or dependent parents. The system of military allowances paid to families of regular soldiers without resources was extended in 1940 to POW families. Regular soldiers' wives with incomes below a certain level could apply to their local government for military allowances. In July, 1942, it was decreed that all prisoners' families were entitled to these allowances, yet for reasons of economy an income ceiling still determined eligibility. *Guide pratique des familles de prisonniers de guerre et de prisonniers rapatriés, droits et avantages* (Paris: Charles Lavauzelle, 1944).

5. Durand, *Captivité*, 200. Under the Geneva Convention POWs' rations were supposed to be equal to those of the German army, but this was rarely the case.

the absence."[6] But others experienced tension: "My parents spoil the children too much."[7]

Being the wife of a prisoner meant making difficult decisions, sometimes for the first time, about the family's income, budget, housing, and so on. Initially, historians might assume that running their households alone would increase women's confidence and perhaps result in more egalitarian marriages after the men returned. But this was not usually the case, since the policy of the French state at Vichy and the corresponding atmosphere in France, both the result of the disastrous defeat of June, 1940, promoted traditional roles for women in the family.

The defeat left France demoralized. The belief that the French army, the victor of the Great War, was invincible behind the Maginot Line was brutally destroyed in what has since been called the debacle of June 1940. Shock, humiliation, and disbelief prompted a search for scapegoats and led to the idea that the defeat was punishment for such sins of the Third Republic as paid vacations, pernod, strikes, bad films, bathing suits, democracy, lack of religion, the low birth rate, and the decline of the French family.[8] Philippe Pétain, head of the new French State at Vichy, believed that "the disaster is only, in reality, the reflection on the military plane of the weaknesses and defects of the previous political regime."[9] Only by returning to the conditions of its pre-republican past could France be revived.

Although not all the members of the Vichy government agreed with Pétain's vision, Vichy's external facade throughout the war was characterized by the traditional Catholic conservatism of Pétain, Weygand, and Lamirand.[10] This conservatism permeated not only government propaganda but also radio broadcasts, newspaper articles and editorials, programs for schools and youth groups, and so on. Pétain called for a National Revolution to undo the work of the 1789 Revolution and restore an authoritarian, hierarchical, family-centered society of farmers and artisans led by a "natural aristocracy." The motto "Liberty, Equality, Fraternity" was discarded in favor of "Work, Family, Fatherland."

Rebuilding the French family and thereby increasing the population was central to this scheme. Pétain believed "a people is a hierarchy of families."[11]

6. *Femmes d'absents . . . Témoignages,* Recueillis par les Associations de Femmes de Prisonniers et le Mouvement Populaire des Familles (Paris: Editions du Cerf, 1945), 15.

7. Ibid., 38.

8. Jacques Duquesne, *Les catholiques français sous l'occupation* (Paris: Grasset, 1966), 26–27.

9. Philippe Pétain, *Paroles aux français* (Lyon: Lardanchet, 1941), 78.

10. Paxton, *Vichy France,* 139–45, 271–73.

11. Pétain, *Paroles,* 128.

Not the individual but "the family is the essential cell; it is the very foundation of the social edifice; on it we must build. . . . In the new order we are instituting, the family will be honored, protected, aided."[12]

Although the Vichy regime blamed the low birth rate and the other "causes" of France's defeat on the Third Republic, the Third Republic had in fact already set in place most of the family and pronatalist policies that Vichy adopted and amplified. Pronatalism had been present in France since before the turn of the century, when a declining birth rate led to predictions that France stood in danger of losing its position as a great power. Concern turned to fear and even panic after the bloodletting of the First World War, and in the 1920s the Republic passed laws against contraception and abortion. Though the case of Nazi Germany demonstrates that pronatalism does not necessarily focus on the family, in French legislation the two were always linked.[13] For example, Nazi Germany rewarded procreation with a Mother's Cross;[14] its counterpart in France, instituted in 1920, was designated the Medal of the French Family, thus explicitly linking procreation and the family. A bronze medal was awarded to the mother of five children, a silver for eight, and a gold for ten; however, the children had to be legitimate,[15] whereas the Nazis encouraged women to bear children of superior racial stock out of wedlock.[16] The Third Republic also created Mother's Day and in its final year passed an extensive Family Code whose stated goals were both to increase the birth rate and to "protect the family cell from a moral point of view."[17] Thus Vichy and the Third Republic differed not so much in their ideas about the family and

12. Ibid., 168.

13. Robert Talmy describes the conflict of the 1920s and 1930s between the pronatalist groups and those whose emphasis was on strengthening the family. Robert Talmy, *Histoire du mouvement familial en France (1896–1939),* vol. 1 (Paris: L'Union Nationale des Caisses d'Allocations Familiales, 1962), 206–309. However, the legislation passed by the Third Republic clearly integrated both pronatalist and profamily ideas (2:5–52, 218, 241). Another discussion of French pronatalism and family movements and their impact on French feminism is Karen Offen's "Depopulation, Nationalism, and Feminism in Fin-de-Siècle France," *The American Historical Review* 89, 3 (June 1984), 648–76.

14. Tim Mason, "Women in Germany, 1925–1940: Family, Welfare, Work," pt. 1, *History Workshop* 1 (Spring 1976), 83.

15. *Les prisonniers et la famille* (Paris: L'Office de Propagande Générale, 1943), 51.

16. Most of Nazi Germany's population policy was directed at the family; however, some policies undermined traditional family values. For example, the status of unwed mothers was improved; Himmler set up the infamous *Lebensborn,* maternity homes for unwed mothers of children conceived by "racially valuable" men, especially members of the SS; and toward the end of the war Hitler considered a policy of selective polygamy to make up for the loss of men, improve the race, and reward the male elite of the Reich. See Richard J. Evans, "German Women and the Triumph of Hitler," *The Journal of Modern History* 48, 1, suppl. (March 1976), 24–25.

17. *Journal Officiel,* July 30, 1939. Thierry Vignal writes: "The creation of the Family Code was

natality as in their approaches. Vichy strengthened many of the Third Republic's laws, intervened more actively,[18] and funded a full-scale propaganda campaign with photographs, newspaper and magazine features, posters, and radio shows promoting traditional and large families.[19] Vichy encouraged early marriage, many children, and domesticity for wives supported by the hard work of their husbands. "Happiness?" asked one publicity insert: "a wife, a home . . . children."[20]

POW families, left in women's hands while their husbands were in German camps or *kommandos* and unable to produce any "legitimate" children, were to Vichy an anomaly and accordingly treated as "families without heads."[21] Vichy's primary effort was to get the prisoners of war home,[22] but it also sought to help their families, which without fathers were believed to be in considerable danger of disintegration. Vichy paid military allowances to families whose income was below a certain level, granted all prisoners' families tax immunity, ordered landlords to lower their rent by 75 percent, and set up a National Solidarity Fund to which wives of POWs could apply for emergency help.[23]

Vichy also attempted to bolster prisoners' families morally. Family and Health Secretary Jacques Chevalier, in a letter of July 1941 to Darlan, leader of the Vichy government, warned of the dangers of neglecting these families. He described the "considerable development of prostitution by women and minors . . . and the numerous births of children with German fathers." To him, it was "a matter of saving women and children for whom the collectivity has responsibility while the heads of the families are captive."[24] Vichy had passed a law in April, 1941, making divorce more difficult to obtain and forbidding it

---

inspired by the thought that a *population policy* was *inseparable* from a *family policy*" [his emphasis]. *Bibliographie analytique de la politique démographique de la France depuis 1939* (Mémoire, Conservatoire National des Arts et Métiers, 1960), 7.

18. For example, although abortion had been illegal before the war, Vichy handed down unprecedented sentences of twenty years to life for performing abortions and one midwife was executed, on July 30, 1943. See Roger H. Guerrand, *La libre maternité, 1896–1969* (Paris: Casterman, 1971), 110.

19. Archives Nationales, AGII 27, 459, 497, 498, 543, 605, F41 291.

20. Archives Nationales, AGII 498.

21. Robert Moreau, "Repatriated Prisoners and the Families of Prisoners," *France during the German Occupation,* ed. Hoover Institution on War, Revolution and Peace, trans. Philip W. Whitcomb (Stanford: Stanford University Press, 1957), 212.

22. Durand, *Captivité,* 312–33.

23. *Journal Officiel,* May 20, October 5, 1939, May 23, November 17, 1941, February 15, July 20, 1942.

24. Archives Nationales, AGII 459.

during the first three years of marriage,[25] but this was not enough. In December, 1942, to "protect the dignity of the household from which the husband is absent due to circumstances of war," a law was passed that punished adultery with the wife of a prisoner with jail terms of three months to three years and fines of 1,500 to 2,500 francs.[26]

While Vichy policy toward prisoners' wives and children was pragmatic, the extension of these policies to the prisoners themselves was curiously fanciful. The General Family Commission put out a booklet entitled *Prisoners of War and the Family* and directed specifically at POWs. The three evils, according to the booklet, were "too few births, marriages too weak, families too weak."[27] Even Vichy must have realized that the prisoners, much as they might have agreed with the goal of large families, were hardly able to remedy the situation while captive. But the government felt that prisoners of war had an important role to play in the reassertion of traditional Christian values. Those who saw France's defeat as punishment for its sins felt redemption could only come through suffering, and the prisoners of war were those who suffered most from the defeat. If they meditated on the "misfortunes of the fatherland" while they were exiled from France, this reasoning went, they would be purified and would return to save the country.[28] With this in mind, Vichy sent many brochures to the POW camps outlining the flaws of the Third Republic and setting forth the reforms of the National Revolution. The commission believed, "France will truly, durably recover only if the French family first recovers."[29] Although the prisoners were removed from their families, Vichy wanted them to consider and renounce such destroyers of family life as childlessness, adultery, divorce, pornography, abortion, egoism, and alcoholism. The prisoners of war could save France "by preparing themselves right away . . . to become good rebuilders of the French family."[30] How were they to prepare? The Commission suggested setting up exhibitions and holding lectures and discussions on the family in the prison camps.

While the prisoners were supposedly meditating on the problems of France,[31] their wives struggled to survive at home, pulled in opposite direc-

25. *Journal Officiel,* April 2, 1941.
26. Ibid., December 26, 1942.
27. *Les prisonniers et la famille,* 10.
28. Ibid., 5.
29. Ibid.
30. Ibid., 66.
31. In fact the 95 percent of them sent to work on German *kommandos* had little time for meditation. Pierre Gascar, *Histoire de la captivité des français en Allemagne* (Paris: Gallimard, 1967), 94.

tions by the demands they had to meet and the conservative atmosphere of France and its government promoting a family ideal they could not hope to fulfill. The prisoners of war led difficult and depressing lives, but they were removed from the responsibilities of a family and had each other for companionship and support. Their wives, at least initially, faced their problems alone. They were not, however, passive victims of external forces. To overcome loneliness and isolation, prisoners' wives in France formed what we would call support groups to deal with their many hardships. "No one better understands a prisoner's wife than another prisoner's wife," one group stated. "Together, joining arms, we will be less cold and have less fear. We will struggle against misery and temptation, against loneliness and the blues."[32]

The two main groups were the Fédération des Associations de Femmes de Prisonniers (FAFP) in the south, and the Service des Femmes de Prisonniers, part of the Mouvement Populaire des Families (MPF), in the north. They threw Christmas parties for the families of prisoners of war, sponsored benefits to raise money for the prisoners or their families, visited the wives of prisoners in hospitals, and carried out and published the results of a survey, two monthly papers, and a short novel about a POW wife. Describing themselves as *soeurs d'épreuve* (sisters of the ordeal), they met to comfort each other and discuss their mutual problems.[33] They also left a valuable record of their views and attitudes, which appear to be representative of prisoners' wives in general.[34]

Although the goal was "camaraderie outside all politics,"[35] one issue of the FAFP's paper pressured the government to increase benefits for wives. Even this rare appeal was framed within the traditionalist rhetoric of the government, since the women knew that their claim was based on their status as wives

32. *Femmes d'absents,* "Fêtes et saisons" (Paris, 1943), 18. Although "Fêtes et Saisons" is the publisher, I will refer to this paper throughout as *Femmes d'absents,* "Fêtes et Saisons" to differentiate it from other works with similar titles.

33. *Femmes d'absents, causerie faite à des prêtres rapatriés* (Lyon: Imprimerie du Salut Public, 1944), 10.

34. The papers the organizations published were apolitical in nature—although they were submitted to the regional censor in Lyon, censoring of the articles was rare (in one instance they were told not to mention the location of a factory where POWs worked). All the women who wrote for the papers were prisoners' wives; none were professional journalists. In May, 1943, the FAFP counted 40,000 members and 1,200 local leaders and associations in every major city in the south. *Compte rendu de la journée des Présidentes* (Lyon: Fédération des Associations de Femmes de Prisonniers, n.d.) After the two groups merged in 1944, they claimed to have 150,000 members *(Femmes de Prisonniers,* "Notre Combat". The survey, *Femmes d'absents . . . témoignages,* conducted in 1943, was published after the Liberation. All these papers and books are available at either the Bibliothèque Nationale in Paris, its Annèxe in Versailles, or the Bibliothèque de Documentation Internationale Contemporaine in Nanterre.

35. "Comment elles s'entr'aident," *Femmes d'absents,* "Fêtes et saisons," 18.

of the "suffering sons" of France. "We entreat them [the public authorities] to remember the promises made by France to its captive sons. . . . All the French are suffering. But are not prisoners' wives seniors in suffering? And this title, together with THEIR RIGHTS, permits us perhaps to claim what we judge indispensable to our dignity and to THEIR DIGNITY, to our life and to THEIR LIFE."[36] The papers dealt primarily with the problems and fears of prisoners' wives, offering suggestions, advice, inspiring stories, and recipes. Much of the advice reveals an internal turmoil which paralleled the confusing external pressures. The independence they gained from taking on new responsibilities contradicted their own acceptance of a traditional family structure and resulted in an uncomfortable ambiguity which emerges in their writings about themselves and their new roles. They describe themselves both as weak and emotional and as strengthened by this experience, as needing their husbands but gaining new, so-called masculine qualities. The papers suggested that one way to resolve this internal conflict was to think of themselves as temporary heads of families without heads.

Maintaining a strong sense of the prisoner's presence while he was away allowed women to adjust successfully to the separation without upsetting the basic pattern of the relationship. Agnès Griot in her article "The Rules of Happiness" recommended simple and tender letters telling husbands everything. The important thing was "to act as if he were there. . . . Ask his advice, because he is still the Father and the Head."[37] Eliane Clause recommended, "[l]ive with him every day. . . . Do everything as if he were there."[38] Living as if he were there, writing him all the details of daily life and asking his advice before making major decisions were the most frequently offered, though not always the most practical, suggestions. Keeping his photo in a prominent place was another. One woman kept several jars of jam she and her husband had made together for when he returned; another bought birthday gifts for him and kept them in a box.[39] Yet another wife wrote, "[f]or me he is still the head of the family. . . . [N]o one sits in his place; his empty armchair is there waiting for him, I never offer it."[40]

Prisoners' wives felt it important to keep the image and memory of the father

36. Fédération des Associations de Femmes de Prisonniers, "Pour notre dignité," *Femmes de Prisonniers*. These papers have no volume numbers, and the publication date is often covered by the Bibliothèque Nationale call number. The only way to indicate a specific issue is by referring to the article on the front page, in this case "Pour notre dignité."

37. Agnès Griot, "Les règles du bonheur," *Femmes de Prisonniers,* "Espoir."

38. Eliane Clause, "Il reviendra," *Femmes de Prisonniers,* "Espoir."

39. Ibid.

40. *Femmes d'absents . . . témoignages,* 69.

alive in the children as well. As Eliane Clause put it, "Make him live in their little hearts. Interest them in the letter received, in the packages."[41] Making his presence vivid reminded children that the situation was temporary and would make the father's return easier. An article entitled "They Are Waiting Too" specifically addressed this issue. It was important to prevent not only the father's becoming a stranger to his children but also his becoming an idealized superman. Children who forgot that their fathers were human would be disappointed when he returned, as "little by little, the hero of the early days becomes a tiresome and disappointing troublemaker." They recommended painting "a real portrait of Papa and not an idealized person. . . . [D]o not represent the captive as a distributor of indulgences and sweets."[42]

This attempt to maintain a sense of the absent men's presence responded also to the prisoners' concern that the country and perhaps even their own families had forgotten them. One M. Peugnat, a recently repatriated prisoner, described his return in the March, 1942, issue of *Femmes de Prisonniers*. After a warm welcome from his wife, he asked himself, "[b]ut what will my little Jean-Pierre say to me? He was so small when I left. . . . Apprehension. . . . Will he say 'Hello Sir'?" To his great relief, Jean-Pierre called him "Papa," and Peugnat praised his wife's efforts. "There is all the work of the mother during forty-one months. She raised the children in the cult of the return."[43] On a deeper level, the prisoners feared the loss of their position within the family and in society itself.

For prisoners' wives, the raising of children brought out the contradiction between the way society and they saw themselves and what they needed to do to succeed. Being the sole parent in a society that stressed the patriarchal family and paternal authority even in the father's absence added to the complications. Many women felt the father should be the one to discipline the children and agreed it was important to "maintain [the] husband's position in the household as well as his moral authority."[44] The confusion they felt over their children emerges from the 1943 survey. One woman wrote, "[t]he big difficulty is raising my children alone." Although she admitted her children were "not very disobedient," still, "the father's authority is lacking."[45] In an even more contradictory paragraph a woman claimed, "[t]he father's absence is detrimental to their education and their character," but, she went on, "I don't

41. Clause, "Il reviendra."
42. Hélène and Maurice Bourel, "Ils attendent, eux aussi," *Femmes de Prisonniers,* "Espoir."
43. M. Peugnat, "Un retour . . . " *Femmes de Prisonniers,* "Fermeté!"
44. Bourel, "Ils attendent."
45. *Femmes d'absents . . . témoignages,* 19–20.

have the impression that if the father had always been present, they would have evolved differently."[46]

Children could also be a comfort. "If children to raise alone are a great worry, a torment, what a consolation! I pity with all my heart the wives who don't have any."[47] Still, childrearing intensified women's internal ambivalence about their proper role in the family because it compelled them to take responsibility for and impose their wills upon somebody else. Some women had trouble asserting themselves with their children, as did the wife who wrote, "[t]he children give me a lot of trouble: neither willing to help nor obedient, especially the eldest whose character is very difficult and who does not help me at all. I lack the desirable authority."[48]

Women who felt uncomfortable being the head of the family sometimes assumed the role of delegate of the father to assert authority over children. The title of one article, "His Children and Me," expresses this view. This prisoner's wife insists, "I need him so much to be a good mother" and agree that one must act as if he were there and let the children know his authority is ultimate. On the other hand, she describes the struggle to overcome her own weakness in order to adopt the "virile qualities of the absent one."[49] The prisoners were also concerned with this problem. Joseph Foliet reported that his fellow POWs wondered, "[i]s she succeeding in imposing herself on the children with difficult characters?" In his view, a prisoner's wife should "replace the father . . . extend his will . . . make herself energetic and virile. . . . At every moment she must ask herself, 'What does my husband want? What would he do in my position?' "[50] Again, the advice is not to become an authoritative mother, but to take on a masculine, fatherly role, which the husband could resume when he returned.

This program of maintaining the husband's presence and raising the children as if he were there is related to another constant motif of this literature, "the wait." Unlike war widows, prisoners' wives were in a temporary situation. Although they avoided the inevitable decline in standard of living that befell German war widows after World War One,[51] the situation's lack of finality left these women in a state of suspended animation. In addition to adjusting to

46. Ibid., 30–31.

47. Ibid., 20.

48. Ibid., 21–22.

49. "Ses enfants et moi," *Femmes d'absents,* "Fêtes et Saisons," 12.

50. Joseph Foliet, "Comment élève-t-elle nos petits?" *Femmes de Prisonniers,* "Ceux qui sont revenus," 3–4.

51. See Karin Hausen, "The German Nation's Obligation to the Heroes' Widows of World War I," this volume.

separation and absence, they also had to focus their lives on a return that would occur some time in the future and that seemed somehow to depend on them. The frequent use of the future tense in these articles indicates this mode of thinking. "He Will Return" is the title of Eliane Clause's article. She claimed that the return would be "what we have made it every day of our wait."[52] A writer named N. Ulrich, writing about the possible problems of the return, could give her fellow wives little specific advice. "But when the absence ends, when communal life starts again, when your mutual life. . . . finds again its great flame that enlightens and warms, the problems of the return will appear to you in their true light."[53]

If little practical advice was offered, the authors of these articles did try to bring the wait into the range of more common female experiences by picturing it in images familiar to them. Clause compared it to the period of engagement before marriage, while Ulrich compared it to the joy of a mother anticipating the birth of her first child.[54]

The wait was a theme that also took on explicitly Christian overtones. Just as the prisoners would be redeemed by the suffering of their exile, their wives would be strengthened by the wait. Even the marriage might be strengthened. One woman wrote to her husband, "[f]or both of us the ordeal will have ripened our love; it will be more beautiful, grander, more noble because it will have suffered."[55] As a Catholic prepares for each sacrament, prisoners' wives were to prepare for the return. The booklet *Femmes d'absents,* published by Fêtes et Saisons, a division of the Catholic publisher Les Editions du Cerf, included a liturgy of waiting.[56]

The problems that might arise after the return were as worrisome to many women as the absence itself, increasing the anxiety of the wait. Hence preparation for reunion was crucial, especially on the part of the wives. One article explained that the success or failure of the return was the wife's responsibility. Marriage created a common flame which separation had divided into little "uncertain and flickering watch lights." Whether the flame would rekindle "depends for the most part on the wife, who by vocation is the guardian of the flame."[57]

Thus prisoners' wives, in addition to running their households alone, were

52. Clause, "Il reviendra."
53. N. Ulrich, "Les problèmes du retour," *Femmes de Prisonniers,* "Espoir."
54. Clause, "Il reviendra"; Ulrich, "Les problèmes du retour."
55. "Elles leur écrivent," *Femmes d'absents,* "Fêtes et Saisons," 20.
56. "Liturgie de l'attente," *Femmes d'absents,* "Fêtes et Saisons," 4–5.
57. "Le feu qui reprend mal," *Femmes d'absents,* "Fêtes et Saisons," 27.

expected to dedicate their lives to preparing for their husbands' return. They had somehow to obtain enough money for their families to survive, decide how to spend it, maintain the house, discipline the children, and at the same time keep his presence alive, ask his advice before acting. They had to replace the father and at the same time "prepare themselves to let him resume his responsibilities . . . because he is the head of the family."[58] This sense of being a family without a head, of being in a limbo of waiting, of being a single parent yet acting as though the other parent were still there, was not simply imposed by a patriarchal society and government: the women themselves shared these views and expressed the resulting anxieties in their writings. Their situation differed, for example, from that of wives of American prisoners of war in Vietnam, who developed qualities of independence and leadership at a time of increased pressure for women's rights.

As Joan Scott points out, since war is represented as disorder in sexual terms, peace is often followed by the reassertion of order and traditional gender relations.[59] Madame Paumier, a POW wife interviewed recently by Yves Durand, summed up the situation: "When one has lived all alone with the children, assumed alone the family responsibilities, one becomes a bit used to this independent existence." She ends by admitting, "[i]t took some readjusting."[60] Another wife wrote in 1943 that her new responsibilities weighed heavily on her. "I will abandon them little by little, with pleasure, to my husband as he readapts."[61]

Many of these French women may have become stronger, more self-reliant and independent, as a result of this experience, but the norms and values of the society in which they lived prescribed that the husband should reassert his authority when he returned. As ideas about POW families indicate, family and population policies and the attitudes underlying them have shown remarkable continuity in twentieth-century France despite drastic economic and political changes. After the war, as Jane Jenson points out,[62] even politicians committed to equal rights for women retained traditional ideas about their role in the family, with the result that married women did not gain full civil equality until the mid-1960s.

58. "Simples conseils," *Femmes d'absents,* "Fêtes et Saisons," 28.
59. Joan Scott, "Rewriting History," this volume.
60. Durand, *Captivité,* 230.
61. *Femmes d'absents . . . témoignages,* 67.
62. Jane Jenson, "The Liberation and New Rights for French Women," this volume.

PART FOUR

Postwar Traces

SANDRA M. GILBERT

Soldier's Heart: Literary Men, Literary Women, and the Great War

This great war . . . is Nature's vengeance—is God's vengeance upon the people who held women in subjection, and by doing that have destroyed the perfect, human balance.
—*Christabel Pankhurst,* The Suffragette

As we have all been told over and over again, World War I was not just the war to end wars; it was also the war of wars, a paradigm of technological combat, which with its trenches and zeppelins, its gases and mines, has become a diabolical summary of the idea of modern warfare—Western science bent to the service of Western imperialism, the murderous face of Galileo revealed at last. That this apocalypic Great War involved strikingly large numbers of men as well as shockingly powerful technological forces, moreover, has always been understood to intensify its historical significance. The first modern war to employ the now familiar techniques of conscription and classification in order

Reprinted in slightly altered form from *Signs: Journal of Women in Culture and Society* 8, 3 (1983), 422–50. This essay is an abbreviated version of a chapter in *No Man's Land: The Place of the Woman Writer in the Twentieth Century,* a sequel to *The Madwoman in the Attic* which I am writing in collaboration with Susan Gubar, to whom I am indebted throughout this piece. The essay also draws upon my "Costumes of the Mind: Transvestism as Metaphor in Modern Literature," *Critical Inquiry* 7, 2 (Winter 1980), 391–417, and I wish to thank the editors for permission to reprint several passages. Elaine Showalter, Elliot Gilbert, Garrett Stewart, and the members of the Summer Seminar for College Teachers that Susan Gubar and I codirected in 1981 have all given me useful advice and essential support. Gayle Greene (at Scripps College) and David Savage (at Lewis and Clark College) shared with me two brilliant student papers by Tamara Jones (Scripps) and Elizabeth Cookson (Lewis and Clark), whose revisionary research renews my confidence in the contribution women's studies has made to the undergraduate curriculum. The illustrations are reproduced with the kind permission of the Imperial War Museum in London.

to create gigantic armies on both sides, World War I, as we have all been taught, virtually completed the Industrial Revolution's construction of anonymous dehumanized man, that impotent cipher who is frequently thought to be the twentieth century's most characteristic citizen. Helplessly entrenched on the edge of No Man's Land, this faceless being saw that the desert between him and his so-called enemy was not just a metaphor for the technology of death and the death dealt by technology, it was also a symbol for the state, whose nihilistic machinery he was powerless to control or protest. Fearfully assaulted by a deadly bureaucracy on the one side and a deadly technocracy on the other, he was No Man, an inhabitant of the inhumane new era and a citizen of the unpromising new land into which this war of wars had led him.[1]

Of course, as we have also been taught, these many dark implications of World War I had further implications for twentieth-century literature. As Malcolm Bradbury puts it, "Many critics have seen the war as . . . the apocalypse that leads the way into Modernism [and] as violation, intrusion, wound, the source of psychic anxiety [and] generational instability."[2] From Lawrence's paralyzed Clifford Chatterley to Hemingways's sadly emasculated Jake Barnes to Eliot's mysteriously sterile Fisher King, the gloomily bruised modernist antiheroes churned out by the war suffer specifically from sexual wounds, as if, having traveled literally or figuratively through No Man's Land, all have become not just No Men, nobodies, but *not* men, *un*men. That twentieth-century Everyman, the faceless cipher, their authors seem to suggest, is not just publicly powerless, he is privately impotent.

Obviously, however, such effects of the Great War were in every case gender-specific problems, problems only men could have. Never having had public power, women could hardly become more powerless than they already were. As for private impotence, most late Victorian young girls were trained to see such "passionlessness" as a virtue rather than a failure.[3] Yet women too lived through these years, and many modernist writers seem to suggest that, oddly, women played an unusually crucial part in the era. In D. H. Lawrence's 1915 "Eloi, Eloi, Lama Sabacthani," for instance—a representative, if somewhat feverish, wartime poem—the unmanning terrors of combat lead not just to a generalized sexual anxiety but also to a sexual anger directed specifically

1. On the war's dark psychological consequences for men, see Paul Fussell, *The Great War and Modern Memory* (New York: Oxford University Press, 1975); and Eric Leed, *No Man's Land: Combat and Identity in World War I* (New York: Cambridge University Press, 1979).

2. Malcolm Bradbury, "The Denuded Place: War and Form in *Parade's End* and *U.S.A.*," in *The First World War in Fiction,* ed. Holger Klein (London: Macmillan, 1976), 193–94.

3. See Nancy Cott, "Passionlessness: An Interpretation of Victorian Sexual Ideology, 1790–1850," *Signs: Journal of Women in Culture and Society* 4, 2 (Winter 1978), 219–36.

against women, as if the Great War itself were a climactic episode in some battle of the sexes that had already been raging for years. Drawing upon the words Christ cried out as he died on the cross, the creator of Clifford Chatterley here presents the war metaphorically as a perverse sexual relationship that becomes a blasphemous (homo)sexual crucifixion.[4] As battle rages and death attacks, the speaker assumes in turn the terrifying roles of rapist and victim, deadly groom and dying bride. Lawrence's perversely revisionary primal scene is made even more terrible, however, by the voyeurism of a woman who peers "through the rents / In the purple veil" and peeps "in the empty house like a pilferer." Like the gaze of the Medusa, her look seems somehow responsible for male sufferings.

Can this be because the war, with its deathly parody of sexuality, somehow suggested female conquest? Because wives, mothers, and sweethearts were safe on the homefront, did the war appear in some peculiar sense their fault, a ritual sacrifice to their victorious femininity? At the center of his poem, Lawrence places a rhetorical question which seems to imply as much: "Why do the women follow us, satisfied / Feed on our wounds like bread, receive our blood / Like glittering seed upon them for fulfillment?" Through a paradox that is at first almost incomprehensible, the war that has traditionally been defined as an apocalypse of masculinism seems here to have led to an apotheosis of the feminine. If we reflect upon this point, however, we must ask a set of questions about the relations between the sexes during this war of wars. What part, after all, *did* women play in the Great War? How did men perceive that role? More specifically, what connections might there be between the wartime activities of women and the sense of sexual wounding that haunts so many male modernist texts? Most important, did women themselves experience the wound of the war in the same way that their sons and lovers did?

If we meditate for a while on the sexual implications of the Great War, we must certainly decide, to begin with, that it is one of those classic cases of dissonance between official, male-centered history and unofficial female history about which Joan Kelly has written so tellingly.[5] For not only did the

4. D. H. Lawrence, *The Complete Poems,* ed. Vivian de Sola Pinto and F. Warren Roberts (New York: Penguin Books, 1977), 741–43. For similar, though more subdued expressions of the sexual anger the war evoked, see Wilfred Owen's "Greater Love" and "The Last Laugh," in *The Collected Poems of Wilfred Owen* (New York: New Directions, 1965), 41, 59; and Siegfried Sassoon's "Glory of Women," in his *Selected Poems* (London: Faber and Faber, 1968), 28. On Lawrence's wartime experience, see Paul Delany, *D. H. Lawrence's Nightmare* (New York: Basic Books, 1978).

5. Joan Kelly-Gadol, "Did Women Have a Renaissance?" in *Becoming Visible: Women in European History,* ed. Renate Bridenthal and Claudia Koonz (Boston: Houghton Mifflin, 1977), 137–64.

apocalyptic events of this war have a very different meaning for men and women, such events were in fact very different for men and women, a point understood almost at once by an involved contemporary like Vera Brittain, who noted about her relationship with her soldier fiancé that the war put "a barrier of indescribable experience between men and the women whom they loved. . . . Quite early I realized [the] possibility of a permanent impediment to understanding."[6] The nature of the barrier thrust between Brittain and her fiancé, however, may have been even more complex than she realized, for the impediment preventing a marriage of their true minds was constituted, as we shall see, not only by his altered experience but by hers. Specifically, I will argue here that as young men became increasingly alienated from their prewar selves, increasingly immured in the muck and blood of No Man's Land, women seemed to become, as if by some uncanny swing of history's pendulum, ever more powerful. As nurses, as mistresses, as munitions workers, bus drivers, or soldiers in the "land army," even as wives and mothers, these formerly subservient creatures began to loom malevolently larger, until it was possible for a visitor to London to observe in 1918 that "England was a world of women—women in uniforms,"[7] or, in the words of a verse by Nina Macdonald, "Girls are doing things / They've never done before / . . . / All the world is topsy-turvy / Since the War began."[8]

"All the world is topsy-turvy / Since the War began." This phrase is a crucial one, for the reverses and reversals of No Man's Land fostered in a number of significant ways the formation of a metaphorical country not unlike the queendom Charlotte Perkins Gilman called Herland, and the exhilaration (along with the anxiety) of that state is as dramatically rendered in wartime poems, stories, and memoirs by women as are the very different responses to the war in usually better-known works by men. Sometimes subtly and subversively, sometimes quite explicitly, writers from Alice Meynell to Radclyffe Hall explored the political and economic revolution by which the Great War at least temporarily dispossessed male citizens of the patriarchal primacy that had always been their birthright while granting women access to both the votes and the professions that they had never before possessed. Similarly, a number of these artists covertly or overtly celebrated the release of female desires. In

6. Vera Brittain, *Testament of Youth* (London: Fontana/Virago, 1979), 143.

7. Harriet Stanton Blatch, quoted in Nina Auerbach, *Communities of Women* (Cambridge: Harvard University Press, 1978), 162.

8. Nina Macdonald, "Sing a Song of War-Time," in *Scars upon My Heart: Women's Poetry and Verse of the First World War*, ed. Catherine Reilly (London: Virago, 1981), 69 (hereafter cited as *Scars*).

addition, many women writers recorded drastic (re)visions of society that were also, directly or indirectly, inspired by the revolutionary state in which they were living. For, as Virginia Woolf put it in a crucial passage from *Three Guineas,* "So profound was [the] unconscious loathing" of the daughters of educated (and uneducated) men for "the education" in oppression which all women had received, that while most "consciously desired" the advancement of " 'our splendid Empire,' " many "unconsciously desired" the apocalypse of "our splendid war."[9]

The words as well as the deeds of these women reinforced their male contemporaries' sense that "All the world is topsy-turvy / Since the War began" and thus intensified the misogynist resentment with which male writers defined this Great War as an apocalyptic turning point in the battle of the sexes. Not surprisingly either, therefore, the sexual gloom expressed by so many men as well as the sexual glee experienced by so many women ultimately triggered profound feelings of guilt in a number of women: to the guilt of the female survivor, with her fear that "a barrier of indescribable experience" had been thrust between the sexes, there was often added a half-conscious fear that she might be in an inexplicable way a perpetrator of some unspeakable crime. Thus, the invigorating sense of revolution, release, reunion, and re-vision with which the war paradoxically imbued so many women eventually darkened into reactions of anxiety and self-doubt as Herland and No Man's Land merged to become the Nobody's Land T. S. Eliot was to call "death's dream kingdom."[10]

REVOLUTION

From the first, of course, as Paul Fussell has shown, World War I fostered characteristically modernist irony in young men, inducting them into "death's dream kingdom" by revealing exactly how spurious were their visions of heroism, and—by extension—history's images of heroism.[11] Mobilized and marched off to the front, idealistic soldiers soon found themselves *im*mobilized, even buried alive, in trenches of death that seemed to have been dug along the remotest margins of civilizations. Here, as Eric Leed has brilliantly observed, all the traditional categories through which the rational cultured mind achieved its hegemony over the irrationality of nature were grotesquely

9. Virginia Woolf, *Three Guineas* (New York: Harcourt, Brace, 1938), 39.

10. T. S. Eliot, "The Hollow Men," in *Selected Poems of T.S. Eliot* (1925; repr. New York: Harcourt, Brace and World, 1964), 77–80.

11. Fussell, *The Great War,* 3–35.

mingled, polluting each other as if in some Swiftian fantasy.[12] Of his "hero," George Winterbourne, for instance, Richard Aldington tells us that "he lived among smashed bodies and human remains in an infernal cemetery," while Robert Graves describes snatching his "fingers in horror from where I had planted them on the slimy body of an old corpse."[13] Even Vera Brittain, safe for a while at home, observes that when the filthy clothes of her dead fiancé were returned from the front, "the mud of France which covered them [seemed] saturated with dead bodies."[14] No wonder, then, that before his death her Roland had written her bitterly about his spiritual metamorphosis and his radical alienation from the "normal" world she now seemed to inhabit without him: "I feel like a barbarian, a wild man of the woods [and] you seem to me rather like a character in a book or someone one has dreamt of and never seen."[15]

"A wild man of the woods": the phrase is significant, for, entering the polluted realm of the trenches, young men like Roland understood themselves to have been exiled from the very culture they had been deputized to defend. From now on, their only land was No Man's Land, a land that was *not,* a country of the impossible and the paradoxical. Here, Leed remarks, "[t]he retirement of the combatant into the soil produced a landscape suffused with ambivalence. . . . The battlefield was 'empty of men' and yet it was saturated with men."[16] Inevitably, such sinister invisibility combined with such deadly *being* created a sense of what Freud called the *unheimlich,* the uncanny. Yet of course No Man's Land was real in its bizarre unreality, and to become a denizen of that unreal kingdom was to become, oneself, unreal. Practically speaking, moreover, such a feeling of unreality or uncanniness was actually realistic. As Graves notes, "[t]he average life expectancy of an infantry subaltern on the Western Front was, at some stages of the War, only about three months,"[17] so that a universal sense of doom, often manifesting itself as a *desire* for death, forced the "wild man" soldier to ask, with the speaker of one of D. H. Lawrence's poems:

Am I lost?
Has death set me apart

12. Leed, *No Man's Land,* 18–19.

13. Richard Aldington, *Death of a Hero* (London: Chatto and Windus, 1929), 429; Robert Graves, *Goodbye to All That* (1929; repr. New York: Doubleday, 1957), 130.

14. Brittain, *Testament,* 252–53.

15. Ibid., 216.

16. Leed, *No Man's Land,* 20.

17. Graves, *Goodbye,* 59.

Imperial War Museum, London

Beforehand?
Have I crossed
That border?
Have I nothing in this dark land?[18]

Catapulted over the frontiers of civilization, the men of war had been transformed into dead-alive beings whose fates could no longer be determined according to the rules that had governed Western history from time immemorial (fig. 1).

With no sense of inherited history to lose, however, women in the terrible war years of 1914–18 would seem to have had, if not everything, at least something to gain: a place in public history, a chance, even, to make history. Wrote one former suffragist, "I knew nothing of European complications and cared less. . . . I asked myself if any horrors could be greater than the horrors of peace—the sweating, the daily lives of women on the streets."[19] Ultimately, such revolutionary energy and resolute feminism, together with such alienation from officially important events, led to a phenomenon usefully analyzed

18. Lawrence, "No News," *Poems,* 748–49.

19. Mabel Darmer, quoted in David Mitchell, *Women on the Warpath: The Story of the Women of the First World War* (London: Jonathan Cape, 1966), 161.

by Nina Auerbach: "Union among women . . . is one of the unacknowledged fruits of war"—and particularly during World War I, there was "a note of exaltation at the Amazonian countries created by the war, whose military elation spread from the suffrage battle to the nation at large."[20] For, of course, when their menfolk went off to the trenches to be literally and figuratively shattered, the women on the homefront literally and figuratively rose to the occasion and replaced them in farms and factories. The propagandist Jessie Pope's "War Girls" records the exuberance with which these women settled into "Amazonian countries." "Strong, sensible and fit, / They're out to show their grit," this writer exclaims approvingly, adding—as if in anticipation of Woolf—an important qualifier: "*No longer caged and penned up,* / They're going to keep their end up."[21] Picture after picture from the Imperial War Museum's enormous collection of photos portraying "women at war" illustrates her points. Liberated from parlors and petticoats alike, trousered war girls beam as they shovel coal, shoe horses, fight fires, drive buses, chop down trees, make shells, dig graves. Similarly, American women found that war, in the words of Harriet Stanton Blatch, "make[s] the blood course through the veins" because, by compelling "women to work," it sends them "over the top . . . up the scaling-ladder, and out into 'All Man's Land' " (fig. 2).[22]

Though it may be a coincidence, then, there is ironic point to the fact that Charlotte Perkins Gilman's *Herland,* with its vision of a female utopia created by a cataclysm that wiped out all the men, was published in Gilman's feminist journal *Forerunner* in 1915; and at least one feminist noted the accuracy of a cartoon in *Punch* depicting two women who "did not think the war would last long—it was too good to last."[23] As David Mitchell observes, "When the time came for demobilisation," many women "wept at the ending of what they now saw as the happiest and most purposeful days of their lives."[24] For despite the massive tragedy that the war represented for an entire generation of young men—and for their grieving wives, mothers, daughters, and sisters—it also represented their first rupture with a socioeconomic history that had heretofore denied most women chances at first-class jobs and pay.

To be sure, that denial persisted for a time. At the beginning of the war only a very small proportion of the women who registered as volunteers for war

20. Auerbach, *Communities,* 187.

21. Jessie Pope, "War Girls," in *Scars,* 90 (italics mine).

22. Quoted in J. Stanley Lemons, *The Woman Citizen: Social Feminism in the 1920s* (Urbana: University of Illinois Press, 1973), 15.

23. Mitchell, *Women on the Warpath,* 380.

24. Ibid.

Imperial War Museum, London

service in Great Britain were given employment. By the end of the war, however, the number of working women had increased by almost 50 percent, and seven hundred thousand of the women employed had directly replaced men in the work force.[25] Replacing men, moreover, these women finally received the kind of pay only men had earned in the past, so that many a working-class girl could join in the sardonic good cheer expressed by the speaker of Madeline Ida Bedford's "Munition Wages": "Earning high wages? Yus, / Five quid a week. / A woman, too, mind you, / I calls it dim sweet? (fig. 3).[26] Many a middle- or upper-class woman, too, could rejoice with Dr. Caroline Matthews, who asserted that because her medical services were needed at last "[l]ife was worth living in those days."[27] Or they could triumph

25. See Gail Braybon, *Women Workers in the First World War: The British Experience* (London: Croom Helm, 1981), 46–47; and Mary Cadogan and Patricia Craig, *Women and Children First: The Fiction of Two World Wars* (London: Gollancz, 1978), 32–33. For further information, see Mitchell, *Women on the Warpath;* and Maurine Weiner Greenwald, *Women, War and Work: The Impact of World War I and Women Workers in the United States* (Westport, Conn.: Greenwood Press, 1980).

26. Madeline Ida Bedford, "Munitions Wages," in *Scars,* 7.

27. Caroline Matthews, *Experiences of a Woman Doctor in Serbia* (London: Mills and Boon, 1916), 72; quoted in Elizabeth Cookson, "The Forgotten Women: British Nurses, VADs, and Doctors across the Channel" (unpublished paper), 17.

Imperial War Museum, London

with the novelist Edith Wharton, who claimed "the honour of having founded the first paying workroom in Paris," an *ouvroir* for "wives, widows, and young girls without near relatives in the army," and who filed for safekeeping the program of a 1917 New York bazaar for war relief called "Hero Land," which excitedly (and efficiently) offered "the greatest spectacle the world has ever known" in response to "the greatest need the world has ever known."[28]

Inevitably, however, the enthusiasm and efficiency with which women of all ranks and ages filled in the economic gaps men had left behind reinforced the soldiers' sickened sense that the war had drastically abrogated most of the rules that had always organized Western culture. From the first, after all, it had seemed to the man at the front that his life and limbs were forfeit to the comforts of the *home*front, so that civilians, male and female, were fictive inhabitants of a world that had effectively insulated itself from the trenches' city of dreadful night. Aldington's George Winterbourne goes to see his wife and his mistress, but "they were gesticulating across an abyss"; seventeen-year-old John Kipling, dead at the front by the time he was eighteen, wrote to Rudyard Kipling, his war-propagandist father, that "you people at home don't realize how spoilt you are"; and, enraged at the smugness of civilians, Siegfried Sassoon sits in a music hall and thinks, "I'd like to see a Tank come down the stalls, / Lurching to rag-time tunes, or 'Home, sweet Home.'"[29]

Ultimately, this barely veiled hostility between the front and the homefront, along with the exuberance of the women workers who had succeeded to (and in) men's places, suggested that the most crucial rule the war had overturned was that of patrilineal succession, the founding law of patriarchal society itself. For, as the early glamour of battle dissipated and Victorian fantasies of historical heroism gave way to modernist visions of irony and unreality, it became clear that this war to end all wars necessitated a sacrifice of the sons to the exigencies of the fathers—and the mothers, wives, and sisters. Even a patriotic bestseller like Ernest Raymond's *Tell England* (1922) implies, eerily, that, in the new dispensation of war, sons are no longer the inheritors of their families' wealth, they *are* that wealth—a currency of blood that must be paid out indefinitely in order to keep the world safe, not for democracy, but for old men and women of all ages. "Eighteen, by jove!" says a comfortable colonel to some schoolboys he is encouraging to enlist. "England's wealth used to consist

28. Wharton's notes on her *ouvroir* and other charities, as well as her program for "Hero Land," are held at the Beinecke Library, Yale University, New Haven, Conn.

29. Aldington, *Death of a Hero,* 259; John Kipling's unpublished letter of September 19, 1915, is held at the Rare Book Room, University of Sussex, Brighton, Eng.; Sassoon, *Selected Poems,* 17.

in other things. Nowadays you boys are the richest thing she's got."[30] Similarly, in "The Parable of the Old Man and the Young," Wilfred Owen retells the tale of "Abram" and Isaac to dramatize the generational conflict that, along with a sexual struggle, he and many other soldiers saw as one of the darkest implications of the Great War.[31]

That such a generational conflict was not just associated with but an integral part of the sexual struggle fostered by the war is made very clear in a poem by Alice Meynell, a long-time suffrage fighter, who accurately foresaw that through one of the grimmer paradoxes of history the Great War might force recalcitrant men to grant women, the stereotypical peacemakers, a viable inheritance in patriarchal society. In fact, her "A Father of Women" seems almost to explain the sexual anxiety of D. H. Lawrence, who lived with her family during part of the war, for the speaker of this verse answers some of the questions Lawrence had asked in "Eloi, Eloi, Lama Sabacthani":

Our father works in us,
The daughters of his manhood. Not undone
Is he, not wasted, though transmuted thus,
And though he left no son.[32]

She goes on to tell "[t]he million living fathers of the War" that they should finally "Approve, accept, know [us] daughters of men, / Now that your sons are dust." Ostensibly so calm and sympathetic, her last phrase can be read almost as a taunt, though it is certain she did not intend it that way. You have killed your sons, she seems to say, so now your daughters will inherit the world.

A devout Catholic and a "poet's poet," Meynell was clearly no war propagandist, yet some readers might well have felt that such a revolutionary vision of patriarchy "transmuted" by war aligned her with more frankly militaristic women writers. And of these there was a considerable number, a phenomenon which would also have reinforced male sexual anger by implying that women were eager to implore men to make mortal sacrifices by which they themselves would ultimately profit. For while their brothers groped through the rubble of No Man's Land for fragments to shore against the ruins of a dying culture, countless women manned the machines of state, urging more men to go off to battle. Robert Graves reprints a famous, indeed infamous, piece of

30. Quoted in Cadogan and Craig, *Women and Children First,* 92.

31. Owen, *Collected Poems,* 42.

32. Alice Meynell, "A Father of Women," in *Salt and Bitter and Good,* ed. Cora Kaplan (London: Paddington, 1975), 187–89.

propaganda in the form of a letter from a "little mother" who argued that women should gladly "pass on the human ammunition" of sons to the nation and declared ambiguously that "we will emerge stronger women to carry on the glorious work [their] memories have handed down to us."[33] Similarly, "Women of Britain Say—'*Go!*'" proclaimed one of the War Office's best-known posters (fig. 4), and the female censoriousness implicit in that slogan was made explicit by the fact that at times the vigorous, able-bodied war girls, who had once been judged wanting by even the weakest of young men, became frighteningly judgmental about their male contemporaries. Speaking with some disgust about "the instinct of pugnacity . . . that [is] so strong in women," Bernard Shaw describes "civilized young women handing white feathers to all young men who are not in uniform."[34] Metaphorically speaking, moreover, popular women writers like Jessie Pope and Mrs. Humphry Ward (in England), as well as more serious artists like May Sinclair (in England) or Edith Wharton and Willa Cather (in the United States), distributed white feathers to large audiences of noncombatant readers. "Who's for the trench— / Are you, my laddie?" asked Jessie Pope in her jingoistic "The Call"; May Sinclair described "the ecstasy" of battle in *The Tree of Heaven,* and Edith Wharton depicted the satisfactions of having "a son at the front" in her novel of that name.[35] It is no wonder, then, that Wilfred Owen's bitterly antiwar "Dulce et Decorum Est" with its violent imagery of gas-caused "vile, incurable sores on innocent tongues" was originally entitled "To Jessie Pope" and then "To A Certain Poetess" before its author decided, instead, on a bleak allusion to Horace's "Dulce et decorum est / Pro patria mori."[36] In the words of women propagandists as well as in the deeds of feather-carrying girls, the classical Roman's noble *patria* must have seemed to become a sinister, death-dealing *matria.*

Even the most conventionally angelic of women's wartime ministrations, however, must have suggested to many members of both sexes that, while men were now invalid and maybe in-valid, their sisters were triumphant survivors and destined inheritors. Certainly both the rhetoric and the iconography of nursing would seem to imply some such points. To be sure, the nurse presents

33. Graves, *Goodbye,* 229–30.

34. Bernard Shaw, quoted in Woolf, *Three Guineas,* 182. It is worth noting, however, that Woolf believed Shaw was exaggerating.

35. Jessie Pope, "The Call," in *Scars,* 88; May Sinclair, "Victory," in *The Tree of Heaven* (London: Cassell, 1917), no. 323; Edith Wharton, *A Son at the Front* (New York: Charles Scribner's Sons, 1923). For a sardonically masculinist view of women's propagandizing, see Aldous Huxley, "The Farcical History of Richard Greenow," in *Limbo* (New York: Doran, 1920).

36. Owen, *Collected Poems,* 55–56.

Imperial War Museum, London

herself as a servant of her patient. "Every task," writes Vera Brittain of her days as a VAD, "had for us . . . a sacred glamour."[37] Yet in works by both male and female novelists the figure of the nurse ultimately takes on a majesty which hints that she is mistress rather than slave, goddess rather than supplicant. After all, when men are immobilized and dehumanized, it is only these women who possess the old (matriarchal) formulas for survival. Thus, even while memoirists like Brittain express "gratitude" for the "sacred glamour" of nursing, they seem to be pledging allegiance to a *secret* glamour—the glamour of an expertise which they will win from their patients. "Towards the men," recalls Brittain, "I came to feel an almost adoring gratitude . . . for the knowledge of masculine functioning which the care of them gave me."[38]

Not surprisingly, this education in masculine functioning that the nurse experiences as a kind of elevation is often felt by her male patient as exploitation; her evolution into active, autonomous, transcendent subject is associated with his devolution into passive, dependent, immanent medical object. Lawrence writes in "The Ladybird" about a wounded middle-European prisoner who tells a visiting English Lady with whom he is falling in love that she must "let me wrap your hair round my hands like a bandage" because "I feel I have lost my manhood for the time being."[39] Hopelessly at the mercy of his aristocratic nurse, this helpless alien adumbrates wounded men who also appear in works by women—for example, the amnesiac hero of Rebecca West's *The Return of the Soldier,* whom a former girlfriend restores by gathering his "soul" into "her soul,"[40] and Lord Peter Wimsey in Dorothy Sayers's *Busman's Honeymoon,* who is so haunted by memories of the war that he confesses to his bride that "you're my corner and I've come to hide."[41]

Where nurses imagined by men often seem to have a sinister power, however, the nurses imagined by women appear, at least at first, to be purely restorative, positively (rather than negatively) maternal. The "grey nurse" whom Virginia Woolf describes in a notoriously puzzling passage in *Mrs. Dalloway* is thus a paradigm of her more realistically delineated sisters. Knitting steadily while Peter Walsh dozes, she seems "like the champion of the rights of sleepers" who responds to "a desire for solace, for relief." Yet even she is not an altogether positive figure. Like "The Greatest Mother in the World" depicted in Alonzo Earl Foringer's 1918 Red Cross War Relief poster—an enormous

37. Brittain, *Testament,* 210.

38. Ibid., 165–66.

39. D. H. Lawrence, "The Ladybird," in *Four Short Novels* (New York: Viking, 1923), 57.

40. Rebecca West, *The Return of the Soldier* (1918; repr. London: Virago, 1980), 144.

41. Dorothy L. Sayers, *Busman's Honeymoon* (1937; repr. New York: Avon, 1968), 316.

nurse cradling a tiny immobilized man on a doll-sized stretcher (fig. 5)—Woolf's grey nurse evokes a parodic Pietà in which the Virgin Mother threatens simultaneously to anoint and annihilate her long-suffering son, a point Woolf's imaginary male dreamer accurately grasps when he prays, "let me walk straight on to this great figure, who will . . . mount me on her streamers and let me blow to nothingness with the rest."[42] Does male death turn women nurses on? Do figures like the pious Red Cross mother experience bacchanalian satisfaction as, in Woolf's curiously ambiguous phrase, they watch their male patients, one-time oppressors, "blow [up] to nothingness with the rest?" A number of texts by men and women alike suggest that the revolutionary socioeconomic transformations wrought by the war's "topsy-turvy" role reversals did bring about a release of female libidinal energies, as well as a liberation of female anger, which men usually found anxiety-inducing and women often found exhilarating.

RELEASE, (RE)UNION, (RE)VISION

On the subject of erotic release, a severely political writer like Vera Brittain is notably restrained. Yet even she implies, at least subtextually, that she experienced some such phenomenon, for while she expresses her "gratitude" to the men from whom she learned about "masculine functioning," she goes on to thank the war that delivered their naked bodies into her hands for her own "early release from . . . sex-inhibitions."[43] Significantly, too, as if to confirm the possibility that Brittain did receive a wartime sex education, Eric Leed records the belief of some observers that "women in particular 'reacted to the war experience with a powerful increase in libido.' "[44] Was the war a festival of female misrule in which the collapse of a traditional social structure "permitted," as Leed puts it, "a range of personal contacts that had been impossible in [former lives] where hierarchies of status ruled?"[45] Certainly the testimony of male artists would seem to suggest such a notion.[46] In *Death of a Hero,* Richard Aldington is explicit about what he sees as the grotesque sexual permission the war has given women. Speaking of George Winterbourne's mother, he re-

42. Virginia Woolf, *Mrs. Dalloway* (New York: Harcourt, Brace, 1925), 85–87.

43. Brittain, *Testament,* 165–66.

44. Leed, *No Man's Land,* 47.

45. Ibid., 45.

46. It seems significant that in *Lady Chatterley's Lover* Ivy Bolton becomes Clifford's perversely sexual nurse and that Mellors's estranged wife Bertha has the same name as one of the war's principal guns—the "Big Bertha."

Imperial War Museum, London

marks that "the effect of George's death on her temperament was . . . almost wholly erotic." Similarly, Elizabeth and Fanny, George's wife and mistress, are "terribly at ease upon the Zion of sex, abounding in masochism, Lesbianism, sodomy, etcetera."[47] Comparable allegations against the deadliness of female desire are leveled in a number of Lawrence's stories, notably "Tickets Please" and "Monkey Nuts." In the first, a bacchanalian group of girl tram conductors band together to enact a ritual scene of reverse rape on a tram inspector with the significant Lawrentian name of John Thomas, while, in the second, a girl in the land army decides to seduce a passive young soldier and manifests the power of her perverse erotic will by putting "a soft pressure" on his waist that makes "all his bones rotten."[48]

Where male writers primarily recounted the horrors of unleashed female sexuality and only secondarily recorded the more generalized female excitement that energized it, however, women remembered, first, the excitement of the war and, second (but more diffusely), the sensuality to which such excitement led. Thus, where most male writers—at least after their earliest dreams of heroism had been deflated—associated the front with paralysis and pollution, many female writers imagined it as a place of freedom, ruefully comparing what they felt was their own genteel immobilization with the exhilaration of military mobility. In her "Many Sisters to Many Brothers," Rose Macaulay articulated their envy of the soldier's liberation from the dreariness of the home and the homefront: "Oh it's you that have the luck, out there in blood and muck."[49] To women who managed to get to the front, moreover, the war did frequently offer the delight of (female) mobilization rather than the despair of (male) immobilization. After all, for nurses and ambulance drivers, women doctors and women messengers, the phenomenon of modern battle was very different from that experienced by entrenched combatants. Finally given a chance to take the wheel, these post-Victorian girls raced motorcars along foreign roads like adventurers exploring new lands, while their brothers dug deeper into the mud of France (fig. 6). Retrieving the wounded and the dead from deadly positions, these once-decorous daughters had at last been allowed to prove their valor, and they swooped over the wastelands of the war with the energetic love of Wagnerian Valkyries, their mobility alone transporting countless immobilized heroes to safe havens.

47. Aldington, *Death of a Hero,* 12, 19.

48. D. H. Lawrence, *The Complete Short Stories,* 3 vols. (1922; repr. New York: Penguin, 1976), 2:343–44, 373.

49. Rose Macaulay, "Many Sisters to Many Brothers," in *Scars,* xxxv.

Imperial War Museum, London

It is no wonder, then, that even the roar of the guns seems often to have sounded in these women's ears like a glamorously dramatic rather than a gloomily dangerous counterpoint to adventure, and no wonder that even combat's bloodier aspects sometimes appeared to them like what Lawrence called "glittering seed" instead of wounding shrapnel. Thinking wistfully of an ambulance unit in Belgium that she had to leave, May Sinclair summarizes this ambiguously apocalyptic "joy of women in wartime" as a vision of high-speed travel through a world in the process of violent transformation. "You go," she tells her former mates in the Munro Corps, "under the thunder of the guns . . . / And where the high towers are broken / And houses crack like the staves of a thin crate."[50] Elsewhere, Sinclair confides about the excitement of combat, "What a fool I would have been if I hadn't come. I wouldn't have missed this run for the world."[51] Just as enthusiastically, VADs, drivers, and

50. Lorine Pruette's comment on "the joy of women in wartime" is quoted in Lemons, *Woman Citizen,* 15; May Sinclair is cited in Mitchell, *Women on the Warpath,* 129.

51. May Sinclair, "The War of Liberation: From a Journal," *English Review* 20–21 (June–July 1915), 170–71, quoted in Cookson, "Forgotten Women," 13.

nurses like Vera Brittain and Violetta Thurstan testify to "the exhilaration" of their departure from England, the "diversion" of bombings, the "thrill in the knowledge that we were actually in a country invaded by the enemy," and the "great fun!" of life at the front.[52]

If the testimony of these memoirists sounds inhumane or even inhuman, it is worth remembering that most are in some sense recounting their feeling that the Great War was the first historical event to allow (indeed to require) them to use their abilities and to be of use. Certainly Sinclair's account in *The Tree of Heaven* of the "exquisite moments of extreme danger" experienced by her heroes reflects a transference to men of the liberation she herself experienced when she worked in Belgium with the Munro Corps.[53] Similarly, when in *One of Ours* Cather celebrates Claude Wheeler's escape from rural Nebraska to wartime France—noting that "to be alive, to be conscious, to have one's faculties, was to be in the war" and associating the European cataclysm with the idea that now "the old . . . cages would be broken open for ever"—her vision of the doomed young man's good fortune is surely a way of dreaming her own release from the deadening decorum of the provincial prairie town where she had always longed to be a sturdy "Willie" rather than a submissive Willa.[54]

For many women, but perhaps in particular for lesbian women like Cather, whose refusal to identify with conventional "femininity" had always made their gender a problem to them, the war facilitated not just a liberation from the constricting trivia of parlors and petticoats but an unprecedented transcendence of the more profound constraints imposed by traditional sex roles. Most dramatically, this transcendence is described in Radclyffe Hall's two crucial postwar fictions—her short story entitled "Miss Ogilvy Finds Herself" and her more famous *The Well of Loneliness*. In the first, the aging lesbian Miss Ogilvy remembers, as she is being demobilized, that her ambulance was "the merciful emblem that had set [her] free," and she mourns the breaking up of the "glorious" all-female unit she has led.[55] Similarly, Stephen Gordon, the "invert" heroine of *The Well,* feels at the outset of the war like "a freak abandoned

52. Brittain, *Testament,* 292; Mrs. St. Clair Stobart, "A Woman in the Midst of War," *Ladies Home Journal* (January 1915), 5; B. G. Mure, "A Side Issue of the War," *Blackwood's* (October 1916), 446; *A War Nurse's Diary* (New York: Macmillan, 1918), 59; all quoted in Cookson, "Forgotten Women," 12–13.

53. Sinclair, *The Tree of Heaven,* 346–47.

54. Willa Cather, *One of Ours* (New York: Knopf, 1923), 416, 291.

55. In Radclyffe Hall, *Miss Ogilvy Finds Herself* (London: Heinemann, 1934), 3–4.

on a kind of no-man's land" (and Hall's metaphor is significant) but soon finds herself paradoxically metamorphosed into a member of a new women's battalion "that would never again be disbanded." For, explains Hall, "war and death" had finally, ironically, given "a right to life" to lesbians like Stephen, women who refused the traditions of femininity and the conventions of heterosexuality alike.[56]

To be sure, specifically erotic release was frequently associated with such a right to life, for Vera Brittain's sex education was complemented by the romantic permission given, in varying degrees, to heterosexual characters like Miranda in Katherine Anne Porter's "Pale Horse, Pale Rider" and to lesbian heroines like Miss Ogilvy and Stephen Gordon. In the first work, Porter's protagonist, falling in love with a young soldier, meditates happily on the "miracle of being two persons named Adam and Miranda" who are "always in the mood for dancing."[57] As for Miss Ogilvy, she goes off on a vacation and Hall grants her a dream of unleashed desire in which, transformed into a powerful primitive man, she makes love to a beautiful young woman, enthralled by the "ripe red berry sweet to the taste" of the female body.[58] Similarly, Stephen Gordon meets her lover, Mary Llewelyn, when they are sister drivers in the allegorically named Breakspeare ambulance unit, and after the war they too achieve a "new and ardent fulfillment" on a honeymoon in Spain.[59] Not coincidentally, perhaps, lesbian writers like Amy Lowell and Gertrude Stein produced some of their most ecstatic erotica during the war years. Lowell's "Two Speak Together," for instance, a tribute to her lover/companion Ada Russell, appeared in the same 1919 volume with her darkly elegiac "Dreams in Wartime," while "Lifting Belly," Stein's most famous encoded celebration of lesbian sexuality, was composed, according to Richard Kostelanetz, between 1915 and 1917, the same years in which, in *The Autobiography of Alice B. Toklas,* she recounts her ambivalently cheerful experiences of the war.[60] Recording "real life," Vita Sackville-West wrote of how her love

56. Radclyffe Hall, *The Well of Loneliness* (London: Cape, 1928), 315, 319.

57. Katherine Anne Porter, "Pale Horse, Pale Rider," in *Pale Horse, Pale Rider* (1936; repr. New York: Modern Library, 1939), 198.

58. Hall, "Miss Ogilvy Finds Herself," 34.

59. Hall, *Well of Loneliness,* 366.

60. Amy Lowell, *The Complete Poetical Works* (1919; repr. Boston: Houghton Mifflin, 1955), 209–18, 237–41; Gertrude Stein, "The War," in *The Autobiography of Alice B. Toklas,* in *The Selected Writings of Gertrude Stein* (1933; repr. New York: Vintage, 1972), 135–81; Stein, "Lifting Belly," in *The Yale Gertrude Stein,* ed. Richard Kostelanetz (New Haven: Yale University Press, 1980).

for Violet Trefusis was finally consummated in April, 1918, when Violet came down to the Nicolson establishment at Long Barn because "the air-raids frightened her." As Vita tells the story, her own "exuberance"—"I had just got clothes like the women-on-the-land were wearing, and in the unaccustomed freedom of breeches and gaiters I went into wild spirits"—finally made the "undercurrent" of sexuality between them too strong to resist. It is no wonder, then, that when the pair eloped to Paris after the war, Vita "dressed as a boy" with a "khaki bandage round [her] head" to impersonate a wounded soldier named Julian. And it is no wonder either that, despite the irony of having been liberated by such an equivocal costume, she later recalled that she had "never been so happy since."[61]

Perhaps more important than the female eroticism energized by the war, however, was the more diffusely emotional sense of sisterhood its "Amazonian countries" inspired in nurses and VADs, land girls and tram conductors. As if to show the positive aspect of the bacchanalian bonding Lawrence deplores in his "Tickets, Please," women like Vera Brittain, May Sinclair, and Violetta Thurstan remembered how their liberation into the public realm from the isolation of the private house allowed them to experience a female (re)union in which they felt "the joys of companionship to the full . . . in a way that would be impossible to conceive in an ordinary world."[62] For Radclyffe Hall, too, the battalion of sisters "formed in those terrible years" consisted of "great-hearted women . . . glad . . . to help one another to shoulder burdens."[63] In a variation on this theme, Winifred Holtby told in *The Crowded Street* how her alienated heroine, Muriel Hammond, finally achieved a purposeful life through the friendship of Delia Vaughan, a feminist activist (modeled in part on Vera Brittain, as Muriel is on Holtby herself) whose fiancé was killed in the war. Not insignificantly, moreover, Holtby dedicated this celebration of sisterly companionship to another of her close friends, Jean McWilliam, with whom she lived as a member of the WAAC in France in 1918.[64]

It is also of course true that, as Wilfred Owen's poems testify time and again and as Paul Fussell has brilliantly demonstrated, the Great War produced for

61. Nigel Nicolson, *Portrait of a Marriage* (London: Weidenfeld and Nicolson, 1973), 105, 112.

62. Violetta Thurstan, *Field Hospital and Flying Column: Being the Journal of an English Nursing Soldier in Belgium and Russia* (London: Putnam's, 1915), 174, quoted in Cookson, "Forgotten Women," 16.

63. Hall, *Well of Loneliness,* 336.

64. Winifred Holtby, *The Crowded Street* (1924; repr. London: Virago, 1981).

many men a "front-line experience replete with what we can call the homoerotic."[65] But the male comradeship fostered by the isolated communities of the trenches was continually countered and qualified by rifts between men that were not just accidental but essential consequences of the war. Most obviously, the No Man's Land that stretched between allies and enemies symbolized the fragmentation of what Sigmund Freud called the "wider fatherland" in which, as Freud sorrowfully noted, European men no longer dwelt, though they had "moved unhindered" in it before the war.[66] "Strange Meeting," perhaps Owen's most famous poem, stunningly dramatizes this disintegration of male love, with its vision of brotherly doubles meeting in a "dull tunnel" where one tells the other, in a paradox that summarizes the perils of patriarchal bonding, "I am the enemy you killed, my friend."[67] But even Lawrence, that notorious celebrant of "blood brotherhood," balances his depiction in *Kangaroo* of the "half-mystical" homoerotic friendship between Richard Lovat Somers and the young Cornish farmer John Thomas with a portrayal of the horror Somers experiences when military doctors "handl[e] his private parts" during an army physical, a trauma so indelible that by the end of "The Nightmare" of the war Somers feels "broken off from his fellow-men . . . without a people, without a land."[68]

But if the war forced men like Lawrence, Freud, and Owen to qualify their dreams of brotherhood by confronting the reality of No Man's Land and imagining themselves as nightmare citizens "without a land," it liberated women not only to delight in the reality of the workaday Herland that was wartime England or America but also to imagine a revisionary worldwide Herland, a utopia arisen from the ashes of apocalypse and founded on the revelation of a new social order. In a range of genres—poems and polemics, extravagant fantasies and realistic fictions—women writers articulated this vision repeatedly throughout the war and postwar years. Gertrude Atherton's popular fantasy, *The White Morning,* for instance, told a utopian tale in which Germany is taken over by an army of women. Their Amazonian leader, Gisela, flies over Munich, noting with satisfaction that the city is "packed with women" who are "armed to the teeth" and carrying "a white flag with a curious

65. Fussell, *The Great War,* 272.

66. Sigmund Freud, "Reflections upon War and Death," in *Character and Culture* (New York: Collier, 1963), 109–13.

67. Owen, *Collected Poems,* 35–36.

68. D. H. Lawrence, *Kangaroo* (New York: Viking, 1923), 261, 265.

device sketched in crimson: a hen in successive stages of evolution" into an "eagle [whose] face, grim, leering, vengeful, pitiless, was unmistakably that of a woman." In less detail, but just as dramatically, Dorothy Harrison, one of the protagonists of Sinclair's *The Tree of Heaven,* has a mysterious epiphany when she is confined at Hollowell Prison as part of the prewar suffrage battle, an epiphany that turns out to be a proleptic vision of how women will get the vote in "some big, tremendous way that'll make all this fighting and fussing seem the rottenest game."[69] Similarly, Eleanor Pargiter in Woolf's *The Years* thinks that because of the war things seemed "to be freed from some surface hardness" so that, as German planes raid London, she and her companions raise a toast "to the New World!"[70]

For many women, such intimations of social change were channeled specifically through the politics of pacifism. From Olive Schreiner, whose meditation on "Woman and War" argued that the mothers of the race have a special responsibility as well as a special power to oppose combat, to Charlotte Perkins Gilman, whose Herland was an Edenically peaceable garden because its author believed women to be naturally nonviolent, feminist activists had long claimed that, in the words of Crystal Eastman, "woman suffrage and permanent peace will go together."[71] Indeed, like the trade unionist Mrs. Raymond Robins, whose opinions were otherwise very different, Eastman had confidence that "it is the first hour in history for the women of the world. This is the woman's age!"[72] Precisely because these thinkers were uniformly convinced of woman's unique ability to encourage and enforce peace, there is sometimes an edge of contempt for men implicit in their arguments. But it is in Virginia Woolf's *Three Guineas,* the postwar era's great text of pacifist feminism, that such hostility to men comes most dramatically to the surface, in the form of violent antipatriarchal fantasies paradoxically embedded in an ostensibly nonviolent treatise on the subject of "how to prevent war." Perhaps, Woolf hints in an early draft of this New Womanly book of revelation, the devastation wrought

69. Gertrude Atherton, *The White Morning* (New York: Stokes, 1918), 165, 147, 146; Sinclair, *The Tree of Heaven,* 142. Atherton's novel was brought to my attention by Tamara Jones, "The Mud in God's Eye: World War I in Women's Novels" (unpublished paper).

70. Virginia Woolf, *The Years* (New York: Harcourt, Brace, 1937), 287, 292.

71. Crystal Eastman, "How I Dare Do It," in *Crystal Eastman on Women and Revolution,* ed. Blanche Cook (New York: Oxford University Press, 1978), 240; see also Olive Schreiner, "Woman and War," in *Women and Labor* (London: Unwin, 1911); and Charlotte Perkins Gilman's comments on the Great War in the excerpt from *With Her in Ourland* included in *The Charlotte Perkins Gilman Reader,* ed. Ann J. Lane (New York: Pantheon, 1980), 200–08.

72. Robins is quoted in Lemons, *Woman Citizen,* 20.

by war is a punishment (for men) exactly fitted not only to the crime of (masculine) warmaking but to other (masculine) crimes: "We should say let there be war. We should go on earning our livings. We should say it is a ridiculous and barbarous but perhaps necaary little popgun. The at-would be a help. Then we should live ourselves the sight of happiness is very make you envious" [*sic*].[73] Even in the more subdued final version of *Three Guineas,* moreover, she seizes upon the imperative to prevent war as an excuse for imagining a conflagration that would burn down the old male-structured colleges of "Oxbridge," representative of all oppressive cultural institutions, and substitute instead an egalitarian and feminist "new college, [a] poor college" where "the arts of ruling, of killing, of acquiring land and capital" would not be taught.[74]

Later in *Three Guineas* Woolf rebels even against the rhetoric of writers like Schreiner and Eastman, observing sardonically that "pacificism is enforced upon women" because they are not in any case allowed to offer their services to the army. Thus, most radically, she puts forward her famous proposal that "the daughters of educated men" should refuse to join with their brothers in working for either war *or* peace, but should instead found a Society of Outsiders based on the principle that "as a woman, I have no country. As a woman I want no country. As a woman my country is the whole world."[75] To be sure, Woolf recommends as part of this proposal a passive resistance to patriarchal militarism significantly similar to that advocated by many other feminist pacifists. But at the same time, with its calculated expatriotism and its revisionary vows of "indifference" to the uncivilized hierarchies of "our" civilization, her Society of Outsiders constitutes perhaps the most fully elaborated feminist vision of a secret apocalyptic Herland existing simultaneously within and without England's "splendid Empire," a righteous and rightful woman's state energized by the antiwar passions the war produced in women. In some part of herself, therefore, Woolf may well have shared the apocalyptic delight that Hesione Hushabye bizarrely expresses when bombs begin falling at the end of Bernard Shaw's *Heartbreak House:* "Did you hear the explosions? And the sound in the sky: it's splendid: it's like an orchestra: it's like Beethoven."[76] As

73. This Woolf manuscript is in the Berg Collection, New York Public Library, New York, and is quoted by permission of Quentin Bell.

74. Woolf, *Three Guineas,* 103.

75. Ibid., 197, 109.

76. Bernard Shaw, *Bernard Shaw's Plays,* ed. Warren S. Smith (1919; repr. New York: Norton, 1970), 147.

patriarchal culture self-destructs, those it has subordinated can't help feeling that the sacrifices implied by "the sound in the sky" might nevertheless hold out the hope of a new heaven and a new earth.

Even as they mourned the devastation of the war, then, a number of women writers besides Woolf felt that not only their society but also their art had been subtly strengthened, or at least strangely inspired, by the deaths and defeats of male contemporaries. Vera Brittain notes that when her fiancé, Roland, was killed, "his mother began to write, in semi-fictional form, a memoir of his life," and adds that she herself was filled "with longing to write a book about Roland."[77] In *A Son at the Front,* the tale of an artist-father whose art is mysteriously revitalized by the death of his soldier son, Edith Wharton offers an encoded description of a similar transformation of a dead man into an enlivening muse.[78] More frankly, Katherine Mansfield confides to her journal after the death of her brother, Chummie, that through his muselike intervention she has been vouchsafed a "mysterious" and "floating" vision of "our undiscovered country," a transfigured land not unlike the state imagined by apocalyptic feminists from Schreiner to Woolf, in which the dead Chummie represents "the new man."[79] What issued from such ambivalent moments of inspiration was her best set of stories—the New Zealand tales, "Prelude" and "At the Bay." Finally, in perhaps the most notable instance of female inspiration empowered by male desperation, H. D. writes in her roman à clef, *Bid Me to Live,* how the various defeats of her husband (Richard Aldington) and her male muse (D. H. Lawrence) transformed her autobiographical heroine, Julia, into a "witch with power. A wise woman . . . [a] seer, a see-er."[80] No wonder, then, that when she later looked back on her experiences in two wars, she revised and reversed the imagery Lawrence had used in his "Eloi, Eloi, Lama Sabachthani." "Am I bridegroom of War, war's paramour?" Lawrence's speaker had asked, and H. D. seems almost to have wanted to answer him directly. Tracing her own growth in an unpublished memoir called "Thorn Thicket," she declares mystically that "the war was my husband."[81] And at the

77. Brittain, *Testament,* 251–52.

78. Wharton, *Son at the Front,* 423, 426. Willa Cather records a similar (and similarly encoded) empowerment of the living by the wartime dead in *The Professor's House* (New York: Vintage, 1925), where the sacrificed Tom Outland gives meaning to Professor St. Peter's existence.

79. Katherine Mansfield, *The Journals of Katherine Mansfield* (1927; repr. New York: Knopf, 1954), 43–45, 49.

80. H. D., *Bid Me to Live* (New York: Grove Press, 1960), 145–46.

81. The manuscript of H. D.'s "Thorn Thicket" is held at the Beinecke Library, Yale University, New Haven, Connecticut, and is quoted by permission of Perdita Schaffner.

very least, if the war was not her husband, it was her muse—as it was Woolf's, Mansfield's, Wharton's, and many other women's.

REACTION

Given the fact that the war functioned in so many different ways to liberate women—offering a revolution in economic expectations, a release of passionate energies, a (re)union of previously fragmented sisters, and a (re)vision of social and aesthetic dreams—it seems clear that more than simple patriotism caused some leaders of the women's movement quite early to recognize a connection between feminist aspirations and military effects. In 1915, for instance, *The Suffragette,* the newspaper of the English Women's Social and Political Union, was renamed *Britannia,* with a new dedication: "For King, for Country, for Freedom." At last, it must have seemed, women could begin to see themselves as coextensive with the state, and with a female state at that, a Britannia, not a Union Jack. And, as we know, the female intuition expressed in that renaming was quite accurate; in 1918, when World War I was over, there were eight-and-a-half million European men dead and there had been thirty-seven-and-a-half million male casualties, while all the women in England over the age of thirty were finally, after a sixty-two-year struggle, given the vote. Not too much later all the women in America over the age of twenty-one achieved the same privilege. For four years, moreover, a sizable percentage of the young men in England had been imprisoned in trenches and uniforms, while the young women of England had been at liberty in farm and factory. Paradoxically, in fact, the war to which so many men had gone in the hope of becoming heroes ended up emasculating them, depriving them of autonomy, confining them as closely as any Victorian women had been confined. As if in acknowledgment of this, Leed tells us, doctors noted that "the symptoms of shell-shock were precisely the same as those of the most common hysterical disorders of peacetime, though they often acquired new and more dramatic names in war: 'the burial-alive neurosis,' 'gas neurosis,' 'soldier's heart,' 'hysterical sympathy with the enemy.'. . . [W]hat had been predominantly a disease of women before the war became a disease of men in combat."[82]

Because women developed a very different kind of "soldier's heart" in these years, however, "wearing the pants" in the family or even "stepping into his shoes" had finally become a real possibility for them. Yet of course that

82. Leed, *No Man's Land,* 163.

triumph was not without its darker consequences for feminism. Because male artists believed even more strongly than their sisters that soldiers had been sacrificed so that some gigantic female could sleep surrounded by, in Wilfred Owen's words, a "wall of boys on boys and dooms on dooms";[83] because they believed with Hemingway that a Lady Brett was a sort of monstrous antifertility goddess to whose powers the impotent bodies of men must ceaselessly be offered up; because with Lawrence they "feared" the talents of liberated "poetesses" like H. D. at least as much as they admired them, the literature of the postwar years was marked by an antifeminism which, in the words of Rebecca West, was "strikingly the correct fashion . . . among . . . the intellectuals."[84]

Inevitably, however, many women writers internalized the misogyny that actuated such antifeminism. Heroines like Hall's Miss Ogilvy and Stephen Gordon, for instance, who were briefly freed by the war, ultimately succumb to the threat of a reconstituted status quo. Miss Ogilvy dies almost directly as a result of the sexual "dying" that climaxes her dream of erotic fulfillment, and Stephen Gordon is assaulted by "rockets of pain" which signal "l'heure de notre mort" as she surrenders Mary Llewelyn to the male lover who she decides is Mary's rightful spouse.[85] Just as theatrically, Gisela in *The White Morning* realizes that she has murdered a man she loves when "all feeling ebbed . . . out of her" because she was merely "the chosen instrument" of woman's revolution; and Katherine Mansfield, even while she is inspired to art by her dead brother/muse, speculates that she too is "just as much dead as he is" and wonders "why don't I commit suicide?"[86] The guilt of the survivor implicit in such imaginings is specifically articulated by one former nurse who defines her culpable numbness in a dreadful confession: "She [a nurse] is no longer a woman. She is dead already, just as I am . . . a machine inhabited by a ghost of a woman—soulless, past redeeming."[87] Most theatrically, perhaps, Katherine Anne Porter expresses in "Pale Horse, Pale Rider" this nurse's feeling (and what might have been a universal female sense) that if men are sick, they must have fallen ill because women are sickening. After her heroine,

83. Owen, "The Kind Ghosts," *Collected Poems,* 102.

84. Lawrence, *Kangaroo,* 253; Rebecca West, "Autumn and Virginia Woolf," in *Ending in Earnest: A Literary Log* (New York: Arno Press, 1971), 212–13.

85. Hall, *Well of Loneliness,* 511, 507.

86. Atherton, *White Morning,* 133, 145; Mansfield, *Journals,* 38.

87. Mary Borden, *The Forbidden Zone* (London: Heinemann, 1929), 59–60, quoted in Cookson, "Forgotten Women," 9.

Miranda, down with influenza, has had a terrifying dream about her lover, Adam, in which "he lay dead, and she still lived," she learns that her disease has contaminated him and, indeed, he has died and she has lived, kept going by a "fiery motionless particle [which] set itself . . . to survive . . . in its own madness of being."[88]

It is not surprising, then, that, repressed by what was still after all a male-dominated community and reproached by their own consciences, many women retreated into embittered unemployment or guilt-stricken domesticity after World War I. "Generally speaking, we war women are a failure," confesses a character in Evadne Price's *Women of the Aftermath*. "We had a chance to make ourselves solid in the working market . . . and came a hell of a cropper in most cases."[89] To be sure, as J. Stanley Lemons and others observe, women's "peacetime levels [of employment] were [still] significantly higher than the pre-war situation."[90] Nothing would ever be the same again. But no war would ever function, either, the way this Great War had, as a battle of the sexes which initiated "the first hour in history for the women of the world." World War II certainly was to be as much a war against women civilians as it was against male combatants, with a front indistinguishable from the home-front. As Virginia Woolf anticipated in *Three Guineas,* in fact, it was to be a war whose jackbooted Nazis, marching for the Fatherland, enacted the ultimate consequences of patriarchal oppression, so that Sylvia Plath, protesting against her imprisonment in "daddy's black shoe," would fear that "I may be a bit of a Jew."[91] In 1944, moreover, in her war-shadowed "Writing on the Wall," H. D. was to return to Radclyffe Hall's definition of "no-man's-land" as a "waste land" for "inverts" (Hall) and "hysterical women" (H. D.); while more recently, in a revision of the metaphor that Hall's Stephen Gordon temporarily transcended, Linda Pastan was to see her own body as "no man's land" over which sons and husbands battle; and in 1981 Adrienne Rich was to publish a poem which despairingly declared that "there is no no man's land," by which she clearly meant that there is still no Herland.[92] Did World War II, with its very name suggesting a deadly repetitive compulsion, usher in what Rich has

88. Porter, "Pale Horse," 242, 253.

89. Quoted in Cadogan and Craig, *Women and Children First,* 47.

90. Lemons, *Woman Citizen,* 22.

91. Sylvia Plath, "Daddy," *Ariel* (New York: Harper and Row, 1965), 50.

92. H. D. *Tribute to Freud* (New York: McGraw-Hill, 1975), 77; Linda Pastan, "In the Old Guerilla War," in *The Five Stages of Grief* (New York: Norton, 1978); Adrienne Rich, "The Images," in *A Wild Patience Has Taken Me This Far* (New York: Norton, 1981), 3–5.

called a "war of the images," a newly ferocious battle of the sexes in which we are still engaged? Did that *second* calamity mean, as Susan Gubar has argued, a "diaspora" for women—and specifically for feminists—because male soldiers (on both sides of the conflict) determined that this time, whatever other defeats they had to endure, they would at least triumph over women?

SUSAN GUBAR

"This Is My Rifle, This Is My Gun": World War II and the Blitz on Women

There is too much fathering going on just now and there is no doubt about it fathers are depressing. Everybody nowadays is a father, there is father Mussolini and father Hitler and father Roosevelt and father Stalin and father Lewis and father Blum and father Franco is just commencing now and there are ever so many more ready to be one.

—*Gertrude Stein*

Gertrude Stein's 1937 protest against "too much fathering" informed the literary responses of many of her female contemporaries, who also experienced World War II as a resurgence of patriarchal politics.[1] It is hardly surprising that the identification of fascism and male domination surfaced in feminist polemic even before the outbreak of the Second World War. As early as 1935, both Mary Ritter Beard and Winifred Holtby viewed "the fascist regime [as] a menace to the liberties of women," and three years later Virginia Woolf characterized the nineteenth-century feminists as an "advance guard" struggling against "the tyranny of the patriarchal state," much as twentieth-century pacifists "are fighting the tyranny of the Fascist state."[2] More striking than

I wish to thank Sandra M. Gilbert and Edward Gubar, the participants in the 1983 and 1984 Six-College Mellon Faculty Development Programs, and my graduate students at Indiana University. Susan Schweik's Ph.D. dissertation, "A Word No Man Can Say For Us: American Women Writers and the Second World War" (Yale, 1985), provides indispensable background information. Figures 2, 3, 8, and 9 are reproduced in Zybnek Zeman, *Selling the War: Art and Propaganda in World War II* (New York: Exeter Books). Finally, I am grateful to the Indiana Committee for the Humanities for its generous funding of my research.

1. Gertrude Stein, *Everybody's Autobiography* (1937; repr. New York: Vintage, 1973), 133.

2. The quotation is from Mary Beard, *On Understanding Women* (1931), excerpted in *Mary Ritter Beard: A Sourcebook,* ed. Ann J. Lane (New York: Schocken, 1977), 144; but see a comparable argument in Winifred Holtby, *Women and A Changing Civilization* (1935; repr.

feminist attacks on father Hitler and father Mussolini, however, were women's critiques of father Roosevelt and, for that matter, father Churchill. Throughout the 1940s, Dorothy Parker, Kay Boyle, and Carson McCullers published fiction about the vulnerability of war brides, women war workers, and female civilians who are threatened less by the enemy than by their so-called defenders, while Elizabeth Bowen composed several works about heroines who fear that, as Bryher claimed, "[t]he First War had opened a few doors but . . . the Second slammed many of them shut again."[3] During the same decade in which Pearl Buck argued that "war to man, like childbirth to woman, is simplifying in its emotions," emotions that have "[set] women back a generation,"[4] the poetry of Muriel Rukeyser, Edith Sitwell, Elizabeth Bishop, Gwendolyn Brooks, and H. D. consistently presented not only fascist but also liberal militarism as the logical extension of misogyny. Why did so many English and American women writers perceive the Second World War as a threat to the second sex?

According to Stein, the First World War was "a nice war, a real war, a regular war," but "[c]ertainly nobody no not anybody thinks this war is a war to end war."[5] As she so often did, Stein pointed to one of the major differences between the two world wars, for the *Second* World War was only one of a sequence of wars. A repetition, the Second World War was approached by both sexes with much less idealism than that with which they had approached the Great War. For literary men, the earlier World War had functioned as a historical and imaginative watershed: "Never such innocence again," Philip Larkin explained in his poem "MCMXIV."[6] For women, and in particular for feminists like Vera Brittain, women's economic decline during the interwar years fueled skepticism about propaganda that implied that women would profit from their war work. Although, as William Chafe has shown, throughout the 1940s a significant number of women were catapulted into the labor force, Mrs. Laughton Matthews, the director of the Women's Royal Naval Service (WRNS), was typical of administrators who feared that, while the war has "shown that women can do anything," female recruits might become

Chicago: Academy Chicago, 1978), 151–70. Virginia Woolf, *Three Guineas* (1938; repr. New York: Harcourt, Brace and World, 1966), 102.

3. Bryher, *The Days of Mars: A Memoir, 1940–1946* (New York: Harcourt Brace Jovanovich, 1972), 120.

4. Pearl S. Buck, *Of Men and Women* (New York: John Day, 1941), 155.

5. Gertrude Stein, *Wars I Have Seen* (London: Batsford, 1945), 122.

6. The poem is quoted by Vernon Scannell, *Not Without Glory: Poets of the Second World War* (London: Woburn, 1976), 17–18. This point is also made by Chester E. Eisinger, *Fiction of the Forties* (Chicago: University of Chicago Press, 1963), 23–24.

"disappointed as they were in many ways after the last war."[7] In addition, both men and women knew that, as an adumbration of a third World War or even a fourth, the Second World War could never be considered a "Great" war. If the Second World War had any singularity, it was as the first *total war,* waged by all against all. Not only the women who were fighting for the first time in the air force and the armed services but the whole female population were no longer insulated from the brutality of the battlefield.

While Sandra M. Gilbert has demonstrated that many women were protected by the sharp demarcation between the homefront and no man's land during the 1914–18 conflict,[8] in World War II civilians in most countries were affected by air raids, blackouts, rationing, or even occupation. By contrast, the technological depersonalization of war waged in large bombers and transport aircraft insulated crews from the reality of destruction: "when those on earth / Die, there is not even a sound," the flyer admits in James Dickey's poem "The Firebombing," and he therefore becomes "enthralled" in "aesthetic contemplation" of the destruction he has created.[9] "You only see the first plume and first fall," John Ciardi's pilot observes in "Take-Off over Kansas," so "You think, 'It was not human after all.' "[10] Many servicemen suffered not only from the guilt and anesthetization Dickey and Ciardi describe but also from dislocation, enemy reprisals, and imprisonment. The irrationality and the deprivations of military life combined with the increased destructive capabilities of the machinery of war to fill many men with dread, although Robert Graves has claimed that a larger proportion of the military was occupied with civilian-oriented duties than ever before, and John Press has argued that some soldiers "enjoying, albeit with a twinge of guilt, the green pastures of Kenya, the pleasures of Egypt, or the imperial grandeur of India might reflect that they

7. William Chafe, *The American Woman: Her Changing Social, Economic, and Political Roles, 1920–1970* (New York: Oxford University Press, 1972). A number of historians have questioned Chafe's view that an upsurge of paid employment of married women during World War II led to the women's liberation movement: see D'Ann Campbell, *Women at War with America* (Cambridge: Harvard University Press, 1984). Mrs. Laughton Matthews is quoted in a work written during the war, *Women at War,* by Margaret Goldsmith (London: Lindsay Brummond, n.d.), 98. Goldsmith also claims that *Our Freedom and Its Results* (1936, ed. Ray Strachey) reveals "how much women expected after the last war and how little, in the professions and in business, they really attained" (145). See also Vera Brittain, *Lady into Woman: A History of Women from Victoria to Elizabeth II* (New York: MacMillan, 1953), 188, 198.

8. Sandra M. Gilbert, "Soldier's Heart: Literary Men, Literary Women, and the Great War," this volume.

9. James Dickey, "The Firebombing," *Buckdancer's Choice* (Middletown, Conn.: Wesleyan University Press, 1964), 17.

10. John Ciardi, "Take-Off over Kansas," *Other Skies* (Boston: Little, Brown, 1947), 21–22.

were a great deal safer and more comfortable than people in the cities and towns of Britain."[11]

From the perspective of both men and women, media coverage brought the war home, as if to illustrate the expansion of the "theater" of war from the battlefield to the homefront, and espionage played a much more prominent role in the Second World War than ever before: the enemy was potentially everyone anywhere. Ending the possibility of a separate sphere for women, World War II seemed less a generational conflict between fathers and sons than a road to universal apocalypse, or so the atomic bombing of Hiroshima and Nagasaki demonstrated. In addition, the only separate sphere imaginable in the context of the other major event that vividly dramatized the war's effect on civilians—the Holocaust—was the ghetto or the camp, where the segregation of Jews into male and female barracks resulted in total depersonalization. That the enemy had also defined itself in explicitly masculinist terms meant that women were inexorably involved in the ideological debates that distinguished World War II from the nationalist struggles of the Great War. Cultural historians from Theodore Roszak to Susan Sontag and Maria-Antonietta Macchiocchi have noted that, because European fascism evolved as a reaction against the emasculation associated with the First World War and the Depression, the fascist "father" regarded his leadership as a sexual mastery over the feminized masses.[12]

Consciousness of the infinite sequentiality of world wars, technological advances in destructive capabilities, the obliteration of a safe homefront, the destruction of whole populations, and the ideological threat of fascism doubtless contributed to the polemical and personal critiques of warfare by literary women from Stein and Woolf to McCullers and Sitwell. Yet such factors hardly account for the belief that women were also victimized by men who were presumably on their own side. To be sure, feminist polemicists as well as women novelists and poets mourned the suffering of their male contemporaries. But, given the sense of grief and alienation that literary men recorded, why did literary women also fear that male vulnerability in wartime would result in violence against women? As an articulation of female dread, literary

11. Robert Graves is quoted in Ian Hamilton's introduction to *The Poetry of War, 1939–45* (London: Alan Ross, 1965), 3. John Press, "Poets of World War II," *British Writers,* vol. 7, ed. Ian Scott-Kilvert (New York: Charles Scribner's Sons, 1978), 421–50.

12. Theodore Roszak, "The Hard and the Soft," in *Masculine/Feminine: Readings in Sexual Mythology and the Liberation of Women,* ed. Betty Roszak and Theodore Roszak (New York: Harper, 1969), 88; Susan Sontag, "Fascinating Fascism," in *Women and the Cinema,* ed. Karyn Kay and Gerald Peary (New York: E. P. Dutton, 1977), 352–76; Maria-Antonietta Macchiocchi, "Female Sexuality in Fascist Ideology," *Feminist Review* 1 (1979), 67–82.

women's responses to the Second World War have gone unheard because we have failed to realize that they were grappling with male-authored images that reified gender arrangements as rigidly as they had been demarcated in the Victorian period, but in a newly eroticized way. Even women occupied at vocational jobs that had never before been available to them could hardly escape the conclusion that the female community had been no less occupied than all the other foreign territories that had been laid waste.

WHO IS THE ENEMY?

Wartime propaganda, both Allied and Axis, did much to underline the idea that fascism directly threatened women. In popular magazines and newspapers, American and English photographs during the war depicted women and children as the predominant civilian casualties of blitzes, while pictures of Allied planes dropping bombs over both the Asian and the European fronts tended to represent the transcendent Allied power without regard to the victims. But a series of posters entitled "Who Is the Enemy?" even more graphically presented the enemy as he who would rape and murder "our" women: whether portrayed as an Aryan-looking mom about to be caught in the clutches of hands that look like claws (fig. 1), a ravaged madonna lying amidst the ruins of a landscape obliterated by the face of Adolf Hitler (fig. 2), or a raped prey draped over the shoulder of a Japanese soldier (fig. 3), the woman figures as "bounty"; that is, as the bountiful fertility that must be saved or the booty that constitutes the spoils of war.

Monitory images designed to illustrate what would happen to women if men lost the war were complemented by glamorous recruitment posters intended to encourage women to help win the war. The girl they left behind was urged to join the war effort as, say, a WAC (Women's Auxiliary Corps) or a WREN (Women's Royal Naval Service) or as a Rosie the Riveter in the factories (fig. 4). Even women warriors and war workers, however, were displayed in quasi-pornographic nudity in magazines throughout the war years, and in 1940 the chorus in London's Garrison Theatre wore and then stripped off their WAAF (Women's Auxiliary Air Force) costumes.[13] At the same time, pinned up unclothed in countless photographs that decorated

13. The film *Rosie the Riveter* presents the dichotomy between eroticized images of American war workers and the difficult realities of their lives. Robert Hewison mentions the strippers in *Under Siege: Literary Life in London, 1939–1945* (London: Weidenfeld and Nicolson, 1977), 25. Susan M. Hartmann discusses how men both trivialized and glamorized the "gals" in the military service in *The Home Front and Beyond: American Women in the 1940s* (Boston: Twayne, 1982), 41.

C–90883 Public Archives Canada

THIS
IS THE ENEMY

THIS
IS THE
ENEMY

Imperial War Museum, London

The Bettman Archive

USAAFTC, Library of Congress

Library of Congress

bunks, barracks, bombers, and artillery tanks named after women, movie stars and models clearly represented what the men were fighting for (fig. 5).[14] Indeed, pinups were used to teach camouflage techniques and map reading to new recruits (fig. 6).

As if to answer Allied propaganda, the Axis powers produced leaflets to divide Allied fighting men over the ownership of women. Japanese posters informed Australians away "philandering" in Africa that the English were cuckolding them back at home (fig. 7) and German posters instructed the French fighting men that British servicemen were enjoying security and sex behind the lines (fig. 8). Much futurist and fascist art glorified the hard, the dominant, the masculine (frequently armored) form. Even more explicitly, fascist ideology set out not only to limit women to traditionally nurturing roles (*Kinder, Kirche, Küche*) but also to promulgate the idea that the women's movement was a Jewish plot. It was singularly appropriate, then, that the first issue of *Wonder Woman,* which appeared in 1943, presented the skimpily clad superheroine battling Hitler and his war machines.[15]

14. Randall Jarrell's poem "Losses" is spoken by a pilot whose "bombers [are] named for girls." *The Complete Poems* (New York: Farrar, Straus and Giroux, 1969), 145.

15. On the contrasting attitudes of America and Germany toward women, see Leila J. Rupp,

The eroticizing of women's image in popular British and American graphics led several cartoonists to represent heroines embattled as much by sex-starved servicemen as by the enemy abroad.[16] But more frequently Allied propaganda spoke directly about and to servicemen's fear of their women's betrayal. Posters enjoining silence as a protection against spies implied that women's talk would kill fighting men: a Finnish poster, for example, graphically suggested that women's lips should be locked up (fig. 9), while English cartoons and posters pictured women as irresponsible in their garrulity (fig. 10) or sinister in their silence (fig. 11). The female spy, a vamp whose charms endanger national security, was not unrelated to the foreign femme fatale whose enticements threatened the physical security of the fighting forces. As in World War I, women posed the threat of contamination, for they could infect fighting men with syphilis. The danger of female pollution was used in a 1938 Pulitzer-prize-winning cartoon against U.S. involvement in the war, a cartoon that personifies the war itself as a syphilitic whore (fig. 12). It is also evident in British posters in which alluring, feminine accoutrements (both the veiled hat and its vaginal flower in figure 13) grace the skull's head that would lure soldiers to dissolution and death.

To a surprising extent, women in war literature by men are portrayed in a manner similar to that of the war posters. Of course, many of the novels and poems about the war focus on military bureaucracy, wartime technology, or combat logistics, and female characters play only an ancillary part. Yet a menacing hostility, as well as a curious unreality, permeates both positive and negative images of women in these works. They are viewed almost entirely as ladies-in-waiting, solacing outsiders or resented beneficiaries of suffering. Even the women who represent the values that men are struggling to retain amidst barbaric, death-dealing circumstances are often identified as the cause of the fighting. At the same time, the vulnerability so many men experienced because of the degrading conditions of combat or the impersonality of military procedures and technology paradoxically led them to escalate the war between the sexes.

Mobilizing Women for War: German and American Propaganda, 1939–1945 (Princeton: Princeton University Press, 1978); and Maureen Honey, *Creating Rosie the Riveter: Class, Gender, and Propaganda during World War II* (Amherst: University of Massachusetts Press, 1984). Mary Ritter Beard discusses Superwoman in *Woman as Force in History: A Study in Traditions and Realities* (1946; repr. New York: Farrar, Straus and Giroux, 1981), 54.

16. The cartoons of Sgt. George Baker show servicemen afraid to shake hands with women after army sex education courses. James Jones, *World War II* (New York: Grosset and Dunlap, 1975), 55.

Stärk
fronten här hemma-
Bygg dammar
för ryktena !

Fougasse, Imperial War Museum, London

Fougasse, Imperial War Museum, London

"Come on in, I'll treat you right. I used to know your Daddy."

C. D. Batchelor, 1937, courtesy of the *Chicago Tribune,* New York *News* Syndicate, Inc.

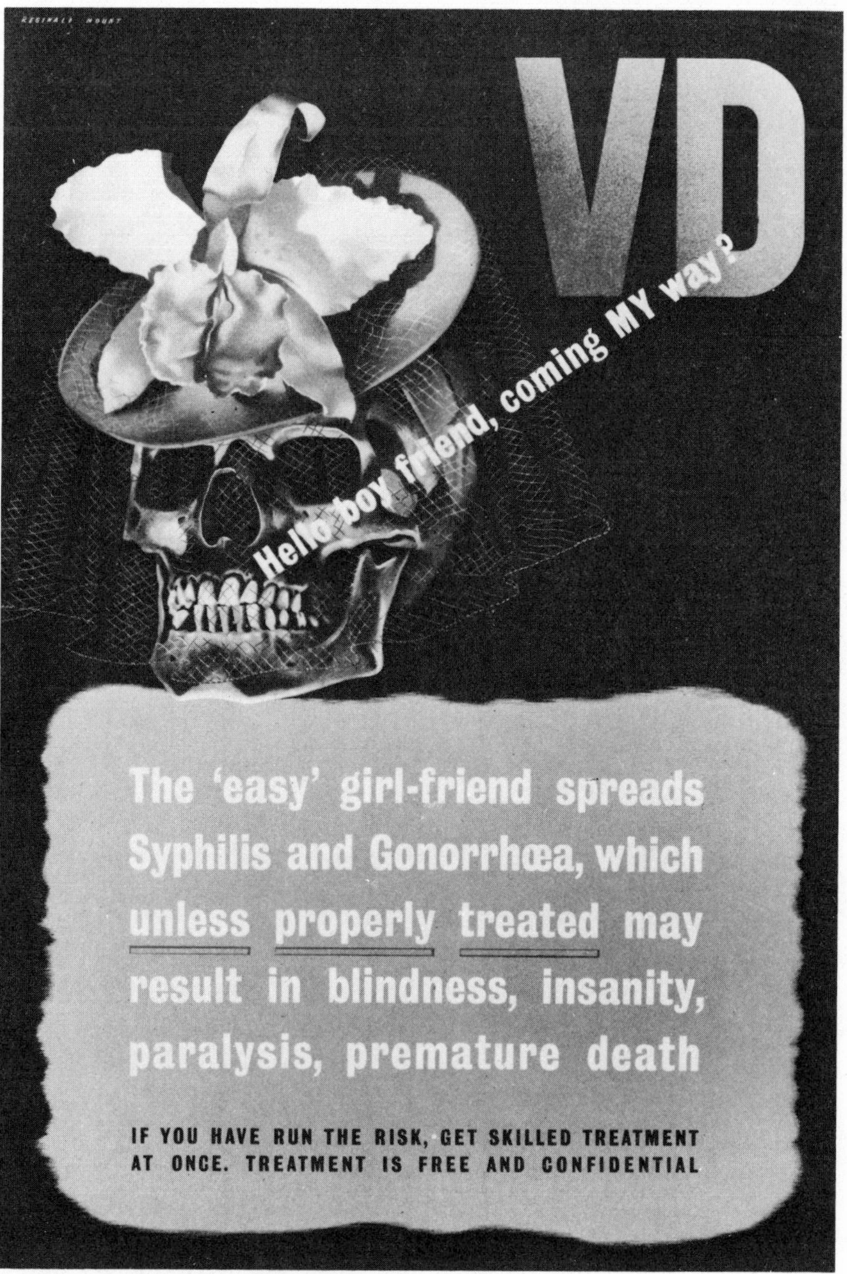

Reginald Mount, Imperial War Museum, London

Whether she is the silent recipient of "V letters" or the photographed face peeping out of the pocket of a dead man, the good girl in the literature of the Second World War is marked by her absence. In Karl Shapiro's brilliant poem "V-Letter," for example, the speaker loves the fair face of his beloved "because you wait" and because "You are my home and in your spacious love / I dream to march as under flaring flags."[17] While Shapiro need not pray for his own safety, "because our love is whole / Whether I live or fail," the dead German soldier in Keith Douglas's poem *"Vergissmeinnicht"* is not saved by his talisman, an autographed picture which is "dishonoured" now that the combatant sprawls in the sun, decaying next to his "hard and good" equipment.[18] As the only witness who would weep to see "the lover and killer . . . mingled" and mangled, the girl he left behind is a repository of the humane values that men must suppress in wartime, and she is therefore rarely present except as a fleeting image or a trace memory. On the one hand, a number of writers express the soldier's guilty sense that his innocent beloved would never understand or accept the person he has been forced to become under the brutal circumstances of combat: "There's the girl I 'left behind,' " the speaker of "Nebraska Gunner at Bataan" exclaims; "I wonder, would she love me yet / If she could watch me grimly kill": and so he wants to "keep her safe back there."[19] On the other hand, many writers express the soldier's anger at the betrayal of the girl back home. In "A Woman's a Two-Face," a "Dear John" letter excuses the female correspondent, who claims to be busy, but the soldier-reader knows "you must be busy, and / I wonder who's the guy."[20]

As Susan Schweik has explained, the predominance of the letter form in World War II literature signals the distance between the sexes.[21] Just as important, men dichotomized women, distinguishing—in the words of the narrator of *Battle Cry*—between "[t]he ones who waited and the ones who didn't."[22] Richard Eberhart's poem about the defence of Corregidor, "Brotherhood of Man," illustrates male nostalgia for a lost female world of faithful-

17. Karl Shapiro, "V-Letter," *Collected Poems, 1940–1948* (New York: Random House, 1978), 87–88.

18. Keith Douglas, *"Vergissmeinnicht"* (1943), in *Complete Poems,* ed. Desmond Graham (Oxford: Oxford University Press, 1978), 111.

19. Corporal Richard F. Ferguson, "Nebraska Gunner at Bataan," in *Reveille: War Poems by Members of Our Armed Forces,* ed. Daniel Henderson, John Kieran, and Grantland Rice (New York: A. S. Barnes, 1943), 71.

20. Corporal John Readey, "A Woman's a Two-Face," in *Reveille,* 215.

21. Susan Schweik presented "Women Writers, Epistolary Form, and World War II," a portion of her thesis, at the Modern Language Association Convention, 1984.

22. Leon Uris, *Battle Cry* (1953; repr. New York: Bantam, 1982), 2.

ness that is identified with the maternal: Eberhart's embattled recruits, vampires "drinking the blood of victims" in a hellish fight, are only prevented from surrendering by a vision of "mother in the midst of terror: / 'Persevere. Persevere. Persevere. Persevere.' "[23] The epitome of what Eberhart calls "Faith beyond reason," the mothers in a number of war novels and poems represent humanistic values at odds with the dehumanizing technology of death.[24] George Orwell's *1984,* for example, contrasts the brutality and lies of Big Brother with Winston Smith's nostalgia for a fantasy world left before the war, when his mother tried to protect him even at the cost of her own and his sister's life. What Smith must learn in Room 101, however, is that he can neither have the mother nor kill the father: indeed, when he is brainwashed and forced to "see" five fingers where there are four, he submits to the power of his persecutor and specifically to the state's phallus, the invisible but potent symbol of authority that no single man possesses. At this point, Smith—"the last man"—relinquishes the oceanic unity he had with his mother for the perpetual warring of Oceania.[25]

Winston Smith's mother is a victim of the war, as she is in countless British poems that elegiacally mourn London as a "mother of wounds," but she is also a mother not good enough to protect her sons from the vengeance of his big brothers. In this respect, Orwell's novel underlines the implicit anger with which many male writers, encased in what they call "the womb of war" or "the steel cocoon," describe the juxtaposition between the biological mother and the military,[26] for the mother who has given her son over to the state has exchanged her birth-giving function for a death-dealing one.[27] One of the most moving American war poems—Randall Jarrell's "The Death of the Ball Turret Gunner"—begins with a divorce from the maternal: "From my mother's sleep I fell into the State." Jarrell then describes how the gunner hunches upside down inside the "belly" of a plane, his "wet fur froze."

23. Richard Eberhart, "Brotherhood of Men," *Collected Poems, 1930–1976* (New York: Oxford University Press, 1976), 101.

24. See, for example, James Jones, *From Here to Eternity* (New York: Charles Scribner's Sons, 1951), 16.

25. George Orwell, *1984* (1949; repr. New York: New American Library, 1981), 81, 206, 222. Daphne Patai also argues that "Orwell assails Big Brother's domination but never notices that he is the perfect embodiment of hypertrophied masculinity": *The Orwell Mystique: A Study in Male Ideology* (Amherst: University of Massachusetts Press, 1984), 251.

26. In Bentz Plagemann, *The Steel Cocoon* (New York: Viking, 1958), 86, a character describes his ship as a "womb." But the phrase "womb of war" also appears in popular poems like "Myself, Soldier," by Pfc. Louis Carpenter, in *Reveille.*

27. In Herman Wouk, *The Caine Mutiny* (1951), and James Jones, *The Thin Red Line* (1962), mothers are blamed for the war.

Awakened by flak, he says, "When I died they washed me out of the turret with a hose." The sleeping mother, oblivious to this cruel substitution of a mechanical for a human womb, seems indirectly responsible for this abortion.[28]

No less guilty, in Jarrell's poems, is the wife of the gunner: in "Gunner," the soldier sent away from his cat and his wife confronts his death wondering bitterly, "Has my wife a pension of so many mice? / Did the medals go home to my cat?" As survivers, pets and wives—presumably interchangeable—are resented as the beneficiaries of men's suffering. Similarly, in "On Embarkation," by Alun Lewis, sobbing women on railroad platforms are "Thinking of children, pensions, looks that fade, / The slow forgetfulness that strips the mind," and in "Christmas Holiday," when the war begins, "The fat wife comfortably sleeping / Sighs and licks her lips and smiles."[29] More comically, in Joseph Heller's *Catch-22,* after Dr. Daneeka has been declared dead by his superiors, his wife is so "delighted" with the insurance payments she has received that she evades his pleading letters by moving and leaving no forwarding address. Like Sargeant Scheisskopf's wife, who wears a friend's WAC uniform in order to take it off for all the cadets in her husband's squadron, Mrs. Daneeka is a predator who stands in marked contrast to the whores who are so happy to "soothe and excite" Yossarian and "put him to sleep."[30]

Countless foreign women in war novels and poems composed before *Catch-22* are praised for their compliant services or damned for their exorbitant prices. As the only available erotic object, the whore sometimes offers sanctuary and sanctity to the soldier.[31] More frequently, however, exotic Eurasian, Italian, French, and African prostitutes are the proverbial solution to the problem of a "rusty load" in popular war poetry like "Lydia of Libya": "Why are the armies of the world / Fighting for that desert land?" if not for "Lydia of Libya, / The lady with the lacy lingerie," who has "passed all her courses" in "harem school" and therefore "devastates our forces."[32] In a more ambitious poem, "Cairo Jag" by Keith Douglas, the speaker has to decide between

28. Randall Jarrell, "The Death of the Ball Turret Gunner," in *The Complete Poems* (New York: Farrar, Straus and Giroux, 1969), 144. Jarrell's poem "Gunner" also appears in this volume, p. 204. In "Two Songs for a Gunner," John Ciardi presents a gunner firing tracers who exclaims, "Look, Mother, how gay / And luminous a sperm I spend in play," and a second who is being fired upon and cowers in "a chaste and sweet . . . womb" which is also "an egg": *As If* (New Brunswick: Rutgers University Press, 1955), 24.

29. Alun Lewis, "On Embarkation" and "Christmas Holiday," in *Selected Poetry and Prose* (London: George Allen and Unwin, 1966), 84, 99.

30. Joseph Heller, *Catch-22* (1961; repr. New York: Dell, 1984), 353, 426.

31. Richard Wilbur, "Place Pigalle," in *The Beautiful Changes* (New York: Harcourt, Brace, 1947), 12.

32. Major Fred B. Shaw, Jr., "Lydia of Libya," in *Reveille,* 217.

getting drunk or "cut[ting] myself a piece of cake, / a pasty Syrian with a few words of English / or the Turk who says she is a princess."[33]

But the rest and recreation furnished by the whore is only a temporary reprieve from the horror of battle: although "Odysseus saw the sirens" as charming, "with snub breasts and little neat posteriors," John Manifold's pilot-Odysseus forgets them when faced with the more portentous reality of "alarming / Weather report, his mutineers in irons, / The radio failing."[34] A poem simply entitled "War" typifies how Homeric allusion allowed a number of poets to contrast men's guileless vulnerability in war with women's guilty safety:

Innocence, hired to kill,
Lies pitilessly dead.
Stone and bone lie still.
Helen turns in bed.[35]

Throughout the *Cantos,* the most famous work to apply Homeric myth to both world wars, Ezra Pound presents himself as an Odysseus dedicated to various embodiments of the principles he associates with the *"pater patriae"* and opposed to a whore figure, Usura, Pound's pointedly anti-Semitic concept of usury. "CONTRA NATURAM," usury is a female figure who "hath brought palsey to bed," and "lyeth / between the young bride and her bridegroom."[36] Associated in broadcasts Pound made on Italian fascist radio with capitalism, warfare, syphilis, and sterility, identified in the *Cantos* with "sows eating their litters" and with "condom[s] full of black-beetles," Usura contaminates the sacred shrine of fertility: "They have brought whores for Eleusis."[37]

Writing from an ideologically antithetical perspective, so many war novelists presented the Eleusinian mysteries inside bordellos that the ambulance driver of Vance Bourjaily's *Confessions of a Spent Youth* equates "a man of war" with "a man of whore": that Bourjaily's hero considers penicillin a far more important scientific achievement than radar, rocketry, or the atom bomb is understand-

33. Keith Douglas, "Cairo Jag," in *Complete Poems,* 97. Also see Bernard Gutteridge, "Sunday Promenade: Antisirane," originally published in *Traveller's Eye* (1947), reprinted in *Old Damson-Face: Poems, 1934–1974* (London: London Magazine Editions, 1975), 43.

34. John Manifold, "The Sirens," in *The War Poets: An Anthology of the War Poetry of the 20th Century,* ed. Oscar Williams (New York: John Day, 1945), 191.

35. Patrick Dickinson, "War," in *Reveille,* 241.

36. Ezra Pound, "XLV" ("With *Usura*" was first published in 1936), appears in *The Cantos (1–95)* (New York: New Directions, 1956), 23–24.

37. See esp. the speech called "To the Memory," delivered on June 13, 1943, in *"Ezra Pound Speaking,"* ed. Leonard W. Doob (Westport, Conn.: Greenwood Press, 1978), 338–40 and "XIV," in *The Cantos,* 61–63.

able, given his most traumatic wartime experience, the bathroom of a hospital in which hundreds of men infected with gonorrhea and syphilis stand, "each with a tortured penis in his hand."[38] The hostility implicit in these portraits erupts in Melvin Tolson's "The Furlough," a poem that describes how a soldier gazes upon the "silken loveliness" of "a passion-flower of joy and pain / On the golden bed I came back to possess":

I choked her just a little, and she is dead.
A furlough is an escalator to delight
Her beauty gathers rot on the golden bed.[39]

As in the posters of the period, the most intense hatred of women surfaces in those poems that identity the "boys" as victims of a war that is personified by the whore. George Barker's poem "To Any Member of My Generation" explicitly identifies the war as a dance "in what we hoped was life"; yet "Who was it in our arms but the whores of death / Whom we have found in our beds today, today?"[40] In "Careless Love," Stanley Kunitz analyzes the erotic relationship between young soldiers and the "dark beauty" of the guns that comfort them, "for what / This nymphomaniac enjoys / Inexhaustibly is boys."[41] Just as Karl Shapiro identifies boot camp with "Virginia," a female state that is sickened "with a dry disease," whose voice "we abhor," and whose sun rises "like a very tired whore" beckoning soldiers to death, Charles Causley exclaims,

O war is a casual mistress
And the world is her double bed.
She has few charms in her mechanised arms
But you wake up and find yourself dead.[42]

When a contemporary writer like Thomas Pynchon redefines the "V for Victory" in terms of the vulgarity, the void, and the vagina of a sinister, syphilitic Lady V, he is no doubt sardonically referring to the phrase "Victory-girl," which was used through the war years as a euphemism for "whore."[43]

38. Vance Bourjaily, *Confessions of a Spent Youth* (New York: Dial, 1960), 322, 345, 353.

39. Melvin B. Tolson, "The Furlough," in *Rendezvous with America* (New York: Dodd, Mead, 1944), 23–24.

40. George Barker, "To Any Member of My Generation," in *War Poets,* ed. Williams, 321.

41. Stanley Kunitz, "Careless Love," ibid., 166.

42. Karl Shapiro, "Conscription Camp," 47–48, and Charles Causley, "A Ballad for Katharine of Aragon," in *Collected Poems, 1951–1975* (London: Macmillan, 1975), 14.

43. Thomas Pynchon, *V.* (1961; repr. New York: Lippincott, 1963), 318. See Catharine R. Stimpson's essay, "Pre-Apocalyptic Atavism: Thomas Pynchon's Early Fiction," in *Mindful Pleasures: Essays on Thomas Pynchon,* ed. George Levine and David Leverenz (Boston: Little, Brown, 1976), 31–47.

B(U)Y BONDS

To focus on the erotic desires and dreads of literary men is in a sense to ignore the major purport of their literature, namely their common effort to demonstrate, in the words of the critic Don Jaffe, "how war stripped man of his manhood, reflected his absurdity and capacity for evil."[44] Indeed, one could argue further that, in response to Axis ideology associating the male with aggression, such Allied writers as George Orwell and Randall Jarrell were engaged in a critique of traditional masculinity. Similarly, conscious of the impersonality and inscrutability of technologically advanced warfare, writers like Keith Douglas and Stanley Kunitz documented how combat was invalidated as a test of individual heroism that could serve as a masculine initiation ritual. Their most telling lesson of war, after their unmasking of what W. H. Auden called the "lie of Authority," was therefore not far removed from Auden's injunction that "We must love one another or die." But, just as Auden rewrote his most famous line to read "We must love one another and die," many literary men bemoaned the inefficacy of love and mourned the insufficiency of women in an absurd universe from which the only exit was a bonding born of brotherhood.[45]

Whether male characters are turned into guilty voyeurs of their own maneuvers or corpses decaying during enemy onslaughts, their authors record a hopeless sense of emasculation. From Ciardi's anesthetized flyer and Orwell's broken "last man" to Jarrell's aborted fetus and Bourjaily's sick "men of whores," male characters are made to realize that the gun always wins in its competition with the penis. The superiority of the gun to the penis led psychologists of warfare like Lincoln Kirstein and John Hersey to examine the war as an assault on or a perversion of male sexuality. Kirstein's terrified soldier turns to masturbation only to discover that the "big load" of the Jerries' "steel-turned tubes" "splashes my small load."[46] Hersey's *War Lover* becomes a sadistic woman-hater: "when he gets in bed," a female character explains, "he makes hate—attacks, rapes, milks his gland; and thinks that makes him a man."[47] The good woman in the literature of the Second World War is therefore the woman whose sexual accessibility, compliancy, or loyalty rein-

44. Dan Jaffe, "Poets in the Inferno: Civilians, C.O.'s and Combatants," in *The Forties: Fiction, Poetry, Drama,* ed. Warren French (Deland, Fla.: Everett/Edwards, 1969), 36.

45. W. H. Auden, "September 1, 1939," in *The English Auden,* ed. Edward Mendelson (London: Faber and Faber, 1977), 245.

46. Lincoln Kirstein, "Load," *Rhymes of a PFC* (1964; repr. Boston: David R. Godine, 1981), 151–52.

47. John Hersey's *The War Lover* is discussed by Joseph J. Waldmeir, *American Novels of the Second World War* (Paris: Mouton, 1969), 27.

states the man's sense of his masculinity without this confusion of love and death, sex and murder.

But allegiance to the gun saves soldiers from dependency on fallible females. More common, then, is the implicit lesson of the famous chant that was used to teach marines how to name their instruments correctly, how, in other words, to distinguish between the rifle in one hand and the penis in the other:

"This is my rifle,
  This is my gun,
This is for fighting,
  This is for fun."

In *Battle Cry,* Leon Uris' squat sergeant patiently explains this lesson, as he hands out rifles: "You've got yourselves a new girl now. Forget that broad back home! This girl is the most faithful, truest woman in the world if you give her a fair shake. She won't sleep with no swab jockies the minute your back is turned. Keep her clean and she'll save your life."[48] True to the squat sergeant's view and typical of the verse produced by members of the forces, "Cannoneer's Lady," by Lt. Morris Earle, contrasts man's love of woman with his passion for "a horwitzer [that] goes to the heart of a man": "In the retch and recoil," he explains, "The cannoneer, loving her, cared for her more / The moment this turbulent outburst began."[49]

Perhaps the most famous novel written about the war, Norman Mailer's *The Naked and the Dead,* illustrates how even those writers engaged in developing a critique of this identification of the gun and the penis paradoxically reified the female to rectify the relationships between men. General Cummings, a Faustian fascist with repressed homosexual tendencies, derives joy solely from power and specifically from the "phallus-shell that rides through a shining vagina of steel," a fantasy Mailer is presumably ridiculing. Significantly, however, Cummings' obsession with coming is explained as the result of the overprotectiveness of his mother and the bitchiness of his wife. His working-class double, Croft, is sexually aroused by a machine gun because his wife has been unfaithful to him. Although Mailer's surrogate, Captain Hearn, seeks an alternative to Cummings' and Croft's dream of a League of Omnipotent Men, he eventually discovers his commonality with them, for what he needs most is "control and not mating." Finally, then, Mailer's novel confirms Cummings' creed: namely, that "[t]he average man always sees himself in relation to other

48. Uris, *Battle Cry,* 48; "This Is My Rifle" appears on p. 53.
49. Lt. Morris Earle, "Cannoneer's Lady," *Reveille,* 31.

men as either inferior or superior. Women play no part in it. They're an index, a yardstick among other gauges, by which to measure superiority."[50]

Whether they are dead, disloyal, or frigid wives, randy girlfriends, or raunchy whores, the female characters in *The Naked and the Dead* play no part in the action except as "gauges" located in the "Time Machine" sections that return us to civilian life before the war. Even the love that saves men from the "lie of Authority" and serves as an alternative to Cummings' philosophy of the will to power is a love between men: when Ridges and Goldstein bear the burden of Wilson's syphilitic body back to the beach at the end of the novel, Wilson becomes their "heart."[51] The brotherhood of Ridges, Goldstein, and Wilson resembles the camaraderie between buddies in countless novels like *From Here to Eternity,* where Jones presents two characters (Prewett and Warden) moving from the here and now of poker, drinking, whoring, and brawling to a fraternity that causes both men to reject their mistresses in order to wed themselves to the military.

Trying to capture the apocalyptic dynamic of war in his 1943 essay "Looking Back on the Spanish War," Orwell fixes on its eroticism when he describes the ecstasy of shaking an Italian soldier's hand:

To meet within the sound of guns,
But oh! what peace I knew then
In gazing on his battered face
Purer than any woman's![52]

Similarly, after describing a prison camp in which "those [who] survived best were feminine," Richard Eberhart claims that "we were at our peak when in the depths," sustained by "visions of brotherhood when we were broken."[53] An index of the enlisted man's alienation from his commander, such male bonding is presented as redemptive when and only when its eroticism does not become overtly sexual, and it is therefore almost always set against male homosexuality, which is usually diagnosed as a sick response to the violence of battle. Worse than being labeled a "whore" is being called a "queer" or a "fairy," for homosexuals are typically presented in World War II literature as guilt-ridden, pathologically violent, and suicidal.[54]

50. Norman Mailer, *The Naked and the Dead* (1948; repr. New York: Holt, Rinehart and Winston, 1981), 568, 580, 322.

51. Ibid., 672.

52. George Orwell, "Looking Back on the Spanish War," in *A Collection of Essays by George Orwell* (New York: Doubleday, 1954), 214.

53. Eberhart, "Brotherhood of Men," 103, 105.

54. The best discussion of the violently destructive, suicidal homosexual in the literature of the

In the effort to differentiate such homosocial eroticism from homosexuality, both the absent woman and the whore play crucial roles, for—as the imagined object of male desire and as the body that links men to men—they ratify men as male.[55] Because literary men could no longer define masculinity in traditional terms, the woman played a tangential but crucial role in their literature, for she was one of the few marks left of their virility. While sailors in *The Steel Cocoon* object to "the whole mess that made [them] need women" and lament that "you never know until the last minute whether you're going to get in or not," often admitting "I just want to get my gun," such sentiments prove that the "satisfying relationship" between men and boys on the ship is "merely a normal expression of the capacity, or even the need, of all men for the love of one another."[56] When pilots, infantry soldiers, sailors, hospital inmates, and prisoners of war become "mates" in World War II fiction, they are united by their love for each other and defended from the charge of deviancy, which such love could otherwise provoke, by their scorn for homosexuals and by the credo that "men like to get their guns off."[57]

Mailer's *An American Dream* goes on to dramatize the implications of such gunnery. During the war Second Lieutenant Rojack kills one German "faggot" with "mother-love all over his face" and one wounded but determined German with "haunting" eyes, and then he returns home, moving back into a "marriage [that] had been a war": after Rojack murders his wife, his eyes are at last "equal" to the eyes of the German with the bayonet and, after he sodomizes her maid, he finally savors what had been missing on the battlefield, the "high private pleasure in plugging a Nazi."[58] Through Rojack, Mailer analyzes why, for example, Ivor Roberts-Jones, a poet who served as an artillery lieutenant, viewed the bombardment pattern produced by "The guns shout[ing] in the narrow valleys" as "little . . . shifts, like a girl arranging her dress, / At the start of the party waiting for the young men."[59] But Mailer also illuminates his own

Second World War is Peter G. Jones, *War and the Novelist: Appraising the American War Novel* (Columbia: University of Missouri Press, 1976), 113–61.

55. I am indebted to Irene Quenzler Brown of the Women's Studies Program at the University of Connecticut for the term *homosocial*. I have also profited from Eve Sedgwick's use of this term in *Between Men: English Literature and Male Homosocial Desire* (New York: Columbia University Press, 1985).

56. Plagemann, *The Steel Cocoon,* 63–64, 20.

57. Jones, *From Here to Eternity,* 643.

58. Norman Mailer, *An American Dream* (New York: Dell, 1965), 11, 42, 47. Kate Millett discusses the aeronautic imagery of Rojack's "solo flight" into Ruta in *Sexual Politics* (1969; repr. New York: Avon, 1971), 31.

59. Roberts-Jones's poem is discussed in a different context by R. N. Currey in *Poets of the 1939–1945 War* (London: Longmans, Green, 1960), 38.

earlier work, specifically the conclusion of *The Naked and the Dead* where, in an effort to foster camaraderie, the major who inadvertently blunders into a successful campaign "jazz[es] up the map-reading class by having a full-size color photograph of Betty Grable in a bathing suit, with a co-ordinate grid system laid over it." Thomas Pynchon echoes this scene at the beginning of *Gravity's Rainbow* with Slothrop's map of London, which is sprinkled with stars—"Carolines, Marias, Annes, Susans, Elizabeths"—each marking the place where he has had an affair and each appearing a few days before bomb sites of V-2 rockets mysteriously appear.[60]

BATTLE CRIES

The pinned-up "bombshells" who become the targets of men's desire unnervingly recall the women in the military who continually confronted, at the camps they called "Wolf Swamps," sexual assaults from men who jokingly translated WAAF as "Women All Fuck."[61] They also recall the WASP (Women's Air Service Pilots Association) pilots who were physically endangered by their male colleagues: according to Sally Van Wagenen Keil, when women pilots towed targets for gunnery training missions, receiving flak from American soldiers, they were like "clay pigeons in a shooting gallery"; when they tested planes for faults or damage, their safety was threatened by mechanical failures which were the result of sabotage, or so they suspected when traces of sugar (sure to stop an engine in seconds) were found in the gas tank of one WASP plane.[62] As auxiliary units, which were ruled by the military but not legally within it, many English and American women's corps received no insurance, no benefits, no ranks equivalent to those of men, and no pockets in the skirts that were designed to head off public reaction against masculine uniforms.[63]

While literary women may not have faced physical assaults, they were bombarded by images that required a retort, or so the surprising directness of much of their literature suggests. No slower than George Orwell to perceive totalitarianism as a Big Brother, literary women did not react to his face with

60. Mailer, *Naked and the Dead,* 721; Thomas Pynchon, *Gravity's Rainbow* (1973; repr. New York: Bantam, 1974), 21.

61. Cynthia Enloe, *Does Khaki Become You? The Militarization of Women's Lives* (London: Pluto, 1983), 2.

62. Sally Van Wagenen Keil, *Those Wonderful Women in their Flying Machines: The Unknown Heroines of World War II* (New York: Rawson, Wade, 1979), 197, 202, 212.

63. Women's uniforms are portrayed and discussed in Jack Cassin-Scott and Angus McBride, *Women at War, 1939–45* (London: Osprey, 1980), 15–18.

Orwell's nostalgia for a pre-War world of renunciatory motherhood or with his longing for a redemptive fraternity. On the contrary, their art frequently begins with a critique of both fascist and liberal militarism and ends with a rejection of precisely the images of women that their male literary counterparts promulgated. In poems, stories, and novels that respond to the ideology of separate spheres that is embedded in so much war propaganda and literature, many literary women resembled Muriel Rukeyser in her effort to get "Beyond the men of letters, / Of business and of death."[64]

Beginning "Letter to the Front" with the assertion that "Women and poets see the truth arrive," Rukeyser analyzed how women represent refuge to soldiers in combat: "now we are that home you dream across a war," she muses, determining to "hold belief," even "though all you want be bed with one / Whose mouth is bread and wine, whose flesh is home."[65] Equally cut off from communication with men are the women portrayed by Dorothy Parker and Babette Deutsch: the wife in Parker's "The Lovely Leave" realizes that her husband has found in the service "companionships no—no—wife can ever give [him]," and his leave proves to her that he has taken leave of her and virtually married his companions in the military, while Deutsch simply asks, "How shall we talk / To you who must learn the language / Spelled on the fields in famine, in blood on the sidewalk?," an idiom that insures her own impotence: "I cannot hide you now, / Or shelter you ever, / Or give you a guide through hell."[66] But, if the absent soldier and the soldier on leave are frightening, the returning combatant is a positive menace. In Elizabeth Bowen's short story "The Demon Lover," a woman is abducted by a man lost in the First World War and found in the Second, while in her novel *The Heat of the Day* the heroine is horrified to realize that she cannot disentangle the identities of her lover and his antagonist, an Axis spy and his Allied pursuer.[67]

What the war teaches women is that they must relinquish any dreams they may have had about joining forces with men. In *The Member of the Wedding,* Carson McCuller's Frankie Addams, a girl who "wanted to be a boy and go to the war as a Marine," envies "soldiers in the army [who] can say we," for the

64. Muriel Rukeyser, "Wreath of Women," *Beast in View* (1944), in *The Collected Poems of Muriel Rukeyser* (New York: McGraw-Hill, 1978), 217–18.

65. "Letter to the Front," in ibid., 239.

66. Parker placed "The Lovely Leave" first in her original *Portable* collection. See *The Portable Dorothy Parker* (New York: Penguin, 1944, 1977), 17; Babette Deutsch, *Take Them, Stranger* (New York: Henry Holt, 1944), 58–59.

67. Elizabeth Bowen, "The Demon Lover" (1946), is reprinted in *The Collected Stories of Elizabeth Bowen* (New York: Random House, 1982), 661–66; *The Heat of the Day* (1948; repr. New York: Avon, 1979).

war "would not include her." Yet, when she turns herself into the feminine F. Jasmine Addams and meets a soldier near a sign that reads "Prophylactic Military," she discovers that their conversation "would not join": her first date talks "a kind of double-talk that, try as she would, she could not follow."[68] Without a member of her own, she learns that she cannot become a member of the war-wedding but must instead defend herself against the soldier who tries to rape her. As if to summarize Rukeyser's, Parker's, Bowen's, and McCuller's insights, in stories like "Men" and "Army of Occupation" Kay Boyle implies that what women face in wartime is not only the unleashed violence of sex-starved men but also the elaborate images such men construct as a compensation for and a retaliation against the sex they are presumably fighting to preserve—but that they are really preserving themselves to fight.[69]

The threat of violent rape also appears in "Serenade: Any Man to Any Woman," in which Edith Sitwell presents a cannoneer who identifies his beloved with a cannon and woos the woman who "Can never see what dead men know!" by asking her to "die with me and be my love."[70] While Sitwell implies that the "universal Flood" of wartime destruction is composed of female blood, Virginia Woolf writes more hopefully about the necessity of "compensat[ing] the man for the loss of his gun" and thereby freeing German and English airmen "from the machine."[71] But in Woolf's novel about the period between the wars, *Between the Acts,* a young woman is haunted by a newspaper article about troopers who dragged a girl "up to the barrack room where she was thrown upon a bed. Then one of the troopers removed part of her clothing, and she screamed and hit him about the face."[72] Although such black women writers as Gwendolyn Brooks and Ann Petry record the suffering of black soldiers in an army as fascist in its racism as are Germany's services, they also present the ways in which even these victimized men treat their women as whores.[73]

68. McCullers, *Member of the Wedding* (1946; repr. New York: Bantam, 1981), 39, 127.

69. Kay Boyle, "Men" and "Army of Occupation," both published in the 1940s, appear in *50 Stories* (New York: Penguin, 1981), 275–87, 439–53.

70. Edith Sitwell, "Serenade: Any Man to Any Woman," in *The Collected Poems of Edith Sitwell* (New York: Vanguard, 1968), 269–70. Also see "Lullaby," pp. 167–68.

71. Virginia Woolf, "Thoughts on Peace in an Air Raid," was composed in August 1940 and is reprinted in *The Death of the Moth and Other Essays* (London: Hogarth, 1942), 156.

72. Virginia Woolf, *Between the Acts* (1941; repr. New York: Harcourt Brace Jovanovich, 1949), 20.

73. Gwendolyn Brooks, "Gay Chaps at the Bar" (1945) and "The Anniad" (1949), in *The World of Gwendolyn Brooks* (New York: Harper and Row, 1971), 48–59, 81–96. Ann Petry, *The Street* (1946; repr. New York: Pyramid, 1961).

It is in this context that we need to read the most ambitious poem written by a woman about the war, H. D.'s *Helen in Egypt,* in which the so-called "cause" of the Trojan War attempts to extricate herself from the guilt with which she has been imbued. Meditating on a question Simone Weil had raised in her essay "The *Iliad,* Poem of Force"—"What does Helen matter to Ulysses?"—H. D.'s epic recalls Weil's answer: "Troy and Helen matter to the Greeks only as the causes of their shedding so much blood and tears; it is in making oneself master that one finds one is the master of horrible memories."[74] Meeting Achilles on the beach, what H. D.'s Helen must confront is an attempted rape by a soldier who can only be redeemed if she can break the "Command"—the "iron-ring"—of the martial brotherhood that has protected him throughout the fighting. H. D.'s exiled Helen illustrates a major incongruity in the literary responses of men and women to the Second World War, for while male artists reasserted an ideology of separate spheres, women writers perceived themselves and female culture to be in danger of destruction.

Concerned less with military maneuvers and more with sexual antagonism, the literature women wrote about World War II needs to be understood as a documentation of women's sense that the war was a blitz on them. From Stevie Smith's *Over the Frontier* to Doris Lessing's *Children of Violence* series, Djuna Barnes' *The Antiphon,* Katherine Anne Porter's *Ship of Fools,* and Paule Marshall's *Brown Girl, Brownstones,* women's literary works depict the ruin of the war as the site for the ruin of women's lives or communities. For Harriette Arnow's Gertie in *The Dollmaker,* it means relinquishing *"her land"*:[75] she is removed from her Edenic farm and catapulted into the industrial hell of Detroit's war factories, where she loses her economic independence from her husband, her children, and her art. For the women who inhabit the Victorian hostel in Muriel Spark's *The Girls of Slender Means,* it means an undetonated bomb that explodes and thereby destroys the last vestiges of the female community.[76] Fittingly, amidst the joyous crowds commemorating V-J Day in the London rally that concludes Spark's novel, a young sailor quietly slips a knife between the ribs of the girl at his side. Like Elizabeth Bishop, who abhorred the medal-dressed, combative "cocks" screaming "unwanted love, conceit and war," many literary women ask, "Roosters, what are you project-

74. H. D., *Helen in Egypt* (1961; repr. New York: New Directions, 1974), 55, 63. Simone Weil, "The *Iliad,* Poem of Force," in *The Simone Weil Reader,* ed. George A. Panichas (New York: David McKay, 1977), 171.

75. Harriette Arnow, *The Dollmaker* (1954; repr. New York: Avon, 1972), 134.

76. Muriel Spark, *The Girls of Slender Means* (1963; repr. New York: Putnam's, 1982), 174–75.

ing?"[77] The literary responses of men to the Second World War help explain why, for so many women artists, the weapons of war—like the canon of combat—could only result in what Sylvia Plath called "Charred skirts and deathmask."[78]

77. Elizabeth Bishop, "Roosters" (1946), in *The Complete Poems, 1927–1979* (New York: Farrar, Straus and Giroux, 1983), 359.

78. Sylvia Plath, "Getting There" (1962), in *The Collected Poems of Sylvia Plath,* ed. Ted Hughes (New York: Harper and Row, 1981), 249.

DENISE RILEY

Some Peculiarities of Social Policy concerning Women in Wartime and Postwar Britain

War throws gender into sharp relief. During World War II, in Britain as elsewhere, women's war work, even when presented as the result of their collective heroic capacity, was seen as work done by *women*. It was permeated by the gender of its performers, and consequently by what was seen as the temporary nature of the work of women who were also mothers.[1] In some ways, the weight placed on gender is unsurprising. Only at a time of exceptional demand for labor—that is, during the war—were all women, regardless of their reproductive status, made publicly visible as workers. But, although in the abstract this might seem to have been the ideal moment to break down the logic of sexual difference, and to push for childcare facilities and better working conditions for women, in fact these goals proved impossible to achieve. Married women employed in industry were never taken seriously as real workers, and by 1945 the dominant rhetoric described the figures of woman as mother and woman as worker as diametrically opposed and refused to consider the possibility of their combination.

Women *when named as a sex* by the formulations of social policy cannot escape being the incarnation of gender as strange or temporary workers; nor can they escape being seen as hovering on the edge of maternity. How did this emerge in British social policy in 1945, the year in which the Labour government was elected? The combination of universal postwar pronatalism with the undifferentiating tones of social democracy was deadly. Rhetorically, women

1. Denise Riley, "The Free Mothers: Pronatalism and Working Women in Industry at the End of the Last War in Britain," *History Workshop* 11 (1981).

were overpersonified as mothers and desexed as workers. There were few institutions or social programs designed to meet the practical needs of working mothers, although women with children did gradually take up unskilled and semiskilled light industrial work. This postwar mood fit in very well with the conditions and forms of women's work during the war years, where everything unusual was explained as being "for the duration only." Far from war work serving to revolutionize women's employment on any serious level, it was characterized as an exceptional and valiant effort from which women would thankfully sink away in peacetime. This characterization was heavily underscored by pronatalism.

It was hard for women to maintain any graceful balance on this tightrope, needing to criticize, on the one side, overemphasis on the role of mother and, on the other, their desexualization as workers. In this climate, one could hardly expect anything but rhetorical feminization to accompany what small admission there was of "women's needs," whether from the standpoint of conservatism or radicalism. It is impossible to imagine discreet, and gentlemanly provision of nurseries and flexible factory hours—given that any new social policy must advertise itself as innovative and will do so in the language of given and recognizable categories. The difficulty is that women as the foci of social policy are always something more than bearers of a sex; they are wives, mothers, sometimes daughters; they were sometimes (but always awkwardly) reasserted as citizens in 1945; and as workers they are seen as saturated in this annoying sex. Hailing one manifestation of the sex often involves contesting the importance of the others, both in social policy and in critical opposition.

The historian faces a dilemma in the task of assessing the rhetorical and excessive feminization of women as both workers and mothers in wartime social policy, which often took the form of attributing "girlishness" to the work force or "brooding maternity" to housewives. The feminist historian finds herself dealing with material that is also fascinated by the category of "women," but in a manner that may well be antagonistic to her own persuasions. This may lead to a contest between conservative social policy and contemporary feminism over some "right" or "better" naming of women when wartime policies on the family are under scrutiny—clearly a fruitless battle.

In Britain during the 1940s, women en bloc were subjected to a barrage of feminizing descriptions that denied or misread the practical requirements of women workers with children. Social policy, addressing "women" as a foreign body, was indifferent to the fact that "women" constituted no uniform category, and real consequences flowed from this; a feminist history must respond to this indifference, but it cannot do so only by means of a blanket denial that women are or want such-and-such or by setting up a rival unified category of "women." Feminist historians will need sleight of hand and elasticity which proved difficult for women's labor and feminist organizations in the late 1930s and 1940s. This peculiarity—the need to seize the opportunity to speak for "women" without adopting the convictions of the dominant pronatalist rhetoric that also claimed to speak for "women"—beset those organizations and faces feminist commentators now. The following descriptions are given to convey the intricacies of that peculiarity.[2]

The Royal Commission on Population was established in 1944. After five years' deliberation, the commission concluded that a series of broad social reforms to aid families were vital to keep the population from sinking below replacement level. Most demographers of the 1930s and 1940s worked on the supposition that marital patterns and mortality rates would not change. In practice, earlier marriage and childbearing threw off their predictions of the number of births necessary to save the population. These demographers set the target at at least three and desirably four children per family, and this was advocated in a context of social reform. Some of these reforms even materialized, although they might have done so even without the pronatalist gift wrapping.

The question of democracy in obstetric help surfaced at the level of official reports: the 1946 *Survey of Childbearing in Great Britain,* by a joint committee of the Royal College of Obstetricians and Gynaecologists and the Population Investigation Committee, referred to class differences in the availability of analgesics and anaesthetics in childbirth. Removing such a lack of parity (partly by supplying midwives with Minnit gas and air machines) fit well with both the democratizing aspirations of the prospective National Health Service and the alarm caused by the decline in family size (in working-class families particularly) to an average of one or two children. A concern for the "quality" of the wished-for increase in the population mixed well with the mood of egalitarianism and the 1945 speech of social democracy. Thus supplying contraceptive devices and information no more ran counter to pronatalist aims than did the improvement of maternity and infant medical care; as pronatalists themselves pointed out, contraception furthered their aims by ensuring the "sensible spacing" of births and encouraging parental "responsibility."

While, on the available demographic evidence (which had not caught up

2. This article draws on material from the abovementioned article and from Denise Riley, *War in the Nursery* (London: Virago Press, 1983).

with the fact that the birth rate was beginning to rise), it seemed reasonable to almost all political tendencies to express anxiety about the low birth rate (both Labour and Conservative programs did so), it was recognized as important not to restrict access to contraception. For the Britons were not Germans. The 1949 *Population Report* again distanced itself carefully from what it understood as reactionary pronatalism. The contraceptive habits newly acquired by the working class were criticized in some quarters, however. The notion that a good example should be set by the upper middle classes, the guardians of racial quality, was stressed by more rightwing pronatalist writers, who also questioned the advisability of spreading contraceptive knowledge further. "Apathy," a low "morale," and lack of faith in the future were cited by these writers as explanations for the contraceptive habits of the working class.

On the other hand, at the end of the war, "materialist" accounts of the seemingly low birth rate blamed the housing shortage. Debating the Housing (Temporary Accommodation) Bill in the Commons in September 1944, Mr. Cocks (a Labour member from Broxtowe) said, typically tying up birth control with housing restrictions, "[t]he Government say they need larger families and have made an appeal to the country for larger families. By erecting these houses [the temporary steel bungalows that preceded the "prefabs"] they are more likely to stop childbirth altogether, and instead of calling them Portal bungalows they should be dedicated to Dr. Marie Stopes."[3] Others rejected such "economistic" accounts in favor of theories of spiritual despair ranging from mild anomie to a profound national world-weariness; and some combination of practical and spiritual encouragements to women to reproduce was recommended by commonsensical members of all parties.[4]

The Royal Commission on Population hoped to set up nurseries, nursery schools, play centers, and laundries to ease the burden of the mother. The recommendations of the Fabian groups within the Labour party—"the general aim must be to secure that reproduction takes place at the age and rate which breeds the best biological stocks"—included free access for all to improved obstetric care, contraceptive advice, and nurseries for "occasional relief." They pointed out "the desirability of preventing any marked difference in the fertility of different social groups." Healthy immigrants would help the population problems and would be "best suited" if they were of European origin: "the eugenics of immigration cannot be overstressed," the Fabians

3. Hansard, September 26, 1944, Commons Debates.

4. See, for example, Roy Harrod, Memoranda Presented to the Royal Commission, *Papers of the Royal Commission on Population,* vol. 5 (London: HMSO, 1950), 85.

insisted; "sound stock" was essential for the "national good."[5] Pronatalist, egalitarian, social-democratic, eugenicist and racialist ideas were all combined. Overt eugenicism was more subdued than it had been in the mid-1930s, yet the intermittent debate about the introduction of family allowances in the 1940s sat fairly close to contemporary pronatalism. Here, too, England was carefully dissociated from the unpleasant practices of fascist Europe. Sir William Beveridge (architect of the Beveridge Report, the blueprint for the British welfare state) discounted pronatalism as the inspiration for the family allowance system, instead emphasizing its social-democratic, ameliorative aspect.[6]

Pronatalism permeated a myriad of social policy issues during and after the war. As one looks through the wartime and postwar literature, it becomes a matter of trying to understand fine shades of relations: how pronatalism prevented family allowances from being captured by the left as an unambiguously socialist program, or how anxiety over the birth rate affected the equal pay debate.

The Royal Commission on Equal Pay (1944–46) was appointed officially, in the words of its own Preface, to "examine the existing relationship between the remuneration of men and women in the public services, in industry and in other fields of employment: to consider the social, economic and financial implications of the claim to equal pay for equal work." Commission members speculated about the effects of equal pay on the birth rate but felt that on that point they could reach "not only conjectural, but meagre," conclusions.[7]

In 1944 the Fabian Women's Group submitted evidence to the Commission, arguing that the introduction of equal pay would not have a "dysgenic effect." Women would not be tempted to flee marriage and maternity for the attractions of an equal wage—if maternity no longer entailed "being a slave to a broken sink or a decayed and obsolete coal range."[8] In this they followed the position adopted by the Standing Joint Conference of Working Women's Organisations on the social need to value the work of mothers in the home adequately and treat them as "workers," too. The Fabian Women's Group had to argue on all sides at once: "We do not . . . accept the assumption . . . that the

5. Fabian Society, *Population and the People: A National Policy,* by a committee of the Fabian Society under the chairmanship of Dr. W. A. Robson (London, 1946), 48–50.

6. Sir William Beveridge, *Voluntary Action: A Report on Methods of Social Advance* (London, 1948).

7. Royal Commission on Equal Pay, Cmd. 6937 (London: HMSO, 1944–46).

8. Fabian Women's Group, Minutes of Evidence Taken before the Royal Commission on Equal Pay, Appendix, xi–xix.

desire for children and for home-making has become so weak among British women that the introduction of reasonable rates of pay would cause a stampede away from the home; but we do not hold that sweating the mass of wage-earning women is a sensible or civilised way of persuading them to have children."[9]

Some conservatives, on the other hand, were prepared to submit that there were "social causes for unequal pay" (that is, reasons for retaining it). One was, according to the economist Roy Harrod, "to secure that motherhood as a vocation is not too unattractive financially compared with work in the professions, industry, or trade."[10] The commissioners themselves commented:

> Ignoring the fluctuations due to war, the spread of feminist ideas has operated in recent decades to enhance the demand for women's labour and to expand the supply. . . . If, now, an upward reevaluation of the occupied women's standard of living were to coincide with a withdrawal of women from the market in response to a swing of social opinion in favour of motherhood and home life, such an improvement of standard might prove to be maintainable . . . even in the absence of a further rise in the intensity of the demand for women's labour.[11]

At first glance the welter of proposed improvements in the lot of the postwar mother and family seems quite dazzling. When it came to mothers, who was not a social democrat? A huge literature, concentrated in 1945 and 1946, argued for nurseries, after-school play centers, rest homes for tired housewives, family tickets on trains, official neighborhood babysitters, holidays on the social services for poorer families, access for all to good gynecological and obstetric help, a revolution in domestic architecture toward streamlined rational kitchens and a good number of bedrooms, and more communal restaurants and laundries. Eva Hubback's suggestions in *The Population of Britain* included marriage guidance clinics, adult education classes to teach "hygiene, family relationships, child management, and the domestic crafts," and a new school curriculum including "education in family living." Houses should be built to accommodate the larger families of the future; women should be able to work part-time if they wished; the bar on women's working in certain professions after marriage should go; and training in civic values and "citizenship" should be diffused through all educational levels. The recommendations of the 1946 *Survey of Childbearing in Great Britain* by the Royal College of Obstetricians and Gynaecologists also mentioned adult education in "domes-

9. Ibid., 84.
10. Roy Harrod, Evidence Taken before the Royal Commission on Equal Pay, 92.
11. Royal Commission on Equal Pay, 118–19.

tic relationships" and "preparation for family life," as well as sex education and courses in household skills in school.

The 1949 Report of the Royal Commission on Population advocated a package of income-tax reliefs, nurseries, improved home design, washing machines on the rent-to-buy system and a network of family holiday camps. The Fabian evidence to the 1945 Royal Commission on Population was also in favor of nursery schools, family traveling opportunities, education in citizenship, and a system of effective financial aids to parents, including a marriage bonus. Cash benefits for new mothers could be supplemented by baby things in kind, like carriages. In 1948, Beveridge himself recommended "holidays for housewives," pointing to the Lancashire Council of Social Services' home, the Brentwood Recuperative Centre for Mothers and Children, as an example. "The housewife may at times be as much in need of rehabilitation to do her job as a crash-shocked airman or injured workman."[12] Beveridge also approved of the 1945 Reilly plan, which proposed "a return to the village green"—making cooking and washing communal to ease the isolation of the housewife.[13]

More examples of these mixtures of practical improvements, domestic innovations, and pronatalist devices—which emphasized the concern about the strains of maternity that was at the bottom of all this activity—could be given, but what I want to point out here is the tight meshing of these elements, which is so noticeable in retrospect. By 1945 the rhetoric of social-democratic policy on the family had been so often invoked that its repetitions began to sound as flattened and exhausted as the housewives' lives they sought to improve. For, insofar as a "family policy" concerns children, and given that the bearing and rearing of children is by biology and custom respectively the province of women, then a main object of family policy is women. The universally pronatalist climate of 1945–47 ensured that the effective target of postwar social philosophy was the mother.

One of the clearest instances of this focus on the mother can be seen in arguments in favor of postwar retention of nurseries. The widespread pronursery sentiments of the late 1940s were perfectly congruent with enthusiasm for the family. Nurseries were advocated as key points for educating mothers through influence and precept, and they were thought likely to raise the birth rate by easing the burden of childrearing. The many postwar proposals for conveying first aid to tired mothers shaded into allegations of "fecklessness" and incompetence, which could be remedied by on-the-spot instruction.

12. Beveridge, *Voluntary Action,* 264–65.

13. Lawrence Wolfe, *The Reilly Plan: A New Way of Life* (London, 1948).

"Help" and "training" were close neighbors in this literature, and a tart comment in *Our Towns,* the result of investigations by the Hygiene Committee of the Women's Group on Public Welfare, makes the underlying attitude clear: "We cannot afford not to have the nursery school: it seems to be the only agency capable of cutting the slum mind off at its root and building the whole child while yet there is time."[14]

Advocacy of nurseries as adjuncts to training for motherhood was adopted not only by classical conservatives but also by Fabian humanists. In 1945 the Fabians again recommended the judicious use of nurseries to promote democracy: "to provide the freedom from family cares which the well-to-do mother provides for herself."[15] The main argument, however, was not egalitarian but pronatalist; or, more accurately, egalitarianism with regard to the family was written into the language of any pronatalism that claimed progressive or democratic ambition, whatever its formal political origin. Yet none of these considerations brought about a national network of postwar nurseries, for the government was not, in the end, swayed into action.

Nevertheless it can be argued—and was argued at the time—that real progress was made: access to contraceptive and obstetric services was improved and democratized; the lives of children in homes run by local authorities received fresh consideration; family allowances were introduced. These were gains in line with the long-voiced demands of women's labor organizations and were significant advances, however imperfect and flawed their implementation. It was widely assumed by contemporary socialists and social democrats that serious humanitarian advances had been put into motion by postwar family policies, even if the material gains were in practice slight—as with family allowances, the principle was respected, while the five shillings a week was derided.

But it is important to notice that, although social policy did in some ways treat women and children as separate family members, for the most part women were considered only as mothers within the family, socially and economically. Questions of childcare and other reforms central to the lives of women and children were decisively captured by a language in which the figure of the mother was continuously produced as both cause and object of all these reforms. Mothers were indeed addressed in their own right, but this was not in itself any guarantee of political advance, even if it held the promise of practical gains.

14. Women's Hygiene Committee of the Women's Group on Public Welfare, *Our Towns: A Close-up* (London, 1943), 105.

15. Fabian Society, *Population and People,* 32.

There is a crucial difference between invoking "the mother" and speaking about the practical needs of women with children: the first is a rhetoric of function and static position; the second discusses sexual-social differences without fixing them under the appearance of eternity. To say this is perfectly compatible with acknowledging that some real, if circumscribed, improvements were achieved in the lives of women with children. But postwar pronatalism did not of itself produce such gains; even if it acted as a spur, the goals themselves had other and older origins. And pronatalist speech imposed a double edge on the articulation of these limited social gains, for this was always at risk of being expressed in a merely instrumental diction.

The risks of the metaphor of the mother as worker in the home in a climate of pronatalism are doubtless clearer in retrospect, as are its temptations. That "housewives and mothers"—the two so often named in the same breath that they might have been one hyphenated occupational category—did "real and vital work" became a cliché of 1945 and 1946. The architects of rational kitchens were fond of it; the Fabian homage to the community and the ideals of citizenship relied on it; and its currency was such that even its manifestation in certain kinds of feminist literature was unsurprising.

Some tendencies, occupied with predicting and influencing postwar family policy, avoided the assertion and counter-assertion about the proper dispositions of "women" by having it all ways at once. The Fabian recommendations to the Royal Commission on Population held that women must be wholehearted full-time mothers yet must not age into being "parasites" on the community. They should be aided by social and economic reforms, so that they might more easily produce more and better children. The Fabians saw the "new marriage" as "teamwork" between husband and wife; Fabian feminism tended to look back, half bored and half scandalized, at the lamentable separatism of its mothers' generation.

In the vision of 1945 progressivism, women in production would work on the same terms as men; women at home—mothers—would pull their weight within "the community," that declassed terrain of pure sociability. Fabian social-democratic idealism, including its feminism, effectively collapsed sexual difference into a brisk citizenship, trampling over the solid intricacies of both class and gender; except in the case of maternity, where it fell in with the tenets of a broad pronatalism, liberally understood. This Fabian influence was clearly present in the formulations of family policy deliberations and commissions toward the end of the war.

In assessing it, we face the difficulties inherent in analyzing social policy from a feminist viewpoint. Feminism insists on full recognition of the special needs of women. But it also quarrels with social policy makers' assessments of what those needs and that sexual difference are. So the feminist critique may attack an unimaginative and conservative stress on gender on the part of social policy—at the same time as it tries to advance its own view of how the unhappiness of women's lives may be improved. But this means that both social policy and feminist critique necessarily emphasize the category of women.

This brings up one of the stubborn questions for any feminist political philosophy: the problem of how to assert a category without becoming trapped within it; how never to overlook or misread gender in its manifestations while also not allowing it to hang like a veil to filter every glimpse of the world; as if we perceived all of it in advance; as if being women or being men produced, out of that very distinction itself, exhaustively distinctive lives. Close attention to the effects of gender must be accompanied by a sense of when it is more appropriate to *deemphasize* some overinsistent naming of women. It is the tendency of social policy on women and the family to excessively feminize, to name the sex tenaciously, as if possession of a gender in itself automatically entailed the smooth generation of a social role. Part of the feminist critique will therefore be, paradoxically, a minimizing of the naming of women. But this does not allow us to turn with relief to the category of "human"—at least, not yet. There have been too many premature hailings of the human in the name of socialism, premature because they have not gone far enough in tracing the fine ramifications of gender everywhere. Yet this is a necessarily interminable business; it may be more accurate to remark that there can be no direct transition from "women" to "human."

Could there be a conservative language which when proposing progressive social policies might be innocent in its effects? On the evidence of postwar Britain, I suspect not; there, it was as if a deeply conventional naming of the mother had by 1948 become a veneer over an altered economic surface; progressively espoused nurseries were transformed into conservatively denounced nurseries, yet each side used remarkably similar rhetoric. A mass of unbroken language, a seamless web of invocations of "the mother, the woman worker" masked profound dissent. Social policy may well be far less cohesive than its own presentation suggests; it may be internally quite incoherent, concealing an elaborate history of submergence and resurfacing. The history of the introduction of family allowances makes this forcefully plain. Or local and central government may be at odds and idiosyncratic policies locally pursued, for example by the medical officers of health who had their own persuasions about the care of children. Yet the language deployed flows across these cracks, creating the appearance of a smooth surface which can exert a powerful appeal.

At other points we can trace the opposite phenomenon: flaws and fissures widening where a contradictory speech breaks apart. Social policy may speak with many voices—some which have a sneaking disrespect for the authority of the others—or older departmental battles may be fought over again under the guise of a more contemporary rhetoric. Government equivocation on nurseries is indifferent to women's needs and wishes except when expediency suggests it; the government struggles over its own problems of how to fund and extend some policy, how to preserve the spirit "for the duration only." For civil servants are not social theorists; they inherit a set of contingencies, and a policy is also a morass of haste, calculation and miscalculation, banality, cynicism, and delay. These contingencies may be supported by theories which, purporting to be drawn from psychology or history, may merely be the traces of an infinite regress of mutual appeals to each others' "expert evidence" of the nature of human or maternal needs. All these observations warn us to adopt caution when tempted to speak of "the language of social policy" or "the rhetoric of maternity."

There would be little gain in attempting to enliven social history merely by adding a new sociology of language. Rather than simply identifying "a language of" something, we need to inch toward some sense of the effects on our lives of ways of talking and reading and being always represented. How to assess, for instance, the impact on "women themselves" of their continually being described as mothers, girlish employees, docile mother-workers? Especially when these "women themselves" may not have access to a contrasting set of descriptions, how does the language *work back* on the consciousness of its ostensible subjects? For sometimes one must speak and act within a language one may feel half-consciously uneasy with, unsatisfied by: *there may be no choice of words.*

So to the difficulty of the overfeminization heavily present in British expressions of policy during wartime is added the difficulty of understanding its resonances in the minds and words of its targets. This understanding is an essential part of deciphering social policy, and not an optional extra for those with a taste for popular psychology or oral history. The difficulties are immense, but surely some speculation is preferable to rigorously shunning the area. For example, I think we can fairly safely suggest that there must be gaps between a psychology and a social policy that claims allegiance to it; between a formal social policy and the practices that ostensibly embody it; between propaganda and people's behavior, which may resemble its dictates but for independent reasons; between the enactment of a social policy and people's acceptance of it—even when they appear to comply. A close examination of the nature of these gaps in specific circumstances is essential to deciphering a social policy.

Essential to this enterprise, too, is considering, even if only speculatively, how the languages of a social policy work in fine detail. For example, we need to interpret the impression it makes on its targets, assess the degree of "consent" to the formulations of, say, a heavily conservative rhetoric of the family. Here, if we speak only of an official rhetoric of the family embodied in policies, and study only its effects measured as compliance (seen from a feminist perspective as culpability) or resistance (seen as a heroic cynicism), we obscure the fact that there are no completely naive or completely knowing linguistic subjects. People may independently adhere to a rhetoric of the family which is not that of officialdom, although it may deploy similar terms, and their use of rhetoric may not mean they are blind to the actual difficulties and antagonisms within families. This adds a necessary complication to assessing social "consent" to family policy; the recognition that an unpleasant rhetoric may superficially resonate with a different preexisting speech, hesitant and contradictory and fully cognizant of misery, about the family. Analogous considerations could also influence our reading of the success of a socialist family rhetoric or discourse on women. In all cases questions of the availability of alternative descriptions of social possibilities for women are crucial; unease or dissatisfaction needs to recognize alternatives to the status quo before it can ascend to a full or "political" articulation, legible as "resistance" to subsequent generations.

A better understanding of the impact of the feminizing speech of wartime British pronatalism demands special attention to the histories of the political and social languages which buoyed it up or embraced some of its terms. For a public language comes with us into the house; but when it crosses the threshold, it will always encounter another and not fully distinct language already installed there.

JANE JENSON

The Liberation and New Rights for French Women

The end of the Second World War and the Liberation was a moment of great change in the status of French women. They were finally granted the right to vote and to run for public office, and the Constitution of the Fourth Republic enshrined the right to work in its articles. These real gains reflected the fact that for France the dreadful experience of the war was also a catalyst for social revolution. Despite pain, death, and loss of national dignity, the war seemed to clear the way for national renewal. Thus, the Liberation was seen as a moment to right wrongs, end injustice, and move the country toward a more equitable and democratic society. As part of this process, it was also the moment to bring women into full participation in the polity and equality in the workplace.

At the same time, however, the Liberation was also a moment of reinforced attention to the needs of workers and their families and to the nation's need for a larger population. Social rights for the citizens of France took a leap forward as the modern welfare state took shape. Some programs were extensions of what had existed before the war, others had been developed by the Vichy regime, and some were new. No matter what their source, however, all these programs were consequential for the lives of French women because they established the shape of women's relationship to the state for the whole postwar period.

Much of the discourse of the policy process included an assumption that women's place was not at work and in public but exclusively within the family, sustainer of the private sphere. Postwar social programs thus emphasized women's family roles. They were designed in ways which encouraged the

This paper is a partial report of a project funded by a Fellowship from the German Marshall Fund of the United States in 1984.

expansion of a gender-defined division of labor between public and private spheres. In addition, the inequality of civil rights which characterized the situation of the two genders before and during the war was not altered at its end: wives remained subordinate to the *chef de famille*.

This essay traces the reasons for the seemingly contradictory results of wartime and the Liberation for women's condition—expansion of economic and political equality and of social rights, yet continued legal subordination within the family. Many of the reasons can be found in the conditions of war, the political struggles which took place from 1939 to 1945, and the balance of political forces that resulted from the Liberation. Only by specifying the overall aims, actions, and possible alliances of the important political participants can we understand their motives for selectively granting new rights to women while leaving intact other forms of legal subordination.

The political situation in France from 1944 to 1947 was dramatically different from either the *immobilisme* of the Third Republic or traditionally conservative Vichy. As a consequence of these differences, citizenship rights were finally extended to women, and female workers were given better access to the paid labor force. But these gains were limited. The discourse and the notions about women that continued throughout the war and Liberation meant that no new rights for women as women were guaranteed in the process of consolidating new social programs. Instead, such programs strengthened the social rights of French men and their families. Moreover, married women's civil rights remained severely constrained throughout the "social revolution" of the Liberation, further demonstrating the inhibiting effect of a political discourse that lacked a notion of fully independent women.

NEW RIGHTS, 1944–1947

The Liberation of France followed almost a decade of deep social and political divisions, which had been expressed in the class antagonisms of the Popular Front years as much as in the violent resistance to the Vichy government and German occupation. The popular discourse of the period portrayed the Liberation as the moment in which old antagonisms could finally be set aside, because a political will and force existed to overthrow the economic structures, social relations, and political forms that had contributed to class warfare and military defeat.[1]

1. This interpretation is drawn from popular discourse. Even at the Liberation many politicians' first concern was to block popular leftist mobilization and ensure moderate government. See Robert Paxton, *Vichy France: Old Guard and New Order* (New York: Knopf, 1972).

Although there were obviously limits to the potential for change, the balance of political forces between 1944 and 1947 contrasted dramatically with those of the Third Republic and Vichy. The Third Republic had been deeply divided by the polarization of the Popular Front. Vichy, in turn, had amputated the left and was dominated by the most conservative and traditional portions of the right. The Liberation, in contrast, was characterized in the beginning by a resurgent and predominant leftism. The Parti Communiste Français (PCF) gained more membership, influence, and credibility than ever before, and the politics of traditional Catholicism was replaced by the initially much more progressive Christian Democracy of the Mouvement Républicain Populaire (MRP).

Out of this balance of forces came fundamental political, economic, and social reforms, which stand as a landmark between 1936 and 1981. Women benefited from these reforms in several ways. First, the blockade of female suffrage which persisted throughout the Third Republic broke up and, on March 22, 1944, even before the Liberation, the Consultative Assembly in Algiers voted to give women the right to vote and run for office. In addition, the Preamble of the Constitution of the Fourth Republic, intended to update the 1789 Declaration of the Rights of Man and of the Citizen, stated: "The law shall guarantee to women rights equal to those of men in all spheres. It shall be the duty of all to work, and the right of all to obtain employment. None may suffer wrong, in his work or employment, by reason of his origin, opinions or beliefs."[2]

To the extent that such constitutional documents can be interpreted as a snapshop of a nation's vision of itself, this clause shows that French women had finally come into full possession of political rights and the fundamental economic right to work. Further reform of the situation of working women occurred with two other actions, both carried out under the direction of Communist ministers. The minister of labor, Ambroise Croizat, established the principle of equal pay for equal work on June 20, 1946; and a statute giving all citizens equal employment rights in the civil service was developed by the minister of state, Maurice Thorez, and put into effect on October 5, 1946.

In addition to the reforms explicitly directed toward women, the new social policies had a major impact on their condition. The Preamble to the Constitution stated: "The Nation shall ensure to the individual and family the conditions necessary to their development. It shall guarantee to all, especially to the child, the mother and aged workers, the protection of their health, material

2. Philip Williams, *Crisis and Compromise: Politics in the Fourth Republic* (Garden City: Anchor, 1966), 510.

security, rest and leisure. Every human being who is unable to work on account of his age, his physical or mental condition, or the economic situation, shall be entitled to obtain from the community decent means of support."[3] The first goal of social policymakers was to implement the philosophy that had emerged from the Resistance, as expressed in the program of the Conseil National de la Résistance (CNR). Hoping to overcome the class-divided politics of the Third Republic and Vichy, the CNR searched for ways of expressing a new collectivist notion of citizenship, in place of what was seen as the rampant liberalism of earlier years.[4] Nevertheless, while these social policies affected the situation of women in profound ways, they did not grant them new rights of their own. This was because, during the upheaval of the wartime and Liberation years, political actors were operating with discourses which dealt with women in contradictory ways. One discourse spoke of universal rights, based on equality, and another emphasized the specificity of women, based on their place in reproduction and the family. Both these discourses were used in the development of social and economic policy during the war and Liberation.

Because of the different interests of political actors and the shifting balance of political forces, one formulation dominated in some policy realms while the other shaped programs elsewhere. When lawmakers reflected on women as producers, they tended to see them as deserving treatment similar to that men received and a discourse of equality was used. However, as soon as politicians turned their attention to questions involving reproduction (social insurance, family policy) all of them—even those who in other realms used the discourse of equality—reverted to a language emphasizing, if not subordination, at least difference. In this way, fundamental contradictions in treatment persisted seemingly without being noticed.

For example, despite the constitutional guarantee of full equality—a guarantee located in a list emphasizing political and economic principles like the right to work and the right to strike—married women in France remained without full civil rights until the mid-1960s. They were legal minors, subordinate to their husbands. A husband could deny his wife the opportunity to take up any activity or profession outside the home, to travel, or to take examinations in preparation for a job if he determined these activities to be contrary to "the interest of the family."[5] Moreover, if a couple were married under the

3. Ibid.

4. See Richard F. Kuisel, *Capitalism and the State in Modern France* (Cambridge: Cambridge University Press, 1981); and Henry C. Galant, *Histoire politique de la sécurité sociale française, 1945–52* (Paris: Colin, 1955).

5. A. Michel and G. Texier, *La condition de la française d'aujourd'hui* (Paris: Gonthier, 1964), 1:79–80.

régime de la communauté légale—as were three-fourths of French women—the husband had complete control over the family's resources and decisions.[6] In a fundamental way, the retention of the notion of *chef de famille,* which was the foundation of marriage law in the Napoleonic Code, was incompatible with any concept of gender equality. A family with a *chef* is not an egalitarian institution.

CONTRADICTIONS IN THE DEVELOPMENT OF ECONOMIC AND SOCIAL POLICY

The constitutional guarantee of the right to work and the commitment to equal pay culminated a set of improvements in the working conditions of women that began long before the war. During the war, however, efforts had been made to interrupt this march of progress. According to the Vichy regime, the German victory was caused by unhealthily individualistic liberalism which produced, among other things, family breakdown. To combat individualism, Vichy proposed to place the family as a buffer between the individual and the state by making it one-third of the triptych *Travail, Famille, Patrie.*

In this celebration of the family, Vichy ideology assigned women responsibility for family harmony. Therefore, policies intended to strengthen the family and discourage individualism were developed. Divorce was severely restricted and the education of young girls was redesigned to prepare them not for a profession but for marriage. In October, 1940, a regulation was passed limiting married women's access to state employment. At the same time the Ministry of Labor encouraged employers in the private sector to lay off any women who were not widows, supporters of a family, single and without resources, or the wives of mobilized soldiers. These measures were intended both to combat unemployment and to contribute to family stability.[7]

The reasoning behind these initiatives was structurally flawed, making them difficult, if not impossible, to enforce. First, it was clear even during the war that sending women home would have undesirable consequences for French capitalism as well as society. The interwar economy had a high rate of female participation in the workforce and compulsory replacement of women workers with men would raise the cost of labor. Second, the state would commit itself

6. After 1938 wives could take some actions independently (e.g., have a bank account and passport, sign and receive a check, enter a sanitorium), but the husband still had the prerogatives of *chef de famille.* Maïté Albistur and Daniel Armogathe, *Histoire du féminisme français* (Paris: Editions des femmes, 1977), 2:584–85.

7. A. Peyrat, "La fête des mères de 1932 à 1950" (thesis, University of Paris I, 1979–80), 96.

to immense costs if it were forced to support widows and other single women, a social category greatly swollen because of the war. Finally, marriage itself would be threatened as a social institution if concubinage were the only way for a couple to retain two salaries.[8] Therefore, little real action could be taken. Despite the ideological commitment of the Vichy regime to restricting women's work and strengthening the family, programs to implement this ideology were limited.

Nevertheless, the formal reversal of this position and legal guarantees of women's right to work came only with the reinforcement of the left in the postwar Assemblies. Vichy's decision to attack state employment for women explains in large part the immediate postwar legislation granting gender equality in the civil service. These actions reflect a long-term commitment on the part of the French left to the integration of women into the labor force—in ways that would not threaten men's wages and employment.[9]

Resistance organizations did have an equivocal attitude to some kinds of women's work during the war. By 1942, as the war situation forced Germany to conscript foreign workers, the government tried harder to integrate women into French production as replacements for male labor. By 1942, however, the Resistance was sufficiently organized and visible to oppose the draft of women into the factories. The Communist women's organization, the Union des Femmes Françaises (UFF), and other committees of women mobilized against the participation of women in war work, under the slogan *Pas une Française pour le Reich!*[10] In fact, opposition to forced war work led many people of both genders into resistance politics, if not into the maquis.[11]

In general, however, the UFF wholeheartedly supported working women's issues; its tripartite ideal for French women envisioned them as mothers, workers, and citizens. Therefore, even as it opposed draft labor, the UFF directed much of its attention toward working women, or, more accurately working mothers. For example, once the Vichy regime declared Mothers' Day a national holiday, the UFF proposed an alternative, politicized fête to mobilize people around the needs of working mothers for childcare, improved maternity leave, and so on.[12] After the Liberation, in June, 1945, the first

8. F. Paris, *Le travail des femmes et le retour de la mère au foyer* (Paris: Receuil Sirey, 1943), 390.

9. Michel and Texier, *La condition de la française,* 2:206; Jane Jenson, "Gender and Reproduction: Or, Babies and the State," *Studies in Political Economy: A Socialist Review,* #20 (Summer 1986).

10. See the poster following p. 224 in Union des Femmes Françaises, comp., *Les femmes dans la résistance* (Paris: Editions du Rocher, 1977).

11. Ibid., 151–52; and Paxton, *Vichy France,* 392.

12. Peyrat, "La fête," 118–20.

Congress of the UFF organized an exposition around the theme "Women's Work across France," which was intended to display women's contribution to the "battle of production" then going on. Even more indicative of the UFF's ideal for women were the two motions passed by National Council of the UFF on September 8 and 9, 1945, arguing, first, that in the battle of production housewives' duty lay in helping working mothers in any way they could (with childcare, hot meals, and so on), and, second, that employers' attempts (as were then being made) to lay off married women must be resisted because *all* women had the right to work.[13]

Thus, in agitating for and gaining this most basic of rights—the right to economic independence through work—the parties of the left, unions, and resistance organizations of women used a discourse that emphasized the notion that women as workers were individuals with the same rights as men. Once women entered the paid labor force they were mobilized around the same programs and policies as were men. Struggles for new rights for women, as for men, were intended by the PCF and its flanking organizations to serve a double purpose—improvement in conditions of French workers and mobilization of support for revolutionary politics. While recognizing the necessity of liberating women from relations of subordination, the left saw this liberation as possible only under socialism. In the meantime, struggles for equality of participation, pay, and treatment would advance that cause by bringing women into contact with political bodies—parties, trade unions, mass organizations—that could lead them to an understanding of the need to engage in the socialist cause.

This notion of equality also helped motivate the Provisional Assembly's support for the enfranchisement and political eligibility of women. Throughout the Resistance the Communists pursued a vigourous united frontism, within which they placed much emphasis on expanded democracy. According to their analysis, one of the causes of the defeat and the conservatism of the Vichy government was a severely limited democracy; the Liberation was to be a moment of social revolution that would expand the boundaries of democracy. The PCF and other left organizations therefore pressed for a strong Assembly, workers' control in the nationalized industries, works committees in factories, workers' participation in social security programs, and full participation of women in politics. In Algiers the Communist representative, Fernand Grenier, advocated full political rights for women over the objections of members of the Radical Party and some Gaullists.[14]

13. Ibid., 120.
14. UFF, *Les femmes,* 258–63.

In promoting his measure, Grenier argued from a discourse of equality. Women "deserved" full political rights because they had, by means of their heroic actions in the Resistance, demonstrated they could no longer legitimately be considered minors on the political scene. If some of the left in the Third Republic had seen gradual acquisition of political experience as the proper route toward women's political participation, the Resistance was interpreted by them as proof that experience had been acquired. Women had shown themselves "equal" to men in performing their national duty.

Once again, it is important to note the crucial effect of the balance of political forces. Only the weakness of the Radicals in Algiers allowed this measure to pass. Radical senators had systematically opposed enfranchising women in the Third Republic; some took similar positions in Algiers. The Radicals there voted unanimously against Grenier's proposition. However, the balance of political forces was very different in Algiers than in the prewar Palais de Luxembourg and the proposal carried.

Even in these debates, however, there was evidence of competing discourses about women. For example, in Algiers some members of the Assembly raised the issue of whether an election held before the repatriation of predominantly male prisoners and deportees from Germany would be "representative." One Radical senator clearly articulated his fears during the 1944 debates: "No matter what the merits of women, is it a good idea to replace universal male suffrage by universal female suffrage?"[15] What was clearly on the senator's mind was the advantage the right might gain from such an electorate. Politicians almost unanimously thought that women were more religious than men and therefore more likely to vote for the right—a belief that the first electoral results showed to be not without foundation.[16]

There was more to the debate than political opportunism, however. These formulations of the question also reflected the notion of the "difference" or specificity of women. While the Resistance may have allowed women to show themselves as capable as men in wartime, reference to their activity also contained notions of specificity. The heroic exploits recited were often actions of women in support of their male *compagnes* or against the occupier who had diverted to his own use bread that was rightfully due French children. These symbolic ideas of difference became very important when attention turned from economic and political rights to social rights.

To illustrate the simultaneous use of two discourses, it is helpful to examine the positions of the PCF, already identified as the major proponent of a

15. Ibid., 260–61.
16. Albistur and Armogathe, *Histoire,* 2:601.

discourse of equality. François Billoux, minister of health in the postwar government, claimed:

We always thought that women ought to be able to choose freely whether to work outside the home. In order to make a real choice possible, it is necessary to provide the means. Such means for choice were not given by firing women on the pretext that they should give up their places to demobilized men, to prisoners of war, or to the deported. . . . From this point of view a thorough application of the Langevin-Wallon Plan, conceived during the Resistance, would have ended discrimination in job training. One of our preoccupations, immediately after the Liberation, was to promote real protection for mothers and children. This preoccupation responded to a double concern: the national interest, of course, and the interest of mothers and children. They are, in any case, inseparable.[17]

This quote is representative of the kind of argument used by the PCF, and it is also a replica of the Preamble to the 1946 Constitution. When women and work were discussed, the focus was on equality; when social policy was on the table, women were folded back into the family and dealt with alongside other "needy" categories like children and pensioners. Moreover, mothers and children were an inseparable dyad in this structure of thought.

In utilizing this double optic, the left's discourse at times intersected with that of the right and with church-inspired notions of women and the family. Throughout the twentieth century, the French expressed deep concern over the low birth rate—the problem of *natalité*. The Third Republic used this social statistic to explain all that was wrong with France, especially the country's military weakness vis à vis Germany. There were, of course, differing interpretations of the reasons for the falling birth rate: Republicans tended to attribute it to declining rural population and values while Catholics emphasized decadence following on the heels of secularization.[18] However, no matter what the cause, all agreed that the solution was to buttress the family via state programs to encourage childbirth. Thus in 1939 the Daladier government produced a *Code de la Famille* which included a series of financial measures (payments and tax reforms) supposed to encourage childbearing.

The Vichy regime made extensive use of this policy and wartime modifications of the Family Code served as the basis for postwar family policy, which in turn provided the foundation for the French welfare state.[19] Family allowance

17. UFF, *Les femmes,* 251–52 (translation mine).

18. R. Tomlinson, "The Politics of Dénatalité during the French Third Republic" (thesis, King's College, Cambridge, 1983), chap. 9.

19. The very wide agreement across time and political groups on these issues is indicated by the fact that Alliance Nationale, the major pronatalist organisation, survived intact and with political power despite having collaborated extensively with Vichy. Ibid., postlude.

payments were a central pillar of this policy. Payments to families with children, as a means of redistributing income—redistributing the costs of children from those with many to those with none or few—existed throughout the interwar period. The earlier versions, however, were established by capitalists primarily as a mechanism for controlling labor and were paid by employers to men and women within their enterprises.[20] The Family Code marked a break with this rationale and represented a greater concern with natalism. It provided payments to men whose wives remained at home, on the hope that they would be encouraged to have more children if the family had a substitute for the woman's income. Under Vichy this program supplemented the income of families with only a single salary (*salaire unique*), recognizing the costs of women remaining at home, which they tended to do once there were more than two children. During the Vichy years, the unlinking of work and family allowances continued, as coverage was extended to more and more categories of the population without salaried employment.[21] The concern with natalism continued into the Liberation period, reflected in General de Gaulle's claim that France needed "douze millions bons bébés en dix ans." Family allowances were raised immediately and other grants which had been provided by Vichy were continued (for example, a lump sum was paid for a first child born within two years of marriage).

But the actual design of family policy can be understood only by examining the balance of political forces in postwar France. The issue quickly became whether family allowances would be incorporated into the social security system being developed. Social security programs were claimed as part of the "victory" of the CNR and designed to grant the protection due the French working class that had been denied by the right. While all the political groups in the postwar majority agreed on the necessity of such reforms, they did not agree on the specifics. In particular, the MRP, the largest party in the second Constituent Assembly, succeeded in extracting family allowances from the general system of social insurance, so it could continue to serve as a pronatalist program.[22] The MRP insisted upon this separation because it wanted a program that would guarantee a minimum family wage, thus ensuring that extra children would not drain family resources. The philosophy of social insurance, in contrast, was to guarantee a minimum income in times of adversity. Under that system families would have to bear the cost of additional

20. D. Ceccaldi, *Histoire des prestations familiales en France* (Paris: UNCAF, 1957).
21. Ibid., 80ff.
22. Galant, *Histoire politique,* chap. 3.

children; the state would guarantee only that the family's income would not fall below an established minimum.

The position adopted by the Christian Democratic MRP reflected its social philosophy. The party's goal was to reinforce intermediary "natural structures," especially the family, between the individual and the state.[23] In promoting these natural structures, however, the MRP was also promoting the Catholic assumption that the only stable family is a hierarchically organized one. This new and very influential political formation therefore did nothing to bring women out of the family or lead them to greater equality in the social policy realm. In fact, it actively inhibited any such change. Thus, Vichy had effected the separation of family policy and general social policy, and the Liberation governments, under the influence of the MRP, consolidated that shift. With the terrain of debate bounded by the family, all political actors were limited in their discourse.

Conflict then erupted about the state's role in supporting particular forms of families. During the war there had been an effort to use family policy to impose a traditional morality. Administrators had attempted to restrict eligibility for family allowances to married women and legitimate children. This initiative was blocked by officials of the Department of Labor and the pronatalists in the Commissariat Général à la Famille, who insisted upon maintaining payments to unmarried mothers.[24] By the end of the war, despite the MRP's hopes of using family policy to encourage traditional, hierarchical families, official policy eliminated any distinction between legitimate and "natural" families (with the exception of the pronatalists' one-time payment for a child born within two years of the date of marriage). By this time the Ministry of the Family had come round to the position consistently promoted by the departments of Labor and Social Security (both under the influence of the PCF) that it was unfair to deny children access to financial aid because of the situation in which they found themselves as a result of their parents' actions.[25]

In this process it is possible to see the effects of the different visions of women that political actors utilized. Those in the parties or within the state who dealt with working women were much less likely to assume that the traditional family was the only kind that existed or that it was necessarily desirable. They understood the real needs of unmarried mothers and protected programs that addressed them. Those more concerned with the family than

23. Ibid., 65–69.
24. Ceccaldi, *Histoire,* 82–83.
25. Ibid., 119.

with women, however, tried to use financial incentives to buttress the moral principles they promoted. The balance of political forces allowed the latter position to predominate to the extent that family policy was successfully separated from general social policy. But its supporters were not strong enough to overcome the alliance of the left and the pronatalists opposed to limiting state support only to traditional families.

Nevertheless, because debate turned on this issue—whether the state should recognize nontraditional family forms—nowhere was there any broad discussion of the real needs of *women*. They were ignored in a debate that centered on legal and natural families. Throughout the postwar period, the French welfare state, founded on family policy, would assume an inevitable connection between mothers and children, as well as linking mothers and the nation's need for a larger population.

In the balance of political forces that produced social policies at the Liberation, there was little opportunity for new definitions of women to emerge. The Gaullists, greatly concerned by the threat to the nation posed by a decline in the number of births, supported all programs that promised to maintain the birth rate at its high wartime level. The MRP adopted the church's vision of the family and considered women only as mothers. The Marxist left, retaining its double optic, considered women either as workers or as a social category—mothers—whose special needs should be addressed by social programs specific to them. It did not, however, see mothers as equal to workers (both women and men), who were in the vanguard of the struggle for socialism. This continued failure to integrate an understanding of the inequities of reproduction into theories of exploitation in production meant that the left continued to approach women from two contradictory perspectives simultaneously. Despite paying a great deal of attention to many kinds of democracy—parliamentary, in the workplace, in social programs—there was no effort to understand the family as a terrain on which democratic struggle was also necessary.

Consequences for women followed from a discourse of difference used to allocate social rights. One consequence was that the new rights were granted to "workers and their families." Social programs were constructed around the notion of a worker with a dependent family. Women workers had access to these programs, but nonsalaried women remained dependent on a male subscriber. Thus the French welfare state, founded on family policy, shored up and cemented a family structure in which wives and children were dealt with as minors and appendages of men.

Even more important, the separation of family allowances from the social insurance system permitted the continued definition of childrearing as a national duty (duly rewarded) rather than as a risk workers faced alongside other risks like industrial accidents, illness, or old age. This programmatic separation could bring payments high enough to encourage larger families and thus discourage women working (since labor force participation is inversely related to the number children a woman has). In this way, the state encouraged women to play only one of their possible roles, that of mother. Moreover, this was a subordinate role, because it was assumed to be played within a family still hierarchically structured by the Napoleonic Code. The Liberation did not include an effort to reform that Code and give married women new civil rights.

Finally, because of the hegemony of this discourse depicting women as mothers, it became almost a logical impossibility to think of them as something else. The virtually unanimous concern for the birth rate and support for the family meant that any efforts to reform the extremely strict 1920 law banning abortion and contraception could go nowhere. In fact, the law was made even more restrictive in February, 1946, by placing new limits on products and reinforcing the penalties on medical personnel.[26] The "social revolution" of the Liberation thus gave women of childbearing age neither the right nor the ability to control their reproductive capacity. Women's actions in this regard were forced into the bleak and very painful world of illegality.

Women workers did gain new economic rights at the Liberation and political rights were obviously greatly expanded. But without full civil rights even these gains were partial. If the Second World War brought new attention to social rights almost everywhere, for French women this attention, reflected in family policy, was confined to their role as mothers within an inequitable family structure. Only mobilization in later decades would bring women onto the political scene as independent social actors. The end of the war did not, then, meet women's needs for Liberation.

26. Michel and Texier, *La condition de la française,* 2:111–12.

ANNEMARIE TRÖGER

German Women's Memories of World War II

The Second World War may be defined as a war against civilian populations. Although in earlier wars, including World War I, civilian populations suffered—a cost deplored as the natural byproduct of warfare or justified as necessary to destroy the supply bases of the adversary—in World War II the war against the civilian population became a strategic goal in itself: the bombings of Guernica, Warsaw, Kiev, London, Coventry, Berlin, Dresden, and Hiroshima allow no other interpretation. The introduction of new technology in warfare may help account for the long-term psychological impact of the Second World War on patterns of thinking; on social myths and meanings ascribed to political and historical facts beneath the level of established ideologies; on the concepts of individual and collective identity, values, and norms; and even on the fundamental *Lebensgefühl* (feeling for life). The impact on older Germans who lived through the war is apparent: the war dominates their memories and life histories.

Even though individuals are compelled to talk about the war, one senses a painful lack of words adequate to describe the anthropological meaning of airborne warfare. The most valid expression even for articulate intellectuals appears to be nonverbal; Picasso's *Guernica* is an example.

It is often said that Germans will be unable to come to terms with their recent past—especially the horrors of the concentration camps—as long as they cannot come to grips with their experiences and defeat in the Second World War. (This may also be said of other nations in other wars). The reverse is also true: as long as Germans refuse to face the concentration camps, they will not be able to understand their own suffering in the war. This inextricable knot is the real barrier to finding a symbolic, that is, a common language to discuss the last war. The problem is not linguistic but psychological: it is the "inability to mourn," attributable to deep, contradictory emotions.[1] Because the Germans have not been able to work out collectively the experiences of the Second World War, individual memories assume more importance—and become a political force themselves.

In Germany, as in many other countries, there are at present two different discourses on war: the official-political one, espoused by political parties, governments, bureaucracy, and institutions; and the discourse of the disarmament movement. They are discourses in the true sense that they have distinct basic assumptions and logics. The official discourse operates with the traditional concepts of two opposing sides, victory and defeat, balance of power, defense, and deterrence. The peace movement, on the other hand, starts with the assumption that there is *one* gigantic, uncontrollable war machine, which, once set into motion, resists interference; it assumes that in an emergency involving this machine there would be nothing left to defend, neither a fatherland nor values like freedom or democracy. Thus the concept of enemy itself becomes obsolete.

It is too simplistic to categorize the official political discourse as masculine and that of the many-faceted peace movement as feminine. It is true, however, that the war narratives of men, especially veterans, tend to follow the official political discourse. And it is therefore striking to find in the war memories of German women of various political inclinations basic assumptions similar to those of the current peace movement. This surprising continuity between the apolitical narratives of women about World War II and the political discourse of the disarmament movement may have a historical explanation. Women's memories of the inferno of burning cities under carpet bombing allow one to imagine nuclear war: destructive forces operating beyond interference, with no visible enemy or front. Perhaps women are better able to convey these images because the culture allows them to express their fears and anxieties and to admit their helplessness. Therefore, what postwar generations in Germany have learned about the impact of World War II has come primarily through the narratives of their mothers and grandmothers. Close examination of these narratives, however, reveals that their message is not one-dimensional or direct but contradictory and ambivalent.

I analyze here some of the inconsistencies using two sets of oral history interviews with men and women who lived in Berlin and Hanover during World War II. The women in both these groups personally experienced the

1. To paraphrase the title of a book by Alexander Mitscherlich: "Die Unfähigkeit zu Trauern."

effects of the most advanced warfare technology. Fifty percent of Berlin and close to 60 percent of Hanover were destroyed by bombs. The Berlin project, carried out in 1978–80 in a working-class neighborhood, focused on the impact of fascism on social relations. The Hanover project, carried out in 1982, centered on gender relationships in the postwar years. The thirty-five respondents in the Berlin project were born before World War I; by 1945, most of them were between thirty-five and forty years old. They grew up during the Weimar Republic and entered the period of National Socialism as young adults.[2] The eighteen interviewees in the Hanover project were much younger. Born between 1920 and 1925, they were part of the Hitler Youth generation; by 1945 they were between twenty and twenty-five years of age.[3] About one-third of the interviewees in both projects were men. Women's accounts compare favorably to men's for their seriousness and compassion. But comparison in depth is impossible because of space limitations.

Neither investigation focused on the Second World War, yet the respondents made it into a central topic in these largely self-directed interviews. The place and time given to the war in their life histories is of methodological interest. The topic of war comes up quite early in the narrative. In the Hanover interviews with members of the younger generation, prewar life takes only a few minutes in the normal narrative sequence. The older Berlin group, interrupting the chronological order, introduces the war the moment the topic of National Socialism comes up in the interview. In terms of "talking time" versus "time talked about," the five war years take more talking time than any other period in the respondent's life.[4] The five years of war almost always take more time to recount than do the seven years of National Socialism prior to the war (1933–39). The uneven ratio between talking time and time talked about is exacerbated in shorter interviews. Longer interviews conducted over several sessions allow the interviewee psychological time to talk about everything of importance. This indicates that war is not necessarily a timespan of which more memories are conserved and about which more events or stories can be related.

2. The Berlin project method used largely self-directed interviews, life history approach, 3 to 5 sessions on the average. The study was financed by the Freie Universität Berlin in 1979–81. See Annemarie Tröger, Lore Kleiber, and Ingrid Wittmann, "Mündliche Geschichte: Ein Charlottenburger Kiez in der Weimarer Republik und im Nationalsozialismus," *Museumspädagogischer Dienst* (Berlin: Sonderheft Industriekultur, 1983).

3. The Hanover project was a graduate course conducted for two semesters at Hanover University in 1982–83. The interviews used the life history method followed by a focused interview.

4. Aside from the favorite topic—specific to every individual—that constitutes a major component of a person's reconstructed "I" or identity.

The number of incidents related from the period of the war is in most cases rather limited, but these incidents are often retold several times, particularly if the interview spans several sessions.

Qualitative distinctions also make the war memories important for interpretation. It is not the drama and singularity of war that make it a prime issue for these life histories. On the contrary, the most dramatic and frightening period, from the winter of 1943 to April, 1945, when heavy bombardments daily threatened life in the cities, is rather vague in the memories of survivors. Their recollections are gray, impersonal, and distant, as if they did not really live through that time or as if they had been in a trance. The descriptions of the bombardments and air-raid shelters are composite; people, incidents, and circumstances that may have been present in various similar situations are often put together in one dramatic story. In these new syntheses social-historical information is relegated to the background and a higher-level, quasi-symbolic significance comes to the fore.

Memories are constantly being recreated; there is no "original" and therefore accurate memory. Memories of 1945 described in 1946 are no more "true" than those described in 1978. We lack comparative oral history material—say from 1946 or 1960—that would enable us to analyze the process by which the war has worked on the human mind. Through the community-study and life-history method, however, we can gain detailed factual knowledge of the social and historical circumstances in order to interpret memories. The relative distance from historical facts and their conscious or subconscious transformation in the narrative constitute the raw material for interpretation.

War memories may after careful scrutiny say something about people's actual behavior in the past. But the past ("what really happened") is not the subject of this article. War works on the mind and is thus part of the psychosocial fabric of our society. Paradoxically, the dynamics through which the war worked on the mind may be traced by examining the ways memory has remade the war. Memories of the war interest us today both as keys to and as active agents in the present. Even our questions about war memories are a product of war memories.

In symbolic terms, the war stories are both individual and collective. They are made of and told as personal experiences but at the same time they carry collective patterns of meaning. These meanings, however, are not yet socially codified and therefore I prefer to call them quasi-symbolic. It is difficult to say how willfully these stories are constructed and how consciously their symbolic meaning is conveyed: these factors differ from person to person and from one story to the next. Even within a single story there are breaks and shifts. For example, a story that sets out to convey a specific message may end with a different, even contradictory meaning.

For purposes of analysis I distinguish three levels of meaning in these war-related accounts. At the first, *existential* level, the individual attempts to describe the heretofore unexperienced—emotions and feelings for which there are no words, no collective language; experiences that have no precedents in one's life. The second, *psychological* level concerns the complex formulation of both individual and collective identity. Then there is the third, *historico-political* level of relatively deliberate, generalized description, which is conveyed at times by metaphors such as "war as natural catastrophe." These three levels, used as methodological constructs, allow one to deal with the complexities of oral memories.

In the following section I examine interview passages, filling in historical or political details necessary to my interpretation. I concentrate here on several questions: How do women describe their experience of technological warfare and what metaphors do they create to do it? What psychological effects does this experience have? And how do women deal with the problematic of recent German history, a history which they did not make but of which they are invariably a part?

The following narrative was taken from interviews with a single woman but the accounts of other women are quoted occasionally as supporting evidence. The decision to restrict the analysis to a single case has not been easy. But the symbolic meaning often appears in the metalanguage of a narration and long quotations are required to capture them. Biographical background also informs the interpretation, so a sketch of the "whole person" must be drawn. In this narrative, all three levels outlined above are present even though Frau Werner speaks usually at the existential level. Her narrative is more complex and less controlled than others, hence more interpretation is required. Her rationale has to be closely followed to clarify the hidden logic of her discourse.

THE STORY OF FRAU WERNER

Frau Werner was born at the turn of the century, the only daughter of an overseer on an aristocratic estate in what is now Poland. She often fondly recalled her childhood and youth in this still semi-feudal world. In her memory, it became an idealized, warm, and protective world that contrasted with her later hard life. Orphaned at eighteen, she followed the usual path of an Eastern (German or Polish) migrant worker to the industrial West. After several jobs in smaller towns as a domestic servant, around 1926 she arrived in

Berlin, where she had neither relatives nor friends. Shortly before the depression she became an assembly-line worker at the Siemens electrical plant, where she worked until the end of the war. In the last year or so of the war, she worked in an underground ammunition production site within the Siemens compound where she was locked up during the day with the foreign forced laborers. After the war she held several jobs, including that of *Trümmerfrau,* cleaning up the rubble of the war from the city. By then in her fifties, she was worn out and remained largely unemployed until she retired on a small pension. Frau Werner did not belong to any party or union; she is certainly not the prototype of a class-conscious worker. In her naive humanism, however, she was genuinely distrustful of National Socialism. Coming from a rural background of dependency and submissiveness, a single woman and an unskilled worker, she was vulnerable and easy to exploit, an Aryan underdog in a Nazi society.

Frau Werner composed her experiences of various bombardments into the story of a single night.[5] Her story presents primarily the existential level in my analysis as she endeavors to express the hitherto unexperienced, to name what she felt during a cataclysm.[6]

The apartment house was small; only eight people were living there. I used to go to the shelter in the house next door. It was larger and I felt more secure there. And when it became so crazy with the bombing [in 1944]—it was a catastrophe, no, really. I ran out of the house into the backyard. It was full of phosphor and my soles were burning. I thought, my God, what is happening to you? You are burning your feet. Where to go? I didn't know; it was coming from the sky. I was completely out of my mind. Suddenly it came to me: you are going to need your quilt. So I ran back into the house and got my down quilt. Then there was the engineer from Siemens. Wait, how was it? Well, I ran into the house and found all the doors had blown open. I saw my landlord lying in his bed. He was blind, you know, and there he was lying on his bed, completely alone. So I ran into the room: "Where is your wife?" "I don't know," he said. He was already rather old, you know. I said, "My God, Herr Wein, get up and get out. The house is already on fire upstairs." And he said, "Oh let me burn!" and I said, "I can't let you burn here, all alone. Where is your wife?" "I don't know," he answered, "she ran away." And later I said to her, "Frau Wein, how could you do such a thing?" "I was completely distraught," she said. "I just ran out of the house; I didn't think of my husband." "Well," I said, "if I hadn't come back he would have burned to death. Well, you are a nice

5. She told the story twice in slightly differing versions, but the main elements remained the same. The following passages are from the second interview.

6. All of the following direct quotes from interviews have been slightly edited and translated by the author. Brackets contain completions or explanations. Ellipses (. . .) indicate phrases or passages that have been omitted. All personal names have been changed. Frau Werner was interviewed by Karin Eickhoff for the Berlin project.

wife." . . . Anyway I just saved my down quilt. I wanted it—really wanted to save it. And there was a crashing all around, and a roaring in the air. I still remember. I stood in the street with my bundle—and I cried and cried. The crashing in the air; I could have been hit but I was so overwhelmed I didn't know what to do next. And it just happened that somebody I knew came by, an engineer from Siemens. And he asked, "What are you doing here?" "I don't know where to go," I said. There I stood with my bundle and everything around me was in flames. Where to go? "Well," he said, "come along." And we went around the corner and there was a military hospital; it was not yet burning and everything was completely dark, because of the blackout. And there was a steep staircase down to the basement [of the hospital] and he said, "Throw your quilt down there!" "I can't," I said. "You have to jump down into the basement," he said. So I threw my quilt down and he—he gave me a push. And I fell down backward onto my quilt. And because of the noise the doctors came out. You know there were a lot of wounded in the hospital and a lot of doctors. That I did not break any bones was really a wonder. And the doctors took me in and gave me an injection to calm me down. I had a real shock you know . . . and then I had to go to the big school building [in the neighborhood]. Well, in its basement I camped with a lot of other people [who had also lost their homes]. I don't know how long I lived down there. It was terrible. I had nothing but the clothes I wore. I could hang them up on one nail in the wall. That's all I owned. And there, in the basement, we got a little to eat, because nobody had anything left. I had only the clothes I wore and my down quilt. Nevertheless I had to go to work every day. . . . And then I had to live with people here and there. I had to get up rather early to get to work so I was disturbing the people I lived with. I went to the office of housing control and said, "Sir, I have become a real gypsy." But I did not get my own room until a long time after the war [around 1947]. . . . Perhaps they, the Americans, wanted to bomb Charlottenburg castle, but they hit us [instead]. It was terrible—I don't like to think about it. I always say I don't want to go through it again. Well no, I don't think that I could bear it a second time.

There is a clear difference in style between Frau Werner's description of the night of the bombing, which has a dreamlike quality, and her report on her daily life after the air-raids. The dreamlike quality is produced by the scenarios, by recurrent metaphors (such as the down quilt), and, last but not least, by the way she collapses different stories into one. The composite character of her memory is most visible in her unfinished story concerning the blind man. If she saved him that night as she says (led him into a shelter and so forth), the following sequence of her standing alone and terrified in the street until her savior, an engineer, came by, does not make sense. The two incidents probably happened in separate, although similar, situations. The recomposition does make sense, however, for the symbolic meaning she really wants to convey. The anecdote of the handicapped, helpless old man functions as a metaphor and not as an actual story in the context of her narrative. It highlights her own feeling of vulnerability and "interprets" her sense of confusion and blindness. Her irrational behavior, standing out in the open during the bombardment clutching her down quilt, is also that of a blind person immobilized, because every step could conceivably lead to an abyss. The story of the blind man's wife conveys the same message: the most simple and basic human solidarity did not function. Yet the wife cannot be blamed because the war also made her senseless.

The symbolic meaning of Frau Werner's story is that the bombings were such a new and threatening experience, so different from all previously conceived dangers, that normal, rational action became meaningless and the established norms of perception, judgment, and behavior were rendered invalid. If Frau Werner had finished the story of the blind neighbor, she would have undercut her message by portraying herself as a rational and responsible actor (which she probably was in the actual situation). Then her story would have become that of a heroine instead of a helpless, confused, and frightened person. Its symbolic meaning would have been reversed: technological warfare is a dangerous yet manageable situation, if only one is cold-blooded or callous enough to deal with it, as most men would portray themselves.

In addition to the bombing, the two other major themes of Frau Werner's war memories were hunger and bad working conditions. These two themes came up in all the interview sessions and were closely connected to the issue of foreign forced labor.[7]

> And, on top of everything [the air-raids], nothing to eat, nothing to eat. I could not sleep at night because I was so hungry, and I paced up and down with hunger-pangs. I got only the fewest ration cards. . . . Then I lost so much weight: I became weaker and weaker. I even broke down on the street. Three times I fell, you know, where the old post office used to be. There I broke down and fainted, just in front of a young man who helped me up. I said, "Where am I?" "Well," he said, "you know you are hungry." He saw immediately what was going on. And I was so embarassed that I said well, yes. "You are just hungry, not sick," he said, "come, let us go eat. I still have some ration cards." So we went to eat and I was glad. I was totally run down. It was [because of] the work. I worked on the assembly line at Siemens. You know what a conveyor belt is? It's very hard on the line; the machines are running all the time, without interruption, and you have to move quickly. . . . The assembly line ruined me. It was terrible. Nobody can bear it for a long time. I always said it made me *kaputt*. Nights we spent in the shelter, during the day we worked with nothing to eat. No human being is able to endure that. I kept thinking, perhaps you should have gone to America. You wouldn't have gone through the war and many things [in my life] would have been better. Well, I don't know what would have happened to me over there.[8]

7. The following passages have been pieced together by the author from different parts of the interviews.

8. In the early 1920s Frau Werner had the vague possibility of going to the United States, but she never seriously pursued it.

The notion of being a victim permeates Frau Werner's description of the work more than her narration of the bombings. In her own way, Frau Werner makes it clear that she is a victim of class society (a term she would not have used), the war epitomizes her situation. Important to her self-perception as a victim is her social status as a single woman, ostracized by official ideology for not having children and by public attitude for not having a man, assigned few ration cards and dangerous jobs. Because of her marginal status Frau Werner believed that any woman "with a man" was treated better than she was. In the interview she continued to harbor this impression: "And if they find out you're single, well, just forget it, you have no chance."

It is significant, given the misogyny of the National Socialist era, that Frau Werner's two "savior" figures in dramatic situations are both men. There are hints in her more factual accounts that she received more consistent help from women, but, given the symbolic valence of men over women, she would be unlikely to construct her dramatic stories around women. Her stories may incorrectly report social historical facts (who helped whom), but as metaphors for the social and political power structure between the sexes they are quite realistic.

More important than the political symbolism is the psychological level in these savior-stories. Both saviors respond to her needs as a human being and not to her civil status, decide for her what she needs, and assume responsibility for her like a child. The need to be treated "like a child," the need for warmth and security, may be particularly strong in the case of Frau Werner, but it is also present in the war narratives of most of the other women interviewed. A woman in the Hanover group from a secure upper-middle-class background related with pride how as a young apprentice she assumed the difficult management of a bookstore during the war and helped organize a community library in the postwar years. Yet she exclaims, "and there we [the female members of the family] were, sitting all alone, without my father or my brother, imagine we women all alone in the shelter!" Here we can trace an important psychological ambivalence in women, accentuated to the extreme in the war situation. On the one hand women were—and had to be—strong, brave, and tough. All are acutely aware and proud of these qualities in themselves, even Frau Werner, who saved the blind man. On the other hand, the difficult living conditions and fear created by the bombing must have unleashed a tide of regressive needs. The seemingly irrational importance Frau Werner attaches to her down quilt in a life-threatening situation, even to the point of putting herself in danger to save it, is a classic regressive symptom. But it was virtually impossible for most women to act out their regressive needs, since they had to be responsible for children, the elderly, and maimed men who had their own regressive tendencies. Adult women could only give expression to these needs in their fantasies, in which, presumably, the powerful and protective man played the leading role. These fantasy men could perform their role better the less they could be verified against actual men in daily life.[9] That strange ideological hybrid of Nazi womanhood, the tough but submissive female, may have reinforced and maintained the contradiction lived by many women.[10] Otherwise, women might have surrendered to their needs or they might have become self-consciously powerful as a people and as a gender. Instead, the contradiction has remained unresolved.

With the defeat, the German masculine mystique fell apart both privately, for individual women, and publicly. This collapse seems to have occurred suddenly and not as a result of a slow erosion caused by women's assumption of stronger roles in German society from 1942 on. Significantly, women clung to their protective fantasy men until they could no longer avoid facing reality. The awakening was no doubt very painful for some of them. A woman from the Hanover group who was twenty in 1945, with two young children and a husband who had become a war invalid in 1943, recounts the last days of the war: "When the Americans came—I cried so terribly [sobbing]. At first our troops came through: [very emotional] beaten down, worn out, and they had nothing to eat. And four days later the Ami [American troops] came: beaming faces, the boys were rested, with gloves and not in rags like ours—it pierced me [tears in her eyes] and it still hurts after so many years."

A short period of individual assertiveness and informal social power on the part of women followed (until the end of the 1940s), again under extreme conditions of hunger, social uprootedness, and scarcity. In the early 1950s a seemingly sudden reversal of women's emancipation took place: the traditional familial roles and gender relationships were reestablished and the majority of German women adapted without resistance. To explain this development, we must assume that, during the short "spring of liberation," the fundamental

9. The National-Socialist ideology of manhood may have helped to direct women's fantasies, but it lacked any nurturing aspect.

10. For views on the double-faced ideology of women in German fascism, see Leila J. Rupp, *Mobilizing Women for War: German and American Propaganda, 1939–1945* (Princeton: Princeton University Press, 1978). For the early formulation of this ideology, see Claudia Koonz, "The Competition for Women's Lebensraum, 1928–1934"; and for its later use in industrial psychology, Annemarie Tröger, "The Creation of a Female Assembly-Line Proletariat," both in *When Biology Became Destiny: Women in Weimar and Nazi Germany,* ed. Renate Bridenthal, Atina Grossmann, and Marion Kaplan (New York: Monthly Review Press, 1984).

contradiction between self-assertion and feelings of weakness remained unresolved while the regressive need to be protected continued to dominate.[11]

The third major topic in Frau Werner's war account, foreign workers, clearly exposes the contradictory nature of her war experiences. The stories occur twice, with slight variations, but the sequence remains exactly the same.

> I never liked Hitler. [Interviewer: "Why not?"] No, I never could stand him. I had then a radio to listen for bombing alerts. When I heard his voice I turned it off. I could not stand him. . . . Well, our foreman was also such a crazy [National Socialist], and the manager, he was also totally crazed. I scolded sometimes. I was not one [a National Socialist]. And once he said to me: "If you don't shut up, then we will see where you will [have to] go." Then I shut up; I was scared. And at the same time, there were a lot of foreign workers at Siemens. They had to work there and they had a camp near Spandau [a town on the outskirts of Berlin]. They all lived there. They were mostly Czechs. Some knew a little German but we were not allowed to talk with them. Secretly we did anyway. I still have the shawl of one women; her name was Vera. "Visit me in Prague!" [she said]; I never got there. [She] meant after the war. Her family owned a concert coffee house [a large, well-known coffee house]. [One day] she said, "I have to go" and then she escaped. It did not take long [and she was back again]. I said, "Vera, where have you been?" And then she told me, "The German police searched for me at home, and I had to come back." At Siemens, you know, that was forced labor! And she cried. And then I said, "Well, Vera, it's not our fault that there is a war: we would rather not have it." Oh well, I still keep her shawl that she gave me as a gift.

> One day I got a notification from the government [ordering me] to do war work, to ammunition production, my goodness. . . . We sat in the basement of the Siemens plant, we worked in the basement, and above us the airplanes were flying. And there was a little stove, and we cooked turnips there with water and salt, nothing else. And the Russians [prisoners of war] wondered what delicacies we were eating; and in the next room there was a pile of turnips. And then, I remember, we had a guard [for the Russians], an older man. Once he came in and laughed. And I said, we don't feel like laughing. And then he told me that he had found a young Russian sitting on the pile of turnips in the next room. He had asked the Russian [trying to be funny]: "What are you doing here, looking for turnips in a pile of turnips?" And the Russian was so scared to death that he said: "Mercy, mercy, Russki so hungry. Mercy, mercy, don't shoot." But the old man didn't even have a gun, you know. And he [the Russian] ran away and turned around shouting, "Mercy, mercy, Russki hungry." Oh, I will never forget it. I will always remember. Isn't it terrible that a human being is so hungry . . . that he doesn't know what to do any more? Isn't it frightening? We have gone through the worst; not only they, but we also.

11. On the postwar "liberation" see Annemarie Tröger, "Between Rape and Prostitution: Survival Strategies and Possibilities of Liberation of Berlin Women in 1945–48," in *A Century of Change: Women in Culture and Politics,* ed. Judith Friedlander, Blanche Wiesen Cook, Alice Kessler-Harris, and Carroll Smith-Rosenberg (Bloomington: Indiana University Press, 1986), in which I analyze the situational factors accompanying women's liberation—which are insufficient to explain the conservative turn in the 1950s.

The last phrase epitomizes the vacillating and mostly unclear sense of "we". Frau Werner clearly did not mean "we Germans." She separates "them up there"—Hitler, Goebbels and the "gentlemen of Siemens"—from "us down here." The threat of being sent to a concentration camp is the crucial link to the issue of forced labor, indicating how close her situation was to that of the foreign workers. In her narrative, she struggles between trying to show that "we" down here were all the same—victims of the war—and having to recognize the reality that there were major differences between "them" (the foreign workers) and "us." The story of the turnips shows the ambiguity most clearly: in her long deliberations on food and foreign workers (not quoted), it sets out as an example that "we" had no better food than the Russian war prisoners. But then the narration turns against the initial intent of the narrator and takes an independent course, since the incident with the young Russian demonstrates that "they" did not even have turnips and risked their lives to steal them. As if to insist on the original message of her story, Frau Werner finishes somewhat abruptly with "we have gone through the worst, not only they, but we also."

In her peace declaration to Vera, the "we" approaches closest to the notion of "we German workers"—without, however, the more active implications of class solidarity, which would at least have meant sharing the relative privileges of German workers. Frau Werner is honest enough not to hide behind the indeed very heavy penalties for giving food to foreigners, as most respondents do; she talks instead about her fears of not having enough for herself. Since proletarian internationalism was too high a goal, identifying with the "internationale of victims" seems to be the only way out of the moral dilemma; it does not require more than having been oppressed. Yet there is still an unresolved "remainder" in her identification with Vera. Vera's shawl becomes important in this regard, for it symbolizes that Vera forgave her. (Personal gifts, especially from Jews, play an important role in many memories.)[12]

In all of Frau Werner's war memories, there is no "our side," no reference to national identity (in contrast to her childhood memories, in which her German nationality is important to distinguish her family from the Polish farmhands). Once she refers to "ours," but in a rather negative way: seeing an American pilot who had been shot down accompanied by German soldiers, she asked what would happen to the "young man." Upon hearing that he would have to

12. Often, these gifts serve as crude proof that "we personally had nothing against the Jews." But there are also the more subtle and serious cases like Frau Werner's where the gift seems to have the nearly religious function of alleviating guilt. These are often persons who helped Jews to survive but in the end could not prevent their deportation.

testify or be beaten up, she reflects: "You think ours were so noble—you'd better not believe it." She seems to have abdicated her national identity for the period of the war: "Perhaps I should have gone to America." Correspondingly, there is no "other side," no enemy, in her war descriptions. The American bomber pilots who destroyed her homes are nearly exculpated; they wanted to bomb Charlottenburg castle, Frau Werner speculates; unwillingly, they hit us instead.

The issue of forced foreign labor is still an unresolved problem in the memories of many working-class people, whereas for most middle-class respondents it does not even seem to be an issue. In contrast to Frau Werner, most Germans, except for old Communists, will not touch the sensitive spot unless asked directly. Yet, in her struggle with her collective identity, this sensitive if apolitical woman presents the objectively ambiguous position of the German working class then and the resulting ambivalent and confused emotions of today more accurately than many of her more class-conscious colleagues.

NEVER ANOTHER WAR

There is one clear and unmitigated message in all the interviews undertaken with German women: never another war—under no condition! The three levels of symbolic meaning introduced above permeate most of the other interviews in the Berlin and Hanover projects. The existential level is clearest in the descriptions of the city bombings. The many strikingly similar stories about putting one's life in utmost danger for a pint of milk or an identification paper convey the message that daily life was a dangerous affair in which one had to be both mindless and brave. They also seem symbolically to express the senseless and nameless death resulting from depersonalized technological warfare in which human life—one's own life—had no value, not even for oneself. The innumerable stories about bombed apartments and the endless and futile attempts to recuperate them do not simply convey the factual information that a home was essential to survival. Rather, they symbolize being thrown out in the open, having no protection against impersonal destructive forces, being delivered over to forces beyond one's control. The soldier in the front-line trench, under fire and crying for his mama, became a famous metaphor for human inability to deal with the new technological quality of World War I. The woman standing in the full blast of saturation bombing, crying and clutching her quilt, is an equally powerful metaphor for World War II.

The symbolic meaning of these war stories on the historico-political level manifests itself through the context and choice of vocabulary. War is often seen as a natural disaster, a catastrophe. This common metaphor is ambiguous; it expresses, for lack of more appropriate language, the feeling of being completely delivered over to forces beyond one's control. It is justified and "real" on the existential level, but it also conveys, implicitly, a political message: there is no collective or personal responsibility for war; it just "breaks out," is not prepared for and not declared. By the same token, the end of the war is often referred to—at least by the loser—as "the change" (*Umschwung*), as if it were merely a change in weather; rarely is it called "the defeat." "War is something beyond politics," one woman remarked. The concept of war as a natural catastrophe rather than the consequence of imperialist drives[13] allows one to be against war—a sentiment deeply felt by the majority of German people since the end of World War I, and even more strongly after World War II—but at the same time to uphold nationalistic values. It allows the contradiction of supporting armament expenditures to "reestablish national pride" while at the same time "praying to God" that another war does not come. Such metaphors allow individuals and nations to shore up inconsistencies that might otherwise break apart. Naturalizing war allows people and nations to be proud of easy victories over small and helpless countries, to rejoice over the booty, be it French perfume or Polish servants, while feeling victimized if the price of death and destruction has to be paid. The subjective level of symbolic expression in the narratives concerns both the experience and the identity of the individual woman and women's social self image. It involves nearly all facets of female subjectivity and provides a psychological base for political metaphors used in the public realm. The symbol of the victim may exemplify the complex relations.

The notion of being a victim permeates nearly all the war accounts of the women interviewed. As a matter of fact, in the second part of the war, the majority of German women, as well as children and others on the homefront, *were* victims in the traditional sense of the word. They were subjected to and suffered under conditions that they did not want and could not change.[14] Thus the image of the victim is an accurate description of the war experience, so

13. *Imperialist* is used here as an analytical concept to designate specific political-economic relations between nations, not as a historical term referring to the German Empire.

14. At what point ordinary people could have prevented the war is a question beyond the realm of this essay; I offer the ironic remark made by Alexander Kluge in one of his films, which portrays a woman in an air-raid shelter about to collapse: "The last chance Mrs. X had to prevent her present uncomfortable position was in 1928."

powerful as to have a lasting impact on the discourse of today's political movements.

But the symbolism of the victim has a meaning beyond the actual circumstances that these women endured; it becomes ambiguous, like the metaphor of the natural disaster, yet it remains more compelling because of its religious roots. The religious and popular symbol of the victim absolves the victim of responsibility and guilt. A victim of the war cannot be responsible for it. In the postwar German understanding, this notion is carried even further: as a victim one cannot be held responsible for fascism. This is certainly one reason that interviewees brought up the war as soon as the uncomfortable issue of National Socialism was raised in the interview. Suffering shields Germans from the threatening and guilt-provoking questions surrounding the issues of fascism, concentration camps, and the Nazis' treatment of Jews.

Women have been victimized, as a group, throughout history. Religions have built female victimization into a positive ideology of self-sacrifice as the highest virtue of womanhood, and fascism thrived on a secularized version of female sacrifice. Thus, the image of the victim is an integral part of women's cultural and social identity. It is not surprising, therefore, that symbolic victimization is much more obvious in women's interviews than in men's. Pleading "not guilty" in all political matters is their favorite answer when they are confronted with their role in the rise of fascism. That victims are responsible too, even for their own victimization, is never allowed to enter their minds. They are dazzled and bewildered when held accountable. German women paid heavily for the deadly adventures of their male ruling elites. But, this only strengthens their already deeply engraved identities as victims. The war, as these memories show, has not broken the vicious cycle.

INDEX

CONTRIBUTORS

YASMINE ERGAS is a member of the Social Science Research Council and author of *Nelle maglie della politica: Feminismo, istituzioni politiche e sociale nell'Italia degli anni '70.*

SARAH FISHMAN is a doctoral candidate at Harvard University and holds a Whiting Fellowship for 1986–87.

SANDRA M. GILBERT is Professor of English at Princeton University and coauthor of *The Madwoman in the Attic* and *The Norton Anthology of Literature by Women.*

JENNY GOULD is working on a thesis for University College, London.

SUSAN GUBAR is Professor of English at Indiana University and coauthor of *The Madwoman in the Attic* and *The Norton Anthology of Literature by Women.*

STEVEN C. HAUSE is Associate Professor of History at the University of Missouri and author of *Women's Suffrage and Social Politics in the French Third Republic* and the forthcoming *Hubertine Auclert: The French Suffragette.*

KARIN HAUSEN is Professor of Economic and Social History at the Technical University of Berlin and editor of *Frauen suchen ihre Geschichte.*

MARGARET R. HIGONNET is Professor of English at the University of Connecticut, author of *Horn of Oberon,* and coeditor of the journal *Children's Literature.*

PATRICE L.-R. HIGONNET is Goelet Professor of French History at Harvard University and author of *Pont de Montvert* and *Class, Ideology and the Rights of Nobles during the French Revolution.*

JANE JENSON is Professor of Political Science at Carleton University in Ottawa and coauthor of *Crisis, Challenge, and Change: Party and Class in Canada; The View from Inside: A French Communist Cell in Crisis;* and *Absent Mandate: The Politics of Discontent in Canada.*

LYNNE LAYTON is a doctoral candidate in Clinical Psychology at Boston University. She holds a Ph.D. in Comparative Literature and is coeditor of *Narcissism and the Text: Essays in Literature and the Psychology of Self.*

SONYA MICHEL is Lecturer on History and Literature at Harvard University, coauthor of *The Jewish Woman in America,* and author of the forthcoming *Children's Interests/Mother's Rights: The History of Public Child Care in America.*

RUTH MILKMAN is Associate Professor of Sociology at Queens College, City University of New York, editor of *Women, Work, and Protest: A Century of U.S. Women's Labor History,* and author of the forthcoming *Dynamics of Job Segregation by Sex during World War II.*

MICHELLE PERROT is Professor of History at the University of Paris VII and author of *Les ouvriers en grève (France, 1871–1890)*. She has just completed volume 4 of the *Histoire de la vie privée au 19ème siècle.*

DENISE RILEY is Research Assistant in the School of Social Sciences, Institute for Advanced Study, Princeton. Her books include *Dry Air* and the forthcoming *"Am I That Name?": Feminism and the Category of "Women" in History.*

PAULA SCHWARTZ is a doctoral candidate at the Institute of French Studies, New York University.

JOAN W. SCOTT is Professor at the School of Social Sciences, Institute for Advanced Study, Princeton. She is author of *The Glassworkers of Carmaux: French Craftsmen and Political Action in a 19th Century City* and coauthor of *Women, Work, and Family.*

ELAINE SHOWALTER is Professor of English at Princeton University. Her most recent book is *The Female Malady: Women, Madness, and English Culture, 1830–1980.*

ANNEMARIE TRÖGER teaches at the Institut für Soziologie at the University of Hannover.

MARGARET COLLINS WEITZ is Chairman and Associate Professor of Humanities and Modern Languages at Suffolk University and author of *Femmes: Recent Writings on French Women.*